An Autobiography

LAURIS
EDMOND

An Autobiography

LAURIS EDMOND

An Autobiography

First published in 1994 by Bridget Williams Books Limited,
P.O. Box 11-294, Wellington, New Zealand

© Lauris Edmond, 1994

Much of the material in this book was previously published as:
Hot October: an autobiographical story, Allen & Unwin/
Port Nicholson Press, 1989 (reprinted by Bridget Williams Books, 1991)
Bonfires in the Rain, Bridget Williams Books, 1991
The Quick World, Bridget Williams Books, 1992

This book is copyright under the Berne Convention. All rights reserved.
No reproduction without permission.
Inquiries should be made to the publishers.

ISBN 0 908912 65 X

Edited by Anna Rogers
Cover design by Mission Hall Design
Text design by Afineline
Typesetting by Archetype
Printed by GP Print, Wellington

I name this place
to find it

by looking truly
I can hear and speak my dream

this is where I stay
also my journey

for nothing rests except
within its timeless motion

the names of things are sleeping
in the way they've come

This is my waking up, my camp,
my resting-place along the never-ending

lines that cross the world. My song
waits here, I sing it.

'I Name this Place'
from *Scenes from a Small City*, 1994

Contents

Author's Note *ix*

Part One: Hot October *1*

Part Two: Bonfires in the Rain *127*

Part Three: The Quick World *293*

Author's Note

This edition of my autobiography is the same in its essentials as the three-volume version published between 1989 and 1992 *(Hot October, Bonfires in the Rain* and *The Quick World)*. It is, however, somewhat reduced in length, and the photographs originally used have been omitted.

My purpose has been a practical one: a single volume is more manageable than three, also cheaper and probably more accessible, especially for publishers and booksellers – and readers – in countries other than New Zealand. The changes are in detail, not in events or themes. Indeed I selected for reduction only those passages where I could simplify the outline without altering the substance, or the flavour, of the existing narrative.

In each of the earlier volumes I acknowledged the particularity of my own view of events, insisting that others would see and interpret them in ways different from mine, and I re-affirm that acknowledgement here. I also record again my thanks to those who have made helpful comments on the earlier manuscripts. I have been greatly helped in the shaping of the present volume by the careful and intelligent editorial advice of Anna Rogers.

It has been a stirring experience to publish this story of a woman's life towards the end of a century which has so fundamentally changed women's circumstances and outlook. With this new edition, I have a unique opportunity to acknowledge my debt to readers – that usually silent company that is every writer's real constituency. Correspondence, from both men and women, has not only been generous in its sharing of experience comparable with mine; it has also continually illuminated the larger questions that stand behind the choosing of directions in every life and, of course, the writing about them in autobiography.

L.E.

Hot October

Part One

Hot October

Chapter 1

'Eighty in the shade' was hot, by Jove. You were brave to be living through it. 'Ninety in the shade', you were verging on the heroic; 'a hundred', and you had joined a beleaguered élite. You stopped complaining; sticky all over, red in the face, you passed the news round the wilting drifters in the playground when you got back after lunch. 'A hundred-in-the-shade, did you know?' 'Oh. I'll tell Madge.' 'She says. Her mother told her.' It dignified us all. Nobody asked why it was always in the shade – surely if it was heat you were on about, in the sun was where you'd get it. But of course I never said so.

In February it happened a lot. The Sugar Loaf and all the other hills went brown, then lighter brown, finally almost white. It never rained. My brother Clive and his friends had bikes and after school they went for swims in the camping ground on the other side of Taradale. The Tutaekuri had good swimming holes there in spite of a few snags he told us, loftily. He did other remarkable things too – caught eels in the ditches near our place and brought them home and hung them on the fence, where he put a nail through the skin and peeled it off like a stocking. He caught them with a jag – a bent nail sticking out of the end of a broom handle, and was of course scornful to his sisters when we asked how the eels felt and why they let themselves be caught. It was much the same when he shot sparrows and chaffinches with his BB gun, and Lindsay and I buried the victims with flowers and a cross of sticks. I was bigger than Lindsay but we were both too small to be of use or interest, to him.

The morning of the earthquake was hot, and muggy as well – strange, thundery weather. The sun didn't shine but it was all the hotter for that. It was Lindsay's first day at school; when the bell rang for playtime I waited at the door of her room and hand in hand we went outside to play. Within moments the world began to blow itself apart in the most extraordinary way – the roof of the school flew off in a cloud of brick red dust, the walls subsided and the roof landed again with a roar on the heap they made. The ground rolled and surged as though it had become water, waves passing over and through the asphalt playground as we sat, or rolled about, on the grass by the fence. We'd clambered through the wire and were gazing in astonishment at that red cloud. Once the school had vanished before our eyes, turning itself into a heap of red rubble and dust, it was hard to know what to do. 'We'd better wait here and see what happens,' I, seven years old, said to Lindsay. 'Oh no,' said she, six (between November and April she was only a year younger than me), 'we'd better go home. It's no good staying here, it'll take too long.' We lived five minutes' walk down Osier Road, but we kept falling over because the ground still rocked so wildly. Just over the crossing we met our mother. She looked really mad – her eyes were wild and in her hand she clutched a young lilac tree we'd had growing just inside our gate. She shrieked and clung to us, crying that we must find Clive.

The pale broad figure of Mrs Pollock from next door loomed up; she had a faded cotton frock and bare feet and her face was red from crying. She left us and climbed through the fence into the paddock by the road, where she wandered off towards the trees calling, 'Billy . . . Billy . . .' He was about our age, Lindsay's and mine, and in the primers too, but we hadn't seen him. As it turned out, Billy had stayed behind to help clean the blackboard, being a first day monitor, and was one of the three children killed by falling debris in the school's collapse. If the earthquake had been five minutes earlier we would all have been crushed and the child population of Napier and Hastings almost wiped out.

We didn't find Clive at first either, but he did appear among the swarms of mothers and children further down the road. He'd gone one better than us, naturally. He was leaning against the school wall eating his playlunch apple when the wall fell back behind him and the roof came down; he had just time to scramble clear and crawl away alive. Doubtless whatever had happened to Fatty Frederickson would have been better still. I had heard him saying to Clive that if a wild bull came into our backyard and he happened to be up on the roof at the time, he'd take one leap down, land on its back and grasp it by the horns and ride it away, tamed. Boys. That's the way they talked.

Our father was a painter and paperhanger, an occupation in which we all had some share. His clients expected him to be designer as well as decorator, and we helped to choose combinations of wallpapers and borders for the rooms he was to paper. The usual practice was to have a main paper up to about seven or eight feet, a narrow ornamental border that picked up on its strongest colours, then a different paper above. Houses in the thirties all had a twelve-foot stud. The family conferences about these choices were long and satisfying. Mum and Lindsay and I said you couldn't have a stripe on the bottom (stripes were popular) and a floral on the top. Ugh! Nor could you have blue and green together, or blue and pink mixed with orange and brown – each was a separate camp. Orange and brown were our favourites (Mum wore them a lot); in their company were yellow and cream and fawn. A border that I loved to choose was a continuous twining garland of nasturtium flowers, yellow and orange and bronze, with the curving of the petals making its outer edge. All the papers were in large pattern books which Dad would bring home and open on the kitchen table in the evenings for us to decide. At times papers went out of stock and Lindsay and I were allowed to take the page out and cut it up to make pictures, or paper dolls' dresses.

On the day of the earthquake Dad was up a ladder, painting tanks for a farmer on the hills towards Puketitiri. As he held up his brush to dip it in the paint pot that hung on his ladder, the tank leaped off its stand into the air and rolled down the hill. He was a phlegmatic man, my father; his main thought was that if he'd been in front instead of at the side it would have taken him too.

At home we passed the wrenched hole where our mother had grabbed the little lilac tree to steady herself, and the rocking ground, opening and closing, had delivered it into her hand. Inside there was unforgettable havoc. The broken glass of preserving jars floated in plum and apricot pulp with soot, broken cups and bowls, the nameless mess from mantelpieces, fallen kettles, ink pots, butter and jam, mingled with spilt tea and sugar to make a ghastly lake on the kitchen floor. There were broken mirrors and windows and light globes in every room, fallen wardrobes and dressing tables, smashed ornaments and clothes and bedding mixed up everywhere. But the thing that terrified us most was that the floor kept moving, it never stopped.

Ours was a wooden house, not brick, but we were afraid of it all the same. There was an open paddock next to us where Lindsay and I played in the long grass and some years my father grew lettuces for the market. There we sat, with a washing bowl of plums and peaches, picked from their trees in the back garden the day before – in another life – and salvaged from the wash house where there was nothing much to fall. When our mother got up, saying she wanted to look for bread and butter, we pulled her down with screams of terror at the thought of her going in there. Outside was the only safety, despite the fact that cracks were already appearing here and there through the grass.

In the afternoon we drove to Napier to see if our aunts and grandmother, my father's family, were safe. Or we set out. On the way we had to cross the innumerable bridges which cropped up on that road, winding as it did through five or six miles of inner harbour. There were cars everywhere, jamming the narrow road, all full of families going, like us, to find relatives in 'town' – though Napier, had we known it, was already beginning to disintegrate in the fire that eventually destroyed far more than the earthquake itself.

Just before one of the bridges there was a traffic jam; cars as far as we could see – slow-moving tourers with canvas roofs buttoned down, and a few sedans. Someone ahead of us had been caught in a crack in the road. It had opened with one earth movement wide enough to swallow the front wheels and closed again quickly enough to wedge them tight. We sat in the hot car for a while, Lindsay and Clive and I together in the back seat silenced by shock, then we found a way out of the confusion and turned back.

No telephones worked, but we found out in the next few days that Aunty Syb and Uncle Bert and Thelma, a glamorous cousin in her teens, were all safe. The other family was Aunty Grace, Uncle Will and a tribe of cousins I was to get to know much better after the earthquake because they moved to Greenmeadows and lived quite near us. Grandma lived with them; she seemed to be always in bed, sitting up with her long grey plait down her back and talking to us in a funny dry voice with a little cackling laugh, She did our family mending and I used to bike round to Aunty Grace's with a bag of holey socks and torn dresses which she would restore with delicate almost invisible stitches. I would talk to her for a while, watch her take out her tobacco tin and roll one of her thin little cigarettes which she then smoked in a tortoiseshell holder, cackling and saying she was wicked and would go to hell when she died. She told me that because I was 'good at school' I must have a career – be a headmistress of a school perhaps. At the end of the visit I would gather up a bag of completed mending and bike home, half pleased, half sorry to leave that slightly musty bedroom. She smelt, like the Christmas cake that was kept in a cupboard for months, with the one bottle of port that we had in the house, of staleness, old clothes, the past. Once she did a seam, finishing off a skirt for Lindsay that Mum did not have time for, and pricked her finger so that there were minute dots of blood all down the side of the garment when it came back. 'Come, come, Grandma, you can do better than that,' said Mum in a wildly funny way she had, Lindsay and I laughing at such delicious impertinence.

But on the day of the earthquake we heard nothing of these people. Only that someone else's grandmother had been in the bath in her house in Napier and the explosion of water pipes had floated her out into the street where she rode along in her white porcelain contraption, naked to the heavens, while the ruins of the city piled up around her. This was a spectacular disaster. We were glad she wasn't our grandmother, for people to see her like that.

For weeks the ground kept moving, off and on. None of us slept in houses at first; we had a corrugated iron garage and some neighbours came and put their mattresses alongside ours and we slept there, huddling together and telling stories in the dark about the horrors we'd heard about during the day.

Going to school changed too. For a few weeks nobody went at all; a lot of families went away for a holiday, to visit relations in other parts of the country. Then it was arranged that we should join classes at Taradale school. Greenmeadows had been a side school anyway, the seniors had always gone to Taradale for their last two years. Some, who didn't go to high school, stayed on and became known as Standard 7. People in this class were well into their teens and waiting to go to work, or in the case of one girl, to get married. Her name was Emily Waddell (pronounced 'Waddle') and Lindsay and I went and watched her wedding in the local Methodist church. As she walked past we stared with a kind of shocked awe at her rouged cheeks and frizzed hair and long taffeta dress. It was as though the still remote adult world had come in and performed a danse macabre for us on our own ground.

We had to walk a mile to Taradale school, a wooden building that had survived the earthquake. Taradale kids were snooty and I was frightened of most of them, most of the time. One day we had a memorial service for the children who had died in our school; a teacher who had been injured but had recovered spoke about their bravery and their devotion to duty in staying behind to be monitors. She cried and was led away. I thought of Mrs Pollock going into the trees calling Billy and felt sick with the strangeness of it all. Then we sang *Abide with Me* and I cried hopelessly too, as I did every time we sang it at Sunday school if someone's friend or relation had died.

We never lost our earthquake consciousness; the moment a light globe began to sway everyone went dead white; it was a kind of suffocating terror – you couldn't breathe for a moment or two. Then you would find out if it was a false alarm – that is, a tremor – or if the slow beginning meant a big one was coming. Both kinds happened often, and we learned to know the difference between the main types, bumpers and swayers. The swayers were worse because you had longer to anticipate the worst without knowing how bad it would be. In May that year there was another severe one, in the late evening. It was nothing like the first, but it sent us all to gather in our mother's bed where we huddled, teeth chattering for hours before we could be persuaded to go back to our own beds. The morning of February 3 when I had said to Lindsay 'Let's wait and see what happens' was a lifetime away. We knew.

Chapter 2

Four years later in 1935 the Labour government came to power. For months before the election we, like most families we knew, had the plump and smiling face of Michael Joseph Savage up on the wall, though in our case it wasn't in the house but out in Dad's office, an old fowl house a little distance from the back verandah. There he did his accounts, mixed pots of paint, wrote letters to the newspapers and read, discovering an obsession that was to last all his life for political rebirth or, as he called it at first, monetary reform. He'd always been interested in ideal societies; many of the books lying about the house had titles such as *Equality* (Edward Bellamy), *Looking Backward* (by the same author), and there was H.G. Wells' *A Modern Utopia* and *The Open Conspiracy*. This was sub-titled 'Blueprints for a world revolution'; and it did seem that my mild and often uncommunicative father was excited by such a prospect. Another was called *Perfecting the Earth*. He believed in this possibility, and after a while so did I.

Other Labour Party members, including candidates like John A. Lee and William Barnard (our member after the election), also didn't greatly distinguish the new dawn promised by Savage and Semple, Nash and Fraser, from the more general reform they encountered in their reading. Thoughtful, unschooled and largely self-educated men were common; for my father the focus increasingly fell on Douglas Social Credit, a faith which came to dominate our household. I think we became a bit cranky in the eyes of people in the town, but at first it wasn't so – didn't the whole world want Labour to win? When it happened, the night of the 1935 election, we gathered in the chook house, all of us, and shrieked and laughed with Dad; we'd wanted Utopia to come, and as far as we could see, it had.

These were the years of the Great Depression, but any connection between Labour politics and the hardships of being poor didn't strike

Lindsay or me. Clive may have been a party to anxious conversations about the family budget, I don't know. Certainly nothing was ever wasted. We grew our own vegetables and if we didn't eat them at one meal they appeared again in another form – meat and potatoes as shepherd's pie, parsnips and carrots mashed as bubble and squeak. Naturally we made jam from the plums, apricots, peaches and melons in our own garden, even green tomato jam from the vegetable patch. I especially liked the evenings when we all sat round the kitchen table and sliced up grapefruit for marmalade or minced peanuts for peanut butter, watching, as the mincing grew to seven (the proper number), the marvellous transformation from dry roasted nuts to delicious soft paste, ripe with oil.

Soap-making wasn't so appealing – the smell of boiling fat and carbolic acid (or whatever it was) filled the house, and there was nothing for us to do. However, the big yellow bars of soap, when they were set, were some satisfaction – the proud sense of having created something out of nothing that was part of all these operations. Since Dad made a good deal of our furniture, mixed his own paint, chopped wood for the coal range, and built the stretchers for our camping holidays, we took it for granted that there was no other way to maintain a family life support system.

Our clothes were made out of bigger garments cut down. Mum spent hours treadling away at the old Singer machine, while Lindsay and I made school classes out of rows of small buttons, with a Big Wheel coat button out in front hectoring them as we knew teachers did. She was clever, our mother, and used all kinds of odds and ends for trimming; for winter coats made out of a herringbone tweed of hers, she made matching berets, half brown velvet from an old evening frock. The lapels were velvet too. Sometimes a difficult part like a lapel or collar wouldn't lie flat and there were endless tryings on, rages, perhaps tears, violent snatchings and wrenchings as we stood there, seemingly still, but getting our chins or elbows in the way so they had to be shoved crossly this way or that.

Lindsay and I always had matching clothes. One of our dresses, brown spotted cotton made from a dress Mum had worn when she was a student at training college, had cream crêpe de chine collars, from a blouse, and these in the making went swimmingly all the way. So there were jokes, singing, stories, games of threatened pricking with pins that made us squeal and wriggle. There was the story about the man who caught a magic fish and because it asked him to throw it back, and he did, it promised he could ask for anything he wanted. And the marvellously repetitive *Old Woman Who Went to Market to Buy a Pig*, which in parts we could all chant together. (Stories at bed time were different – a series of episodes in the lives of Nancy and Betty, two girls our age whose adventures bore an amazing similarity to our own.)

Even if Lindsay and I didn't notice we were poor – and thought a ha'penny a week to spend at Tronson's Store quite enough – of course we were. Clothes were always passed on from one family to another; not neighbours or friends, but relations. Mum came from a family of twelve, most of them brothers who were farmers or in some way connected with farming. We visited their families regularly. One sister had died young and there was an older sister who had married somebody grand, the son of a titled landowner in Gisborne, and lived in Tolaga Bay on a station (not merely a farm). This was Aunty Clara and we thought of her with a respectful anxiety. In my mind she was surrounded by a floating whirl of silver cutlery and swishing skirts and white linen tablecloths. We didn't visit her.

Another sister, Aunty Alice, was closer in age to Fanny (our unfortunate mother's only name); she lived in Wairoa and we exchanged visits often with that family. There were three children, roughly parallel in age and certainly in sex, to the three of us – not counting John, our late baby, born when Lindsay was six and I was eight. They were great friends those sisters, and at the same time fiercely competitive, particularly about their children. There was never a time when I hadn't known that Garth, the eldest, was a paragon, a perfect boy – presumably in his mother's eyes, but most of the time in our mother's as well. He was held up to Clive as a model of discretion and self-control; his was a faultless boyhood. Clive killed birds with his shanghai and later with his gun; Garth was gentle and compassionate. Clive got doubtful school reports; it seemed he could be lazy, dirty, cheeky, loud. Garth was none of these things. Clive teased and tyrannised over his sisters, Garth was kind to his. When we stayed with them or they with us, Garth seemed much the same sort of boy as Clive, but this didn't change our mother's view.

There was one major crime that apparently tempted the susceptible Clive, but I never found out what it was. Occasionally the air would be charged with a sort of black electricity, Mum and Dad would whisper or mutter to each other, Clive would cry. Lindsay and I,

11

baffled, were bundled out of sight and told to mind our own business. One terrifying evening we came back down the passage, unable to help ourselves since Clive was crying stormily and Mum was raging, though in a low voice. We saw him in his room crouching down, crying, and her at the door tall and terrible, like an avenging angel, holding, of all monstrous things, the carving knife from the kitchen. We were paralysed with fright, yet we didn't for a moment think she wanted to kill him – the talk of 'cutting it off' was something different, something forbidden and dreadful to which we didn't want to give a name. We crept back to bed, not even able to ask each other what Clive's crime might be. We were very nice to him the next day; he had somehow entered a male world forbidden even to him, and we were for once prepared to be humble. Girls might be insignificant and foolish, but there were ways in which we were safe.

Indeed the rivalry between Alice and Fanny didn't seem to affect girls much. Dorothy and Valerie were good at the piano, but then so were we – or passable anyway; they were clever at school, we were that too. Nicely behaved girls are. It wasn't a problem. We played with them hour after hour at their house, where we used to go down to the river, and learned about tidal swell and the bar across the mouth of the Wairoa River. When they came to stay with us we went for swims too, but also climbed the Sugar Loaf (they didn't have hills) and had picnics in special places in hills or by creeks on the way to Rissington.

In one way we were inferior to our cousins – we were worse at being homesick. On the first night in Wairoa I always cried, and usually for several other nights as well; Lindsay was a bit better, but not much. When the Powells came to Greenmeadows they launched into the business of the holiday without fuss. I said to myself that I would be like this too, but when the time came I would be engulfed again in the despair of being far from home, darkness coming down and no way of finding my way back to familiar things.

The habit of exchanging parcels of used clothes continued long after the Labour government had come and gone and the leanest times were over. One of these parcels, sent in the usual way, suddenly offended Fanny – or was it Alice? – and it was bundled up again and sent back. It came back. It was returned again. Indignation mounted, and wretched garments became horrible, unwanted by either of these two tall, powerful and extravagant women. Fanny had not only a taste for drama but a flair for it. She was full-bodied, voluble, regal in her rage. Everything began with WHO does she think . . . WHO am I . . . HOW DARE . . . and so on. We quailed, clustered round, felt the indignity with her. They wrote furious letters, sometimes they rang each other up and were lofty and withering on the phone, at least our mother was. We listened, impressed and appalled.

In the end it all died down and there were Christmases and birthdays marked only by dreary reproaches and miserable self-defending expostulations. Finally silence; and only years later a kind of comprehension of their loss, a real, if lame and ungracious, capitulation on both sides, and a shaken autumnal friendship.

There is no doubt that it was a dramatic family. The brothers – our uncles – were endlessly interesting to us. There was a typical Price face and physique which some, like Fanny, clearly possessed, and others had traces of. It was a lean face, with straight lines in the nose and chin, straight eyebrows too, and penetrating eyes; blue like some of the uncles, hazel or brown like Fanny's and Alice's. They had wide smiles and – the thing I liked best about them – they laughed in a way that was more than hearty, it was helpless. There was a sort of wheeze about it, they lost their breath, couldn't speak, everything in the world suddenly became so preposterously funny there was no way to stop yourself joining in. Uncle Bert was like that – though at other times he was desperate with rage about his poorly fertilised hill country farm. Alice, riper and plumper, had the same abandonment, and Tom, the charming failure who never got his own land, but turned up from time to time to stay overnight when he was on the road cattle droving. He sat under the willow tree with me and taught me how to cheat at cards as though it was a great joke. He had bright brown eyes and brought stories with him that made Fanny laugh till she was nearly sick. I loved them all, but this thin, laughing rascal was truly precious.

Then there was Grandfather Price. A white-moustached old gentleman in a basket chair on a verandah in a house in Hastings. Married to an unlikely shadow of a woman called Violet, he was disapproved of by everyone for leading their adored mother a dog's life (she had died before I was born). This gave rise even then to whispered conversations about 'celebrating again'. Celebrating what? I naturally asked; someone's birthday? A memorable snub followed – I was to go away at once and not listen to what wasn't my business. In fact for me he was a hero. Reprobate he might be; my friend he also was, and fascinating. When we went to visit him on Sunday afternoons I gravitated at once to his verandah and his chair, and there we played the most stunning games of wit and skill. Problems you had to work out in your head, reasoning your way out of certain death by crocodiles, the rope, or the electric chair. Nobody had ever made me think so hard. I tingled with the difficulty of it.

Chapter 3

Despite the daily frugalities of our household we always had a car, and indeed a truck as well, which Dad loaded with ladders, paint pots, a blow lamp for burning off, bundles of wallpaper and pattern books and a toolbox. He always had 'the men' with him, Bill Jackson and Stan Cawston and Ernie Rispin. They arrived in the morning and conferred about the day's job in the yard outside Dad's fowl-house office, talking in an offhand laconic way that utterly separated them from us, the insiders. Some of his strangeness clung to our father even after he came home, took off his paint-smothered overalls and washed and dressed to sit down with us.

Mum served tea straight out of saucepans on the range or the bench, though she talked about the vegetable dishes (in the china cabinet in the front room) as something she knew she ought to use, and one day she would. Serviettes too were in a drawer in the front room, but we were in no doubt about their importance; we even knew you weren't supposed to call them serviettes, but table napkins.

After tea Dad was often preoccupied with decisions about prices, specifications and jobs, which he would talk about to Mum, not us. He seemed at times to notice with some surprise that we were there, and would give his funny crooked smile, making us feel shy even of him. His nose had been broken when he was a boy in an accident on a bike, one night when he was riding without a light, and it made his whole face look slightly askew. He had nice brown eyes and square hands which he'd put together between his knees, palms together, as he sat and thought in front of the fire on cold nights.

Sometimes it was the open fire in the front room, but that was when relations came to stay, or perhaps when Mum had ladies to afternoon tea. Mrs Turton, Mrs West and Mrs Madison. There were teacups in the china cabinet for these occasions, small curved or fluted cups with gold edges and matching saucers and plates; they mostly had flower designs and printed on the underside was 'Royal Albert China' or 'Royal Stafford Bone China' (whose bone, I wondered) or – and Mum said these were the very best – 'Royal Doulton'. 'Oh good afternoon, Mrs Scott', they would say as she opened the front door. 'Mrs Turton, Mrs West . . . do come in', and then they would talk about their children. The ritual was unshakeable: sandwiches first, on the top plate of the three-tiered cake stand, then pikelets or scones, cakes on the bottom. Our mother didn't have a silver teapot though. Hers was aluminium; a misfortune.

When I began to write poems and keep them, carefully printed in a black notebook with a shiny cover, she wanted me to come into the sitting room and recite them to Mrs Turton and the others. I did once say A.A. Milne's *The King's Breakfast*, red in the face and trembling (but with my feet correctly placed, ankle to instep and turned slightly outwards), but I refused to say my own.

They didn't belong with rooms and conversations anyway, but to wandering about alone in the long grass in the paddock, climbing the plum or apricot tree, or 'round the side of the house'. This meant the 'dark' side, a shaded strip of path and garden between the house and the hedge into Pollocks'. Several peach trees grew there and were among my subjects for verse: their leaves 'curled like tiny boats' (they must have had leaf curl; peach leaves are flat if the tree's in good health). There were also poems about the open country, changes in the seasons, the hills (on which the small slips made by erosion were 'giant fingers scratching'). Staring was one of my chief occupations, and making something of what I saw a secret delight. Mum and Lindsay might see the poems when, rhymed and ready, they were copied into the black notebook, but nobody else.

It was round the side of the house that I saw my first and only fairy. It was quite close, sitting on a branch of one of the peach trees, dressed in pink as a fairy should be, with pink gauze wings and a very tiny face. As I watched her she got up slowly and flew to a higher branch where there were more leaves. I couldn't see her so well there, but it didn't matter; it had been an encounter of the profoundest pleasure, one I would never forget.

John, as he grew out of babyhood, proved he had the same taste as I did for drifting reveries in the paddock or garden, or 'out the back' where the chook houses were, and the plum trees and vegetable garden. Sometimes we wandered about picking grass or leaves, not talking much, half alone, half together. He also had imaginary friends who became familiar to us. Gilligan rode everywhere with him on his tricycle, and there was a lesser character, Wollawobbler, who sometimes accompanied them. I think John had more compelling solitudes in him even than I did. A late child, he mostly played alone till he went to school.

Every summer we went camping. Not usually to one spot, but to several, taking again and again to the dust, rock and limestone tracks that most roads were. We piled our gear into the trailer and ourselves into the car, whichever one it was – they changed quite often. The best was a big Buick that had dicky seats behind the main front seats and there were fights to get these uncomfortable places, which conferred an undoubted cachet on the occupant. You saw the road and clouds of dust and passing trees and hills from your own personal angle, and if nobody pinched you from behind (though sooner or later they would) you could just sit and gloat.

Usually we stayed several days. Waking up at first light you lifted the edge of the canvas wall and there you were, lying on the floor of the world with grass all around, the smell of it in your nostrils, and the first birds whispering somewhere above you. If Lindsay and I woke up together we didn't talk, just looked and breathed. But even cooking and washing up, conducted at ground level, had an excitement in it, as though we were playing house with the universe. Once it was the Hawera racecourse, with the grandstand as free entertainment, then we took the road over Mount Messenger to Taupo. It was rough even by our standards, and made slower by the opening and closing of rabbit gates at each bridge (when it was my turn I always had a moment of panic as the car and trailer rattled by in case they forgot and drove on, leaving me alone with that huge silence). The rabbits we never saw unless we drove after dark. We camped by the Waikato, there a powerful and dangerous river, very deep and green. That night Lindsay walked in her sleep, passing out of the tent in her long white nightie just as Mum woke; for the rest of our stay she kept Lindsay by her on the double mattress, their two nightgowns joined by three large safety pins.

Coming home was queer. The house was hot and airless, the floors sloped, dead flies blackened the window sills; but then there would be summer days at home, fruit on the trees, hot and buzzing places in the long grass to lie in and stare up at the sky – all before school began again. And bike rides, to the fruit farm for apples and pears, or the camping ground for swims, our togs and towels rolled into two tight sausages that fitted behind the seat while Lindsay and I took turns riding and being dubbed. When we got home Mum would be bottling in the boiling kitchen, and we needed at once to make her a cup of tea. Very weak, with two slices of bread buttered on the loaf and cut as thin as paper; we sat down with her, and if there was a knock at the door one of us had to go.

It might be the Rawleighs man, or a man selling laces and ribbons or rolls of material, or wool and crochet and knitting needles and patterns. Then Mum would come out herself and spend a long time examining their goods and weighing up the possibilities of getting a bargain, but when she'd decided – and often it was to buy nothing – she was authoritative, even peremptory. Lindsay and I wished she would apologise for not buying, or talk about the weather; but no. It was 'none of this is worth the money' or 'poor quality for the price' or, some awful times, 'shoddy, I'm afraid, just shoddy'. The salesmen, meek as they were, never complained but packed up their scattered wares and went off round the corner of the house, with their shabby suits and neutral expressions. Neither hope nor disappointment showed in those thin faces. Mum wasn't unkind – and often put fruit or scones or a partly worn shirt out at the gate for the swags (of whom Lindsay and I were terrified). It was just that she didn't see any sense in not saying what she meant.

Coming home meant re-discovering the piano too, and having to practise. Lindsay and I each began to learn the piano when we were seven. There was a convent across the road and Sister taught in a small side room which you reached through a foyer. I tiptoed over its polished floor in breathless apprehension, not daring to look up at the statues of the Virgin Mary in their alcoves above me. They smelt like a church, only more so. Sister said we must sing a prayer before we began every lesson because that way I would get a brighter crown in heaven. Heaven I already knew was full of people wearing crowns and wings, walking round on gold pavements with God in the middle on His throne, gold too and layered like a Napoleon cake. Although singing the prayer was embarrassing, it did confirm my impression that this world and the next were connected by furniture and equipment.

Once when the foyer was being renovated Sister took me out through the main building and in another corridor I saw the spectacle of Jesus, his robes undone at the front and his very body opened to show his heart, big and shining and dripping with blood. This seemed so macabre that I had a bilious attack when the time came for my next lesson, and had to make it up at the end of the term.

But we were Anglicans. Our parents didn't go to church themselves – indeed Dad was increasingly attracted to something called Theosophy – but we were packed off to Sunday school. God was apparently for children, like bread and milk when you were sick, or going to bed early. Lindsay and I despised Sunday school: they praised you excessively for learning simple texts by heart – 'In my Father's house are many mansions' or 'Blessed are the meek for they shall inherit the earth'. Mostly they told Bible stories and then asked questions, as though begging us to give the right answer. The cards were all right – pictures of disciples, rich men, beggars, all in white robes, and Jesus with a halo – but there was no advantage in going regularly for that, because at the end of the year they gave them to everyone anyway. I liked the hymns best, and used to sing O *Worship the King* and *Sun of my Soul* for hours, idling on the swing or up in the willow tree.

Later on, in a fit of intense religious fervour, I reproached my mother for never having had us christened; this meant I couldn't receive confirmation, which I passionately desired. She said reasonably that if I wanted to be christened I could be, so Lindsay and I stood awkwardly round the font one Saturday, with Aunty Peggy as godmother and Uncle Mortimer as godfather. Unfortunately I had reached that stage where I could lapse into desperate giggling, and I heaved and spluttered through the formal exchanges as through it was a scene from the Marx Brothers. I finished with a sort of bray when the vicar made the sign of the cross on my forehead with his cold wet fingers. Mum was furious, but of course I couldn't stop.

The nearest thing I had to a revelation happened when I was in bed one night, lying awake tormented by the impossibility of ever being good enough – not only good enough to please Mum, but *good*. I knew I wasn't. Lindsay was, but not me. I was cruel to her, insulting to our mother, lazy, a sneak (I went into the front of the house to do the Saturday jobs, tidying, dusting, bath and basin, and stayed to read in secret, knowing it was wrong). I took advantage of being 'good at school' and made other people feel they weren't, because I was basically selfish and self-important and didn't care for other people more than myself. I thought despairingly about all this, and then over the pine trees across the road (my bed was by the window; Lindsay had accepted the wall – another proof of my selfishness) came a huge yellow full moon. It sailed through the sky, coming down and down, ever closer to where I lay cringing in bed. It had a dense if shadowy population on it; they seemed to be standing up, and the closer they came the more it seemed that they stood round the central figure of God, sitting on His throne. I could not bear it; there was no doubt that this was the Second Coming, and that all the evil in my heart would be revealed to the remorseless eyes of the Lord and His angels. I would wake up in the morning and find myself dead, and would have to begin at once on my eternal damnation. There was no changing it, and after a while I went to sleep. In the morning it was fine, and Saturday, and I was still there, alive after all.

Chapter 4

The year of the earthquake Fanny's favourite brother came to live with us. Big Clive, to distinguish him from Little Clive, whose room he shared. He was the youngest of the Prices, he had just finished training as a teacher and came to do his probationary year at Taradale school. He was my teacher in Standard 1.

At home he was wonderful, clever and funny and affectionate; he played euchre and five hundred with us, crib and draughts and dominoes, and of course General Knowledge. He sang *Abdullah Bulbul Amir and Ivan Skavinsky Skavar*; leaning back in his chair while refrain after refrain rolled through him, and I sat on his knee, then leaned against his chest to feel the buzz of the song inside him. At school however he was Sir, and we couldn't look each other in the eye. He heard my reading, reproved me for untidy writing, glared at me if I talked in class, just as he did all the others. Spelling had to be heard daily; you learned your list, handed it to him and spelt each word from memory. One day he asked me for mine; 'I did it before,' I muttered. He didn't remember. Could I explain please? Mumbling even more, reluctant to the last degree, halfway up to the front and penned between rows of desks, I was obliged to squeak, 'When you were shaving, Sir.'

Worse was to follow. Sir hated cheating above all other crimes; Valerie Langley and I cheated at spelling. We copied each other's so that both got all the words right. Instead of keeping our arms round our own page on the desk we shared, we lifted them at the elbow so the other could see underneath, and walking down the rows calling out words, Sir saw us. Spelling stopped; he dragged us both out to the front of the class: 'Look at them!' he roared. 'Cheats! Both of them – cheats!' Valerie and I shrank, wilted, cried. No explanations were possible – nothing about being friends and helping each other. We crept back to our seats. It was worse for me because he was a hero – in my not very densely populated landscape, *the* hero; it helped not at all that afterwards, at home, he made no reference to the incident and appeared to have forgotten it. I never quite lost an anxiety that he would in some other unexpected but terrible way 'find me out'.

Towards the end of the year Mr Tooman the headmaster came in to examine the class. Sir stood at the back and did not speak, a ghost of himself. Mr Tooman asked us who King John was and how to spell 'arithmetic'; he read a story and asked questions about it, we said the six times table. At the end he asked the date of Christmas Day, choosing Cecil Hunt to answer. Cecil Hunt was one of those unfortunate boys who got everything wrong; he did not know when Christmas Day was. Mr Tooman was amazed and horrified, Cecil hung his head, his straight fair hair fanning out over his cowlick; I looked at my desk and hoped not to be the one to tell him – not because I didn't know, but out of some dim desire not to connive at his disgrace. Eventually Evelyn McKenzie told him and Cecil Hunt sat down.

The next year we had a slight, bloodless woman called Miss Butcher. She had short straight white-blonde hair, invisible eyebrows and eyelashes and eyes of the palest blue, remote as a polar iceberg. She was thin and shrill. Every day we recited our tables in the comfortable singsong that was an essential part of learning them ('seven sevens are forty-nine, seven eights-a-fifty-six, seven-nines-a-sixty-three' – in a slowly rising crescendo – 'seven-tens-a-*seven*-tee, seven-elevens-a-*seventy*-seven and' – the climax – '*seven-twelves-are-eighty-four!*') while Miss Butcher walked up and down the rows with her stick in one hand, tapping it on the palm of the other, and leaning over close to our faces to find out who was chanting, and who was merely mouthing. The mouther would be dragged from his seat by the ear (boys, with their short hair, were more prone to this disaster) and punished by two cuts, one on each hand, the strap whistling through the air and down on to the skin with speed and precision. If Miss Butcher was bloodless, we were not; the hot tingling of pulled and twisted ears and stung palms gave a physical urgency to all our learning.

Miss Shugar, teacher of the primers and friend of our mother's, taught us sewing. She was a large threatening presence with her hair in a bun, a house near the school to which we sometimes had to go on visits, and in the house an ancient crone of a mother, a parrot that shrieked and cackled, and the shadowy figure of a man said to be a boarder and addressed by Miss Shugar as 'Goo'. She taught us to make samplers with rows of running stitches, hemming, herringbone, featherstitch, cross-stitch and double hemming. Mine was a dreadful object, a small piece of lawn tightened out of all recognisable shape by crabbed stitches, smudged with dirty fingermarks, stained by occasional bloodspots and pock-marked with holes left by unpicked stitches; an object of despair, mortification and hopeless, thwarted ambition.

Miss Shugar had no opinion of my sewing, nor, I suppose, of me. When I began to giggle and talk, as a kind of natural distraction, she was at once in a fury; I was cowed, but temporarily. Days at school continued to be followed by command visits on the way home to that macabre household where Miss Shugar became noisily festive and offered Lindsay and me pieces of seed cake on little curly plates, and put a shawl over the parrot if his screams became too shrill.

One day I went too far. She shouted that if I talked and giggled any more the next time would be the last. It was. In front of the other sewers, thankfully keeping their eyes on their samplers, she really bellowed. I was a terrible child, a failure at all useful activities, a nuisance at school and a disgrace to my family, who must be constantly ashamed of me. I was in fact a disaster wherever I went and could only be described as the King of Mischief Makers. I didn't wonder why not the Queen; I was already too overcome by shock and humiliation and crying so hard that no one, not even Miss Shugar herself when she eventually began to try, could stop me. I cried all the way home, Lindsay and my friends Josie and Chrissie ministering to me as best they could. When our mother saw my sodden state she at once went to the telephone and abused Miss Shugar so violently that even I stopped to listen, and felt some consolation in having such a champion. Miss Shugar was much less of a power after that. Some time later her aged mother died and at once, almost the next day, she married Goo. I had always assumed that Goo bore the same relation to her that we did – fancy marrying such a creature! I was impressed by his bravado, and sorry for him now that he would be gripped for ever by those remorseless talons.

There was one other teacher who interested me, but he appeared much later, when I was in Standard 6. He was thin, dark and sporty looking; he wore blazers and cream shirts with open necks and light shoes, and he was the most wonderful man in the world – for a while I loved him more even than the uncles. He was quiet and humorous, he asked questions it was fun to answer, partly because they were difficult (they reminded me of Grandfather Price's tricks that made your brain work so hard); partly too because he was himself pleased and perhaps amused when you got it right. If you didn't he just asked someone else. The only frustration was that once he got the idea that you often would, he didn't ask you very often, so that some of us spent long times not merely waving our arms in the air, but shaking them, beating the air violently, as if by the very force of our frenzy we could compel him to say, 'Yes, what is it then?' One day he asked us what was wrong with the sentence 'The farmer went out to the paddock to look at his sheep and saw that he had less than the day before' and I was the only person in the class who knew it should say 'fewer'; I thought I would die of happiness. We knew his Christian name too, which added to his splendour. It was Roland.

Towards the end of that year it became known that girls could sit for a scholarship to Iona College, one of the private schools in Havelock North, that centre of Hawke's Bay gentility. Mum was enthusiastic. I sat the exam and was awarded a scholarship. However I wanted to go to Napier Girls' High School with all the other Taradale and Greenmeadows girls; for once I put my foot down, and the next February caught the bus to Napier with the others and continued my public schooling as nature, perhaps, intended.

Lindsay was my natural ally at home, but at school she was inconvenient, a junior in another class; my two friends there were Josie and Chrissie. Josie was a small freckly girl who lived round the corner, a couple of hundred yards from our house; closer, if you cut across the back, but I was wary of the swamp, especially of the noises it made at night when a chorus of frogs resounded through the neighbourhood.

Our mother was very interested in Josie's family; she half envied, half despised them. Mr Alexander was a maths teacher at the Boys' High School in Napier; Dad was a painter and paperhanger. One, she said, was called 'profession', the other was 'trade' and we were in no doubt about the drawbacks of the second. At the same time Mrs Alexander was stout, comfortable, loud; Mum felt her superior refinement and laughed at Mrs Alexander for saying 'kids' instead of 'children' and talking of giving the family 'a big fish tea'. (Mum had thought I would meet the daughters of professional fathers at Iona, and overcome the handicap of having one in trade, as well as reinforcing our natural delicacy.)

But despite her ambivalence, the Alexanders and ourselves had many neighbourly connections. There was for instance a burst of parties – uncharacteristic for us – at which carpets were rolled back, cream cakes and lemonade offered round and evenings given to dancing and singing and romping about. The families vied with one another in the sumptuousness of the supper and the joyfulness of the atmosphere. Through several winters we took turns; other neighbours joined in when it was at the Alexanders', so theirs were larger than ours and a bit more hectic. (One miserable time I took a piece of toffee out of a jar and found it was rosin used by Josie's older sister for her violin; her smile claimed a point to them.)

Josie was one of twins and her brother Joe and I, amply supported by our mothers, were rivals for the first place in every class through primary school. When we got to the end there was a terrible climax. I beat Joe in the final exam and so had to be given the gold dux medal (which, to my furious embarrassment, was presented in our sitting room by dark-suited men from the Education Board and the School Committee, because schools were closed all that summer for a polio epidemic). Joe was very upset and I felt pretty uncomfortable myself. 'I'll beat you at high school!' he hissed, but before that could happen he went up to play on the roof with Fatty Frederickson, still full of bravado; there he slipped, grasped a naked electric wire and was killed instantly. There were no more parties after that, no more ebullient talk of big fish teas and the like. Josie and I were in different forms at Girls' High, and our lives took different paths.

But while we were still small, she and I played companionably for hours, building houses with the lettuce boxes (in the years Dad grew them for the market), climbing the willow tree, playing families with dolls in the long grass beyond the plum tree, sitting on comfortable branches in the plum or apricot trees, eating our way through the summer crops. Lindsay was a part of all these activities, through the timeless summers that childhood is composed of, and remained my true favourite; nevertheless Josie and I sometimes felt it necessary to exclude her from our secrets. When Josie, and Chrissie too if she was there, had the spike with me, Lindsay had to be hastily reinstated. She was wonderfully good-tempered about these sudden changes of status, my sister.

When the house-building phase was at its height, Lindsay and I called in aid from an unlikely quarter, and asked Clive to help build a platform in the fork of the willow tree where we could have a real house, one in which we could sleep all night. This became a devouring ambition. We thought of nothing else for days; it was the May holidays and Josie and Chrissie were both away. Laboriously we nailed the boards for the floor to bits of branch or trunk, tacked sacks higher up so we had walls and a place to crawl into. There wasn't a lot of room by the time we had furnished the room with cushions, books, dolls, apples, biscuits and all the other paraphernalia of occupation.

On the night we were allowed to try, darkness seemed much delayed; Lindsay and I went to bed about a thousand hours before dusk even began. However it did slowly, slowly come; we wriggled into better positions, changed back, tried other angles; Lindsay's knees grew huge and bony, she said I had to turn over, I said I'd stick out through the wall, she said I was stopping her going to sleep, I said she was too fat to sleep with anyway. The morepork that lived in the bush over the road behind the pine trees hooted sorrowfully; we looked out to see if the kitchen light was on or if they'd gone to bed and left us out there all alone. It was on; we agreed not to talk for five minutes while we went to sleep. When it was nearly morning and we'd tried every way to stretch out but couldn't, and had nevertheless heroically slept for hours, we thought it was fair to go inside, and finish off the night in our beds. When we got to the kitchen Dad was still up, reading. It was nine o'clock.

Chapter 5

Greenmeadows was a village, and we took part in local activities and performances without question. Our mother was a faithful member of the Women's Institute, intermittently secretary or president of the Gardening Circle and always president of the Drama Circle. They wrote away to Samuel French and Co. for hired sets of plays, English drawing-room comedies mostly, and either rehearsed and performed them in the Taradale Town Hall or did readings in one another's sitting-rooms. When it was our turn there was much preparation, the making of peanut brownies, rock cakes, Sydney Special (a concoction of rolled oats, coconut, sugar and butter, otherwise known as Doormat) and orange cake.

Sketches were often preferred to plays, and our mother soon took to writing these herself. You took an incident – someone's cow breaking a fence and getting into a patch of prize cabbages grown by a hated neighbour . . . There would be talk of gentle swishing sounds heard outside the window, dreamy speculation about visitors, the sound of a sudden loud moo . . . then confusion, outrage; the reckoning. This kind of scenario produced highly popular comedy, especially when local names and street addresses were included. I myself came to have an enthusiasm for mimicry and self-dramatisation and took to doing solo acts ('This is a youthful portrait of Miss Dolores Swinburne the famous actress who is paying her first visit to friends in Greenmeadows New Zealand . . . '), but of course I performed these in strict privacy at home. I also impersonated screen heroes and heroines; George Arliss was my great triumph; Joan Blondell I wasn't bad at either, but when I did Charles Boyer (divine creature) they thought I was just myself, simpering.

I too wrote some plays, which Clive and Lindsay and I, and John when he was old enough, performed on the front lawn, with the flowering currant bush as backdrop. Our audience was Mum and Dad, with any visiting aunts and uncles and cousins, sitting on chairs brought out from the kitchen. But when I was about twelve, and Lindsay ten, we were invited to perform in the Taradale Town Hall at an evening of plays and sketches, real public ones, organised by Mum's Drama Circle.

Our piece was called *The Bathroom Tap* and consisted of four scenes showing the same incident. The first was set in New Zealand: the tap blocks, father knows all about plumbing, mother grieves that the children will go to bed dirty, father unblocks the pipe, mother hails him as a hero. In the English version mother rails against the servants, father wears a bowler hat and is pompous. The tap is fixed by a relation of the butler's, visiting below stairs. The Italian scene was one of wild confusion with the characters running about the stage waving their arms and shouting. The last scene was the Russian one, and our downfall. Lindsay and I sat on either side of a table, front of stage; at long intervals we were to say with a profound sigh, 'Ah it doez not matterrr. Eet eez all one. The waterrr runs . . . the soul endures . . . ' while other people rushed in and out shouting that the tap had burst, the floor was flooded, the cat was drowned and so on. The pensive silences in the face of all this fuss were too much for Lindsay and me. The audience began to doubt us, started to laugh; we smiled, screwed up our faces to make them stop, put our hands over our mouths, braced our shoulders. In the end we lost all semblance of control and shrieked with laughter ourselves, beginning again each time we tried, 'Eet does not matterrr . . . ' Finally the audience began to stamp in a way that told us unmistakably that we had done our time. We crept away still shaking, a disgrace to a great profession.

Clive and I also experimented with a different kind of performance; the creation of Ikey, the smallest man in the world. Clive, wearing a celluloid nose, fluffy black moustache and blue woollen hat, appeared before the curtain as Ikey's head; his chest, dressed in the rest of the blue woollen suit – an old one of John's – was Ikey's body, and his hands in small shoes stood on the table as the little man's feet. My job was to crouch behind Clive and reach through to provide the hands. We set up a tent at a school fair, and there Ikey chattered and told stories and jokes in a voice we imagined was foreign, dancing on the table and waving his hands about. Teddy Tronson took the threepences. He lived at the end of Osier Road and was entertaining to us, it has to be admitted, because he said 'w' for 'r' and recited 'Gwasshopper Gween' ('Gwasshopper Gween is a comical chap . . . bwight little twousers jacket and cap . . . '). However, he controlled our audiences, and we made ten shillings and sixpence.

We had our part to play in the Garden Circle too. Every year there was a Flower Show in the Taradale Town Hall and every year Lindsay and I entered the junior sections; we made tight little posies, arranged collections of wild flowers (which always died before the judges had appraised them) and, most importantly, created miniature gardens in trays of sand. These had pebble paths, lawns of scissored clippings from the real lawn supplemented by moss, ponds made of handbag mirrors, flower beds of heads of geraniums, geums, thrift and daisies. You could make a bush out of a forget-me-not spray, a rockery from a pine cone, fences and gates out of sticks. They were magical creations, the most elegant kind of playing house, yet as earthy as mud pies. They took hours and hours the night before the show; last-minute replacements of wilting grass or flower heads had to be rushed through early in the morning, before Mum set out to carry them, with her own exhibits, to the hall. Dad had to be home that morning to drive her there; we had to go to school but of course paid it no attention, merely sitting out the time till we could get out at two o'clock (as you did on Show Day) and race round to the hall to see who'd got the red, blue and yellow tickets for first and second places and highly commended.

For city children there must have been other textures and smells and colours, the things that make up a permanent memory in your hands and body, the shape of what you most often touch and hold. The sensations I kept were the wrenching, piling, caressing heaps of grass, picking the slender stems of wood daffodils (the small all-yellow ones, the only daffodils with a perfume), drawing words and pictures on the glossy surfaces of taupata leaves with a stick or nail. And of course the whole-body sensation of lying in the hot-scented grass, crouching in the dark prickles of the underside of the hedge, or flying, exhilarated and appalled, too high on the willow tree swing; scrambling up its rough trunk to the windy places above and there, at the right time of year, picking sprays of catkins – the word, which I liked to say over and over, as satisfying as the little fuzzy heads themselves.

Grass itself was not one thing, but a whole population in the small hot countries of summer playing in the paddock. Prairie grass was the aristocrat, its seed heads were the tallest and its seed shells, lapped over one another like the wing feathers of a sparrow, were good to hold. Brown top was shorter, more plebeian, its head squat and hairy, rye grass all sheen and smooth overlapping – besides being the instrument for 'Tinker tailor soldier sailor richman poorman beggarman thief', as plantains were for soldier fights with Lindsay. There was another, nameless, grass with a sharp prickly head, the stick-like ends of each seed turned back to front; this made them uncomfortable to handle, but they were dangerous as well – if you got pricked with one of these sharp sticks it would go into your body, follow your bloodstream to your heart, where it would prick you till you died.

Outside we were on our own. Inside were our parents, and occasions of another sort. Lindsay and I made presents in secret for Christmas and our mother's birthday – handkerchiefs in sachets, oven cloths decorated with the fancy stitches we'd learnt from Miss Shugar. They were lumpy, asymmetrical, puckered, but the revelation of our secret was always delightful. Mum gazed at them as though they were embroidered on the finest damask, turned them over, praised and admired. We squirmed in our happiness, telling her, at last, of the times she had nearly caught us at it, of the desperate hiding of evidence, of the horror of discovering, with only days to go, that MUMY was seen to be a letter short, of the nights crouching over our art works by candlelight, the early mornings when we woke each other when the house was still quiet and the sparrows just beginning to whisper outside our window.

I think our parents loved each other. They laughed together often, and seemed to have an array of shared occupations that suited both equally. They read to each other for instance, Dad doing rather more than his share because Mum usually had hemming or domes and hooks to sew on dresses or shirts while she listened. Wodehouse's Jeeves books were among their favourites; they read the series through and then at intervals did them all again, falling about laughing at Bertie Wooster's wounded dignity and Jeeves' calculated deceptions, his suave 'Yes, sir', 'Indeed, sir? I am sorry to hear that.' They sometimes sat at the kitchen table in the evening with a Jeeves volume, forgetting the time we were supposed to go to bed. 'Great Scott, Jeeves! Look at that girl just coming on to the pier,' Dad said in his Bertie Wooster voice, 'I never saw anybody so extraordinarily like Miss Wickham. How do you account for the resemblance?' 'In the present instance, sir, I attribute the similarity to the fact that the young lady is Miss Wickham.' 'Eh?' 'Yes, sir. If you notice, she is waving to you now.'

30

'But what on earth is she doing down here?' 'I am unable to say, sir.'

We could probably have stayed up for hours before they noticed the time. But Lindsay and I had our own business to attend to. Some time before, the light bulb in our room had blown and we began to use a candle. We had an enamel candlestick with a handle to put your finger through, the kind Wee Willie Winkie used in nursery rhyme books, and a brass snuffer-out that Grandma had given us. An elaborate ritual had grown up round these possessions: we had to stand together at the far end of the passage by the kitchen door and race for the door of the bedroom because only there could our bagsing begin; first finished – with bagsing I mean – had all the best things to do. 'I-bags-lighting-and-snuffing-out-the-candle-bags-you-fold-the-bed-covers' was thus shouted in a high babble, no single word distinguishable from another; the one who got finished first could play with the candle and its warm and plastic wax for as long as she liked, while the other morosely spread out the bed covers on the floor to get the edges straight. Other details were later added to the struggle – bags-you-open-the-window, bags-you-push-the-door-stopper-round (a flannel-covered brick that lurked behind the door during the day) and even bags-you-do-all-the-dusting-on-Saturday, but this, my idea, proved unworkable. When Saturday came, Lindsay claimed she couldn't remember and that I'd made it up.

When I was a few years older, I stayed up in the kitchen myself, long after the parents had gone to bed. There I devoured *The Mill on the Floss, The Cloister and the Hearth, Silas Marner, A Tale of Two Cities* and all the A.S. Neill books – *A Dominie's Log, A Dominie Abroad* and so on. I read as one addicted, fearing nothing except the moment when I had to stop or the story came to an end, and emerging to find real life unfocused and shadowy by comparison. Lorna Doone was especially magnetic; it was winter, and I raced back each night to my craving, symbolised by the faintly sweet smell that clung to my bookmark, a piece of raisin packet. The aura of danger and daring that clung to the Doone outlaws, the earthy reality of the moors, the wild weather and the waterfall up which John Ridd must eventually climb to reach the lovely Lorna at the top, all echoed my own sense of the drama of the earth and its wild places (though Greeenmeadows was clearly tamer than the moors of Exeter). When I came to *Wuthering Heights* a lot of my pleasure came from the physical reverberations of the place itself, and the sensations associated with that dramatic weather.

But this did not rule out delights of a different kind – Georgette Heyer's elegant club-and-drawing-room romances, and Edward S. Ellis's Deerfoot books, which I borrowed from Clive, weeping bitterly when Deerfoot, having survived every terror in the woods of the American West, as the white frontiersman cleared the Indians out, died of a broken heart at the loss of his squaw. Scott's *The Talisman*, tale of the Crusades, was riveting too, and of course *Jane Eyre*, when I came to it, I read so often that much of it I came to know by heart, as I did *Pride and Prejudice*. The world you entered by reading was a vast, various place centred in England but including America too, and a past which was more or less indistinguishable from the present. Pretty well every time and place in fact, except New Zealand.

It was Clive who introduced William into the household; the sight of him sitting at the kitchen table or out on the verandah or in the willow tree laughing his head off – not privately, inside himself, but loudly, helplessly, a wild cackle – aroused everyone's curiosity; in the end we all read them, all insisted on reading bits aloud, even to those who knew them already. And the series went on and on, there seemed no end to the disastrous child's escapades. Clive's laughter was like the uncles', possessing him completely; every now and then he would cry 'Crikey!' or 'Stone the crows!' as he took breath. The perfect recommendation.

Long after I could read myself, Dad went on reading some things to me. All of *Alice in Wonderland* and *Through the Looking Glass* he read in his quiet musical voice, while I lay in bed listening to him dramatising characters like the Gryphon or the Red Queen or Tweedle Dum and Tweedle Dee. I think this habit began when I had tonsilitis and had to spend time in bed anyway. I often had sore throats and despite friar's balsam inhalations and sulphur lamps in our room, they wouldn't go away. Dr Will, dark, dignified and doctor-smelling, came and looked down my throat, listened to my chest with a stethoscope, made me say ninety-nine, and decided that I should go to Napier Hospital to have my tonsils out.

Lindsay wrote in her diary 'Lauris went in to the hospital to get her tonsols out and John has to get his out soon. I have to do all Laurises jobs we went to see her today. Mummy has got the flew but she will not go to bed . . . Lauris is home now and I always get her tray ready. She had bread and milk becos it is soft Josie brought some pretty violets. Laurises throat is sore and she gose to bed first and I go after.'

Greater drama was to follow. The wound, made by surgical scissors, healed but the sore throats continued. Dr Will came one day and exclaimed with great excitement that my tonsils had grown again. Back to hospital I went to have the offending organs burnt out; I had to stay several days in the children's ward, which as it turned out opened up a territory so forbidden that to enter it made me feel wicked indeed. In a word, it provided comics.

Comics were not allowed at our place; other children might wallow, we must not. It's hard to say how I knew even their names *(Tiger Tim, Chuck, Beano)* or that the stories were in little boxes alongside pictures, and were racier than 'real' books. In the hospital ward there were two other children, Madge and Jimmy, who had piles of comics which they took for granted I must have my turn to read. They were also wonderfully naughty, cheeked the nurse, jumped out of bed and ran round the room as soon as she'd barred us from putting a foot to the floor, made dirty jokes about bedpans. They giggled wildly, and so did I. My cheeks were hot all day with excitement and guilt; I read the comics down to the last ragged page and didn't say a word to Madge or Jimmy about how 'good' I really was. At night I fell into a flushed and exhausted sleep, like a drunk sleeping off the excesses of the day.

Madge and Jimmy didn't have visits from their families every day as I did. When mine came, my evil companions were silent, pretended not to look, and never referred to this interruption once the bell had gone. Mum smiled at them in a way that I suppose was gracious as she walked out; they pretended to be asleep.

At home and convalescent, I received visitors; girls who lived across the road in the new St Joseph's Maori Girls' College and shared with Lindsay and me a craze for autograph books. The girls were all beautiful, we thought, brown and smiling, and what's more they had spectacular handwriting. It made me very proud to have even the least remarkable autograph ('By hook or by crook I'll be first/last in this book') inscribed in my book in their graceful curves and twirls, especially on the capitals. Huia, my favourite, wrote a longer piece: 'In the wood box of your memory regard me as a chip'.

I also wrote to pen friends, an English second cousin, a boy in Sydney, Lexie, a girl exactly my age who lived in Wellington. In 1940 when the Centennial Exhibition burst into amusement parks, fair stalls and circus acts she invited me to stay with her; I spent a dazed week riding the scenic railway, firing balls at the open mouths of wooden clowns, gabbling tongue-twisters into a 2ZB microphone (and winning a box of small dry chocolates). We took photos of each other standing in our Deanna Durbin halo hats on the steps of the museum, and promised to be friends for ever.

Chapter 6

The Napier Girls' High School motto was *Ad Lucem*, Towards the Light. Its uniform was a navy blue serge gym frock, white long-sleeved blouse and tie, blue blazer, black woollen stockings and black brogue shoes, laced; a navy felt hat with hat band in the winter and white panama in the summer. During my years there a merciful regulation was introduced which allowed sockettes and sandals to be worn at school, but not outside the school gate. You had to make a cloth bag with a string through the top to carry your change of footwear. There was also a white piqué gym frock for sports days and special occasions, and you could get permission to wear it on ordinary days. The material crumpled so badly that instead of the deep pleats neutralising the adolescent bulges of our bodies, by morning interval you looked like a basket of white washing.

Girls from Greenmeadows and Taradale caught a school bus – vehicles which, we believed, were given to the school when too broken down for the ordinary run. They graunched and clanked up Shakespeare Road so slowly that local girls passed us, walking to school; on the steepest bit at the top we had to get out and walk too. The long bus rides, winding through the damp post-earthquake country of the old inner harbour, were times for finishing homework, for gossiping, exchanging secrets, sometimes for quarrelling. Girls of twelve to eighteen, squeezed up together, smell different from small children; it's a more womanly body smell, of sweat, hot skin (sometimes pimple-infested), oily hair, and the peculiar dark reek of blood locked into sanitary towels, fresh or stale. At least a quarter of the thirty or forty girls in a busload would be having their 'pain' (we had never heard the word 'menstruating') at any one time, and in the summer, especially on the way home on a hot afternoon, the stink was pleasurably strong – pleasurable to me anyway, because when I first went to high school I hadn't 'started' at all, and was deeply envious of girls who had. They felt their superiority too, and conferred with one another about the annoyance of unreliable safety pins, the bother of having 'it' on sports day, and the trial of little brothers and sisters.

I had first learnt of the strange phenomenon from Marcia Redgrove, the daughter of a Social Credit acquaintance of my father's; I'd met her at a Social Credit camp. She was a bit older than me and had a worldliness that I found fascinating and slightly sinister. Not that she wore sophisticated clothes, or was 'smart' like the families of some girls at school; Marcia went to a private school so I only saw her on arranged visits. She had a style that seemed to me darkly Victorian – lisle stockings, high-necked blouses, horn-rimmed spectacles. She had a swarthy skin and a faint moustache. When I went to her house her two parents, immensely old, withdrew after shaking hands and left us alone in the 'drawing room'. There Marcia showed me their art books, finding in each the female naked figures which she dwelt on with a lingering intensity, stroking their nipples, the shadows of their pubic hair, the curve of their thighs. Flushed and alarmed, I agreed from time to time that this was of *course* what I wanted to do.

My initiation came at a Girl Guide camp when I was about eleven. In between expeditions designed to help you get badges such as Tracker's (for which you had to learn to recognise signs left on rocks or trees by other Guides) or Fire Lighter's (without matches and in the rain), Marcia and I managed to find time for secret talks. She told me that it was 'that time of the month' for her, and that she had awful pains 'down there'. She began telling me by hints – a raised eyebrow, eyes rolled in 'that' direction – when she was going to the sack-enclosed cubicles that were our latrines, and intended me to follow her. I was afraid I was going to have to enter the same cubicle, but she merely gave me a running commentary through the sacking wall of how awful it was, more blood than yesterday, how she had to change frighteningly often, far more than other girls. I smelt the fearsome odour, listened aghast to the details, mourned my own body's childishness.

But the information was useful at school in fending off the dreaded question: 'You mean you haven't started AT ALL?' When at last I did, and Mum gave me some of her own little towels and made me others, she didn't tell me – and neither did anyone else – about the connection between this and the birth of babies. In Standard 6 groups of girls used to huddle in corners of the playground talking about things I knew were 'dirty'. 'Go away!' they would snigger in rude voices when I approached, 'You're not allowed, you're too good.' I ate my lunch alone, hating my difference, mystified about what it was.

Eventually on a camping holiday when I was fourteen, Mum took reluctant action. She suggested we go for a walk, and broached the subject of period pains – were they bad? Did I talk to other girls about them? What, if anything, had I said to Lindsay? At last, with much hesitating, did I know why I had them? When she told me the rudimentary facts, I asked why I didn't have a baby then, since I'd begun the other thing. She struggled through an outline of the process of copulation. Did people do that every time they wanted a baby? Yes, they did. With supreme heroism she added that sometimes they did it anyway. 'What for?' I demanded, incredulous. 'You mean they do it for lust?' I don't know how that word suddenly appeared, but it silenced her for a while. 'I suppose you could call it that,' she brought out in the end, miserably. 'Shall we go back now?' And in separate thoughtful silences we walked back to the tent together.

My agonies at being a goody-goody and sometimes friendless in Standard 6 vanished with a change of school. Suddenly I was among people who thought as I did – or, more importantly, didn't care whether we thought the same or not. When we talked, differences were interesting rather than an offence, and after a whole school life where everyone was located according to their house or street, I found it tantalising to guess why girls were as they were and what other lives they might have, hidden in a past or present I could not know.

We had all sat an entrance exam and according to our results been advised – or our parents had – about the most suitable course to take. I wanted to 'do academic' anyway; although I'd learnt no language except English (and a few words of Maori), I was keen to try both Latin and French, the two foreign languages the school offered. Competitiveness remained part of the natural order – you were always better or worse than someone else, as I well knew from the years of rivalry with Joe Alexander, not to mention the fierce competing of Fanny and Alice, the jealous sisters. In any case I found the new subjects a pleasure and didn't think much about results. French, Latin, Algebra and Geometry – I adored them all. Algebra was especially satisfying – to extract patterns of reality out of x's and y's without ever giving them the ordinary old names like 5 or 9 took me into new kinds of thinking, with the weight on the oblique, not the direct, yet it was an indirectness that called for the greatest possible precision. It was not unlike the experience of poetry, though I didn't associate the two just then. Latin too had wonderful inbuilt rewards, like the pleasure of getting case and gender exactly in line; even French, a living language, had this quality. Although we learned phonetics and practised all the new nasal sounds with relish, we didn't seriously think of it as a language some people speak all the time. It too was a 'subject'.

There was a more personal aspect to French in that I got a crush on the teacher. She was a tall, erect figure and wore dresses in gold and bronze colours; she strode rather than walked about the school, her black degree gown billowing out behind her. Miss Moncrieff – she had wavy brown hair, an angular face that I thought of as 'sculptured', grey eyes and a wide mouth. I loved her so much that I had to pretend to much greater ignorance than I felt, and arrange to have special coaching alone with her in the classroom at lunchtime.

There she would go patiently through parts of irregular verbs and exceptions to rules while I stood adoringly at her side. From time to time she would say 'Do you see now?' and I would frown, afraid the sessions might come to an end, and say cautiously, 'I think I do, I'm not quite sure Miss Moncrieff . . . ' Just saying her name, there in the intimacy of our tête-à-tête, was a delight.

After Easter she came back to school wearing a diamond ring on her engagement finger; at once it changed her. Perhaps I had wanted to marry her myself; at any rate I stopped pretending I didn't understand French, and joined as volubly as anyone else in the intense discussions we held between periods, or at interval and lunchtime, about who he was, how he'd proposed, what she'd said, and how obvious it was that for weeks she'd stood by the window gazing dreamily into the courtyard behind the school, and now she never bothered, but went briskly about her business. You could see she'd come down to earth now she'd got her heart's desire.

At first I knew no one, being the only girl from Taradale school in 3A, but gradually a group of us began to find some common cause. Teachers were mostly a joke; theories about the meaning of life very serious – atheism, theosophy, rationalism, universal equality. But the most absorbing subject was ourselves, what we planned to do with our lives, how awful our parents were, how victimised we were by the twin powers of home and school, their general failure to understand our quality. The one who had the clearest sense of her future was Daisy. She was going to be a novelist. In fact she had already written most of her first book, and could and did tell us about it, showing us pages of her crabbed markings with a mysterious and triumphant air. It was about a young girl locked in a castle by a handsome desperado who threatened to kill her if she didn't do his bidding – cooking and cleaning for the twenty soldiers of his personal bodyguard. In return he would make her co-ruler of all their territories. According to Daisy he would ravish her as well (the word sounded as though he would stand in front of her, too star-struck by her beauty to do anything at all, but even to me that seemed improbable). We said it sounded marvellous. I secretly thought it silly, but admired unreservedly the purposefulness of her ambition. My writing of poems was nothing like that, and I never mentioned it; it was clear that Daisy was a real writer and I was not. I did, it's true, write poems for the school magazine, and the supposedly witty Form Notes, but that was hardly remarkable, to Daisy or to me.

Daisy was a boarder in the school hostel, and, with two others, she sometimes visited me on Days Out. The others were Jemima, Jim for short, who lived on a sheep station in northern Hawke's Bay and was placid and matronly and benign, and in my eyes terribly mature; and Beth, the most worldly-wise of the four of us. She had a quiet unsurprised way of listening to our ravings, particularly Daisy's and mine, as though she 'knew about that' already.

These visits were regarded by my family with a mixture of unease and gratification. I would go to meet my friends at the bus stop struck by a sudden shyness: there they were in their navy blue suits, boarders' dress uniform, looking polite and formal. We walked back to the house, they exclaimed artificially about the countryside, I droned on about who lived in each house we passed. They didn't seem to care; I fell silent. When we got home it was worse. They stood about saying 'Yes, Mrs Scott' and 'No, Mrs Scott' to Mum's attempts at being jolly. John came in with mud all down his front, blushed and ran out without speaking; the hole in the lino under the kitchen table grew enormous – they surely lived in mansions and were used to great grandeur. Lindsay came in, I glared at her, but she refused to look at me and said cheerfully, 'Would you like a ride on Tommy?' Tommy was the badtempered Shetland pony from the farm at Patoka; Uncle Bert had sent him into isolation at our place. He had bitten me the day before, and the previous weekend had come right up to the back verandah and eaten a loaf of bread Mum had taken from the oven and put out to cool.

'They don't want to do that!' I said at once. But I was wrong, they did. What's more they wanted to change out of those stuffy uniforms and borrow clothes of ours. 'I'll show you,' squeaked Lindsay, thoroughly above herself. Whether I liked it or not, off we went to catch Tommy; at the end of the afternoon they said, 'Oh thank you, Mrs Scott, we've had a terrific day.' But afterwards when Lindsay asked 'Shall we play Grab?' trying to lure me into our room, I just said no, I really couldn't be bothered.

On sports days my mother turned up to watch; like other girls' mothers, she was an embarrassment. I talked to her as little as possible and tried not to let anyone find out which one was mine. One year the Duke of Gloucester visited the school, and we crouched down in formation to make NGHS, before we sat in rows to listen to his and others' speeches. We did not know till afterwards that the reason members of his party stood so close was that he was usually drunk, and they did not want him to fall over; I did not pass this on to Mum at all.

As we grew up, Clive continued to have the fiercest rows, but mine too could be sustained and violent. Usually my crime was that I was selfish, but sometimes I was stubborn as well. For instance about Joyce Paterson's party; she had an older boyfriend whose family had parties where they played 'Postman's Knock', pairing off to kiss on the porch or in the garden. I had been to one and was scared to death of going again, but Fanny was convinced it was part of my social education. In the end my obliging throat was sore, I couldn't go, and she and I established a suspicious truce.

But she was all co-operation with my friends. Avis was another, much closer than the boarders, who arrived suddenly in Greenmeadows with her mother and sister to live in a house in Osier Road. The sister was Lindsay's age and they came to assume a position halfway between friends and family. The sisters were darkly beautiful, and they had a beautiful mother too. She, in a rather more guarded way, made friends with our mother, though they never got further than 'Good morning, Mrs Stenson' 'Ah, Mrs Scott!' Mrs Stenson had a glamorous history into which we were slowly initiated. She had been an interpreter with the Maori Land Court in Rotorua; and indeed the brown eyes and olive skin we admired so much told us they were Maori themselves, though nobody said so. Mrs Stenson had come to fulfil the conditions (a period of separation) for a divorce. She was to marry another man – rich, something to do with an oil company – who lived in Australia.

Lindsay and I looked at each other in wonder when we heard this. We didn't know anyone who had been divorced, and were really a little shocked, though loyalty to our new friends prevented our saying so. Avis and Betty seemed perfectly at home with their bizarre destiny and referred to it, if at all, in the most offhand way. Mum never mentioned Mrs Stenson's past or future; ours went on being the usual sort of parents, Avis called for me to walk to the end of the road to catch the school bus every morning, God went back to his heaven.

After a while Mrs Stenson took a house in Napier and Avis and I began to spend weekends in each other's houses. This induced much greater intimacy, particularly when we sat late over the fire on Saturday nights, made toast with a long toasting fork, and drew plans for the houses we would one day live in. We pored over these for hours, changing rooms and porches and staircases and copying ladies in fine clothes from Mum's dressmaking pattern books, to show ourselves walking about our houses and gardens. Avis told me that in Rotorua she had fallen in love with her cousin, and her family disapproved; it's dangerous to marry a first cousin because your children would be cripples or mongols and anyway he was a Maori and they wanted her to marry someone white. She still loved Ted though, they wrote to each other in secret and were going to wait till they were twenty-one.

My knowledge of love was suddenly paltry. It included Miss Moncrieff, a brief passion for the head prefect in my first year at high school, and Mr Samuel. He was the young Tongan Methodist minister who rode past our gate every day on his motor bike, and for whom I attended a great many Sunday school teas with Nona, since she was a Methodist and I was not. And a freckly boy in a motor camp one summer. Not much, really.

When Avis announced that we should go to dancing classes in Napier, I agreed with proper humility. She would shine like a star, I would be in a corner shrouded in the invisibility I knew shyness confers. There were two tutors: Madeleine (she told us this wasn't her real name) wore a pink dress with a full skirt and black patent leather shoes with high heels. Richard's shoes shone too, his trousers were tight on his long legs, and he wore a black bow tie. He looked like the dressed-up eel shown simpering at Father William in the *Illustrated Alice in Wonderland* we had at home.

The girls stood in a line spread across the room (upstairs, above Mason and Mason, Barristers and Solicitors in Dickens Street); Madeleine, with her back to us, out in front, did each step and we followed. 'Back slide close,' we chanted, shuffling backwards for the modern waltz, and 'One two three, one two three' while Victor Sylvester and his dance band uncoiled, smooth as a velvet ribbon, out of the gramophone. When we took partners, Avis came into her own. Richard himself often asked her to dance; so did Larry, a sleek youth who was said to work for T & G Insurance. The only person who seemed to want to dance with me was Stanley, who was heavy on his feet and smelt of fish paste – so strongly that sometimes I thought of asking him what he'd had for tea. 'Slow slow quick quick slow,' we intoned together. Anything was better than conversation.

Chapter 7

There was another girl in my form who had grown up in Napier, been to intermediate, knew heaps of girls and was in every way an aristocrat. She had parents who went to cocktail parties too; she was stylish, but not unduly superior. On the contrary, she was rather shy, and seemed not to be aware of her natural advantages. She had a straight jaw and nose, high cheek bones (a bit like Miss Moncrieff) and slightly buck teeth that gave her smile a wonderfully amused quality. Her name was Molly. I got to know her slowly, but by the end of the second year she was unassailably my best friend and we had begun to spend weekends with each other's families and in all ways to share our secret lives. Eventually it became necessary to spend most afternoons after school together, and then go home and ring each other up for hour-long conversations. These were toll calls, and our fathers came to have strong views about them.

Molly's family lived in a two-storeyed gabled house in a garden dim with overhanging trees; a row of huge palm trees stood along the front of the house, giving an exotic touch to its wide verandahs and low eaves. The family had a way of acting out their lives as though every moment was a dramatic performance. Molly had an older sister called Renée, who had the same artlessness of manner that allowed them both to appear wide-eyed ingenues and at the same moment conscious young sophisticates. They would rush breathlessly upstairs to their rooms to confer about some tremendous trifle – that Renée's young man, when he came to take her out, wore an impossible shiny jacket . . . his feelings must not be hurt, but clearly one of us must invite him to take it off, another engage him in conversation, a third lose it. They did not shriek and giggle as Lindsay and I did; they were brilliantly funny by being serious.

Mrs Magnus was beautiful, gentle, sweet-tempered, perhaps frivolously social (casual references to cocktail parties and dinners seemed to say so). She was unmistakably not the one in charge of the household (unlike, I realised, my own mother); Mr Magnus was. He was smarter than his wife, but had none of her grace or good looks. He was considerably shorter, rather red in the face, beginning to go bald, and often came home smelling of liquor, his flush and gaiety more hectic than usual. He was affectionate and tolerant towards Molly and me, treating us as mildly amusing pets, though he sometimes pointed out details of our clothes or hairdos in a way that made me uncomfortable and Molly full of indignant protest. She would lecture him, and he would smile as if to say, 'My daughter has such spirit!'

One evening when we were in the sixth form and going to a school dance, Mr Magnus came in from Bowls as I was talking on the phone in the hall, while the family were sitting in the dining room. He came straight up to me, ignoring the phone and my conversation, and began kissing me closely and urgently. I sat there, completely helpless; I could not move, or think. At last the dining-room door opened, he made some jolly remark about how pretty my dress was, appeared merely to pat my shoulder, and went upstairs to change. Then he came in to dinner, and neither then nor at any other time did he show any sign of remembering this astonishing event.

That same year, during a weekend at my place, Molly and I had to share a single bed; Lindsay couldn't move out of hers, as she usually did, because the stretcher was used by a welfare boy Dad had decided to 'give a chance' to by offering him an apprenticeship. This boy, Ron, lived with us, sleeping in a porch Dad had built enclosing part of the front verandah, but he stole money from Mum's purse, and the night after she and a visiting welfare officer questioned him about it, he peeed all over the wall of the new little porch. Dad was devastated, crushed for a time by such disappointment.

But the weekend Molly came, Ron had just arrived. He slept on his little porch, eating with us in silence and going off to his room at once. Molly and I went for a walk to see Nona, my Methodist friend who lived in Taradale; the evening was cool and pleasant. Nona's mother was the usual sort, stout, always wearing an apron, able to produce biscuits on sight; she gave us some shortbread and a cup of malted milk. Coming back down Osier Road in the dusk we sniffed the osiers' herbal scent and remarked that Nona would get fat like her mother and we were lucky our mothers were thin. After we'd gone to bed, and ostensibly stopped talking to go to sleep, we began slowly to caress each other's bodies under our pyjamas. We stroked each other's breasts, I at first lying behind her with one arm across her waist, then by a silent consent turning over so she could do the same. Then, holding this embrace, we went to sleep. The next morning we made no reference to this queer burst of intimacy. It just sank, I suppose, with all the other extraordinary events that seemed to mark one's progress towards adult experience, into that private limbo where it would never be revealed, and never forgotten.

On my sixteenth birthday I had a surprise party, the only one I had ever been to. The day was a Saturday. At breakfast Lindsay had given me some slippers, Mum and Dad *Pickwick Papers* (which I'd started to read at school, and liked), Clive a ruler inlaid with New Zealand woods which he'd made at woodwork, and John an embroidered handkerchief. Avis (living with us while her mother was in Australia) did me a watercolour of the flowering currant bush. We were going to spend the evening at home as usual – there would probably be *Dad and Dave* on the wireless, or *Eb and Zeb*; or we could play gramophone records, or sing. Why then did Avis start urging me to change my clothes? It's silly, I said, they're for going out. 'Oh go on,' she begged, 'it's your birthday, isn't it? Everyone dresses up a bit for that.' In the end she persuaded me, and then enticed me to go, wary and unco-operative as I was, into the sitting room with her. Ah, that moment of revelation . . . five dressed up girls, all my special friends, sitting around the room smiling . . . the amazement, the confessions, the tales of being smuggled in the back door . . . the discovery that after tea we were to go to the pictures in Napier, to *Pride and Prejudice*, everyone's best-loved story . . . the appearance of Clive, sheepishly dressed up too (he was to be allowed to drive us into town). We floated in a froth of delight, they were the cleverest, most deceiving plotters in the world, I the most enchanted victim.

Lindsay had been a great help with the preparations, but she wasn't allowed even to ask if she could go with us. However the next morning I did have to thank her, and properly too. 'I already have,' I said rudely, gripped by my social hangover.

Clive was beginning to fall in love with girls. He fell for Avis first, then Molly; wanted to borrow the car to take them to the pictures, to hang around when I was talking to them. He was awkward and eager, which annoyed me greatly; worse, he was trampling on my cherished friendships by introducing these two, in turn, to experiences they could not describe to me in the colourful detail we liked and practised.

Avis was a more elusive, more dangerous prey, and stalking her made Clive much more anxious – so much so that he was several times known to 'drink beer' (in Mum's ominous phrase) to get his courage up. At least that's the reason he gave me, as we walked down Osier Road together after separate visits to friends one Saturday afternoon. I complained that he smelt nasty and it was a silly thing to do. He was massively indifferent. Clive was used to being in trouble; rows and upheavals surrounded his every action. Even when we were small, he often got the stick, the willow switch raising red weals on his thighs, though usually I think he'd merely wanted to be like other boys, to go birds-nesting instead of practising the violin (which he played beautifully and came to hate), or play cricket, or camp out.

Beer drinking was his worst crime; the very idea of it sent Fanny into a kind of frenzy, and one day when I was home from school with a cold and she began to tell me stories about Grandfather Price, I glimpsed the reason. Sometimes late at night her father would arrive at a place where the farm met the road, several paddocks distance from the house; there he would stand and holler, loud, drunken and peremptory, and Fanny, at eight or nine, would have to go and lead him over stiles and through gates, put him on his feet when he fell over, and deliver him to her mother, whose job it was to undress him and put him to bed. Sometimes the 'Old Man' gambled, playing cards with his cronies by the fire and drinking poker beer. On those evenings she and the other children might see them, drunk and careless, relieving themselves outside the back door. I pictured the scene; recoiled, shocked. How extraordinary it was though, that these grotesque tales referred to the benign and intelligent old man I knew, chuckling over his wizard puzzles in the big bath chair on his Hastings verandah.

Clive 'touched drink' usually after long Saturday or Sunday afternoons with his friends, tinkering with some car or motor bike engine. He really loved engines. When we were children, every family journey by car had as its accompaniment Clive's high-pitched nasal whine, 'Zooming along at eigh-tee nee-ow nee-ow nee-ow', on and on till we all wanted to kill him. After he'd left school, and the war had begun, he applied for entry to a naval training course as an engineer. Because he was under twenty-one his father's permission was needed, and our parents simply decided, without a word to Clive, that the Navy was too dangerous and they refused to agree.

This curious decision fitted into a pattern of nervous protectiveness the war aroused in our parents. By the time I left home in 1942, the war had been going on for over two years, Pearl Harbor had been bombed and New Zealand was at war with Japan; over 60,000 New Zealanders were fighting in Egypt, the Middle East and the Pacific, and many more were in camp at home. In the month I departed for Wellington and left Greenmeadows behind at last, the Japanese bombed Darwin and began reconnaissance flights over New Zealand. Yet for all we realised these as events of national significance in our family, the war-makers might have been a party of gremlins we could keep away by chanting a few incantations.

The truth was that our father had by then such long and engrossed association with the Social Credit movement that he thought of all political events as evidence of international monetary plots. We'd had a copy of *The Protocols of the Learned Elders of Zion* in our house for years, and he completely accepted this proof of financial conspiracy, authorised and controlled by the Zionist faction of the Jewish people. The enemy was all the more sinister for being hidden, and wars between nations merely brought further evidence of the power of the financial network, since it supported armament manufacture everywhere and was indifferent to national borders. Social Credit would create an ideally balanced society in which everyone had equal access to wealth and advantage – consumption would equal production, as we were fond of saying. News of the dumping of cotton and coffee and other crops while millions starved (which was not published in the newspapers but brought to Social Credit meetings) outraged and horrified us. It was not clear, to me at least, how the international monopolies were to be made to relinquish their hold, so the just society could come into being, though we did know that the world's first Social Credit government had been elected in Alberta in Canada.

In the meantime there were enemies closer to hand in the form of 'orthodox' beliefs – in politics, in medicine and health care, in religion. If we had a faith, this was it. Anti-orthodoxy (our routine connection with Anglican church and Sunday school did not seem in any way incompatible with this). I embraced it easily: at high school when we talked about serious matters, nobody minded if I mentioned it, but the talk could never go far because nobody knew what to say. It was a sect, a cult, and once you were in it, you felt its rightness – as we used its symbolic green ink.

As for the war, such a faith enabled Mum and Dad to consider threats of invasion in almost entirely personal terms. 'If the Japs came', we as a family would pack up and go to the country, to Uncle Bert's farm in Patoka and, taking food and clothes, hide in the bush. At the same time Mum was a member of the local Patriotic Committee, and became its president, showing an unexpected flair for public processes; this didn't strike anyone as inconsistent with our private plans for escape. She also brought home skeins and skeins of khaki wool which she and Lindsay and I knitted into socks and balaclavas, but that still didn't make us feel that our destiny (or our safety) was to be shared with our neighbours. We would decide what to do for ourselves.

In those last years at home I sometimes thought I had an inkling of why people in our town drew back from us, treated us with a slight formality. There was some kind of haughtiness in us. For all that we so badly wanted to make friends, and agonised over our awkwardness in doing so, we thought of ourselves as in some way more interesting than other people. In the days when we'd had parties with the Alexanders, ours had been to prove ourselves, not just to have fun. We were actually very good at enjoying ourselves, but didn't know how to do it naturally and placidly with other people. We knew how to perform, but that's quite a different thing.

Chapter 8

When Clive left home, two years before me, it was to go to training college. There had been talk of him doing what many boys did, 'going into his father's business', and indeed he had sometimes gone on painting trips in holidays. But this is not to say that our parents were searching for the career that best suited his tastes and talents, or Lindsay's or mine either, though there had been some wondering whether Lindsay could be a nurse and I a librarian. They wanted very much to ensure that we made the best of ourselves. Professions were better than trades, jobs in offices more dignified that jobs done in overalls, and we were 'clever' children, we had all done academic courses; it seemed to them that we must enter the world at the proper level, secure a suitable share of its advantages (especially Clive) and make the right friends (Lindsay and me).

The career we knew most about, apart from Dad's business, was teaching, because both Fanny and Big Clive had made it familiar; in the end all three of us went to training college and learned how to be teachers, and it suited none of us, though this didn't become clear till a long time later. John was so much younger that he was almost another generation; all his experiences were different from ours, and when he was seen to be 'brilliant' it seemed natural for him to go straight to university. This was partly, I suppose, because by then I had at least become familiar with its milieu, even if I hadn't exactly done it justice.

Clive soon began to come home full of excited talk about 'Training Coll' and tramping; he brought friends. He even took me to a dance in Hastings – and introduced me as his kid sister with the pink hair ribbon. He began to address me as 'Sis', though I wished he wouldn't, and to tell me about girls who were 'bloody glorious', which made me squirm even more. He also produced Sandy, who chattered to me and to Molly, whom he quickly met, about the life we would lead in

Wellington, as if he was the only authority we would ever need, which we instantly believed.

We had by then both been accepted for training college, and written to Victoria House, where Mum had once lived, to ask for a shared room, though I was still unsure of some crucial details of my future. At the start of the third term of my last year at school I had suddenly decided I wanted to sit for a university scholarship and, whether I got one or not, leave school. The school frowned on this idea. No one would set or mark work or give me time off from ordinary work. I was on my own. I rather liked that, and came out quite well in the end. I didn't get a scholarship, but my name appeared at the top of something called the credit list, which was the next best thing. It gave me enough money to be a full-time university student, instead of going to training college. My last weeks at home were dense with argument and speculation. What exactly should I do?

These discussions took their place among the flurry and fuss of making clothes. We hunted for bargains in Napier shops, examined plain cottons, floral cottons, serge for a good skirt, piqué for a trim one, seersucker for pyjamas, viyella for blouses. It was an exciting time, slightly frightening for me, momentous for us all. We were a committee grooming our candidate for the election; we pictured the avenues of fallen admirers through which I would walk, and rolled about laughing. Naturally we ignored the fact, known to us all, that in these fine garments I would be more socially and conversationally inept that many in plainer clothes.

We played the old silly games, Mum chasing us with threats of needle pricks, luring us close to pinch our squealing, contorting bodies. We sang quite a lot, sometimes the old war songs Fanny had sung years before when she'd been helping Alice tend patients in the flu epidemic in 1919. There was the quaintly poignant

> Good byee, good byee!
> Wipe the tear baby dear,
> From your eyee,
> Tho' it's hard to part, I know,
> I'll be tickled to death to go.
> Don't cryee! Don't sighee!
> There's a silver lining in the skyee . . .

or, much more rollicking,

> Tramp, tramp tramp the boys are march-ing
> Who's that knocking at the door?
> It's the Kaiser and his wife
> You can stab them with a knife
> And they won't a-come a-knocking any more.

There were the usual stories to be told . . . Clive's elaboration of a forbidden newspaper picture showing the rope around a murderer's neck and huge shiny drops of blood leaking out of his suitcase . . . Fanny trying to scold and being overcome by laughter . . . the day Lindsay and I starved for our health and had to be succoured in the evening with Christmas cake . . .

I suppose we were gathering up the years to put them away, our shared childhood, Lindsay's and mine, the mixture of devotion and bossiness and sheer enjoyment that made Fanny the kind of mother she was. There were darker currents below this surface, but we had no idea of them then. How do you know, before a perfect circle breaks, what new shapes it will form? It had always been hard for us to leave home even for short times; what none of us realised was how little Fanny herself, despite her eagerness to foster each departure, was equipped to let us go. For the moment we sewed and sang, and played out the drama that being our family was, and left the future to itself.

As the time to go came nearer, I more and more shied away from old ties, old habits, old fixations and fancies. I didn't, for instance, want to play games with Uncle Mortimer when he came to tea on Sunday nights. He was Dad's bachelor brother, and when he came he and I made toast on an old kerosene stove kept in the wash house, while Mum concocted the tomatoes-and-bacon, or onions-in-cheese-sauce, or whatever it was to go with it; we played loud and (I had once thought) hilarious games, addressing each other in phrases like 'My Lord, what is this repast?' Then in the evenings we played paper games, especially General Knowledge, which we'd taken seriously for years.

Now I was to be grown up, I didn't want the riding round Green-meadows on my bike, down to the camping ground for swims, or out to Red Cliffs or Waiohiki for picnics with Nona or Joyce or Lindsay or any of the boarders from school. I would not be there to sing *The Ash Grove* or *Danny Boy* or *The Keel Row* while Mum played her chords, or Lindsay and I tried turning the accompaniments into duets, nor to play tennikoit on our small front lawn, or climb the Sugar Loaf, or eat chocolate peanuts all the way to the late bus with Molly after school, or practise diving for a brick in Napier Baths to get my life saving certificate. I'd finished even with my triumphs, like becoming a maker of impromptu speeches, and winning the huge silver cup for oratory with a speech about Bernard Shaw when I hadn't read a single one of his plays, only the Hesketh Pearson biography. Behind me too lay the anguish of those terrible fights of Clive's with Fanny, and the sickness of my crying over mine; and the old nightmare I'd had for years about a light outside the stained glass of the top half of the front door, and my knowing I had to go and open the door, even though what was outside would kill me (though I always woke, shaking and crying, just as my hand touched the knob). And John singing *The Merry Peasant* ('at the dawn of day, Tra la la la, Tra la la la') and calling it, in his piping little voice 'the Mary Pheasant'; and Dad laughing while he wrote out recipes that Mum dictated in the kitchen and putting 'Steamed Apple and Pig Pudding' and 'pig' again every time she said 'apple'. The morepork at night when we camped in lonely places, or the hush above our crunching feet as we walked home late along the country lane that Osier Road really was, and the brilliant umbrella of the stars quivering and shimmering above us. It was time to go and leave it all.

The Napier express departed at 8 am, as usual, on the last Saturday in January, and with my finished clothes, my pile of music, *Jane Eyre* and *Pride and Prejudice* and my sheets and towels for the hostel, I said goodbye, cried, got into the train, sat down beside Molly, and we were gone.

Chapter 9

February 1942, Victoria House A. I had a bad bout of homesickness last night. I'd been visiting other rooms with Molly and having visitors here in ours, and suddenly couldn't bear any more chit-chat and laughing at nothing (though we are both getting much better at it and are even becoming renowned humorists) and – well, you know the feeling, I wanted you all awfully. However, the Training College Welcome Ball was on and we had to go, of course expecting to have a fearful time. We were sunburnt from a picnic at Days Bay, but I plastered Molly's dark suntan powder on and lots of lipstick (we both looked pretty ghastly).

There were heaps of Air Force boys, enough men altogether and some over, so we started to dance immediately and went on all the evening – pretty nondescript partners, though I had one or two mildly interesting second years and one staff, and Molly won the Monte Carlo and looked sweet. Afterwards I couldn't find her and went back to the cloakroom and she was talking to Sandy! Wonderful to find someone we knew – we sat and talked for a long time and unburdened ourselves about whether you have to have duty dances, and who with. Then we locked up the hall and went over to college where Sandy gave us cups of milk and bits of supper and we sat in the Exec Room feeling gloriously proud to be there. Then Beetles came in – he is an ungracious, tall, long-legged, clever young man, very amusing; College Treasurer and of course on the Exec. They walked home with us to the hostel and although Molly prattled inanely and I was gloomy, we felt secretly proud all the time. Sandy is such a good little thing, not at all disillusioned and blasé but full of enthusiasm – and he has such an alive little face, is alive altogether – I am thoroughly fond of him. Quite a lot of second years I've been introduced to say, 'Clive's sister! Good Lord!' and grasp me by the hand. Or else, 'You're Scotty's sister?' It seems to make them simply totter with amazement.

I went to see Mr Lopdell about training college or varsity, which it's to be, and he said much the same as Sandy, about corporate life and investment in self and personality and the richer life at TC: I told him you thought I was a bit young to go full-time to varsity and he said he thought so too, but I could take up the bursary next year perhaps, and go full-time then. But I was to think it over for a few more days – so you see I've successfully managed a bit more procrastination.

Shall I give you a day's programme? 6.30 a loud bell ringing (isn't it humiliating) upon which we have to go down and cut lunches of tomato sandwiches which later become what I call Sog; you almost need a spoon to eat them. Then we make our beds and have a cold shower (I'm so glad the habit was established at home) then 7.30 breakfast, stewed fruit and toast or sometimes a sort of tomato glue or fritter things. 8.30 depart for TC and start there with an assembly; we sing songs like *Waltzing Matilda* and the President gives out notices – he's a second year of course, tall and good-looking, but all talk. At the end of the day (I'll tell you about the lectures later) we go into town just for the fun of being in Wellington; twice we've been to the dear railway station to have a cup of coffee and a ham sandwich. When we get in to the hostel we always have to mark ourselves off the signing book; after the ball we were all supposed to be in by 1.30 and we weren't till 2.30, but it was quite all right, we were just at the gate with Sandy and Beetles talking about whether TC people are intellectual snobs and why Beetles is blasé and Sandy is not. You know, if I'm to stay here I am determined to enter into everything and do my very best to get somewhere. I am sorry that at the hostel already Molly and I are regarded as great wits (it's because the others are such idiots) – we're going to put a stop to it because it will do us harm and stop us getting on with things.

It feels funny to be writing to you after talking to you such a little while ago (it only cost 8s 2d which I can easily afford and anyway I wouldn't have missed it for worlds). I could see perfectly John, little darling, standing palpitating beside the cupboard in the passage where we always stand when Daddy or a distant relation or someone rings. Also I felt beautifully important dancing round all over the place waiting for 'my call'.

On Friday night there was a Bob Hop. I wore my sheer and it is a sweet frock but I find that after all our deliberating it is a bit long, I think I'd better take it up. Molly was more of a success than I, but neither of use were belles. In fact I was feeling thoroughly disgusted – couldn't make any decent conversation to Sandy at all, I never can at dances – and as the last straw we came home with two youths, Molly's a nondescript first year, mine a pretty awful idiot, a second year. And Sandy was waiting outside! We are both sure it was to walk home with us – and I like him and I don't like the other boy at all, Mervyn someone. We walked home together, the four of us, and talked odds and ends and then went straight inside. Thoroughly prosaic from beginning to end (still, I'm overwhelmingly relieved to find that such people don't expect you to be sentimental, and kiss them and things, as Clive warned me everyone would).

Molly has gone out tonight, the first visit either of us has made alone. Her mother's here because a sister-in-law has died – after years of half aliveness, so it's not so bad. I didn't go partly because I thought she'd sometimes rather see her mother alone (as I would if you came) and a good bit because I hated the thought of going into the house. Silly I know, but I couldn't help it. Later. Just at that moment I heard my name called loudly several times and of course that means telephone – I was so excited I dropped the pen and went downstairs shaking all over with expectancy. Well, to my amazement and joy it was Sandy, wanting us to go for a walk; I explained about Molly and he wanted me to go anyway. I'd been reading a fearful murder story of Ngaio Marsh's that we have to do for English, and it's easy to get depressed alone in your room so I was glad to go out. We walked for miles and miles up and down streets and past houses and trees and trams and eventually got down to Tinakori Road, so we came round Parliament Buildings and back through the town. We stopped at a Tip Top Milk Bar in Lambton Quay and had a milkshake and since there was one biscuit left Sandy made me take it and we shared it later on. We talked about TC and tramping and whether it's a good idea to be in the limelight running things or not, making them work by being on committees. It's one of his ideals to work undercover and he tried to explain why; he's resigning from the Exec because you can do more good by being in the opposition. We talked and talked and eventually and I suppose inevitably, came to socialism and Social Credit. He's hopelessly prejudiced against SC but we weren't serious all the time – we stood a door or so along from Vic House and both talked at the same time – or shouted – without a moment's pause for about three minutes till we were quite breathless. I got in about ten. It is wonderful to be able to talk on an entirely equal basis with no question of sentimentality or anything. We think he's a natural bachelor.

On Monday we began lectures and I feel already that education is a tremendously worthwhile thing to study. One thing they stress is respect for the practical type of child with no brains, just as much as for the academic type. In the afternoon we went down in the cable car (still irresistible) and had our hair set – but it isn't worth it and we won't do it again, mine's a fizz. Today was Culture Clubs and of course I joined Drama, then Sports – you remember I asked for my racquet but don't bother – we're both changing to swimming because there's absolutely no chance of coaching.

I've told Molly that as soon as she's out of the room I'll cut a hole in her blue gingham that she's going to wear on Thursday – that's the day the second years are in college and we always wear our best things to dazzle Sandy. We spend quite a lot of time you know in vigorous and highly diverting rivalry over the poor little thing. We both like him tremendously and you've no idea how amusing it is to compare our triumphs; I am in the ascendant at the moment because of our solitary walk. He little knows what innocent delight he creates.

After the Bob Hop Beetles called a meeting of everyone interested in tramping, so of course we went. It was decided that there's to be a day trip to Catchpole (I think it's called) – you go to Eastbourne and up over the hills from there. It wasn't as good as I expected – the hills are lovely, but not really the people, though I expect it was my fault. It's small talk that is lacking. In a way I don't mind, I manage without it, but I wish I knew how people do it all the same. Molly says I've got everything, music, intellect etc etc, but that doesn't seem to have much to do with it.

They say the Japs are coming in thirteen days. Do you think they will? I miss you all.

Just for you Mum – nobody here uses little towels, they all buy them every month. The only things people wash are sheets, towels, pillow slips, and serviettes; I don't want to spend 3s each month, but I don't know what else to do.

Some days ago I asked a girl at the hostel about music teachers and she said she'd ring hers, a Miss Corliss and she'd probably recommend someone; well, she rang me herself and said to come to her place next

Thursday afternoon and bring any old thing to play. I went, and played the Debussy *2nd Arabesque* and Grieg's *To the Spring*. Then she gave me some sight reading and lots of ear tests and at the end this is what she said: that I have a splendid, extraordinarily good ear, my sight reading is not so good but can be improved with practice, whereas the ear is natural and cannot be trained much (she is not an over-enthusiastic sort of person, quite quiet, so I felt thrilled about this). She said I had such tremendous possibilities (!) that she'd like to take me herself because she could do such a lot with me, but she gave me the name of a young teacher who was a pupil of hers and even rang up to ask her fees which are £2 2s for half an hour a week; if you do Diploma (I presume this means Letters), it is a guinea more. Miss Corliss herself charges £4 4s a term for three-quarters of an hour a week – she won't take less time than that. She said I was to feel perfectly free to do what I liked and I said I'd write to you – what do you think? I did suggest that I might be able to pay myself, but I won't really know till after we get our first pay.

I must say listening to the lecturers fires you with enthusiasm for the new kind of education – freedom for the development of the individual, an end to all the old regimentation, an equal chance for every kind of child. I wouldn't miss the chance to be part of that for anything. The hostel isn't nearly as stirring, and even at college the women talk about silly things and the men talk to one another. Today I went to Drama Club and a young theatrical-looking man came and talked to us; he seemed to know an awful lot about stage production, but was even more interested in his own profile which he several times turned to show us, leaving it there for so long that he and everyone else forgot what he was saying. Also his voice was so theatrical that even when he was front on I wasn't sure he was speaking English; he rolled his eyes up to the ceiling quite a lot too while we sat humbly in our rows being struck by it all.

I went to see Loppy (the Principal) about my varsity course and whether or not I take the bursary and go full-time (I can do some subjects at varsity while I'm at TC). He looked at my marks and was much impressed, specially when he knew I did it a year before the others and by myself. The course he mapped out is thus: 1942 Latin I; French I, History I; 1943 English I, Education I (that will be a busy year at college, if I stay here); 1944 English II, French II; 1945 English III,

Psychology I – BA, then MA in English and possibly French as well. It all sounds wonderful, but I've had doubts since about taking three this year. The first three weeks is to be a trial – I have to pay £5 of the fee for the third subject myself.

Last night Molly and I had dinner at the Vegetarian Café with several Napier girls who were on their way to catch the boat to Christchurch. Already I feel our horizons are bigger than theirs – they seem ordinary, and even Sophie who is here with us seemed no more elastic than she ever was at school, absolutely no sensitivity to influences such as TC, no impressionableness. However many degrees there are to get, if there were fifty of them I could have, I wouldn't want to if it meant doing only that, without being sensitive to what's happening all around me. And I don't want to teach secondary school; here you feel as though it's almost a crusade, helping to mould children while they are still plastic and responsive. When I look at Sophie I just think thank the Lord I can change and be influenced and altered and impressed by – oh everything there is.

The Education lecturer is charming and friendly, so much so that he seems a trifle cloying at times, and you can see he loves to be popular, but I like him and think he's helpful and sincere. The Science lecturer is one you have to beware of, he's clever and cynical and amusing but he finds out all about you and you have to watch out or he'll embarrass you in front of everyone. There's a woman Science lecturer too, nice, but has the queerest back view I've ever seen, especially at the top where her hair is in little shelves sticking out from her head. Scotty, English, is marvellous, wonderful, the most stimulating person I've ever heard. He asks you questions about what the English language means that turn your brain inside out, you can almost feel it happening inside your head.

They divided us up into groups at Drama Club, so we could do three one-act plays. Molly, lucky thing, is in one with Sandy and lots of other people we know but mine is awful – there's only one girl I know at all and everyone else is ghastly. I daresay the RIGHT THING is to stick it out in the interests of learning more about acting – I know I'll get a letter from you Maman saying I must love everyone in my hateful group and then Everything Will Be All Right.

After dinner last night two girls who have heard some extravagant things about my playing dragged me to the hostel Common Room, and I played very badly and sketchily and they applauded awedly and entirely indiscriminately, not knowing a thing about it and not even listening properly (which is perhaps just as well). I felt rather lugubrious afterwards, though writing home cheers you up.

I am in a gloomy frame of mind, depressed about how unnatural everything is because of the rotten old war – several second years went into camp today and more will go soon. That sounds as though I think having men to talk to and do things with is all that's important, and of course I don't – but it is a special part of this new life, sharing everything among men and women alike (so different from school), all having the same pursuits and interests and so on. There's a beautiful companionableness about it, and it's a broad enough stream to take in every kind of person; each one, from Beetles to the Hearties, contributes to its breadth and richness – does that sound pretentious? I hope not.

Leisure time here is often painful because of the futility of the women and the intelligent men who have no taste for intelligence in women. But the lectures themselves, and the general breadth of ideal (I suppose I mean ideology) and the sincerity and earnestness of all the lecturers (or nearly all) so manifestly trying to put their principles into practice – all that makes me feel proud to be associated with education as at TC. I wouldn't be out of it at varsity now for pounds.

Tuesday I began at Kelburn School. Oh Lord, a whole new field opens and this is page nine! I had a Latin lecture so didn't get there till about 20 past 9; the teacher's Miss Sullivan, attractive and brisk and, you discover after a while, as hard as nails. She's taught all kinds of children in the Islands, and being a teacher with style she calls the children 'the kids'. It seemed to me, watching her that first morning and the kids responding, that teaching must be the most wonderfully interesting job to do – but I don't know how long I'll think so. When they all clustered round at playtime I told them they could remember my name, Miss Scott, because I had spots on my frock, and after that of course the little fiends called me Miss Spots, Miss Spotty etc, especially the boys, and I blushed all the time and hated it. Kids are very bumptious; at the moment I am their favourite (there are four students in this class) but it won't last.

Everyone here is rushing about in a frenzy because it is the Varsity Freshers' Ball tonight. Molly's gone down to press her frock, but I have woes heavy upon me. I don't want to go one bit. I just know what it will be like – everyone will be enraptured with Molly and I won't have a word to say (wouldn't I just sell all my intelligence in a moment to be rid of this shyness and have a bit of sex appeal instead) and oh I'm homesick too and I love you all so tremendously (one's emotion rises and floods over with a touch of homesickness). I suppose I'll have to go and collect my confounded frock (had to have it cleaned).

Later. Question is: Freshers' Ball. All right or awful? Millions of things have happened since, but I'll put you out of your misery and tell you. The frock was lovely and only cost 6s 6d; we arrived about nine (such an elegant hour) and found to our horror that people were sitting on forms singing varsity songs – an old custom it seems. Then everyone went upstairs to a smallish hall which became so packed that you couldn't dance a foot without getting very buffeted. The first dance I had with a quite eminent (though pretty silly) second year – I felt proud; Molly had a first year who was quite struck with her, but we don't like him. Then we both had lots of varsity Freshers (a superabundance of men, so there were only about three wallflowers the whole evening) interspersed with dances with nice TC people. It's no good telling me anything about that pink frock or *mentioning* psychological effect, simply no good because I know my darlings that it has a special charm over it and is a *wonderful* frock, the old blue rag can't be compared with it. By supper time I was feeling thoroughly gay and bumptious because of being grabbed at the very beginning of every dance (of course nearly every girl was) – then the rest of the evening became a glorious whirl. Between dances I sat and held audience with others and boy oh boy they kept booking dances ahead and very early one of the medical students – there were two – asked to take me home. Success goes to your head, you can talk so gaily and fluently and suitably without the least effort, and to have people rushing after me to claim the next dance – oh intoxicating! We walked home to the hostel. (I don't like coming home from dances with swains though, I invariably talk in a rush about stupid prosaic things, hostel meals or something. As a matter of fact unless Molly and I are fundamentally cold-blooded it's all a farce about *that* sort of thing – we've had no advances from anyone.) He – my m. student – is going to ring me up and I hope he does. He was delightful. I wish though that we could just simply fall for the people who are attracted to us. Sandy now could have transformed the evening for us both, instead of which the little wretch ignored us from beginning to end.

On Monday night we went to a Welcome Lecture for Freshers at varsity. Fairly trite – all about traditions of learning – but oh it felt lovely to be ascending those broad steps at the entrance, and stopping to look round in the lofty hall and thinking, 'Here I am standing casually in the great front doorway of the University'. I've been several more times now and always I have this little thrill of excitement, especially, I don't know why, about nine in the morning. It's exhilarating to stand at the top of the steps in the sunshine for a few minutes before leaving. Since you bid me, my Lords and Masters (not to mention their advice here), to drop one varsity subject I will (I have to). French, I think, and I'll keep on Latin and History. I told Sandy you thought three was too much, with TC as well, and he said you must be moderately reasonable as parents – he really is the most presumptuous little creature.

I don't think I want any money – I'll go on using that £7 (now £6) – for music and everything else for the moment. By the way I don't think I can enter the competitions – we only get half an hour a day to practise and it's not enough.

Tuesday I went to a French lecture and then History, and afterwards loitered on those wonderful steps talking to Sandy before walking home with him. I'd only been inside a few minutes it seemed and the phone rang – oh the number of times we've raced down those stairs in case it's Sandy, and this time it was, with some tail end of the conversation (about how socialism changes people inside, not just outside). He told Molly – she got there first – and I could have wept at the unluckiness of it. I'm afraid Sandy's creeping into my letters again and that *mustn't* happen because we have both simultaneously and finally relinquished him (we do from time to time). I'll tell you what his attitude is. He's pretty condescending about us both and in fact regards all women as quite subsidiary and having nothing to do with the business of living. If they are amusing, all right, be amused, until you cease to feel interested. A man's whims must be right.

You mustn't mind if I sound gloomy sometimes. I'd rather be home, and I'm living for Easter, but really I suppose I have settled down. Neither of us yet feels that these are the happiest days of our lives, as everyone insists they must be.

Chapter 10

Training College, Kowhai Road. I'm in the Women's Common Room, lockers all round the walls, some dilapidated oilskin mattresses, one seat along the wall – not an exhilarating atmosphere, but it suits the gloom in which I find myself. I've had my morning of classroom control, and if I thought the others were hopeless I was appalling! Tomorrow I have to take Singing and though I like the songs we've learnt (I'll sing them for you at Easter), I'm scared to the point of paralysis to think of doing it in from of those smart children with their silly grins, waiting for me to make a fool of myself – which of course doesn't take long.

Monday I was going to practise on the college piano when I met exciting Bruce Mason. He's a famous second year and brilliant at everything; he seized my Bach and talked a bit about it and then sort of dismissed me, so I just trailed off to the piano (I didn't have anything to say about Bach, of course). I only get half an hour at a time at the piano, not enough. Then Molly and I went into town for an ice cream. In the milk bar in the next little compartment were some American sailors (there are crowds and crowds of them all over the place) and they were black! I was really excited, especially when they talked – I never expected to hear real American voices except in the pictures. They wanted to shout us ice creams, but of course we didn't want that, it was just their charming way of talking (we told them so). Can you imagine the sheer joy of sitting there and watching and listening to a true American accent and manner and style, in real life? They came from California and one said he lived in Hollywood (do you think that was true? We couldn't decide). And the person sitting with them was someone we knew, though we don't think much of him; he's twenty-three, an accountant, but it was sort of useful that he was there. The one from Hollywood (if he was) kept saying May Gard (My God) in a slow drawly way, every second word.

By the way, here you learn to appreciate the real delicacy and subtlety of well-used and discriminating swearing – I wish you could hear Beetles cursing softly and sincerely and fluently. Everyone does it in some way, and it's not unpleasant at all, just companionable and amusing and comforting. I can't do it, but I envy the swearers profoundly.

Another thing about Monday – at lunchtime we had an Open Forum, at which students' views can be aired. A second year called Terry was chairman but the one person who knew anything about procedure, and who's got a more nimble and brilliant and clear cut mentality than all the rest of them put together, was dear Beetles. Sandy was as obstreperous as a little dog, jumping up the whole time to say things, till the whole meeting was *seething* with irritation towards him.

A lucky thing has happened – Trevor Edmond (a rather famous ex-student, finished TC but comes back from camp sometimes) knows Miss Sullivan very well and the other day was apparently talking to her; he told her what a nice person I was, and how keen to learn the job and all the right things. I saw him a day or so ago at varsity and told him I hadn't noticed any great increase in warmth in her manner, so he said he'd tell her again, though of course if I don't look like a good teacher there's no reason for her to think so. I do so awfully want to be good at it. Thank the Lord the kiddies still like me – I thought it wouldn't last – though I don't think I've got much patience. Some days my knitting group are sweet and I feel so buoyed up, then another day they're little brutes; one in particular I just want to drop her out of the window and on to the concrete.

Student Opinion (the Training College monthly paper) is out – some of it is very good indeed, some pretty juvenile. I intend to write for the next issue. Sandy is Business Editor and Bruce Mason Editor – I've told you, he's a brilliant actor and writer and musician and everything all at once; he's also tall and curly haired and delicate, sort of feminine-looking. Oh and I've been to Music and she was there this time, and delightful, asked me to play for her again and said Yes it was as she'd thought, I had the real feeling for music although technically I'm rusty. It appears I am going for Performers' LRSM. You have to choose three pieces out of about ten, one from each of three lists; I've started on a Bach prelude (she played them for me and it was so beautiful – there was an intoxicating sort of thrill about being so close to that lovely music that made my heart beat and my whole – well soul, I suppose – feel excited). The other two are a Chopin scherzo (very difficult interpretation but she says that won't worry me, and technically it's not too bad) and a Beethoven sonata which is simply glorious – I'll have to buy them all. Is that all right?

One night we went to *Thunder Rock* by the Wellington Repertory Players – an excellent play, presented the problem but not the solution, so you came away thinking about that. We walked back with Sandy and Beetles who to my disgust talked about it exclusively to each other (after all we were just women!), though Sandy was a little redeemed the next day when he did talk over the acting, and the fundamentals of the play, with me. The Drama Club, by the way, is going to do *The Man Who Wouldn't Go To Heaven* and I'm Mrs Muggins – not that that tells you much. Molly's group did a reading of Barrie's *Shall We Join the Ladies?* and by some evil working of fate she was Sandy's wife; they were, however, at opposite ends of the stage (to her chagrin and my relief), but then at lunchtime he talked to me and ignored her – swing of the pendulum, an important factor in our lives.

But I must tell you about the last ordinary dance. I wore my limp blue with one of those artificial blue flowers Molly's mother gave me in my hair, and started off the Gay Gordons (you change partners all the time) with Terry, that second year who chaired the first Open Forum, and when the music stopped I couldn't believe my eyes, there was *Clive!* I hadn't expected him till Saturday's train, but of course we had to pass on almost at once to other partners, and when it all stopped Sandy rushed up and lots of others, and shook hands with him (Molly and I watched from a distance and felt marvellously proud of him). Then I had several dances with interesting, conceited Bruce Mason and talked about music and literature and agnosticism and ourselves; he said how old was I and when I told him not yet eighteen he said I looked twenty at least and was doing awfully well (an enigmatic comment, but I accepted it gratefully). Then Clive came up and we began to talk, but Beetles moved him aside and we danced and he said Clive was a great chap and not just because he's my brother, and we kept on dancing till the end of the evening, when he was very frisky and laughed his horsey laugh and said he'd had a great time (you don't know what that is for Beetles – he thinks women the most supremely uninteresting creatures in the world – it's just because we are witty with each other and we do get on nicely). I had to wait for him to lock up and then we walked home – and do you know the whole way we had a gooseberry with us, someone who lives near him – I wanted to say 'we don't need a chaperone' but of course I couldn't. I was pleased partly because Clive was there and I'd hate him to come back to TC and think he has to save me from the wall at dances.

Victoria House A. Thank you enormously – it arrived on Wednesday afternoon when we were having Needlework (ugh!) and some second year brought it in; I felt so important having a crackly yellow telegram envelope handed to me and was only sorry it wasn't an ordinary lecture because then everyone would have seen it (deplorable tendency I know, this hunger for publicity). The fruit arrived in good condition, tomatoes very good, plums superb, shortbread climax of all mortal bliss; now we have fruit we don't have to go down to breakfast. I went last Friday and succumbed to the temptation of scrambled eggs (leaking all over the plate) and toast like rubber – I was punished for the mistake though, I felt like a lump of wood all day.

I'm writing in the hostel garden (if you can call it that), there's a bit of pale sunlight and a restless, cold, disturbing wind – I think our room is better, but Molly says it's a hole and am I a Fug Person? I seem to have been here for ever, having been interrupted almost at once by Betty, one of the nondescripts – nice enough I suppose, but I am utterly sick of being cheerful with her, and what did we talk about? The names people have, dress materials, food, going to the pictures, Wellington shop girls, oh Lord – this is why I've stopped going down to the hostel Common Room. It's just eking out evenings in empty flippancy and is hopelessly pointless – I hunger for some depth and intelligence somewhere. When I come home for Easter can we talk about the Great Abstract every single day and night? Even people like Sandy I'm disillusioned with – after all in spite of everything he's like other men, and underneath thinks women are just to look at and play with and talk nonsense to. I'm beginning to see it as part of the great obstacle women have in front of them wherever they turn.

I am a bit worried about this letter because it is, I think, lugubrious, I'd hate to have you worried over trivialities. As a matter of fact I *am* still waiting for the tranquil happiness which proceeds from real fundamental contentment – as at home. I've been sick (sore throat, as usual) but an early night on Friday seemed to cure it. On Saturday morning Molly and I went to town (I wore my grey jumper and skirt, turquoise coat, scarf tied skinned-rabbit style round my head and looked *jolly* nice). We'd only gone a little way when we met blinking little Sandy; at first he was easier with Molly (you know all about this cursed shyness of mine, which after all your training must be somewhere in my bones still), but afterwards – let me cling to it – I did make him laugh a lot. We had to separate, and when I met him again on my own we got on famously.

Molly and I decided when we got home that we were equal again, and perhaps I was on slightly higher ground. Sandy is entirely a creature of impulse and responds to whatever appeals to him at the moment. Molly is without question the prettier of the two of us, as feminine creatures, and consequently can expect a more constant success with men, though I think more know me and come and talk to me. Sandy likes us both I suppose, probably respects me more but likes being near her better.

Sunday night I went in to the Common Room and somehow began reading aloud from a stupid book I found there called *My Heart and Susan*, then Molly took over and I put in asides till we were all in tears with laughing. Then I found *A Dominie's Log* and read it to myself and got really absorbed – A.S. Neill is a genius yet the way he gives you his ideas about education is so simple! Then they wanted me to play so I did for a while, with people saying insincerely Oh how lovely – then they went back to their talking and I played for ages just for myself. Sometimes I feel so starved for music – the piano here has got a loud harsh clanging tone and anyway I get exactly half an hour a day on it and only occasionally can play on and on. And of course we never hear any radio music; there is one in the Matron's study and I believe you can ask and go in there and listen to the War News if you want to. As though you'd want to!

Playing again after so long of just practising – which is different – puts you in an emotional state of mind, and when I feel like that Molly, who is so excellent nine-tenths of the time, seems miserably inadequate. But it wasn't her fault – I'm feeling very strongly at the moment that I want to get away from people for a while. There are so very many of them – nearly all the time it's all right, but occasionally you pine to be entirely alone. You get out of the habit of thinking smoothly and tranquilly because you so seldom can, and – this will sound weird but it's true – I keep thinking of unpeopled open hills, as at home in the evening, just hills and beautiful silence. There is so much of everything here – people and buildings and noises, you can't help it getting on top of you and making inroads on your particular privacy and sort of suffocating you. Actually Molly isn't here at the moment – she's gone to a play practice – and I don't want to do anything but sit in dead silence and think – it's so *long* since one has thought, so much *doing*.

Wednesday morning I got permission to go and see Clive off to camp – they all have to go, you know, unless they're unfit. We walked up and down the platform talking (one of the things he told me was that I talk like a perfect fool – small talk is all very well but it has to be interesting – not just about what you're doing!). It was lovely to see him – this may sound peculiar, but honestly I've never been half so fond of Clive before – not counting that he is my brother – as I was when he was here this time, and I know I've never got to know him so well.

Friday morning I had my morning of Control and felt like a wet dish cloth afterwards. Tables and spelling went off beautifully, then reading, then writing – good in a way, except that I taught them fs the wrong way, and they all did them so they looked like qs. The worst of it is that you mustn't say Oh sorry children, that was wrong – whatever happens, once you've started you must go on. Then, oh Lord! An Oral Composition lesson – the children supply ideas and everything and you write it all up on the board. It was an utter failure of a lesson – the kids wriggled around and chattered and played about till I could have wept – I'm sure they weren't faintly interested.

Miss Sullivan told me afterwards she knew it would be a flop, and that other teachers said they never gave Oral Composition to students, it's too hard. Apparently she herself doesn't believe in the orthodox method of teaching English and has written a thesis explaining her method (it would be published but for the war). She must get results because she says she's got some excellent essays done last year by subnormal kids – I may be allowed to read them. I stayed after school till about four talking to her – or listening.

Then I had to go over to TC – I'd promised to help get things ready for the evening. The dance began all right – I danced with an Air Force man I quite liked, but he had to go back to camp at ten; then I was *most* honoured to get a soldier who was President of the Exec last year and apparently quite a personage (he knows Beetles and Trevor Edmond of course very well; he – Trevor – was there with his woman whom I talked to, and she's perfectly sweet). Another soldier who was Treasurer of the Exec last year was there too and we made a party and sat in the middle of the floor and had supper (saveloys etc) while he and Trevor talked reminiscences.

Chapter 11

Victoria House A. In the tramping hut (I decided to go) the person who outshone everyone by miles was of course Beetles. I've never in all my life met anyone who makes me laugh so much; he affects a gloomy manner, swears as I've told you with great conviction, and is the ugliest person I've ever seen – rather like a horse. He has an utterly infectious and irresistible loud laugh and is of course beautifully intelligent. I giggle with pleasure just to think of him moaning about things or chewing an apple and looking owlishly round at us in the hut when he first woke up on Sunday morning, or cooking sausages over the fire and being extravagantly resigned when I accidentally kicked his billy of tea all over the floor. We left on the 1.30 bus Saturday and got to the Orongorongo River about six – it's a fairly civilised track but steep and you just trudge along in single file not talking because it's pretty hard going all the time and you need your breath. Towards the end the track gets to be a foot or two deep in mud and water; you get so entirely used to sloshing through it that when it comes to wading the river – nearly up to your waist – you just go in without a word. No one thought of taking off shoes or socks or anything. I got the most terrible blisters again – those brown brogues are too short with thick socks (we bought a pair each for 1s 6d). I don't know what to do. Molly wears her slip slops (16s 6d) but I don't want to, as I wear them to TC nearly every day.

We found the last part of the river too swift so turned back to a hut a bit further back, only to find it inhabited by five varsity trampers. That made about twenty in the hut, nearly everyone slept on the floor and we only got about three hours' sleep – also after getting wet nearly up to the shoulders we had to stand in freezing wind, so my cold is miles worse. The varsity men were what Neville Mitchell (a very nice man indeed who had two years at varsity before he came to TC and knows them) calls Half Baked Intellectuals. They read modern poetry all the time and quote from it and talk most wittily and emancipatedly. One was called Hubert and I called him Ethelbert or Ethelred, can't remember why, and he called me Gwendolyn, and bet he could spell my real name and lost the bet and had to pay me (only 1d, alas). One was English – he never gets any subjects at varsity because he's such an inflammable Communist. We got home worn to shreds and blistered and dirty about six, had a bath, and slept till after the rising bell this morning, at least I did.

Later. I've been reading *The Lonely Plough.* I think the style is forced and unconvincing, the language often far fetched, but I'm enjoying reading it all the same. It's by a woman – you can't help remembering that all the way through – Constance Holme; have you read any of her novels? She's written a lot I think, all about the Power and the Passion of the North, i.e. the North of England. Then I've been reading a lot of that little volume of Longfellow out loud, and it's so disappointing – really unenterprising, such a passive philosophy and so excessively *rhymed*. I suppose he lived in a restricted age, but it seems very lifeless and trite compared with Milton or someone – as for comparison with Shakespeare, you just couldn't! Molly and I have been talking about progress – in general I mean, not our own – and how each generation starts off young and full of enthusiasm, then sinks into lethargy and prejudice and old age. So it's only a little step forward each time, like the pace of a team being that of its slowest member. We went on talking, about how terrified we both are of middle-aged placidity, and how Joan Swan and Nancy Broughton (you know they were at school but not in our class till the sixth form) are like glasses of boiled water that all the bubble has gone out of, and how we'd rather be wild foolish unbalanced creatures all our lives than lose our *bubble*. We go on to assure each other that one's bubble is a fundamental thing, which can stand the test of even middle-aged stolidity and lethargy. This morning we walked down the hill to go to town (and to Kirks for morning tea) and oh the gay proud consciousness of being young! we told each other. Does this sound pretentious? (I had to look up that word in a copy of *Stud Op – Student Opinion* – because I knew the one I wanted but had forgotten its spelling.)

Monday and Tuesday History lectures at varsity – there are two lecturers, Wood who does European history and Beaglehole who does colonial stuff; both are delightful and give you the whole broad full sweep of the subject – I can see History being my favourite subject –

there, not at TC. The European lecturer is gentle and serious and his lectures pass as though an hour is a minute; the other one is interesting too, though he does look at you with a sort of tranquil curiosity and in dead silence when you come in late. There's an amusing ugly first year, Trixie, who calls us The Habituals because we're always late for Latin and sometimes for History – I think I'm going to like her, though we're only gradually getting to know her; she recites bits from T.S. Eliot all the time, especially *The Hollow Men* in a suitably hollow voice which just goes with her funny puckered-up face.

Well, Wednesday. My class was at the Museum for the morning (I took them to the Maori Club, other choices being Insect, Animal, Other Places), then we all came back in a tram from Courtenay Place. Wellington is a *lovely* place, with its rowdy old trams and its endless rattly lifts and vast ugly old buildings covered with Victorian ornaments, and its rude crowds (they are, you know, they glare at you perpetually and never apologise if they bang into you). In places it's very pitiful too – you just ought to see the miserable old shops in the extreme upper end of Willis Street, smelling of fat, and advertising on dingy spotted old cards. Flounders to Take Home, We Specialise in Grills, and one has a lump of stale fat cake with pink icing and a miserable third-rate statue of a ridiculous child holding up its skirt.

Another History lecture and afterwards we stayed on in the varsity library, doing a Latin prose and translation till half-past nine when the Librarian sent us out. It's a wonderful place, so lofty and calm and proud and aloof – you sit at long tables with little lights on stands beside you; we were opposite a man trying to concentrate on an accountants' journal but we drove the poor thing away by staring at him under the little light shade and trying to read his page upside down.

The next night a lovely thing happened – we went on students' tickets (only 1s 6d) to a production by Maria Dronke and her Dramatic Art Studio (she was very famous on the Continent before she came here) of *Shakespeare's Women*. It was absolutely glorious – I'm sending you the programmes, with notes about what each bit was like. The next day it still poured, but we had to go to town to Whitcombes to look at book titles because the Bop Hop that night was fancy dress and we had to go as the title of a book. They gave us a catalogue and at eight o'clock we were still poring feverishly over it but in the end Molly chose *The Compleat Angler* and took the wooden black-out curtain rod and tied some string to it and cut out a paper fish. I selected *A Crown of Wild*

Olives by Ruskin and went out in the teeming rain and got several dripping branches from a sort of mulberry tree next door (I suppose they'll complain to the Matron) with enormous flat leaves, and tied it with string into a crown. You've no idea how queer I looked with those huge swaying leaves framing my head and face – trying for a sort of feeble coincidence I wore that maple leaf frock. When we got there someone said was I *Under the Greenwood Tree* so I changed to that – then someone else thought I was the Greek maiden who turned into a tree. Molly had the last dance with Sandy and I did with Beetles, who walked home with me, and even though two friends of his tacked themselves on I didn't mind much, I just felt so proud I was sort of tingling with it – oh Mummy darling, such a lot of things happen to you, don't they? Such funny funny interesting things. I *hope* I don't forget about any of them ever.

Well I have sworn to stop on this page – but I must tell you that we've had one emergency practice here at the hostel, going down the fire escapes, one at TC finding cover under the trees, and at Kelburn School the kids have had one. Also we have to supply ourselves with a ration of biscuits, raisins and chocolate (which I expect we'll eat when we get it) and have warm clothes by our bed every night. Does this mean the Japs are coming after all? I found out the other day from Sandy that he and Trevor and all those who are down for the Navy or Air Force have to go into the Army till they're wanted; they are just having to stop their courses, including varsity lectures, and for Trevor his school class, all for nothing – I don't suppose the Army even *wants* them, oh it's perfectly lousy. Thank you for the coat – no more tramps for the moment with Sandy and everyone in camp. Beetles, to his great glee, is unfit – flat feet or something. But there's talk of a trip to Kapiti Island at Easter. I am rather tempted, but of course I want to come home, you know that. I don't know what I'll do.

Chapter 12

Kapiti Island, Easter. Wet Tent. Wet Miserable Ghastly Kapiti. I suppose you have to do things to learn that they're no good, and perhaps this terrible awful business is a good thing and will teach me a lesson. I'll tell you about it – on Friday morning at 7.30 I rushed over to John Dew's place (a second year I know a bit) to borrow his pack, put shorts and a few things in it and went down to the station, imagining after all my doubts that I'd decided the right thing, though when I'd taken the plunge I felt horribly homesick and envious of Molly when she left on the Napier train. Bought my ticket and got into the train with a whole crowd of cheerful people, not knowing any of them better than to exchange half-hearted platitudes about fares etc. Hoped miserably that it would be all right later on – at Paekak had wild visions of getting off the train and waiting for the Napier one but of course I couldn't publicly take my pack out from the pile and just leave. We waited at the Paraparaumu Station for the bus; I didn't know who to talk to but Peg Crabtree was there and didn't know many people either, so I talked to her a bit. The only other first year woman (except for two who were at varsity last year, so it's different for them) is a girl called Ann Heyden who is breezy and calls men Twirpy and ruffles their hair and as far as I can see has no trace of sense or intelligence at all, but because of aforesaid breeziness gets on well with everyone. The bus let us out by the beach and we waited for the launch, and the dinghy that was to take us out to it. Beetles was counting everyone and I heard him say 'There's one too many – the twenty-one are here and there's one to come.' I felt terrible because he'd told me to ring him when I'd decided, and I hadn't (he told me afterwards that it wasn't me, it was someone else who came uninvited). I waited for the second launch trip, feeling a little better but still shy and bewildered.

The launch trip was rather nice, smooth and sea-smelling, with the water very close to us, and arriving on the island was fun too – the launch anchors quite a long way out and you transfer yourself and your gear to the dinghy again. The first party were there to meet us and took us up a steep path to the clearing where we were to camp.

Victoria House A. Later. We stayed longer than Easter itself because the launch couldn't get across to pick us up, the sea was so rough – six days altogether, a long time really. One day Peg and I and one or two others walked to the end of the island, to the homestead – nobody home, so we picked some passionfruit (of a different kind, long and yellow, tasted much the same) from beside the track and walked on through a valley right to the other side of the island and got a magnificent view from a hilltop of all the west and most of the north coast, far below us, with the sea just a white curly edge round the rocks. Lovely. We got back after dark, in fact George came to meet us with a torch because they thought we were lost. That night the division began – not a sharp one, but real – between those who did or didn't go up to the big tent in the evenings (as Beetles put it 'for a three hours' dose of bawdry'). There were two people who slept in the big tent who seemed different from the rest of us and quite special – Don and Marj Clendon, both old, about twenty-three. He is a big name at varsity, used to go to TC – studied law too, before that – and now teaches in Northland. They are very smart, belong to a fast set at varsity, but are friendly and nice too.

Anyway, that night everyone collected in the big tent at first, but since the intention was to tell dirty stories and sing dirty songs, as always on tramps, the presence of young people like me and several nondescripts made awkward silences. Some left and went to bed, I just sat there feeling uncomfortable (I couldn't go because they'd laugh and say, 'Is it too much for you?' and treat me as a child afterwards) but fortunately someone came and said the water was leaking through my tent so off I went, rejoicing at the release. The next day Beetles said, 'We shocked you, didn't we?' and I said, 'No, not a bit' (which was true) and he told me all I needed to do was laugh, and I must remember that. He's very nice. After that I always stayed. A couple of nights later we stayed singing and talking till about two and then someone said, 'Let's go up the mountain', so we put on our coats and set off in the dark. The path was very slippery, up up up, slipping on wet leaves with the dark trees all round us and only a torch for light – the top is 1700 feet. A weird journey, silence all the way except for the rests (we had about three but couldn't stop for long because we got so cold). You felt yourself separate and alone in the darkness smelling of trees and earth, no sound but people slipping on the mud.

I've realised that when I'm paralysed by shyness, it's much worse with people who are shy themselves – like Beetles, despite all his talk, and Sandy; now Don, this older man, isn't shy at all, so I never was either, or it didn't matter. But some of the time at Kapiti I did feel half dead with misery – that's why I said at the beginning of this letter that it was so awful it surely must be good for me in some way. Once it starts I seem to get further and further away from everyone till I'm really frightened – I looked at Peg with her easy jolliness, and the breezy girl being breezy, and they just seemed like a different species, and I started to feel a sort of loser, as though I would never catch up with these people who seem so at ease all the time.

In the end the person who helped was Peg – she came back from fishing the afternoon after our night climb and said, 'Let's go for a walk by ourselves', a lovely thing to say. She told me that the only way she can bear all these people is to go off by herself sometimes – I was amazed that she feels like that too, and afterwards I did go, a long way along towards the end of the island, and it was a wonderful relief after being so close to everybody all day, and a good bit of the night too (we always stayed by the fire singing or talking till after midnight). On the way back it began to teem with rain so I took shelter in the little dinghy shed and looked out to sea and the faint line of the mainland and let my mind go blank and just enjoyed the softly hissing silence and being alone. Two of the varsity girls came along and I walked back to camp with them; later on Beetles made me go and change because I was so wet and the only dry things I had were that old purple checked skirt and pink jumper so I put them on. Everyone seemed to think it frightfully funny that I was suddenly so well dressed (not really, but we were mostly so dim and muddy looking) and gradually I started to feel a bit better. That night I slept in Peg's tent, and we talked for hours (or she did) and I started to think perhaps we would be real friends.

The next day was an extra one because there was no launch; some people went for walks, some fished – I did both for a while, then just before tea fell asleep in the tent and woke up feeling horribly sick and bilious. Beetles made me get into his sleeping bag (real down and thicker than mine) and I slept till about nine. Woke feeling splendid, so I walked down to the fire and they were all really nice; Beetles said Loppy had made him responsible for us all and he'd have had a hard time explaining my death, and Don put his arm round my shoulders. Beetles said I was a silly ass to get up and I'd better sleep in the big tent for the rest of the night (a great honour). I did, but I didn't sleep till after midnight because Beetles kept us all helpless with laughing. Some of them had 'tomato sauce' (camp name for beer) but I didn't want any. Beetles doesn't drink either.

Then another day with no launch. We packed everything up, and since we'd used just about all the food there wasn't any of that to carry; some of them slept in the boatshed, but I went back to the tent we'd left up – we didn't exactly worry, but you did begin to wonder what would happen when we got really hungry. However the next morning was suddenly clear and sunny and the launch came. A beautiful trip across – the water calm and shining and full of colours; then we chartered a bus to Paekak. Peg's mother lives there so we went around to her house for a cup of tea, finally caught the Napier express at about four and at last got to Wellington Railway Station at six. Some of us walked through town to the cable car, dirty and dishevelled as we were, with our packs on and singing *The Red Flag* (which I'd learnt over the weekend) and other songs, liking it that people stared. When I got in Molly said I nearly knocked her over with the Kapiti smell. It was hard to believe that she'd been home, and seen you all, and I'd been living this strange wild rough life – you know that feeling that something's happened but it must be to someone else, not you?

This letter will be late I'm afraid, but things do press in on you here – there absolutely isn't a minute; that's half the pleasure of it, this intensity. But at the same time, even though life is full of THINGS, I still feel nostalgia for something more substantial than all this flibberty gibberty business of being amusing and criticising things and people and being ostentatiously unconventional – yet nearly everyone is basically very conventional and susceptible to what Scotty would call the Fear of Social Non-Conformity. There's a sort of upper layer here – I suppose there is everywhere – and in it intelligence is taken for granted. What counts is whether you're a 'decent sort' or not. The human element is the important one – yet perhaps I'm wrong, intelligence does count an awful lot too. As a matter of fact I have settled into the atmosphere very quickly – no credit of course, I have always been susceptible to influences and atmospheres. Molly has not changed nearly so much; she does take in the new ideas and standards but is changing in accordance with them more slowly. One dreadful thing is that you tend to regard popularity and being a success with people as an end in itself and all-important. We are horrified sometimes to find ourselves saying that if one of us is having a burst of popularity everything must be all right. But I am probably boring you to distraction – I think it's events you like to hear.

By the way, you ask if Beetles has faded out of the picture; in fact we are getting on beautifully – but you can't be interested in the same kind of anecdote about him over and over, He is an entirely inimitable personality, and I do think he likes me and we like being together – at least I do, you can't ever be entirely sure with him – and have a lot of fun. At the moment it's often about Kapiti (thank Heaven I did decide to go); even while I'm writing this and I think of his colossal boots and spindly white legs and that convinced and convincing swearing and his moaning voice I am helpless all over again.

Our play. The day of the dress rehearsal I went over to the hall in the afternoon and found Trixie there seeing about props and staging because our ineffectual producers had done nothing, and she is a strong-minded and determined person, almost masculine. She is remarkably ugly but most intelligent and amusing – she and George and I became sort of unofficial producers and did all the work in the end. We stayed right through till the evening working out Heaven, our chief piece of staging, consisting of white steps leading up into what I thought looked like a Victorian bedroom but which was really Heaven. A few of us went and had tea in the staffroom before we went back to finish. We worked in bursts, with lots of stops for talking – then it was time, and we were on.

Scotty came and criticised the play for us, and several second years from camp (most seem to be in the Infantry), and Peg to find out about the next tramp, and in the end there were knots of people all round the hall and we wandered from one to the next talking about it – oh exhilarating. I may as well tell you that I have made quite a stir with my Mrs Muggins – lots and lots of people, even now, days later, rush up and tell me how marvellous it was. Everyone is sure I'll get into the major production, the big play that Scotty puts on in the second term – and I would love to. It's funny because nobody, not even me, ever dreamed I could act before, except just mediocrely. I went home about twelve with Beetles and one or two of the others; he was rude of course but really nice too. (He's entirely different with men – I think he's rather on the defensive with women.)

On the Friday of the play I got to TC about 7.30 – ours was second – in shorts and jumper and socks and slip slops, all ready to leave afterwards, had just time to rush up and get made up by Fitzwilliam-Smith (second year, rather grand), slip on my frock, wrinkle up my stockings and ruffle up my hair and run breathlessly into the hall, Sandy rushing after me powdering my hair, which he kept doing right up to the last minute, All the make-up was excellent – I was almost unrecognisable and looked a *terrific* hag. THEN the play (oh my darlings I do love acting and drama itself and all the thrilling things connected with it!).

In the beginning we had an enthusiastic response – they simply howled with laughter at almost every word, and I felt quite bewildered; they seemed to be missing any point the thing had, but of course it was gratifying for us in a way. Then we had some awful mishaps – the Angel (Thariel – like St Peter) was supposed to sail majestically across the stage and up the steps into Heaven while we all stood tense and still – and so he did till the top step, when crash wallop he tripped and collapsed, lurching and stumbling into Heaven amid shouts of delight from the audience. Someone else galloped up the steps and ripped the curtain down and ended up scuffling under the steps: the wretched audience howled with laughter. We heard a woman say afterwards, 'Oh I thought the second play delightful – such an impromptu air about it!'

I got a tremendous lot of congratulations, the most prized being that I was 'bloody good' from Beetles. Supper afterwards – a lot of important dramatic people were there and we are getting a complete criticism in Drama Club on Thursday. Saturday morning we woke up late, packed our last few things and caught the 10.30 ferry with Peg and George and several others – wonderful trip, I do *love* the smooth calm flow of the ferry and the way we always sing TC songs, ending up invariably with *Turnanog* – the only one that is never sung with any embellishments or nonsense; I'll sing it for you in the holidays, a lovely thing.

At Eastbourne we changed into boots (thank you so much for sending them, I don't know what I'd have done without them). The first hill, the Wainui, is a long long pull, very tiring because it never seems to end, you just grind on and on for ever. Then there's the GB (Guts Buster) a shorter, steeper hill – while you're on it you think it will kill you, but it doesn't; lunch at Catchpole, a lovely beechwood place with leaves carpeting the ground and the Log Cabin showing through the trees. To rest you sit on a log or a stone with your head right down, letting go all over, the way a horse does when it's standing still.

Then there's the Five Mile, through bush all the way – not that you look at it, your eyes are glued to the track which is feet deep in mud in some places – but you feel it there and smell the wonderful cold mossy smell, and then when you do stop, at the hut, and look round it's all above and around you, most gracious and lovely. For the last bit you cross the river and go up a little steep track and suddenly find yourself at the door – it's hidden in the trees from the river bed. Saveloys and bread and butter and of course billy tea waiting for us – it was four o'clock. Margot and Brenda made stew over the fire for tea and then we sat round the fire for hours talking and singing and being funny and clever and making puns about everything. Two strangers came in, two men but the poor things didn't get a look in at all, we were all so busy carrying on at the tops of our voices and laughing our heads off (it's a strange thing there in the dark bush and miles away from everyone, just our special selves round the fire – I can't tell you how it frees you from all the ordinary things you've left behind). About 4 am Bruce Mason and Neville Mitchell arrived – Neville was our leader, coming back; he's a dear little creature and a very experienced tramper. We sang all the way in the ferry, then I walked halfway home with Sandy and then Molly and I came on by ourselves, hot bath (how you love it!) and about ten or eleven hours' sleep, and we're not even stiff. Oh I forgot to tell you, Bruce absolutely *fastened* onto me the whole time – we had a lot of fun, but I don't want to be fastened on by anyone except – no, not by anyone. He says he wanted to nominate me for the Exec. I, needless to say, was nothing loth so he did on Monday – he's on it himself now. I had to refuse two other nominations afterwards – hostel girls. There are about a dozen women nominated so the voting will be complicated – I'll let you know what happens.

NB All the enlightened people here are Communists, the unenlightened nothing at all. No Social Credit.

Chapter 13

*V*ictoria House A. It seems strange to be writing after I've talked to you so short a time ago; I can still hear John's shrill little pipe and Daddy's deep voice, and Lindsay's soft breathless one, and your – well just your voice Mother dear. I am feeling utterly wretched. Those blue and white shoes let in the water, and I'll have to get them soled, and then there have been lots of late nights (I thought I'd become immune!) – I've got a rough loud cough, purple eye circles – general effect, utter hag, and I *feel* so awful. I've been in bed all day and although the cough is still booming away down in my chest I feel slightly better. Molly has been very sweet and good all the time, I think she quite likes ministering. I read *A Room with a View* – E.M. Forster – and you must read it, I thought it beautifully sympathetic and subtle.

One day when Molly and I were in town an American sailor in a milk bar wanted to shout us an ice cream and while we were saying No two negroes came and asked us to go to a dance. We were a bit scared, though you get so used to soldiers and marines speaking to you in the street you hardly notice, and I've got quite good at telling them to go away when they follow me home.

Well, the elections for the Exec are over. The last two days seemed *interminable* – everyone, including of course Molly who has been constantly encouraging, was thrilled about my nomination and certain I'd get in – but of course you can't help feeling insecure. Wednesday afternoon Beetles told me what to do about the voting – it's preferential, and I must put myself first and my most dangerous rival last (he said it was Lovey Reihana, a perfect idiot of a girl – nice enough but an ass, a good-looking Maori girl – in the end she topped the poll!). Thursday morning, everyone being very sweet about wishing me luck – the most prized being Beetles who walked nonchalantly past me in the hall and smiled significantly when nobody was looking – he really is terribly kind when he thinks you need it. Then two agonising lecture periods while the scrutineers counted the votes. Then the announcement. Blankness, perfect numbness while I applauded for the others. Then the Social Committee, a sort of second string to the Exec, and Gillian Brown (the other good candidate who should have got onto the Exec) and I were both elected to that. Everyone profusely congratulated us both – I didn't know what to do (except pretend) – I was so disappointed I could have burst into tears, yet people kept saying Isn't it wonderful and Good for you, etc. Of course Molly knew how I felt, so did Bruce – and Sandy turned up and was very kind and tactful. The rest of that Friday was quite nice despite the feeling of crushedness and humiliation. Talked to Bruce a lot and then after lectures finished I was 'on cleaning' and he stayed behind with me, kept saying he wished I'd got on the Exec (not half as much as I do!) and then in a burst of confidence that he was very fond of me. He has a rather charming boyish manner sometimes and of course I do like him, very much, but if we saw any more of each other than we do he would get on my nerves and I would bore him I'm sure.

Several days later. My cough didn't go away, it got worse and I couldn't go to college for a few days; I missed a riotously funny play at Drama Club, Bruce the central character. Although he's always too much himself he never fails to bring the house down when he's doing comedy – he's absolutely wonderful.

I have parted my hair in the middle and taken down the verandahs so it's all loose. I've been wondering why some people look so like Madonnas and some so unlike – now I know. I'm in Major Production – can't now imagine life without it. *The Man Who Came to Dinner,* with Bruce (in a wheelchair) the central character. I'm his half-witted nurse.

One night I went back after rehearsal to get things I'd left there and was talking to Sandy and Bruce in the hall when we heard Beetles' voice from up in the ceiling of the stage. Was that his darling come back? I stayed on then and we had a perfectly lovely time except that Bruce got so fierce, he was like a bear with a sore head. I've never seen him so cross and bad-tempered. I was looking for a form (for travel to schools) and asked everyone if they'd seen it; Beetles said he didn't want to do anything with my form – roaring with laughter – but Bruce came up and hissed at me, 'That was a pretty thin excuse to hang around Beetles!' I was speechless at first, then furious – he apologised almost at once but then said, 'If you're so upset it must be true' and then we did have a short sharp argument and I went home. I was horribly depressed and miserable afterwards; talked to Margot a bit about it, then about half past nine the phone rang and it was Bruce really apologising and saying he had no intention of being malicious but he was just venting his ill-humour on someone else. I replied that I liked staying talking and he said yes he and Beetles always wanted me to and I wasn't to think any less of him etc etc. I do though – I've lost a bit of respect for him (but then I've never had half as much as for Beetles or even Sandy). He told me the next day that it had got back to Beetles, but all he said to me was 'I hear you two had a row' and chuckled, so I suppose it's all over. You'll think it was nothing much, but I minded *extremely*. I like Beetles more and more and I can't bear it if anything goes wrong, or looks as though it might.

MP (Major Production) is getting close now. After all these rehearsals I still find Bruce frightfully funny, sitting in his wheelchair delivering insults to everyone – especially me, his dopey nurse; I am the feeblest, most timid creature in the whole world, at least Miss Preen is, my character. Last Sunday we spent the whole afternoon doing it, as usual. It teemed with rain as we ran along Upland Road and I got my good coat wet but it didn't hurt it; came home with Beetles about midnight.

Chapter 14

July 20. *So that's that. Yet it can't be – he's not like that about women, I know he's not, he's on another sort of level. She just flirts, I've watched her doing it with everyone in turn and either you're taken in by it or you're not. I'm not, of course, but I'd have been utterly sure he wouldn't be either. The way she looks up at these tall men (well she's so small they're all tall to her – and boy does she make the most of it) – the way she giggles at them – doesn't she know how obvious it is? Good God, doesn't he? And I thought him so different from everyone else in the world! We're all doing the big play and she's doing a little play of her own all the time. Ugh! I despise her.*

Victoria House, July

It's wonderful that you came and I wish you were still here, but not that the play was still on. The delights of life at training college are greatly over-estimated. The beastly Vic-Weir House dance is tonight but Molly and I are going to give our 1s 6ds to Margot and go to bed. I wonder how you liked all the people you met the night you saw the play – I think Beetles is horrible but all the others are nice enough. I want to come home for the holidays instead of staying here and being Manpowered into tram conducting or something. I still feel very nostalgic for hills and paddocks and trees and views and silence, but for the first time since I came away I don't find writing to you very easy. It doesn't seem worth while to bother with all the trivialities, descriptions of people; I'm completely anti-social. There's a boy outside – it's about six, quite dark – and he's crying *Spo-o-orts Po-o-ost* in the cold and dark and it sounds the most mournful sound in all the world.

Nine o'clock. *In bed, face all red and eyes swollen with hours of weeping – at least nobody can see me, or hear what I'm saying (a kind of relief, I can say anything I like here), Maybe I'm just tired and need an early* night – it's just that I can't get it out of my mind. Last night, Beetles dancing every single dance with the nasty wily scheming pretty creature, and then waiting for her outside the cloakroom and taking her off with him in that possessive way – just like any other man. Is this what I mind most, that he's suddenly different because of her? that I'd got him wrong? I don't know, it all hurts, horribly. And for him to ring up tonight and ask if I'm going to the Vic-Weir Dance! No, I haven't got anyone to go with, you have to have a partner, I said mournfully (though heaven knows I tried to sound natural) – and for him to say he wasn't going either, and then to take her to the pictures – and why would Sandy ring up to tell me that? I wish nobody on earth had rung me up, I'm sick and tired of the telephone. I wish I didn't mind so much.

Sunday. When I woke up this morning I found I'd slept through the biggest earthquake Wellington has had in years. My bowl of violets tipped over and my drawer was full of water; it also made the TC roof shift about a foot and there's a gap of daylight showing through, and a great big triangle of wall fell out the end. If anyone had been on the stage they'd have been killed. Tonight a crowd of us went to a Russian film, and Beetles arrived late, just before we were due to go in, walking up Cuba Street with Brenda. I just felt silent and numb, but of course went on talking to the others, Sandy and Peg and George.

Varsity Library. *I'm going to keep on carrying this round with me – I'll keep it with me so no one can find it and read it, anywhere ever. Anyway the times I have to write in it come unexpectedly. Like now, Beetles and Brenda have gone off somewhere; she's supposed to be at History and so am I, but I just can't make myself go, I'm so full of how much I hate that greedy unscrupulous little pig (she's always doing it with someone, I just never thought it'd be with him) – I even hate that little blue jacket she wears with the white flowers – I'd like to cut it into the tiniest morsels.*

I have to think though, and make adjustments, I've depended on him too much, or the idea of him – I don't know where one begins and the other ends. Perhaps I didn't realise how much I'd come to think about him – yet I've always known I liked being with him better than with anyone else, I must have gone on about him in letters home till they're probably sick to death of the sound of his name.

Well, no more of that. Something's gone though, some lovely comfortable feeling at the back of my mind. Perhaps it was a kind of support, a being secure. Am I a sex-starved cobra after all? Molly says yes.

What am I to say to Mum? – she says I 'often swap ideas with Beetles' and surely this is the same even if he has other friends? Oh no, no, no, I don't know how to say it, but it isn't like that, not at all. He was always giving me ideas and it was exciting, but it wasn't just that. It was fun too, for one thing. He made me happy I suppose. As for talking to him now, I can't, I just can't. There's a paralysis in both of us. I can see that this Brenda business doesn't make any difference to some people, like Margot, but it does to me, and I can't help it.

    I think of us all being in a big net, we clamber and swing in it, going up and down at different times and laughing and calling out to one another. Suddenly there's a hole right under me, and other people try to scramble about and get closer to me so I won't see it, or anyway won't fall through. Nobody says so of course, but they do special things – George taking me to the French Maid, after Sandy and I had made the lists of food for the tramp, and waiting so long till I was ready. And then Sandy coming too and being sweet to me – and it was fun, though I think I'm half acting all the time. I laugh and talk just as usual (I think) but it's all put on. Perhaps I should be glad I can, and be weak and feeble here, in secret.

I wanted to come back after the August holidays, of course (despite telling Mother I didn't) but it's strange and hurtful now I am here. Beetles and Brenda both live in Wellington and there are all sorts of rumours about how they spent every minute in each other's pockets. Either it's true, or people make a point of saying it to me to see my face (I try so hard to smile, or look indifferent, but I bet I don't manage it). But I really am working hard on getting through all this – today I was cheerful and even zestful, I felt as though I'd cast out some devils and that had left me clean though weak. It's nasty waking up in the morning though and collecting my thoughts as you do, and remembering Brenda, and knowing there's no way to make her go away, or Beetles go back to how he was. Or how I thought he was.

    Today he said that at the varsity dance tomorrow night he'd 'dance with me if I'm good' – what a nerve. I suppose he thought he was being funny – I snorted but I wish now I'd been really rude. Not that I ever can. I won't go at all.

September

It's strangely depressing being back again – nobody seems pleased the holidays are finished. I am melancholy myself – Molly says I'm changed, I'm quieter, missing a certain vitality; she also said a nice thing, that I have a genius for friendship! Fancy that. She's a dear creature. There is actually a cloud hanging over us all – we can't use the TC building while they rebuild it after the earthquake, and are crammed into varsity buildings, not quite belonging, yet not quite able to have our own communal life. We are too close I think and everyone is bad-tempered.

I'm on section and have a Standard 1 and 2, absolute dregs, exceptionally dull children, but a teacher who's pleasant and patient and even quite amusing about the job. And in spite of – or perhaps because of – their dullness, the children are very, very nice. If someone gets more sums than usual right the others all rush up to tell you, and if one is in difficulties you just can't keep the others from helping him. You have to be careful though – never give two formal lessons together and always for the last hour morning and afternoon give them things that need no concentration. I'm quite enjoying it, though the thought of taking a lesson scares me.

Later. I've done it, for a whole hour and I've never spent a more terrible time in my life, I felt *shrieking mad* at the end, and in fact did break a precious rule and lose my temper (I'll be a hopelessly intolerant and short-tempered teacher) but it did no good whatever. For ages afterwards I felt both limp and hysterical; the worst of it is I don't know how to do it any better next time; if they're not interested in school work, they're not, and even if I were to dance and sing I can't see what difference it would make. When something like this happens you notice other conditions of classrooms – that smell, so strong, so unlike any other – I don't know what it's made of, children's little bodies and dirt and chalk and shut windows and smelly feet.

Coming down the Church Street steps Beetles' mother saw me and gave me a huge bunch of lilac. Then Beetles himself turned up and wanted to ask my advice about Ako Pai, the annual magazine; he thinks I should be the Editor but I don't think I know enough about it. He talked and talked – I must be everyone's favourite Family Friend and confidante – ugh!

When we break up in a month's time we all have to do some war work; the others are grumbling but I think it will be good to earn some money. Maybe their purses aren't always empty like mine.

Chapter 15

Victoria University, February 1943. So, another year. Molly and I are pleased to be back in our ugly little room – in fact are quite skittish tonight (bark of derisive laughter from Molly – 'not all of us', she says). You'll never guess what we did last night. Sandy turned up during the day from camp so we had lunch with him but then Beetles asked him and Brenda to tea (Paul has gone back to camp, having re-established his claim over Brenda, or so it seems – but I don't think much about her any more; she's beyond jealousy, she's so unlike the rest of us). Oh well, I thought, that's that, and went down to the Music Room with Gillian. We simply wallowed in a beautiful Tchaikovsky piano concerto and then, remarkably, Sandy came and found us and insisted we go dancing with them. Gillian went home but I agreed and so found myself in, of all places, the Empress Ballroom! A dimly-lit den full of American sailors and marines and weird female creatures dressed in satin and net, all jitter-bugging wildly, a blue smoke haze over everything. There was a real fight too, which drew everyone in the hall except a few blasé ones like us. We just danced grimly on (sounds a bit contradictory I know). There's a sort of rosy glow of light over the entrance to the place – I felt deliciously sinful being there.

What else has happened? Oh Beetles came down to get me to go to his place the other night; they were all home and we talked and ate fish and chips for tea and I tried to remember what you said about sharing people. It isn't the same with his mother and sister there because they both talk without stopping, but I don't care about being alone with him now anyway. It's partly Gordon I suppose. I haven't told you much about him but he's nice and I feel at home with him in a way I never did with Beetles, I was always so impressed by him.

Gordon is clever but too solemn and dances with his feet flat on the ground all the time, as though he's got to clear away heaps of mud or something, a sort of shovelling action. He and I are doing some research in the library and get let off tons of lectures – we get interrupted a lot though (especially by the lecturer in charge of the library who has, according to Gordon, 'the energy of the chronically inefficient'). One day we had a new student to come and observe us – a fine-looking girl with red hair and yellow eyes and long tawny lashes and orange and yellow clothes; not in the least intellectual, but sweet. Gordon of course shut up like a clam so I had her to talk to by myself all day. I want to shake him at such times. I know all about being shy of course, but he is somehow so *surly* about it.

Sunday. A lovely day, sunny and cool, and I have it entirely to myself because Molly is away on an all-day tramp. I got up late because I wanted to finish my book – *East End My Cradle* by Willy Goldman – an unadorned tale of London slum life, done with an amazingly philosophical tone and outlook. The worst atrocities of daily living are described faithfully but without bitterness or resentment. I wondered if as a social indictment it loses something because of that, but on the other hand it gives you a new angle – these things are, and I'm showing you them, something like that.

We have a room on the third floor of this building I love so much – it belongs (the room I mean) to a varsity English lecturer and with our stuff as well is very cluttered, but there are two enormous windows with wide sills where a solitary librarian can lean her elbows and look at the street below and the world passing by along it. There is ivy growing over the bricks and this makes it all more venerable and dignified. Sometimes I lean my chin on my hand and know what it is like to be a princess in a castle – except that this is an intellectual citadel and thus much more splendid.

Gillian is a continuing disappointment. When I first got to know her she seemed wonderfully grown-up, very charming and intelligent – and worldly too. But if being intelligent is grasping the subtle shades of meaning in a situation or phrase (which I think it is) she's not that at all. She just uses what she has so well that people think her quite outstanding.

Interruption. Beetles and Trevor Edmond came in – both are teaching in Wellington this year and I've seen Trevor several times and liked him a lot. We were to have lunch today but unfortunately Molly told him I was at TC not varsity and he missed me – very disappointed, so he said. He is notorious for his dealings with women – always has a different one, but everyone seems just to laugh about this because they love him. He did have one woman for a whole year but she has now thrown him over – these little tragedies are always passing before our eyes (or closer still). They were going to a Communist Party meeting later on; Trevor is thinking of joining too. Beetles says he gives me a couple of years. *Later.* There was a CP social after the meeting and it was *terrible* – awkward and boring. I'm glad I wasn't there.

Varsity Freshers' Ball the other night – odd to think of the last one when Molly and I were such children. I went with Gordon, Peg and George came too and Paul Meredith brought Brenda (Beetles stayed home); very crowded and not wonderfully entertaining. We all seemed so settled somehow. It's funny, I used to try and try to get hold of someone to make a couple with; now I have, I have wish I were roaming about frightened but exhilarated about the possibilities. And Gordon is so serious.

I spent the afternoon going to a *Salient* meeting with Beetles (you know, the varsity fortnightly paper) – he wants me to write for it. The room, a grubby hole in the gym, was full of foreign-accented intellectuals and I would have been scared of them if Beetles hadn't been with me. I can't imagine I'll be good enough to do anything for them, I don't know why he is so sure I can. I've been thinking about it since, and I think I'll tell him that I'll try some reviews of plays, making them a discussion about the contact a play sets up between the audience and the players, a kind of organised conversation – but of course they might not like that at all. I'll get Beetles to put it to them, I couldn't.

I am at Mount Cook school which has a terrific reputation for TOUGHNESS. My teacher is the nicest I've had so far, young, pleasant and human – I think I'd even like her out of school (which you don't usually). It's Primer 2 so they're only five or six, extremely smelly little kids, but sweet. I don't have any Chinese (though there are lots at the school) but there are two lovely little girls from the Hindu quarter, little black shiny heads, hair dragged tightly back into a pigtail, black black eyes – and a funny, garrulous, somehow maternal air about them. Sante, the most talkative, knows *everything* about the rest of the class and insists on telling you with a funny concerned grave look on her brown little face. At morning talk time the words just tumble out, so fast you're lucky if you recognise one here and there. One child, a bit briefer than Sante, came forward yesterday and blurted out to the class, 'Me father's comin' out of camp in a week!' and rushed back to her seat.

You ask about Health and Happiness. The first is fine, I don't have a cough at all at present. The second is more difficult to describe. Something is not going right but I don't know what it is. Molly and I are liking living together and we see a good deal of Peg and George who are visibly happy; Gillian, however, has turned out a fraud. Underneath a bright and versatile exterior there's a horrible nothing – she doesn't want friendship or affection at all, just success. Molly and I have been useful and pleasant but we're not really any good to her now, she's got to know our friends and we think that's mostly what she wanted.

Another thing, I've decided I can't conscientiously go to Communist Party meetings unless I've got some sort of aim in view, or see myself properly being a part of it. I've told Beetles I can't, and so haven't seen much of him for a while. I haven't usually stood up to him I think, but have been soft and weak; now I do say what I think it seems to make us both feel awkward. And I don't think quite so much of Margot – she's left college of course but comes to things a lot; it seems to me that under her stoutness and seriousness she's actually rather uncharitable and only tolerates people like herself. At the beginning of this year she wrote to Molly saying my relationship with her was just a matter of good company, then when Molly took a long time to reply – and I didn't, to my letter – she began to ignore Molly and concentrate on me. She's hurt us both quite a bit. Like so many people she just follows whims, which seems to me very undisciplined. Oh I know I am too, but at least I don't pretend to myself that it's all right. As you see, I am rather fed up with everyone.

There's Gordon of course, silent and faithful and ready to be interested in whatever I do without demanding a thing, company or conversation even. Certainly he does a lot for me, which is handy, and is always there at dances, but sometimes it drives me mad to be with him, knowing he's so good and intelligent and faithful and steady and yet nothing *happens* when we're together. I suppose I should be more strict with myself, and try harder to be tolerant. I don't know if I can. I'm quite frankly not terribly happy at all, haven't been all this term. I thought I'd love being a second year, but that's something that worries me too, what a milk-and-watery lot we are – the majority are really uninspired, but there aren't any grand figures like Beetles to drag them out of their apathy. *Stud Op* is most anaemic and there's an Open Forum in a week and I'm supposed to think of topics and can't conjure up one matter of great importance. The war, but we've said everything so often. Loppy has even recommended *Stud Op* in Assembly – it must be tame. I was quite ashamed.

I am working hard, handing essays in at varsity and TC on time, and that's something. Perhaps I need an occasion to rise to, like most of our family – don't you agree we need that to be at our best?

Have been having a talk to Gordon about his letter. I've just come home and fortunately Molly isn't here. What does he mean writing to me like that about 'the state of our relations' and saying I have to tell him 'where he stands'? Help! It's like something out of a Jane Austen novel, not the present day. I didn't know what on earth to say to him; in the end we went for a walk and after he'd mumbled away for a while about how his peace of mind is thoroughly upset I tried to reply, feeling like an actor in a melodrama – none of it seemed real. I like to talk to him, dance with him (I didn't say he could be a bit less of a clodhopper) but I don't feel differently towards him from the way I feel about lots of other friends – what else could I possibly say? Anyway I said it, earnestly I daresay, and did it satisfy him? By no means. He said he was resigned to being unhappy, but said he had to know. Heavens, it was getting more like a romantic novelette – I could hardly believe it was happening to me, nor that all the time I've supposed we were just friends he's had all these theatrical ideas. He's nice though, and sensitive and intelligent and I wish I could have said something better. What is it makes some people desirable and others not?

You are very good to send back such positive and confident replies to all my complaining. I don't think anyone should burden other people with problems of that kind though. Perhaps I haven't quite realised in letting it pour off my pen, that of course I must settle these things by myself. And not let any of it show while I'm doing it – damn difficult that is though, I must say. It is easy to theorise when you feel all right. However, next time it might be better if you ignore what I say, or maybe stand on my toes a little, instead of giving it all such consideration. Which isn't to say I don't enjoy letters and encouraging advice (the one that arrived on Saturday was simply balm). Perhaps I am a mirror, and so I need to choose my company carefully; since I'm not awfully tolerant, perhaps that's easy enough. Anyway, happiness, misery, incompleteness or the opposite – fulfilment I suppose – they all depend on one another and must rub together to make a balance in anyone's life. Or so I think.

There was an earthquake just now – they're much worse here than at home, when they come. One thing (not to do with earthquakes) I've learnt in education is that most of your characteristics can't actually change – you can make much or little of them perhaps, but you can't give yourself new ones. You inherit your basic temperament and for better or worse that's what you have to keep. By the way what do you think of *Stud Op*? A lot of the stuff sent in was unspeakably awful but we dragged stuff out of our friends – people like Gordon and Molly and Beetles – and while I suppose you shouldn't do that, we were glad we had. I hope you like my article. I wouldn't like too many people to know what piles of rubbish we rejected and how much of it we had to do ourselves. But actually now we feel quite proud of it.

March

I've enrolled for English I and Education I at varsity – this means with music at four to five on Thursday I have every afternoon taken up. It's quite good really, you can waste a lot of time here just talking to people. This way, with lectures or music from four till six every day, I can work in the evenings or write letters – though there is the phone, a great trap. Talking of that, Beetles rang me last night and talked for *an hour and a half* (I said nobody would be able to get through, and he said it was his revenge because he'd tried so often and been thwarted). He rang primarily to take me to task for a poem I wrote for *Stud Op*; as poetry it's good he says, but the attitude behind it he thinks dreadful and knowing it to be perfectly sincere he's worried. I seem to be drifting with nothing to hold on to, nothing I firmly believe in. I said it's a reaction, a state of mind, but not the only one, and he says I shouldn't have such reactions or moods. Despite everything that's happened, he is nice, he makes me feel different, self-respecting. He really wants my life to be right for me – it's even worthwhile disagreeing with him.

There'll be no parts in Major Productions this year because I've joined the Choral Club. Molly and I were sick of the same people running Drama all the time, and it is rather exhilarating to sing in a large choir. Tommy Young, who takes it, is a wonderful little creature, small and delicate and pliable, as though he hasn't got any bones.

I don't know what's the matter with us – we've all become quiet and sensible. Saturday I was supposed to go out to Paekak with Peg, then Neville came and begged us to go to his place, but I simply had to get my *Stud Op* article written so I stayed home. And Sunday I couldn't go anywhere either because *Stud Op* had to be printed and we do that at varsity. Janet Broadhead is the Editor at present, though her literary ability and judgement are hopeless (she's a nice girl though).

April

My birthday parcel is divine. Every little thing is exactly right, truly – the 30s (I'll get shoes) and the little silver box (John dear where did you get it?) and the scarf and – this made me laugh – the absurd satin panties. Are they to wear? The stockings were superb too and the book; as you know I like Saroyan very much. I got two more books from Peg and from Gillian a book of poems written by a cockroach that couldn't reach all the keys on the typewriter so couldn't do capital letters – archy, his name is; it's funny and nice. A framed print, Gauguin, from Molly, and Neville took me to dinner and Sandy, on leave, to *Twelfth Night*. So – no complaints at all! Beetles forgot till late in the day and rang up and made a speech to me then. And Lindsay my love the cake is delicious. Now that's enough.

Tonight Molly and I have been to a rhythmical gymnastics class. She went to a display of it about a fortnight ago and came home very excited; an Austrian woman called Gisa Taglicht is starting a class for students, and tonight was the first one. You feel like a flying elephant flinging your arms and legs around all over the place, but it's exhilarating too. Eurythmics means expression by movement of sound, usually a drum beating. The first story I ever wrote began with 'a lithe young girl' (you won't remember but I do) so now you see I'm really going to become one.

Chapter 16

Section Reports have come in and mine from Primer 2 is excellent – apparently I have a delightful manner with small children and at the same time am quietly dignified! They caused quite a lot of excitement – but we all know that everyone gets a good report from Infant teachers, they get out of the habit of being harsh, or even direct. Encouragement is the thing. Well, I don't mind.

I'm sorry my letter depressed Clive. You say he needs to be interested in a girl, and I know that, but to set about preparing a selection of unattached women, as his letter said, seemed horribly mechanical to me, and I just said so. He has a difficult and perhaps lonely temperament and seems to learn his lessons, whatever they are, terribly slowly – in fact we all do (Scotts I mean). I seem to be spending a lot of time lately emulating other people, as though they'll tell me what sort of person to be, and then worrying about whether I choose the right ones to admire. Perhaps Clive does that too, do you think? Is it just being young, to feel so uncertain and undecided and copying other people, right or wrong? Of course it's a family characteristic to go to extremes.

I worry too at the moment about whether I can carry all the responsibilities I seem to have – *Stud Op* most I suppose; I love being on it and seeing it get worked out each time, but am terrified in case we can't. Or I can't. To do these things you need a lot of drive or else a very 'sound' temperament – the sort people rely on – and a lot of organisation as well. I seem to do things in such a big rush, and then suddenly I'm beset by uncertainty in case that isn't the right way after all. The only thing I don't get like that about is what I write myself – I'll argue with anyone about it and not care, I don't know why it's so different.

You ask what I mean when I say, as I did on the phone, that I have no more illusions about Beetles. Well, at one time I think I built a half fantastic structure about him and set him apart from ordinary people just because his personality is extraordinary. Now I don't. I know him better and see that he has faults, he's intolerant and can be hard; I like him just as much but I fancy it's the real person I like now, not some fiction I made up in my own mind. I called in at his place the other night and Brenda was there, and I was struck by how different everything is from last year. Not just because she's decided to keep on with Paul Meredith, but because I myself don't want to be a rival of hers, or anyone's – I wanted him all to myself last year, now I don't. He's just another person, though I'll always think of him as having something special about him. There, that's the answer. I like the black and yellow taffeta by far the best of the slips you sent.

Scotty has asked the English second years to write a review of *NZ New Writing* (I don't do English at TC because I'm taking it at varsity this year) and Beth Gould, a hostel girl, asked me to do hers for her so I did, and then when he gave them back she didn't get hers. She asked him why and he said he's keeping it to read to all the sections, it's head and shoulders above all the others. Fancy that – Beth said she felt an awful hypocrite, but we're both pleased; she says he treats her with a new respect! I wish, rather unworthily I suppose, that he knew it was mine; in theory it's enough to know myself. It's funny, though, Scotty made a point of stopping me in the corridor the next day to tell me how good Miss Gould's review was – 'really excellent' he said; I just blinked innocently and said Was it? Do you think he'd guessed?

One night, when we got home from the last tramp, we all met in town to go to the pictures but couldn't get in anywhere so we went and danced instead. It was mad when we were so tired, but getting into nice clean clothes – and having a bath of course – makes all the difference in the world. I felt wonderful. It was a public dance but naturally you don't dance with other people or go in chain dances or anything, you just stay with your party; Aren't I a horrible little bourgeoise?

Last night Gordon and I went to *Fantasia* – it's marvellous; do you think abstract designs moving on the screen like that is the coming thing?

Isn't 19 an interesting age?

June the something, 1943

Last Wednesday, I had a *Salient* meeting, then helped to get *Stud Op* ready for publication, and then there was a meeting to elect the Business Manager and Editor for *Ako Pai*, the annual magazine – and I'm

Editor! I feel pretty awful about it because I don't in the least know if I'll be able to do it properly, or even quite what what's expected of me.

Since then I've had another *Salient* meeting – which I spent writing and writing, before, during and after, to get my stuff in time (a review of a book of Russian short stories and a piece about that film *The Great Lie*). And I've had my first *Ako Pai* meeting; the committee are nice, but I'm still very apprehensive. One thing, I'm afraid that with this magazine as well as all the other things I seem to have to do, I'll have to give up music. There really isn't time for it – I feel terrible because I know she's outstanding and it's a chance I may not have again, but the fact is there simply isn't time. Bernard Shaw says that when someone says 'the fact is' they're going to tell a lie, but this is a fact, and not a lie. I'm sorry to tell you this, but I have to.

The next night I prepared lessons for school. I'm rather enjoying having older kids and had offered to do Literary Appreciation with them. I chose a part of *All Quiet on the Western Front* and read it to them – it's very gripping and they listened with eyes like saucers. I pointed out that it was written by a German, suggesting that war is just as terrible for them as it is for us. The dedication is to those who 'even though they escaped its shells were destroyed by the war'. They are very conscious of political and social questions and discussed it most intelligently. A good class – maybe I'll like being a real teacher, though mostly I think I won't.

Came home to the phone ringing. Trevor Edmond, out of camp at Blenheim for a few days; we talked for a while – I always enjoy talking to him, he's so easy and charming – and then I said I'd see him at the Folk Dancing the next night. And then worried because the last time I saw much of him was at Welcome Ball, I'd been with Beetles and felt my social best and I didn't think I could repeat that. Since then he's written to me and that's been quite pleasant. Anyway the dance was fun – I seem to have learnt how to behave like a little minx and played Gordon against Trevor with great satisfaction, so they both wanted to come home with me . . . what a silly rigmarole to be telling you, the chronicle of a man-hunting butterfly. There are more important matters. For instance I'm a bit concerned about Clive who, after all the looking forward to coming out of camp, isn't enjoying college. He wants to hurry things too much, won't let them take their time, and so doesn't seem to be getting to know anyone. He just sticks with the one or two old tramping mates he's got and dismisses everything else as puerile. A lot of the students are puerile, and very blatant about it too, but there are some very nice men if he bothered to look for them. Is he unsettled by the long time in camp do you think?

Trevor has gone back. We went to the pictures one night, and for a long walk on Sunday, both interesting and nice. I think he needs feminine company and I 'speak his language' and will do. We might go with more of a swing if I were interested in him but I'm not, I just like him, without getting excited by his famous charm. So that's all right.

Ako Pai is going well and I feel much more confident than before. The Business Manager, a first year and hitherto an unknown quantity, is turning out beautifully, sensible and competent; he's very important, and it's a relief to know we haven't got some moron, which I fully expected. A lot of the men are such children. That reminds me, Clive has recovered his senses and is working quite seriously to get a returned man on the Exec; he's been talking a lot, in a sane and capable way. I'm very pleased with him.

Trevor is coming again soon – for final leave! The second time I went out with him this visit I enjoyed as much as any afternoon I remember, it was just lovely. I wasn't going to tell you just now, in case you took fright, but he was going to come home to Greenmeadows next holidays; however he can't because he's been given this frightfully short notice that he's going overseas – to the Islands. He'll be here for a week or ten days first though. I suppose I'll have to go out most evenings – I'd better get some sleep while I can. Ah the summer of the butterfly!

Lindsay my dear, it's a pity to be so discontented with school; much better to like it as well as you can while you have to be there and see all the limitations when you've changed to something else. Whatever you do afterwards – TC or anything – will be all the better by comparison. In fact, the sudden realisation that school was so awful is half the pleasure when your start something else. And you can't really compare school with this life we lead – they're too different. Anyway there are the dreary and disappointing bits to this too you know. I sound like the traditional older sister saying 'Your time will come' I know, but don't be put off. I love you to write and tell me about it. And tell Tommy to stop bucking John off or I'll whack him on the rump when I get home. End of your bit.

I'm following last week's lesson on Literary Appreciation with *The*

Golden Journey to Samarkand, a poem by James Elroy Flecker – you must read it (it'll be in some book of Lindsay's). This bit is especially lovely, it makes me shiver when I read it:

> Sweet to ride forth at evenings from the wells
> When shadows pass gigantic on the sand,
> And softly through the silence beat the bells
> Along the Golden Road to Samarkand.

Tuesday I spent in bed with another bad cough booming away down in my chest. The Matron came in during the morning to say the mail might cheer me up – and there were four letters – yours, and a long one from Peg, one from Trevor, the second in three days, and – almost too much pleasure for one morning – my account from Whitcombes and it's only 7s 6d! And it was a cold wet day so I could relish not being in a draughty classroom – they are the most miserable places on earth.

While I was in bed I read Antony and Cleopatra. *It left me simply gasping; read slowly it is absorbing, thrilling. You seem to grow bigger all the way through to the end, as though you have to, to fit its own huge size. I don't know what it would be like on the stage, almost too much perhaps. All the time I was reading I could smell the honeysuckle on the hedge next door, through the open window, and in the afternoon the sun shone through its leaves so they were little green windows.*

Trevor's final leave is over. I was in a flurry all the time, going to pictures and dances and to the Gardens for walks and to college with Peg and George and to a Repertory play and a Choral Society concert – that bit was with Gordon, an old arrangement, and while the music was heavenly – mostly Russian – he spent the time reading the Sports Post *and telling me all about being ill; I tried not to be bored but the contrast with Trevor's charming, funny, alive sort of conversation was just too much. The truth is that nothing like this has ever happened to me before, this extraordinary excitement (when he begins to kiss me) – it's something I've never felt. I didn't know it existed – how remarkable that it does! It's like a room that you thought was just a piece of wall and suddenly someone has unlocked the door and turned on the light. And I'm in it – wonderfully, unbelievably in it.*

Chapter 17

*T*oday I feel so happy, so very happy – Heavens I sound like a Methodist Sunday school teacher chanting Crusader choruses but it can't be helped; all this week I've felt contented and tranquil inside, as internally peaceful as a fat old munching cow. It's all to do with those two lovely weeks when Trevor was here; if I thought it would make me unsettled (because he was leaving to go overseas) I was wrong – it's the opposite. At the moment it doesn't matter much whether I see him again or not (though I expect that will change when he comes back); the intimacy and harmony was something perfect in itself and if it turns out to be a closed chapter that seems all right. It isn't just a passing elation at all, it's a solid smooth block of happiness underneath everything. It doesn't even seem strange – it's as though it's always been there, a heater I've always been warmed by and only now have I noticed where the glow comes from.

It's made everything else look different, more in place somehow. Beetles for instance (well, he isn't exactly a thing) – on Saturday morning I asked him to come to town for morning tea, and I paid. It was a birthday present (I make such a fuss about my own, the least I can do is recognise other people's); it's the first time I've been able to talk to him since Trevor went and I felt we were two individuals meeting on equal ground at last. We had a very good time; went on to Modern Books and poked about there, and he bought me some violets because he thought it so nice of me to have taken him to tea, and I thought that nice of him – oh we glowed with niceness . . . He told me he was really worried because he thought I might have fallen for Trevor; of course if we both meant it he'd be pleased, but he'd seen it happen too often to think Trevor could possibly be serious.

I reassured him, said I knew all that perfectly well, and that Trevor understood I wasn't 'falling' nor intending to, so it was all right. He was enormously relieved. When I got home there was a wonderful letter from Trevor, also one from Neville saying much the same things as Beetles but in a rather scathing tone. I could not possibly be happy making such a mistake – well he's wrong because, as is so extremely obvious, I am happy and I shall write and tell him so.

I was in town today and saw the men just returned from the Middle East and they looked so thin and haggard and even the young ones so old, I couldn't help wondering if any belief or any country has the right to demand what has been demanded of those men – and taken too. It isn't as though conditions after the war will be so much better – if they were, it might be worth it, but they won't be. People are too apathetic and they won't change. Remarque talks of a whole generation of restless frustrated young men in All Quiet on the Western Front – we don't see them now because they're in uniform, but we will again. Pro-war feeling is very high here at the moment, and I think everywhere. I wish I felt this conviction about winning the war – everyone else seems to.

One night Trevor and I went to a CP meeting, but I must stop going – they take it too much for granted that I'm about to join, and I'm not. Another night he had to have dinner with some National Party friends of his father's – he's a Communist and thinks it's terribly funny to have come from such Tory stock; but I think he and his father quarrel about it too. I can't imagine that – he's so nice to be with, you can't help feeling happy and responsive; he likes women but everyone says he's the one who always cools off (that's why I keep getting these warnings); however it's all right for me. He's got fewer complexes and inhibitions than anyone else I've known; dozens of people rely on him, men go to him for advice. He really is a quite wonderful person and even though I realise all this is just temporary for us both, I think I'm lucky to be having the experience. And just to add an extra touch of bliss, several of the nights we went out he brought his parents' car! A beautiful little modern Hillman and there was I driving off in opulent state (you get a petrol allowance for final leave), all comfortable and private. One night we sat in it and talked for hours about things at college and people who are our friends, and ourselves, and how we can have a light-hearted attitude to life in the middle of the war, and what a thing it is to be happy; some of the time we were very flippant and amusing, or so I thought, some of it quite serious. When we got out of the car to go into the dance, very late, there was Gordon glowering like death at the feast; it was terrible. Later I had a dance with him and tried to be pleasant and gay and all he said was, 'You're very easily amused tonight aren't you?' in a bitter tone. I wish Gordon didn't seem to keep getting the worst of things – it wouldn't matter if Trevor did, *because he's happy anyway, and always falling in love with somebody or something.*

At midnight Trevor and I drove George to Seatoun where he lives – I'd never been there and loved the long drive through the city, then the hills and finally out to the sea. I was quieter than usual coming back, because for the first time I wondered if, after all I've said, I actually am beginning to fall for him a little bit. I don't know. It did seem like it that night and hasn't had the chance to be disproved because the next day he went away. I expect it's all right, and was just a passing mood.

Everybody says I look different, my face has more expression, I look more alive and in a state of semi-excitement all the time; they all declare it's to do with Trevor, and they've noticed it since he went. I gazed in the mirror today and it seemed to me that it's the same old face, but I suppose they know what they're talking about. It is true that I'm simmering with something, happiness I suppose – but I *promise* I won't start on that again. George and Peg are properly engaged; she has a tiny delicate solitaire ring and they're radiant all the time. It is wonderful too, they bring out the best in each other; he needs a confident open person like her, and she wouldn't be happy with someone less shy and unsure of himself than George.

Last week Clive and I went to *This Above All*, enjoyed it despite omissions and an undue emphasis on the patriotic; I suppose you have to expect that during the war – also perhaps the concessions to morality (they weren't allowed to live harmlessly in sin as in the book). Another night we went with that rather bouncy friend of his from Napier, Pete McIvor, to a film that was really nothing but a brutal exposé of a German concentration camp – none of us could believe in it; every German official was the same – they bark instead of speaking, walk stiffly like puppets, they aren't recognisably human beings at all. Can a system like Nazism do that, do you think? I can't imagine it.

Sandy too has been on final leave – and what a day it was, the last before he left. Walking about in the grass up at the wild end of the Gardens, and sitting under trees, and Sandy being half sad and half flippant about leaving . . . it's queer, once Sandy filled the whole horizon when Molly and I were seventeen; now he isn't a joke, then what is he? A young man about to go to the war, wanting to kiss me and only being able to play a game with a straw (we were to chew our own end and gradually come close enough to touch), and giving me advice about Trevor (like everyone else!). But in a way it's Trevor who's to blame when I just feel calm and vaguely helpful (as I did, about the straws) – he – Trevor – is so much more in authority, he just stops the car and turns and puts his arms round me and at once I am kissing him as though I've floated off from the edge and he is the only one who knows where we're going.

That was the day Sandy really knew he was going. The inimitable Air Force doesn't tell you at first of course, just leaves you to wonder till you've got about two days to go – there was all this mystery and muddle when Trevor was going too. Sandy just rang up that day and said he couldn't concentrate on anything and could we go for a walk, and I didn't know for ages that he'd had his news; but anyway we both had our cameras for once, and took photos of each other, and had this funny gameplaying. I couldn't really want to kiss him or anything, he's always too far away. If something had happened I can imagine him taking fright and running a mile straight afterwards.

Wednesday. Working all the time in a sole charge would quickly turn you into a hag of about ninety, so exhausted would you be every minute of the time. Especially if you're a born spinster, as most of us will turn out to be, and if all country school kids are as moronic as these. However life is good if you take it lightly, as I do at present – and how easy our life here is, I can't help thinking that over and over. If the rest of mine is to be awful, it will have to be very awful indeed to make up for the present, and even that won't matter too much if I remember to look back and say Ah well, look at what it was like till I was twenty! In answer to your question Mum about washing my face with soap, no dear I don't wash it with hot water or soap, in fact I hardly wash it at all – does that satisfy you? I should tell you though that I intend to save that bit in your letter and when people notice I stink, I'll show it to them to prove what kind of upbringing I had.

And your question about our playing golf with Beetles and Gordon – they wouldn't call our game golf mind you, because they both can play, while Molly and I mostly swiped the air, but it was wonderful out in the wind. Anyway, it's not too late in the season, you can play all the year round if you like, especially unmarried school teachers when they get to the stage of having sporty clothes and lots of make-up and brown faces and that huntress's look when men are about, and bright forced smiles and lots of conversation about school and the air of clinging to straws . . . you'd better not send Lindsay to college after all, one of those is enough in any family.

November

The election is over – as you know of course. What maniacs voters are – they vote entirely by habit, that's why the contest is always the same old Labour-National one and the new parties so ignored. But they don't know how to do it, if they do have some new ideas – putting up a lot of funny-looking people ranging from representatives of the Real Democracy Movement to 'Savage Labour' (I love that one though). Molly and I were scrutineers but that, as it turned out, only involved counting about twenty votes and feeling important. We went to Beetles' place at night to hear the results and spent most of the time planning our own new party (vastly superior to all the others of course).

Beetles has been giving me advice again, hours and hours of it, at his place, going to the pictures, walking round Oriental Bay one night (we tried to have a cup of tea in a tea shop but were told that only a milkshake was possible, there was milk for that; why couldn't we have some of it in our tea? Because it's 'different' – however after a lot of arguing and pleading we did succeed in getting our tea, with 'different' milk that tasted exactly the same as any other). Off and on all the way he keeps on telling me in a serious, almost fatherly tone that I am glamorising Trevor, and Gordon is wonderful in a different way – but I don't see it (I don't know how he's proved that I make these comparisons – if I do it's because they're like that).

Also the usual old thing about how he – Trevor – is always genuine in his interest while it lasts, and I haven't nearly enough to go on yet, to know if it will last this time or not (well of course I haven't – but I'm not the one making such a point about it). As well, he thinks I'll change a lot after I leave college and meet lots of other people and even though some time I might, at the moment I don't really want either of them (true, true); I must go on living a normal life, keeping in touch with both of them and whatever I decide, about them or anyone else, marriage lasts a long time and it's important to WAIT; if they, both or either, are genuine they'll wait too, and anyway they are at opposite extremes as to temperament and there are plenty of people in between . . .

He really is quite wonderful, Beetles I mean, I know he's full of faults, but he's truly wise and kind. Is he right about all this? Goodness, I don't know. Getting engaged is in the air certainly – Gillian has received a card with different sized holes for her to fit her finger into the right one, so that when Arthur comes on leave he will be able to bring her engagement ring. He's much older than her and plump and scornful about culture, and (people say) not good enough for her, but I think he'll do very well, and she is certainly happy and excited.

The Kitchen Tea for Peg and George is looming up – I wish I'd never thought of it now; I won't know what to do, you couldn't give these people the kinds of silly games people play at such parties, they'd laugh them to scorn. I'm horribly apprehensive; it will cost money too, so I might come creeping along at the end of the month asking for a small sum (how false – as though it hasn't happened hundreds of times before). Anyway, everyone's asked, and seems to think it's a good idea, that's something.

Later. Well the Kitchen Tea was a hideous failure. It was arranged that we should go to Neville's place and then the night before some of the men got together and made arrangements to buy some beer and bring it. As it was our idea not theirs, and in honour of a girl who doesn't drink, I was furious, and suddenly visualised all sorts of disasters at the party, so when Gordon suggested making it a picture party in town I let myself be persuaded.

He felt more strongly about the beer than I did – but I should never have listened to him, I've never made such a blunder in my life. Neville was annoyed and disappointed – understandably – and would not come, and the fact that he was the ringleader in the drink plan didn't make me feel any better about that. Gordon is narrow and uncharitable and I hate to think that I allowed myself to be too. Clive wouldn't come either, though I spent hours trying to persuade him.

Anyway we went to the pictures and had supper afterwards and everyone was quite pleasant of course, but I feel as though I'd lost every particle of respect I ever had from Beetles and Neville and Clive and perhaps others. There it is, I had to tell you; whatever you think about it, I know I'll never *never* be persuaded again by anyone so rigid as Gordon, and I'll never again be so intolerant myself about a stupid thing like a few bottles of beer. All I've succeeded in doing is insulting everyone and nobody can say anything that will make me feel any better about *that*. Please don't mention it when you write.

Gordon isn't coming home with me in the holidays; it's better if he doesn't and in fact I don't think I should go out with him again. He made one of his solemn statements after we went to the pictures tonight, and I do see the point; 'nothing can be done in your direction till Trevor comes back' (Trevor himself would never talk like that). Of course he isn't the sort of person to carry on together if there isn't really any object in view. I thought of this fancy we have that Trevor and I should get married (Peg and George are really going to, in January), and Molly and Sandy too – though they don't know it yet – and all go to Nuhaka and live together. Poor Gordon – he would have had the most awful fit if I'd told him that. It's all a bit of a mess; I wish Gordon didn't have any feelings – he's straight and loyal and intelligent and firm. I rely on him – but that's all.

December

I'm sorry I haven't said much about the Tauranga project – but I loved the photo of the house and all you said about the little farm (but will Lewis really hand the business over to the men and retire? Could he?) Now you talk about chicks in a coop and cows and calves, and the garden on the slope, and the lemon orchard – it sounds simply heavenly, truly a kind of paradise and I can't wait to be there too and explore every inch of it. It still seems extraordinary to have to stop thinking of Greenmeadows as home. But that brings me to another thing – you know I wanted a third year in Music, well when we were doing the applications I talked to them (a committee of lecturers) and they told me that it would be hard to get Music, because there could only be one and there were several people in my year who had specialised far more than I. What about applying for Speech Therapy instead? I didn't even know what it was, but Gillian told me she was thinking about it too and together we found out a bit – not much I must say, but it seems you go to a Speech Clinic at the Normal School in Christchurch, and do some subjects at Canterbury University. That means of course that I wouldn't come home for a probationary year, but since it isn't going to be home for you either I'd still only see you in the holidays.

Anyway I thought I might as well, mostly because I just don't want to be a PA – Probationary Assistant – in a school in Napier or Hastings – or anywhere else for that matter; suddenly now we're all having to decide, I know I don't want to be a teacher much at all.

Later. They made up their minds almost at once – and I've got the confounded thing! I'm not pleased, only amazed that I am going (if I take it, and I daresay I will) to leave here for something so utterly unknown. I have no idea if I want this to be my career. I don't even know what it is, except that it's not speech training (I couldn't bear that). I suppose I am a little bit excited about going to the South Island, especially now our trip to Queenstown is off – I've never seen any of it except on that trip to the Sounds.

Molly and I passed English and Education at varsity – I got an A in Education, can't imagine why; one of the questions was 'A democracy should educate its people for democracy' and I really went to town on that and wrote such a lot of stuff I thought they'd sack me at once but they must have thought it was all right. A's are given to those who 'have an excellent grasp of their subject and express themselves with clarity and style' – which does make me laugh, I wrote such a lot of sheer rubbish. However it's nice to have the passes and to feel that the year's work (what there was of it) wasn't wasted.

Ako Pai has finally gone to the printer. I've been writing things for it for ages, worrying over what's been sent in, and having committee meetings – but not that so much, once the real work began. I took all the stuff to the printer and he looked at it and said, 'Well I'm not dealing with this. I say Joe, you're doing this Pie magazine aren't you?' I managed not to laugh and gave it to Joe – it's wonderful to have it finished and out of my hands at last. It really has taken hours and hours and hours. Did I tell you that Clive wrote an article on 'Why Climbers Climb' which was commended by the judges of the prose competition and has won him the huge sum of 5s! I went to get the poetry entries back from the judge (Beaglehole, one of the history lecturers and a poet too) and was horribly embarrassed because I'd put mine in under another name and he wanted to keep talking about it – it didn't win but was very interesting he said, looking as though he knew it was mine. I just mumbled and got away as soon as I could.

I am going to Paekak for the weekend after we break up and then coming back to Wellington on Monday to post *Ako Pai* – I really can't come home till I've done that and we couldn't get the wretched things done in time to be given out in term time. I hate finishing college and can't really imagine any other life – it's as though I never was anywhere or even *anybody* before these two years, and I cannot see myself doing other things or being away from here. Sandy came back not long ago on final leave – he's going to the Islands too and thinks he'll be there for at least a year; none of Trevor's letters say (or I suppose can say) anything about how long he'll be there. Sometimes I badly want him to come back now, before we're all scattered – this was what it was like in that golden time before he left, with our friends round us. We'll be on our own anywhere else.

Beetles has started organising workers' movements in factories, a wonderfully practical way to deal with 'Workers of the world unite'. I think he will really make some contribution to social reform. When Trevor was here we made great plans one night (at a dance at the Brougham Street Hall) to go somewhere with Peg and George – and Molly and Sandy should come too we thought, and all live together and establish an ideal school along A.S. Neill lines; we would initiate a significant social experiment we said, and have a good time as well. But already we are beginning to go in separate directions – Peg and George are going to teach in Native Schools (they'll get a cheap house that way) and Sandy and Trevor are still overseas, and Molly's going to be a PA in Napier, and I'm going to do I don't know what in Christchurch.

The proofs of *Ako Pai* came back remarkably quickly – Joe must be a good bloke – but after I picked them up I got a terrible fright, I lost them in town! However it's all right, I went back and found them in a shop. I must keep packing. There'll be another box at Napier station early next week. Would you send my new brassiere, the one I haven't worn – it's in the bottom drawer of the dressing table in my room.

Reading Trevor's letters is like drinking cream. Does he mean all these warm and tender words? Am I in some way accidentally the last girl before he left or would he feel like this anyway? Perhaps I don't care. I couldn't bear them to stop coming, I know that. I read today's letter up in the cemetery where we go to swot – it's been a hot day and sitting on the cool stone and rubbing my bare legs on the mossy side of it made a perfect little island of silence, with just me and Trevor's letter alone in it. He was disconsolate though – there seem to have been no mails for ages; it touches me that he who is so cheerful and funny when you're with him can be lonely and far away, and that he tells me. I thought too, sitting there, how I'll miss Wellington, how absolutely I have come to live here – for once it was a still day and as you walk up Varsity Hill from the cemetery to the gym – where I had to pick up a Salient *– you see the sea gleaming in the sun on such a day, and everything fresh and alive, as if holding its breath. In all my life, no matter where I live, I'll never forget* this old path through the gorse, and the leaning stones of the cemetery, and the dirty green wall of the gym as you go on to the steps up into varsity itself. Trevor says 'All my love' at the end of his letter.

Will I know the others, as I've thought I would, when we're all gone away? Will we write as we say we will, and spend our holidays together and know all about one another, next year? For ever? It makes me shiver even to wonder. Perhaps Beetles will leave his school and become a trade union worker, a politician even, and I won't know what that's like because I won't be there . . . and I'll come to Wellington one day and see his mother in the street and she'll look unhappy because she never sees him; I must stop saying these mournful things, they make me want to cry. Perhaps I should go on that last tramp after all – but no, I don't really want to.

I am determined that when I leave here I won't be afraid of growing up and taking things seriously, and getting them done without caring how I appear to other people or what they think. I must try not to be swayed by every little wind that blows, and remember that if I just act in my own way, without pretending, nobody can stop me. I think of myself now like a person leaving the house (not any one house) and closing the door and going out into the street alone, not knowing which way to walk (up there towards the hills? down to the corner where the road leads down into the city full of crowds I don't know and can't speak to?). I am afraid but excited too. All those plans about six of us living together in the country – did we believe them? It's never mentioned now. Peg and George are going to a real house and they don't want us, of course. That's what it is that makes us all on our own – we want to be. I will see Trevor somewhere when he comes back, and it'll just be me, and I think I'll want that too.

Chapter 18

So I went to Christchurch, and became a lady. Or so I said to myself, once I was installed in the Staff House of St Margaret's, a private school for the daughters of the refined and well-to-do. A teacher from the school had come to the Speech Clinic on my first day there, asking if a speech therapy student would be willing to 'live in' and do supervision duties in return for free board. By great good luck, I was the only one in the room at the time. I knew all about student penury, I accepted without a moment's hesitation.

It was a curious, austere life, unlike anything in my previous experience. The devout Anglicanism of the other resident staff, and their fascination with church gossip, suggested at times that I had stepped into some antipodean *Barchester Towers*. They wore plain, rather spinsterish clothes, and held serious conversations about the question of 'going to Rome', their Anglican faith being High Church and close to Catholicism. My impassioned discussions with Sandy and Beetles about the merits of Social Credit and socialism seemed worlds away. This was the England of my childhood reading. Indeed the city itself, with its Gothic churches and the quiet curves of the River Avon moving under stone bridges between English willow trees, seemed to come directly out of one of my Victorian novels.

We lived in an old, rather pleasant house at the far end of the school grounds. I had a room of my own, and a fireplace in it, not to mention the greater luxury of having a maid to come when I was out, to replenish my firewood and do my housework. I wrote gleeful letters to Fanny about these marks of high status, but in the whole year of my residence there I never managed to think of the staff house as home. Yet the quaint ladies of my new acquaintance were kind to me, regarding me at first, it seemed, as some sort of domestic pet; and later in the year we did become friends.

But in any case I was aware that living at St Margaret's was a kind of working for my living. I had to accept, and administer, rules governing every nuance of schoolgirl behaviour which seemed laughably formal to me. They must, for instance – and we must ensure that they did – eat their dessert with a fork (spoons were vulgar, the word 'pudding' irredeemably so); they must refrain from asking for anything to be passed at table (you had to offer some item first, however superfluously). They must pray before and after meals, never speak first to a teacher. On my weekends on duty I marched them to church in a long green-clad crocodile, walking at the back so I could observe misdemeanours such as getting out of line. I wore a hat borrowed from one of the Staff House ladies and, I hoped, a severe if not commanding expression on my face.

The senior girls were only a year or two younger than me, and occasionally it struck them that I had recently left school and ventured out into the world, as they would shortly do. Then, perhaps after 'prep' or hockey practice, they would ask about my occupations during the day, when everyone except me in the entire establishment went to school. I would point out that there were other kinds of school in the world (my socialist – or Social Credit – conscience called into service at last), and the children I saw at the Normal School were in need of special help, which I was learning how to give.

A few days earlier, a younger child had said to me at the dinner table, very pertly, 'You teach the poor children don't you, Miss Scott?' This sounded like pure private school complacency, one of the evils my recent training in educational philosophy had taught me to mistrust, if not despise. Talking to the senior girls, I became fired with proselytising zeal, I held forth on the subject of opportunities for all. My sixth form audience melted away.

But in fact the Speech Clinic did have something of the character of a missionary training school. Speech therapy training was new; we were among the first students to enter the Christchurch Normal School course. As the year advanced we became ever more passionately committed to the task of saving handicapped and helpless children from the worst of their sufferings. 'Speech is morning to the mind' was the epigraph on the speech therapy newsletter, a phrase we often quoted as the perfect encapsulation of our own aspirations.

For the first few months I, and the other five speech therapy students, moved about the clinic, observed the teachers working with individual children – cases, as we were proud to call them. Sometimes we joined in card games (which we were careful not to win) designed to encourage good speech but not offer direct instruction. This accorded with one of our basic principles, that speech correction must always include 'the growth of self-confidence in the child'. We learned this, and a great deal more, in lectures given by Miss Saunders, the clinic's Head. She was an inspiring teacher, and we quickly became inspired. I was soon convinced that there was no greater service I could ever render the human race than to cure its children's speech defects.

We also went to university. Canterbury College was grey stone, architecturally English and grand, formal in a way Victoria had never been. We took Education and Psychology, a natural extension of our daily inquiry into the intricacies of human behaviour. I wrote to Fanny, assuring her that I now felt a far greater enthusiasm for 'educational principles' than I ever had while learning how to apply them in an ordinary classroom; also that I couldn't wait to have my own children.

Making friends was another matter. Of course there were the speech therapy girls, who were friends of a kind, companions certainly; in fact, though I wouldn't have thought of using the word, we were colleagues. We worked together. Only Gillian, who had come with me from Wellington, suggested we should sometimes go out together, but her engagement was in force and her fiancé was often in Christchurch so most of her outings were with him. I did go to one party at her instigation, and wearing her clothes, much sleeker than mine. There I was given a large glass of rum by a smooth young man who assured me it would do me no harm to drink it straight down. This was what a cold Christchurch night required.

The result was sensational, yet disappointing. I became more or less incapable of speech, but did not lose some residual determination to hold onto something that I supposed was my dignity. In a sort of walking coma, I left early and wheeled my bike all the way home through the icy winter night. The young man gave me a disgusted look as I left.

It did seem, however, that the time had come to learn some of the mysteries of the alcohol habit. Wigram Air Force camp was close to Christchurch and, introduced by a friend of Clive's on a brief visit, I met some of its inmates when they were in town on overnight or weekend leave. This began a series of visits to the Winter Garden cabaret, where we smuggled in bottles of wine or brandy hidden in coat pockets and under skirts, drank the contents when the lights were low and talked merrily of the risks we took. In the intervals I danced with the four or five airmen in the group. This was high life, sophistication, I felt sure. It was odd that it wasn't more of a pleasure.

I joined the university drama club. On my first evening there a tall, gaunt woman spoke about 'Drama for Undergraduates'. She was mannish in style, had short hair, a deep voice and a long, clean stride. Her name was Ngaio Marsh. We had read one of her famous murder mysteries in Scotty's English class; I was deeply impressed by her powerful presence, her air of authority. She would hold auditions the following week for a new play. I didn't know its name, nor have the faintest expectation that I would be included in its cast, but I decided at once that, if I did nothing else, I would attend that audition.

I did. I fell under Miss Marsh's spell. I tried with every cell in my brain and body to win the part of Emilia in *Othello*, one of the two plays – the second was to be *Hamlet*, performed in modern dress – that she intended to produce in Christchurch and then take on national tour. And I nearly succeeded. My downfall, at the last minute when she had already commended the energy and conviction of my playing, was my voice. Not exactly my voice, my accent. My New Zealand way of speaking which lacked the rounded vowels she believed necessary for good stage performance. In other words, English vowels. It seemed that ever since my arrival, that pervasive Christchurch Englishness which I had ridiculed so often (if secretly) had been lying in wait for me. Now, when I felt a dazzling destiny almost within my grasp, it leapt out and defeated me.

I could, though, be a court lady in *Hamlet*. I could go on tour, saying 'rhubarb rhubarb' through the crowd scenes.

December 1944. *Trevor is back. He sent a telegram from Auckland but I don't know when he'll turn up here, nor how I'll feel. It's all a rather queer mystery. It's one of those times when everything changes, a sort of universal Gay Gordons in which we all move to another place in the chain and another partner – whether we're ready or not. The Wigram boys have finished their course and are going away for final leave; Pete is lovely, but nothing between us seems to go right. We had a farewell party at the Winter Garden on Saturday, the same six of us, same crazy performance with bottles and glasses, same sense of shallow sophistication I always have there. But we never manage the coming home part – he's excitable, so am I but then panic-stricken, he's offended, I bleat apologies, we fall into a silence that echoes with embarrassment and foolish regret . . . I'm rather glad he's going away – and yet I'm not. He's too beautiful for a man anyway.*

I've applied for two speech clinic jobs, in Hamilton and Wellington; I'll probably not get either – certainly not the Wellington one, though that of course is the one I think about. It's Lower Hutt – how unimaginable to live in Wellington as a real grown-up person in a house or flat and go to work, catching the tram in the morning with the other working girls. A sort of mixture of Mr Polly and Ann Veronica, learning to have a life and live it.

Friday. *Trevor is here. He's staying at Foster's Hotel – a curiously respectable place (it's quite expensive, mostly businessmen use it) but that's because it was arranged by his father. It's nice to see him, he's still easy to talk to – in fact he seems exactly the same, but I don't think I can be. I talked to him right through dinner with (I imagined) a crust of pleasant poise over me, but inside I felt quite dead. He was sweet and entertaining and told me stories about the Tongan children he'd taught, and a mate called Jack who had a wife in New Zealand and a mistress in Sydney and sent each of them a letter intended for the other. (Can this be true? Do people do such things?) I listened but kept thinking that it – we two – would never come to anything after all. He can't come to Tauranga because his leave finishes at the end of December and he wants to be home for Christmas. I don't specially want him to anyway. This is worse than a separation, to feel you've grown away from a person. Perhaps we built up too romantic a picture of each other in all those letters saying 'All my love' at the end – perhaps really I was no more than his final leave girl; they all want someone then. We're going for a ride on the Avon today and I'll wear my green. However, nice as he is, I do think this will be the end of it.*

Chapter 19

It wasn't, of course. The drama club tour took us eventually to Wellington where Trevor, working at the Meteorological Office, was ready for the after-the-show outings even with an actress without a part. Wellington was the last city we visited and the ban on late outings, never wholly observed, became weaker every night of the week-long season. Peg and George, married and teaching in a Native School in Hawke's Bay, had come to Wellington for the summer, and showed an overpowering enthusiasm over every sign of intimacy between Trevor and me. When we met at the French Maid in the mornings Peg spent the entire time telling me what a good friend he was, and instructing me to ignore the warnings of a year before, so ominously pronounced by Gordon and Beetles. 'They were prejudiced,' she sniffed, 'look how they've gone off to the Southern Alps in a huff now he's back.' 'They wanted to go tramping,' I said mildly, and then we fell back into one of her 'isn't Trevor delightful' routines.

We went tramping too, the four of us, while *Othello* played and I was free, off into the familiar green shadows of the Orongorongo track.

I found it a delicious mixture, the recovery of cherished habits, and the sense that we were acting out a newer and more sophisticated drama, a later scene in a perpetually engrossing comedy of growing up, being an adult. We were learning to be lovers, Peg and George were our instructors, Trevor and I initiates into the charmed society of the partnered. This is not to say that we had (as Peg and George, being married, quite properly did have) double sleeping bags, nor that we ever left our single ones. But we lay side by side in one of the bunks and spent a good deal of the night whispering and kissing and believing we were falling in love. Our tutors in their bunk on the other side of the fire were pleased with us, as we were with ourselves and each other.

Several months later, when Trevor's parents went away for a few days, they invited me to stay in their apartment with him, on the assumption, which neither he nor I questioned, that we would sleep separately. Although we had by then openly declared our engagement, we were rather less at ease there, on our own, than we had been in the encouraging company of our friends in the tramping hut, we didn't know why, and of course didn't ask each other.

In the meantime, other phases of the tour also had some of this quality of replaying old friendships in a new and grander milieu. The Auckland season coincided with visits from Clive, Sandy and Peg. Beetles too had not then left for the South Island and was doing time in a pseudo Air Force camp for the Air Training Corps to train school boys. Union work seemed not to earn any money; he was finishing his degree and planning to go high school teaching. These four all came to the last night of *Hamlet* in His Majesty's Theatre and we went afterwards to the Royal Hotel where, abandoned to its stunted luxuries, all except Beetles were staying. We sat on the bed or the moth-eaten chairs in Clive's drab little room, drank some beer, talked of Ngaio Marsh and her production which they, like me, thought the most wonderful theatrical event, far beyond anything they had thought possible in New Zealand – or anywhere for that matter.

We talked too, of course, about ourselves, each producing a faintly disappointing array of sober facts about jobs and money. There was a taint of betrayal in the admission we all tacitly made about new ambitions and loyalties, separate accommodations. I had just heard I had the job in the Lower Hutt Speech Clinic; Beetles assured me I wouldn't find a flat in Wellington because there weren't any. I would have to board with a family. 'Just like the hostel again,' I objected, 'Miss Scott, we can hear your heavy feet all over the house . . . Miss Scott, what time did you come in last night . . . ?' 'Doesn't matter what they say, you'll still have to do it,' he said. He seemed a bit old hat somehow, Beetles, his jokes all sounded the same, though he himself laughed at them reliably as ever. I saw that he wasn't a miracle of a man after all; after a few more minutes of his rather peremptory advice I turned and talked to Clive.

The tour had begun quite differently. For one thing, the plays themselves were so compelling that I had watched them from the wings, *Hamlet* in between my own scenes, *Othello* all the time, every night of the Christchurch season and all but one in Dunedin. Each time Hamlet mourned 'O! what a rogue and peasant slave am I' my heart contracted; when he said with a sorrowful conviction, 'There is a special providence in the fall of a sparrow. If it be now, 'tis not to come – if it be not to come, it will be now – if it be not now, yet it will come – the readiness is all', I seemed to grow prematurely resigned myself. And at 'Goodnight, sweet prince' I always wept.

Othello was different. Paul Molineux as the blighted prince was splendidly serious and dignified, but didn't have the fire of Jack Henderson's *Hamlet*, nor indeed the sinuous cunning of his Iago. But it was wonderful too.

On the first night of *Hamlet* I suffered a major awakening to the realities of the theatre. After 'the rest is silence' and the soldierly resolutions of the last lines of the play, and then the curtain, Jack Henderson got up from his death, swaggered across the stage and said petulantly, 'Oh God, what a silly bugger he is!' I couldn't believe my ears, couldn't bear such a betrayal of the solemn and searching wonder of the play – and from Hamlet himself! Only slowly did I learn to think of acting as a profession, a job, in which the performer lends, but does not give, himself to the part; that night I was just shocked. I went home dejected and perplexed. The world kept dividing itself like an amoeba, it seemed, just when you'd come to appreciate the shape of its wholeness.

Beetles' advice, whether I liked it or not, was sound. I did find board with a family – friends of Clive's and in a rather removed sort of way of mine, the parents and younger sisters of the Paul who had won Brenda and removed her from the passionate battlefield on which Beetles and I had both been losers. They were kind to me, rather homely and gossipy, masters of a kind of ordinariness my own family had never achieved and which I therefore admired. What we had in sandwich fillings for our weekday lunches was a real question to discuss; the world and its directions we didn't tamper with. I was bored but grateful, and I began, as I had imagined, catching the tram to work – or to the railway station, where the train to Lower Hutt left to take a few aberrant citizens like me away from the metropolis in the morning and back again at night. Trevor rang every night, and we went to the pictures or for walks or to drink tea or coffee in town; we became a couple. I felt happy and secure, God was obviously safe in his heaven.

The Speech Clinic was a revelation. A remarkable woman a few years older than me, Evelyn Widdowson, was in charge of it and I was her assistant; she taught me how to handle parents, when they brought their children into the clinic, in a way that made me think of cubs being roughly but affectionately cuffed by their mothers. We had every kind of case, including several very severe spastic paralysis sufferers; Evelyn took these herself, but slowly and warily allowed me to spend more time with them; sometimes I felt on an endless probation, but in fact she was, like a true professional, making sure the children ran no risk of obstacles to their progress towards intelligible speech, which was in any case agonisingly slow.

We worked in a small building that also housed a Manual Training Centre where Hutt Valley school students came to learn to cook. Evelyn and I ate our lunch, spent our tea breaks and sometimes our bus or train trips, with Olwen, the Nutrition teacher; she was small and smiling and shrewd, and we became great friends. This was indeed the world of the working girl, and I loved it. Each of us had a 'steady' who shortly became a fiancé and with whom we planned, in the wartime manner, short engagements and early marriages.

One Saturday at the end of February Trevor asked me to marry him. We'd met for lunch and then wandered about the centre of the city, unsure where to go next; our rather awkward mention of the subject was really the sanction for something we had already tacitly declared. Later we felt very proud of ourselves for having managed to articulate the charged words, however haltingly, when we learned that Peg and George had not managed to say them at all; they had just assumed it was going to happen and gone ahead. We selected a solitaire diamond ring, not too expensive, at which I gave constant gloating glances as I sat in the tram with other girls in the morning. We also suddenly discovered dozens of other engaged couples, people we'd hardly known before, and began to spend evenings with them, gleefully comparing our plans and prospects. It was wartime, nobody thought of having money or a house, but there was a kind of satisfaction in being bohemian about these things. We found out that Don and Marj Clendon, whom I'd so admired on the trip to Kapiti Island in my first year at training college, had got married in a registry office in the hour between two afternoon lectures at varsity, and eaten fish and chips as a wedding breakfast; this seemed splendidly modern and free. I relished saying that my glory box was three enamel plates and a frying pan that I kept under my bed.

We went to Pyes Pa for Easter and Trevor formally asked my father's permission for us to marry. Like all good parents, mine were pleased and proud, and Lewis shook Trevor's hand with a flourish of masculine approval, Fanny and I laughed in a pleased, self-conscious way. Like so much else we did, it was a game – seriously and carefully played, but a game nevertheless. As we were to discover, Trevor and I did not have the remotest idea how we would live together as man and wife, and only the vaguest and most superficial image of each other's real nature, or how one would take the other's measure. But we were bold and unconventional, we were sure, because we laughed at so many of other people's tricks and habits, like the clichés of their small talk. Anyone saying 'No sugar thanks, I'm sweet enough' produced in us (when we were alone) pleasurable trickles of self-satisfied laughter, we were so far above such trivialities.

But of course the important rules, like not sleeping together till we were married, we unquestioningly kept.

Trevor had an older brother, who shared his father Charlie's Calvinism (though not his expansiveness) and had spent the war working as a YMCA secretary, and a younger one, tall and astonishingly good looking in his Fleet Air Arm uniform. Both were, like their brother – and thousands of other young men – in marrying mood. Don married a week before we did, Brian not long afterwards. When the three boys were at home together in the Oriental Bay flat, a jovial and physically exuberant maleness took possession of the household. They talked endlessly about games of rugby or cricket they had played in or watched or heard about, they shoved and cuffed one another, they showed off, they swaggered. Their mother, Ada, they treated with a sort of absent-minded affection, as though she was half a child, half a servant; but there were elaborate gestures of helpfulness too, carrying dishes to the table, washing up, making tea and insisting she sit down. Trevor said he was recognised as her favourite; it appeared they had a long-established, if undefined, partnership against the more powerful figure of his father. This made me vaguely uncomfortable, though I could see that Trevor was quite different from his brothers, more thoughtful, more bookish; the clever one of the family. He shared their excitement in physical prowess, though, and had in fact been given a third year (like my speech therapy one) in Physical Education, which had been deferred till after the war.

The shadow boxing and horseplay the three boys practised Trevor sometimes tried on me. My family's sparring had all been verbal; to be twisted about and held down on the floor till my conqueror let me go was surprising and funny. I was strong but inexpert; for him physical skill was to be taken for granted, the romping at home a natural counterpart to earning places in the A team at school or in sports clubs.

Sometimes we went out – to the pictures usually – after tea. This made sense because there was virtually nothing to do in the evening except wait for Charlie to speak or read aloud. It's true his remarks were often shrewd and entertaining, as long as we listened with docile appreciation; however, although he would have jocular disagreements with me about minor matters – high or low heels, straight or curly hair – he was a fierce and intractable adversary if you seriously opposed him. All money his son had ever borrowed while he was growing up Charlie noted in a little book, and when Trevor went overseas – and part of his salary was sent as a compulsory allotment to his parents – he deducted every penny from it. I, who had received small gifts of money from my parents ever since I'd left home, not to mention having occasional troublesome bills paid by them, was appalled. His family was visibly more affluent than mine; such strictness seemed barbaric.

Chapter 20

A week before our wedding the armistice in Europe was declared. All through my year in Christchurch the war had been changing, as though it was preparing to end – which was indeed what people said, though you could never find out how they knew. D-Day – the invasion of Europe that startled the world – happened in June, and from then on more and more New Zealanders had been recalled from military service and put to work in essential industries, to increase exports to beleaguered Britain. Trevor had come back from the Pacific among the last to leave there; most of the Americans had already gone home, or to the Pacific to fight, or perhaps wait, as Trevor said so many of them had to do, hanging around the camps, standing in canteen queues for ice cream or tobacco, seducing the local girls.

The real war seemed much further away – though ever since the bombing of Pearl Harbor we'd known this wasn't entirely true. But certainly there was war in Europe – as the casualty lists from Cassino and the River Arno testified – and another smaller closer war in the Pacific. And that is how it ended – Victory in Europe Day in May, and Victory over Japan Day four months later in August, after Hiroshima.

About mid-morning on VE Day everything came to a halt – Trevor rang up to say come to town as soon as we could, and we did manage to send our children home and scramble onto a train at Lower Hutt station before they too shut down. The city was a vast carnival, the shops shut but every street packed with shouting, shoving, abandoned crowds. Pubs were open and women were in them drinking, something we'd never seen before in our lives. I had never been closer to a bar than to sniff its beery smell as I walked past the door, crossing to the other side of the street if it was just after six and the rowdy crowd was lurching out as the bar closed. On that day, however, I too milled about in the bar in a Willis Street hotel, talking, or shouting, to people I'd never seen before who suddenly seemed lifelong friends. People we knew did turn up, though, and we gradually became a small crowd of our own. Fitzwilliam-Smith appeared and, in his excitement, seized me and kissed me so extravagantly that Trevor angrily intervened; but nobody could be really ill-tempered as the crowd buoyed us up and carried us on, members of itself and lightly, thrillingly anonymous.

The oddest thing was that I somehow recognised the whole scene, as though I had been there before and knew this is just how it would be (except for the hotels and their bars). This I supposed was because Mum had talked of Armistice Day in 1918, which, now I thought about it, was just before she was married. What a queer continuity things had, hidden deep inside them, I thought, swirling along the street and eventually to someone's flat for a long party. Nobody seemed to have brought anything to drink, but that of course did not matter. We floated along all day and most of the night on the same wave that swept the whole country and half the world.

A few days later I went to Tauranga, where one of us had to live for three days in order to qualify for a marriage licence. Trevor's family had produced a Methodist minister who would marry us in the Pyes Pa garden, Fanny had borrowed a cottage a mile or so up the road so that our friends could stay overnight. I thought of Kafka's fragmented story *Wedding Preparations in the Country* – Kafka, with Koestler, Marx and Engels, George Orwell and the political poets of the thirties, Auden, Spender, Day Lewis and MacNeice, having been required reading when I first came to the 'political university' three years before. Now I pondered the names of guests and wedding styles as the Taneatua Express snailed across the farms of the Waikato. In my suitcase I had the blue woollen dress I was to be married in (exceptional in that it was bought ready-made), the black suede shoes, and a collection of presentable but casual clothes to wear on the honeymoon – a prospect that loomed ahead, vaguely frightening, a test of unnamed and unexplored powers I might or might not be shown to possess. Autumn in the green Waikato was a clear sky and almost bare willows and poplars; we stopped at another small market town – Matamata? Putaruru? – I didn't notice. Suddenly I was gripped by a quick shock, and wanted above everything to stop, go back, escape from this inexorable propulsion forward into a marriage I couldn't imagine, with a person who was still largely a stranger. I was violently shaken, and very nearly got off the train. However, I reminded myself instead that marriages don't have to last for ever. If I didn't want mine, I wouldn't have to keep it; and with this simple-minded conclusion my panic subsided and we chugged on towards Tauranga.

My wedding day was a play, designed by the cast with myself in the central role. About thirty of our friends came with sleeping bags, and a few relations we liked; Molly naturally was my bridesmaid (and Lindsay gracious at not being chosen); Clive made a stiffly pleased best man. Everyone stood about on the lawn looking sheepish, the minister performed the rites and we mumbled our vows. Then he lectured us about the spiritual aspect of married love while we stood still, eyes downcast, unimpressed; like young voters, we were far more dazzled by the discovery that we could vote than by ideas of what we might be voting for.

We had afternoon tea in the elegant living room in the new house, everyone kissed the bride and shook the groom's hand; Sandy, who had surprisingly come, took me aside on the verandah and said, 'When this goes wrong, don't forget I'll always be waiting', after which unanswerable remark he took himself off and hitchhiked the six or seven miles into Tauranga. After tea there were drinks, my parents heroically subduing the panic alcohol usually induced in them, though later in the day Lindsay found Lewis hiding bottles of beer in a cupboard in the kitchen because Fanny thought some people looked like 'going too far'.

We meanwhile were preparing to leave, as newly married couples must do. I was disconcerted to find that I envied those staying behind and planning a party in the borrowed cottage for that evening. However, our car, rented for a week and filled with the three or four gallons of petrol we were allowed, was being decorated in mock secrecy with noisy tin cans, our luggage had for sure been filled with handfuls of confetti, and off down the road to Rotorua and into the larger embarrassments of married life we went, smiling like mad.

People already married seemed not to talk about their honeymoons, and during five days at a Ngongotaha Fishing Lodge, in the off season, in winter, I found out why. It was an uncomfortable time. Our job was of course to discover sex; we had read Marie Stopes, who advised frankness balanced by discretion (don't for instance destroy the mystery by cleaning your teeth in front of your husband or wife) and a book on birth control which recommended the diaphragm. We both had years of familiarity with the smutty innuendoes of tramping hut stories, we were full of a loving optimism which had looked like confidence, but was not. Intercourse hurt so much at first that I couldn't help crying; my young husband may well have shared my 'Is that all?' reaction, but we naturally didn't speak of it. Instead we wrestled valiantly with the much greater problem of what to do in those long, empty, featureless days, the eternal tête-á-tête of the couple that has declared its desire to be left alone – or the marriage-and-honeymoon institution has declared it for them. True, we could go for bush walks, look at trout streams and hot pools, go to the pictures at night; and on one really satisfactory day we begged some extra petrol coupons from a garage owner who was himself newly married, and drove for miles and miles about and beyond Rotorua.

When we came back to Wellington I had violent pains which the doctor explained with a slight smirk were due to an 'internal chill' – common at such times. Trevor went back to the Weather Office, I took two weeks' leave from the Speech Clinic, recovered at once and had to spend the rest of the time listening to the chronicles of insignificance that made up my mother-in-law's conversation. Every afternoon when the *Evening Post* came out I rang all the phone numbers for flats to let but they had always been taken already.

It became a year of contrasts and contradictions. We found a flat, part of a spacious old Wadestown house in which we could begin the playing house that was for me one of the most alluring prospects marriage had to offer. (Occasionally I thought of Avis, who lived in Colorado and was married, not to her young Maori cousin but to an American marine.) The flat was roomy and charming, with a panelled dining room in which friends – the new couples who now populated our social landscape – came to dinner with us. I would sit in the tram in the mornings considering whether to buy steak or mutton chops on the way home, and gloating at the delicious complexities of my days and nights. If there are times of safe arrival this felt like one to me, and I savoured it with a profound joy.

However, I was neither safe nor arrived. Trevor was not nearly as enchanted by our new quarters as I was, and minded far more about the intrusive curiosity of the landlady, a fussy, self-admiring, middle-aged singer. When he was on night shift she complained that she could not feel free to practise with someone sleeping in the house; when we left a heater on she came in and found it, and expostulated loudly; when a friend left a cigarette burn on a bathroom cupboard the sky fell on our poor bald heads. I was quite prepared to survive these inconveniences, but unfortunately the wretched woman rang Trevor's mother to talk it over and at once I was outnumbered and outvoted. We moved out, and lived for the rest of the year in the flat at Oriental Bay, sleeping in the single bed Trevor had occupied as a boy.

In July the family gave a party for its three sons and their wives; they hired a reception room in the city and gathered a crowd of relations and friends and business associates of Charlie's. Among so many unknown people, who all treated me with an instant jocularity, some of my old shyness returned. I also found it galling to be introduced as 'Mrs Trevor', but beyond protesting afterwards to Mr Trevor, I didn't see what I could do. We assured each other often that it was wonderful to be together at last, but I began to have the first intimations of how separate we also were. The natural union with another family was not natural at all, but fraught with strange difficulties which I must solve alone, if at all.

In August we went to Pyes Pa, and heard the incomprehensible news of Hiroshima which marked the real end of the war. We had puzzled conversations about Rutherford and the atom, we read macabre facts about a heat that peeled the skin off people a great distance from the source; we tried to fit this into the pattern of wartime tragedies we already knew – if dimly – and failed. At the same time, and by a strange contradiction, living my parents' new life of rural industry was full of surprises, and some of them were amusing.

Trevor and Fanny sparred amiably, arguing about Social Credit and socialism, Lewis proudly showed us his lemon orchard, so over-composted with pigshit (which he called 'beneficial manure') that you didn't dare walk between the rows for fear of sinking into it. We ate raw fruit and sometimes raw vegetables, but drew the line at starting each day with a sugarless lemon drink, one of Fanny's articles of faith in the natural diet doctrine they both fanatically espoused. Trevor seemed to enjoy all this, though perhaps a little less than I did. Only slowly did I recognise this slight reserve for what it was – much the same sort of hesitation I felt when we were in the Edmond ménage in Wellington. A sense of strangeness. Could such people become one's family?

And then we went away. His third year in Physical Education could be claimed now the war was over, the Phys Ed School was at Dunedin Training College. To the far south we went, clambering, as I had so often done on my own, onto the unstable deck of the Lyttelton ferry. There was the same oily smell in the tiny cabin, the same lurching and rolling in a swell in the Strait, the same dreadful cup of strong tea with a sweet biscuit in the saucer thrust at you in the light from the passageway, wrenching you from that deep before-dawn slumber . . . except that this time there were two of us. We were excited about the journey, eager to try ourselves out in a new milieu. Perhaps we had some sense that we were finally about to begin translating our fantasy, our children's game, into a real occupation that would bear the stamp of marriage – but I don't think we did.

I was seasick – as I had spent a notable part of my childhood being carsick – and as I clung to the railing on the deck, miserable enough to jump over, Trevor stood close and held me, insisting that if I resisted it in my mind I would overcome it altogether. This wasn't entirely true, but I felt a new kind of reliance on him, a new pleasure in the compact of mutual responsibility we had so casually taken on, to find he supported me in that unlovely state.

Did I – did either of us – have the faintest premonition of the upheavals waiting for us, the hurt and exhilaration and terrible griefs of all the other journeys we were beginning in that one? No no, of course not. We simply went to a new town to live, caught the train at Lyttelton and rattled through the plains of South Canterbury, yellow in the February sun, speculating about nothing more far-reaching than the possible quirks of our landlady in an unknown flat, secured for us by a friend who lived in the same street, in Maori Hill.

Part Two

Bonfires in the Rain

Chapter 21

Our landlady in Dunedin was a bit of a floosie. An actress just past her prime, Merle taught drama and elocution in a room in town, and occasionally got parts in Repertory plays, but her greatest attention was given to the dramatising of her own uneventful single life. The fading blonde curls, shrinking complexion and roly-poly body dissolved into the treacherous beauty of a Cleopatra (her favourite Shakespeare character) if there was the slightest hint of an audience. Then (as one of us tiptoed down the passage to the shared kitchen) she would leap out and with her plump little hand to her bosom cry: 'Give me some music, moody food / Of that trade in love . . . ' This was embarrassing for me, but excruciating for Trevor because she gave him a much more powerful dose, and usually tried to draw him into her cluttered and shadowy sitting room. 'He's speaking now, / Or murmuring 'Where's my serpent of old Nile?' / For so he calls me. Now I feed myself / With most delicious poison . . . ' While she walked up and down wringing her hands and giving him sidelong glances, Trevor would stand near the door, trapped, with a pound of onions or a piece of cheese promised for dinner clutched in his hand.

We rented the two front rooms, both large and square with sash windows facing the street across a few bushes and a small front lawn. In one was an enormous feather bed with four brass knobs. It had no apparent base or foundation: getting into it was a dive into limbo, a formless enveloping softness with an occasional feather floating above your head or into your nose. There, in the central hollow of the bed, we made love gleefully – and actively, since beating off the enclosing advances of the mattress was always necessary. One night when we had been in residence for two or three months the bed collapsed. We had perhaps shifted its epicentre, if it had one; there was a groan, a crack, a deep yet fluffily muffled crash, and we were suddenly splayed out on a rocking slope of blankets and pillows, feathers rising in clouds above us. For days afterwards we dreaded Merle's questions, but there were none.

If the bed was unusually large, the fireplace in our sitting room was so small and narrow that in cold weather we sat in front of it with our coats on. One evening, shivering, we measured the grate before lighting the fire and found it was just under three inches from front to back. Wind came down the chimney too, when it was from the south, filling the room with smoke, and sometimes we could only buy brown coal which smouldered so reluctantly that we spent whole evenings with the metal guard clamped in place and the fire roaring unnaturally up the chimney behind it, out of our reach.

For all that, we rather enjoyed the cold climate, our austere circumstances, and that sense of living in a superior outpost that Dunedin seems to confer on its citizens. The severe spire of Knox Church in George Street, the Gothic archways of the university and the old-fashioned stylishness of many of the public buildings combined with the thin cold Leith and its stone bridges to shed an atmosphere of dignity and permanence. Rather unexpectedly, I responded to this; perhaps it simply merged into my pervasive satisfaction at having achieved the married state – and status – that every girl unconsciously desired. The inner promptings that had guided (or compelled) me were, like everyone else's, so little examined that I took them to be natural and inherent. Being married made me feel proud, excited, safe. A grand romantic momentum propelled both of us, in fact, through this early part of our marriage – and so easily, so strongly, that it would have demolished much greater difficulties than ours. We were cold, uncomfortable, occasionally lonely; I was secretly bored by Trevor's preoccupation with sport, he was visibly uninterested at my disappointment in relieving teaching – but none of this really mattered. We could have lived waterless in the Sahara and still found it fun to be together.

One of the pleasures was that we, being married, had constant visits from friends who were not; we had a household, they had rooms and landladies, communal dining rooms if they were in halls of residence. One was a medical student living slenderly on a bursary; he could just afford books, fees and board, but not clothes or cigarettes or outings or even tram fares. On Saturdays and Sundays Hugh Marwick would walk from the house in Leith Street, where he had a room (and 'found' so he did not actually starve), up Maori Hill to our steep little street, laden with stories about the cadaverous life of the Medical School, ripe for the telling.

A law of the school was that students wore suits to their viva voce exam. You simply could not appear before a board of doctors and professors, to be tested for your fitness for a great profession, dressed in loutish tweeds – in other words, the sports coat that was a man's everyday wear. Hugh, like Trevor, like all the other young men we knew, had a couple of shirts, one sports coat and one pair of flannel trousers – the grey strides that Peter Cape was to immortalise in his song *Down the Hall on Saturday Night* – ubiquitous as denim jeans later became. The question of his acquiring a real suit, perhaps a pin-stripe (which meant hiring one), became for all of us a major issue. Not a sartorial, a moral question. To wear his sports coat would be a gesture of democratic protest; it would shake the ancient system, usher in an era in which vision and insight triumphed over money and position. In the end he wore the sports coat, was reprimanded, passed with brilliant marks. We glowed with righteousness.

Married and grown-up we might be, but of course we still behaved like students. Trevor and the others were genuinely studying, but for me too everything was an experiment, and I relished the sense of playing a new part in the unfolding drama of my life. Miss Dolores Swinburne, my youthful transformation, the Hollywood star who had adopted grand postures to impress my little sister when I was thirteen or so, was not really very far behind me. Every time I served a meal, or opened the door to a visitor, or slid into bed with my husband, I acted as one self while another stood by and marvelled at such extraordinarily convincing proofs of maturity. I was impressed by every performance of the young married couple, most of all by my own part in it.

We had our mentors too – the Parsloes, Noel and Beata, who lived just along the street. Trevor and Noel had been in the Air Force together and we had spent a weekend with them in Renwicktown in Marlborough the year before – a delicious winter weekend of long cold walks, chopping wood and gathering vegetables from the garden, cooking on the coal range, talking late by a log fire at night. The hard work and the freshness of that country cottage life, the cold, the hours of intimacy by the fire, had for me some of the quality of the old student tramping trips. Noel and Beata were a little older than us, serious and funny, gentle and shrewd; they were also much more experienced at being married, and I found the tone of slightly arch defiance in their sparring altogether charming. I wondered if we could become as lively, as confident, as vital. Certainly there was much that was frolicsome and funny in our lives together, but the Parsloes' verbal acrobatics, performed with such assurance, impressed me the more, I daresay, because we weren't quite capable of that ourselves.

They were living with Beata's parents while Noel too went to training college as an older, post-war student, and we used to visit them in their part of the house. They had one child, a little boy of two who, according to his father, was adept at devising 'punishments for parents'; put outside the door in disgrace, he overturned a vase or pee-ed on the carpet, then waited with satisfaction for the erring parent to appear. At home we wondered about this occupation of being a parent. Once they gave John a quarter of an aspirin when he couldn't sleep; owl-eyed with disapproval we assured each other we would never violate our children's bodies in this way. They were good parents; we would be perfect.

Beata, whose unmarried name was McCahon, had a brother, Colin, who also lived in Dunedin and did odd jobs so he could have as much time as possible to paint. They were strange, brooding paintings; Beata and I found they disturbed us, and were not sure we liked the sensation. Why did he want to do those dark Madonnas, and the other sorrowful biblical figures? we wondered. 'He feels he has something he must say,' she told me. Colin and Ann, his wife, painted children's pictures full of boats and trains and cars and aeroplanes, all crowded into landscapes that existed solely to hold this riot of moving machinery. They were pot boilers, but funny and charming. Noel and Beata gave us one to keep for our first child.

They also behaved like neighbours, the first we'd ever had. They came to visit Trevor, who for a week of the freezing Dunedin winter was in bed with flu. I, for my part, ministered to his needs, sympathised, encouraged him to recover. This was partly because the date for a university dance was approaching and I wanted to go, but during the week a solution to my problem, if not to his, appeared. Wilfrid, one of our student friends, suggested he should take me. I rushed into the bedroom, bursting with eagerness. It seemed however that the flu was much worse . . . I must do as I thought best, of course, but Trevor was feeling extremely ill. Anyway he'd never heard before that Wilfrid liked dancing, what a strange fellow he was, not as likeable as he'd seemed . . .

how cold it was; could I make him a hot drink? Now? During the evening at home neither of us spoke of the dance. Wilfrid later confirmed that he didn't care for dancing much, and Trevor took this as proof that it had been right for me not to go. I, on the other hand, received it as a subtle compliment.

We had moved to Dunedin for Trevor to take up his third-year Physical Education course; I expected to find work as a relieving teacher and hoped it would be in a speech clinic. Sure enough, there was a clinic, and in the first few months of the year a vacancy on the staff. I confidently wrote out an application, and was highly disconcerted when a local teacher, untrained in speech therapy, got the job instead – and all the more when despite my furious protests the Education Board refused to change its mind. I visited the secretary in his dim panelled office in Moray Place, where I raged and expostulated; his red face remained blank, the heavy jowls didn't even quiver.

'We are not interested in red tape here,' he said at last, 'we leave all that to the folk up in Wellington.' So much for outposts.

Speech therapy was my passion, it was unthinkable to give it up without further struggle – and yet I did. Did marriage weaken all other resolves? Perhaps so; I continued to be a relieving teacher in whatever school asked for my services. One was Kensington, the oldest school in the city, the province, probably in the world. Its floor undulated over rotted piles, its walls were peeled and pitted, its roof leaked and the entire building, with its playground, flooded so badly after more than two days' rain that it had to be closed. As well, the railway line passed almost over its head along a high bank, so close that every time a train came the teachers on the near side had to stop till it had roared and clanked its way past. A fine rain of soot then blew over the playground and the school. I taught Standard 2 for three months during the winter and had a total of nine days off for bad weather. I thought venomously sometimes of the cuckoo in my true nest, imagining the speech clinic a place of warmth, quiet and dignity, while I cajoled, bleated, trumpeted at my slum kids in the soot-begrimed brick heart of the city.

Later in the year I was sent to Forbury, a school in a more discreet part of town. There my experience was almost totally conditioned by the presence, next door to my Standard 2 classroom, of John Melser. He was young, lively, flirtatious – at least, the hysterical chases we had brandishing rulers round my classroom after school had sexual overtones obvious even to my inexperienced eye. Flushed and a little ashamed, I would emerge at last and hurry to catch my bus. But we talked too about our history, ourselves; John thought me amazingly ingenuous – 'You mean you didn't copulate at all before you were married?' What a word – it made us sound like animals. 'Well we – ' I tailed off, talked again of school. He told me not to worry about Nature Study, Comprehension or Junior Science, or any other items on the afternoon timetable; eight-year-olds like to draw. Let them. He lent me crayons and paper, piles of it. We were striking a blow for freedom, I understood, though where he may have acted from principle I merely took the line of least resistance. Perhaps I still cherished a grievance against the Education Board and thought I owed them only token service.

John carried an aura of sexual and intellectual relish about with him that both excited and repelled me. When Trevor and I visited them the children were always naked, and in hot weather he and June also shed their clothes and romped about with their children like domesticated pagans. Their uninhibited style was very self-conscious, yet they carried it off with conviction. Perhaps, though nobody had yet heard the word, they were hippies, arrived before their time.

Weekends we mostly spent at home. All through that year we were trying, on the whole conscientiously, to learn hospitality, a working routine, shared friendships, diminished privacy, sex of course – all the separate parts that made up the central occupation of being married. Still fresh from our single lives, we found the state of partnership endlessly intriguing. On long Sunday walks in warm weather through the scarcely settled foothills of Mount Cargill, the open rolling country behind Maori Hill, we sometimes found in a grassy hollow an adventurous seclusion for making love, with only the sky and birds for bedroom. Once in winter we picnicked far enough up the big hill for the sun to set at two o'clock in the afternoon, a phenomenon we treated like the discovery of a new planet, both cosmic and personal in its implications. We laughed a lot. We traversed, with a kind of cautious astonishment, new territories: maleness, for me, femaleness, for Trevor.

He had no sisters and even the ordinary facts of women's dress – how the shaped panels in a brassiere were put together – were noteworthy for him. I discovered what a wet dream was and some of the Air Force slang that applied to it, such as 'they put kill-cock in your tea', to keep you quiet on long spells of overseas duty. I had my first glimpse of a male world in which salacious stories about women expressed an aggressive, half-scoffing yearning, and I wonderingly compared this with the girlish rivalries, that innocent game-playing, Molly and I had enjoyed over Sandy.

Our landlady maintained her curious, exasperating and sometimes pathetic presence as backdrop to our own domestic experiences. Occasionally we sat in the immense dim clutter of her drawing room and drank tea while she chattered about her pupils and herself, reminding us of her great dramatic gifts, her reputation, her popularity. One wintry Friday night, coming home about six, Trevor had a glimpse of her that gave the lie to this glamorous image. He had turned out of George Street to begin the climb to Maori Hill and there, huddled in a doorway and hidden from late-night shoppers in the main street, Merle was greedily stuffing fish and chips into her mouth, out of a newspaper packet. She looked urgent and guilty; he turned away, and hurried past.

We ourselves thought fish and chips, especially straight out of their newspaper, a great treat, just as we relished smoking the dreadful (but dirt cheap) Napier-manufactured Riverhead Gold and Desert Gold cigarettes; but Merle's falling from her shaky grandeur was another matter altogether.

So our year in Dunedin settled, became habitual, slowly passed. My life spoke of itself in plural pronouns; 'we' had almost entirely replaced 'I'. We despised such clichés as 'the other half', yet living with another person day and night did make me think of two wandering semicircles, like the halves of a cut apple, coming together and forming their natural whole. We even found ourselves authorities on the subject when one of the other Phys Ed students came to ask us, in all seriousness, if, when he and his fiancée married, they should bath together.

The idea, if not the fact, of pregnancy was in our minds a good deal. We met and visited a young couple, Alan and Shirley McCurdy, who were having their first child, and Shirley took me into her room to show me the stretch marks on her swelling body. I gazed at the faintly luminous patterns on her skin, mauve-coloured like veins, with a mixture of envy and embarrassment. How extraordinary everything was! The scent of the new was everywhere – you had only to lift your nose into the wind of the world and it came to you, full of strange and perplexing auguries.

Of course our days were spent apart, and differently, but at home in the evenings I described mine in minute detail to Trevor. I went to other schools, met other characters – like the man who never slept but proofread for the *Otago Daily Times* all night and taught school during the day. I went, rather superficially, to the university by taking a short course in music appreciation in the third term. Whenever I encountered people I liked I 'asked them round' so Trevor could meet them too. For the first time in my life, living in a new place, I made no new friends of my own. Even Beata, the woman I liked best and was most interested in, was part of the Noel-and-Beata combination and I hardly ever saw her alone.

I embraced the new mode with my natural wholeheartedness; if anyone had asked me what I expected from marriage, I would probably have replied 'everything'. Yet even I could see that happiness didn't just fall into your hands like a ripe plum from its tree. There had been the disappointment of the dance Trevor could not go to, so I must not either; and towards the end of the year it happened again, only this time it was a whole series of outings, rehearsals for a play in fact, and they were Trevor's not mine. Dunedin Training College decided to produce Shaw's *Pygmalion* and cast two of their older students in star roles, Trevor as Professor Higgins, Noel as Colonel Pickering. They enjoyed themselves enormously, probably in all the ways I had a year or two before in *The Man who Came to Dinner*. I was envious; the in-jokes using lines from the play were not all that funny surely . . . When the long evening rehearsals ended with Trevor arriving home very late and full of jollity I couldn't control my petulance.

However, if the world had taught me (through a thousand stories in books and plays, and especially in films) that marriage meant happy-ever-after, Fanny had added, in the long, searching, satisfying conversations we'd been having for years at home, the lesson that you had to work hard at being a wife, being a friend. You had to understand the other person's point of view, put yourself in their place, shift your ground. I concluded that my job was to recognise Trevor's pleasure in the play, and in his own performance, and to struggle with my unsuitable feelings as best I might.

During the year Fanny had been part of my thinking anyway, in a quite new way. By 1946 she and Lewis were used to retirement and had securely established Pyes Pa as the family headquarters, the place where we all naturally gathered in holidays. John of course was still at school in Tauranga, but was the kind of student who could easily take time off: they decided to make their first trip abroad. It appeared that Lewis had always wanted to visit the Pacific, and in April the three of them set out for Fiji.

No one in our family had travelled further than the South Island. Suddenly there were constant bulletins of strange new information – wog waggoning, Indian tailors, Fijian gardeners, cane knives . . . Everything was unexpected and fascinating; indeed, Fanny and Lewis in no time had decided they wanted to live there permanently. They bought a cottage. Lewis would organise a Fijian branch of his painting business. One of 'the men' would manage work in New Zealand, we would all come for extended Pacific holidays, possibly come to live there too. Jobs might be found . . .

Mad, said Trevor. Entirely impractical. Of course he was right, and in fact the disadvantages of the scheme very soon became apparent to the travellers themselves (the heat made John ill, Fanny began to think about distance and isolation). For all that, I was rather proud of my enterprising parents. Others travelled – Trevor's own mother and father had recently been to England – but, naive as mine might be, they had thrown themselves into foreign travel with a freshness and excitement one didn't usually expect of middle-aged parents.

Chapter 22

We were all at Pyes Pa for the August holidays. John had gone back to Tauranga Boys' High School, Lindsay came from Auckland where, contrary to the warnings Clive and I had given, she was greatly enjoying training college. It was, as we'd said, not at all like Wellington; she made friends none of us had heard of, went to places we didn't know, seemed always to be 'out with a boy' when Fanny rang her. Clive arrived on a train from Ruawai in the far north, where he was teaching; he was newly nonchalant and terribly worldly, he talked of a drinking game called 'Cardinal Huff' which Lindsay and I were not to know too much about because anything could happen to a girl who finished up under the table. He brought with him a friend called Claire who'd been to a private school and was refined. Lindsay and I were polite but a little stiff with her.

We were excited to be together. Fanny, relieved not to have to live hundreds of miles away from us after all, had a particular radiance. She was freshly enchanted with the house and garden at Pyes Pa, its atmosphere of fruitfulness, its expansive lawns and trees, and the view of the Mount, framed by the low hills that led to our own higher ground. It felt like a conferred paradise to us all. None of us had learnt to think of anywhere else as 'home', and Fanny and Lewis encouraged us to think of the new place as ours. These two weeks restored her sense of the oneness of the family that our leaving several years before had shaken but not destroyed. Probably she didn't believe it could be destroyed, ever.

We all in fact took a proprietary interest in one another's new activities and plans. For Trevor and me it was one of a series of visits that with only slowly diminishing force drew me away from him for a while and back into the circle of Scott conversation, Scott jokes, Scott histrionics. It became a romp, the best of the old times at home, polished with the new gloss of our conscious sophistication, our adultness.

Trevor, despite some unease between us, took his part. He was a more truly experienced social creature than any of us, having always put less store by the special privacy of family living; Lindsay and Clive were impressed by his worldliness. It seemed part of him, not recently attached, like Clive's.

The days were hot, as though it was already summer; I had to borrow some of Fanny's clothes – we were much the same shape and size. Every day two or three of us took the car and shopped in town for the large dinner to be cooked at night. We investigated Lewis's new crops – feijoa bushes that had flowers like pohutukawa and fruit that tasted like scented soap; Chinese gooseberries, huge floppy vines that produced sweet green fruit encased in a hairy skin, and tree tomatoes, dark red ovals full of seeds and sharp-tasting flesh. All were remarkable, exotic, part of the other-worldliness of the place. We spent long delicious days roaming about or gathering in the house to talk, eat, drink tea. Lewis was constructing a ram, an engine and pump to bring water from a spring up a steep bush-covered bank to irrigate his garden and fruit trees, and Clive and Trevor and John worked on the project with him.

And there was Angelina to milk – though in the end Lewis was the only one who seemed any good at it; Lindsay and I poked and squeezed ineffectually, Fanny mostly didn't even try. We three women (Claire had gone home) worked in the dairy, as was proper for our sex, separating milk and cream, sometimes making butter. We fed the fowls, we carried compost. It stank intolerably and we all complained, but Lewis was not the man to be deterred from following his newest star, stained as it might seem to us. He was always good-tempered, didn't in the least mind our ravings, and smilingly ignored us all.

After the first few days the party swelled – Peg and George, those old friends from my student years, came from Rotorua, Peg thinner and quieter than I remembered her. During the year she'd had something called pregnancy in the tube, and because they were now teaching in a remote Urewera school and the hospital was far away over difficult roads, she had haemorrhaged badly and been seriously ill for several months afterwards. Doctors had told her to resign herself to permanent sterility; they talked, a bit sadly, of adopting a baby.

Molly came too. Though we didn't now meet very often, I still thought of her as my 'best friend'. She was teaching in a small school at Onga Onga in Hawke's Bay; there was a great deal of news to exchange.

Fanny and Lindsay were almost as pleased to see her as I was, that too being part of a habit we could still easily revive. And Clive asked an old tramping and climbing friend, Graeme Robinson, who promptly began to fall in love with Lindsay. This was a diversion which aroused a great deal of popular interest, though in their company we made some attempt not to notice.

We examined the photos of Fiji, teased John about the glamorous white trousers he'd brought back; we set up the old tennikoit net on the lawn and played again the chaotic, largely rule-less game we'd perfected in Greenmeadows. Skill resided in one's wit at devising new rules (advantageous to oneself) rather than the actual throwing and catching of the rubber quoit.

And then we departed to take our various directions – south, for us, and south again on journeys that brought us into a cold Otago spring and our last term in Dunedin. By the time we returned to Pyes Pa for the summer vacation, an unexpected and far-reaching change had taken place there. In October Fanny had a haemorrhage of the lungs.

It had always been necessary for us to write 'Yes' beside the word 'Consumption' in the list of diseases on school record cards filled in each year; our mother's mother – the grandmother we knew only from photos – had died of the disease before any of us were born. That meant it was 'in the family'. I had thought of this fact with a certain satisfaction. It was an 'interesting' disease, sensitive people like Katherine Mansfield had it. When it entered our lives as a crisis, none of us knew how to greet this unpleasant stranger.

Lewis wrote me an awkward, scrappy letter saying that Fanny was in Tauranga Hospital but was coming home soon and we were not to worry All the best Love Dad. From Fanny herself there was a small inconsequential note telling me that the flowers in the hospital garden were wonderfully looked after and she didn't want to be treated by orthodox medicine. Was it a crisis? This made it sound like a small matter, hardly more than an inconvenience.

Trevor was preoccupied with trips to Dunedin schools to organise their athletics open days; Physical Education specialists – the Fizzedders – gathered in town in the mornings, joyfully caught their trams to St Kilda, St Clair, Port Chalmers, and met again in the afternoons in town for a beer. When we sat down by our tiny coal fire in the evenings he was vague, though sympathetic, about my worried questions. I didn't know much myself about Fanny's real condition, for all my secret pretensions over the report cards. A haemorrhage of the lungs must mean that blood spouted out of your mouth, but I could not mention this horror even to Trevor, certainly not to Fanny herself.

The next news from Tauranga took a different form. After explaining that doctors believed the disease could have been making inroads on her lungs for as long as twenty years, Fanny announced that they needed one of us to come home to manage the household. (Daughters, not sons, had this obligation.) I was the elder, so they asked me first. The letter precipitated a minor crisis.

Trevor and I didn't know much about rows; we had a row. We had little experience of feeling rejected, misunderstood, betrayed – at least by each other. We felt all these things. Trevor did not seem even to take the request seriously; I agonised over it. I could not think of going, he declared. She had no right to ask. But it was all so awful, I insisted, you had to see how they felt . . . nobody knew what would happen . . . look at Elizabeth Coldstream dying at eighteen, while I was at training college. That wasn't of TB, he pointed out; the anaesthetic went wrong when they collapsed her lung. I was both pleased and puzzled that he wanted to keep me near him. Families – why did they make claims on one another? I remembered Fanny telling me years before about the pioneering Price family she'd grown up in; how keenly they watched over brothers and sisters, parents, children, relations. Without money or friends in a new country, family was all they had. But it wasn't really like that any more; I wrote to her with elaborate assurances of sympathy and concern but said I couldn't come. She was hurt and disappointed; I felt callous, ungrateful, insensitive, but held to my refusal. I had not really made up my mind to it; caught between parents and husband, I simply bowed to the more immediate pressure.

Lindsay, however, did leave Auckland Training College a little before her two years there was finished, at the end of 1946. She wrote to tell me how the matron of her student hostel had called her to her study and shocked her by giving, with little preamble, the details of Fanny's haemorrhage. She was sent to the principal, given her certificate without sitting the final exams and went home.

In Tauranga Fanny was still in hospital; Lindsay visited her, and discovered that she and Lewis were insisting, in the face of massive opposition from doctors and nurses, that she could treat her own illness at home. These authorities could not know, of course, that my parents saw 'orthodoxy' as an enemy greater than any disease. Defeated, they gave comprehensive instructions about protecting the family from infection. So Lindsay began at once to take over most household responsibilities. She wore a handkerchief over her face when she made Fanny's bed, made sure her linen and utensils were kept separate, became a sort of assistant nurse to Lewis. Sickness, and the nursing of the patient, became accepted as simply part of the Tauranga project.

The day came when living in Dunedin was suddenly at an end. Had it really lasted a whole year? We were to live in Wellington, the place we both thought of as our natural home, to rent for a year, perhaps two, a house in Kilbirnie owned by a friend of Trevor's who had gone to Auckland University to study architecture.

We started to pack in December. Our two rooms looked shabby and forlorn without the photos of Pyes Pa, Lewis and Fanny smiling on chairs out on the lawn; my Gauguin print, the small Toulouse-Lautrec Lindsay had given me, Trevor's framed photo of a school friend killed in the war. We pulled out all the tacks from the faded floral wallpaper, we set out on a last walk over the Balmacewan Golf Course and up towards Mount Cargill. And we said goodbye to Noel and Beata with considerable regret, to Merle with none at all. We told each other it had been a good year and we were sorry it was over, but I was privately surprised at my own detachment. No leave-taking could possibly be like the one I'd made at the end of 1943 when I'd finished training college. It had seemed to me then that I must walk away and leave behind my whole life – all there was of it, except my childhood. Perhaps marriage was a small shell, the house I now took with me, wriggling more and more closely into it, unable any longer to imagine myself uncovered and alone.

For all that, I had an occasional sense of being invisible to Trevor when he didn't approve of what I did. And sometimes when I spoke or acted with particular passion and abandonment I had a curious feeling that he was nervous, embarrassed: such bursts of exhilaration (which he called my 'silliness') could not be shared between us because he mistrusted them. I was disappointed, but thought that no great matter, no more than a grain of dust caught inside the enclosing marital shell.

At the ferry wharf in Wellington Trevor's parents met us and obligingly drove us to our new address; there we surveyed our meagre possessions, separated winter from summer clothes (there weren't many of either) and left again to spend Christmas at Pyes Pa. So anxious was I to be off again that I scarcely noticed Trevor's hesitation or his mother's faint protestations about 'staying a little longer'. The Scott family, and Fanny in particular, had still moved only a short way from the centre of my consciousness.

We found at Pyes Pa another summer idyll in the full hot bloom of the season, along with stronger undercurrents of anxiety – Fanny's health (however it might be 'positively thought about'), John's schooling, John's isolation.

Curious as we all were about our parents' new neighbourhood, we accepted, soon after our arrival, an invitation to a card evening. Five hundred. Farming folk; local gossip, local jokes in all their incomprehensible triviality, ourselves blankly staring, not smiling, not joining in. It was rustic farce, and became a tale often retold, a joke in itself, though whether against our hosts or ourselves it would have been hard to say. Because we were all scrupulously polite and superficially (and in fact genuinely) friendly, we supposed that nothing of our real attitude showed. But we were never asked to another such gathering. The idea that Fanny – to whom it really mattered – might enter their world, or they hers, was a piece of social naivety for which she would sooner or later have to suffer.

But not just then. What actually happened was that she set up, or found herself part of, social networks that were as brittle and formal as the ones she'd left behind in Greenmeadows.

All this mattered much less to Lewis. Fanny was at the centre of his social world anyway, along with his correspondence with Social Crediters in various parts of the country, and at home he passed quite easily into the retired life, cultivating his orchard and garden, delighting in sharing with her the new expansiveness of his thirty acres. He couldn't bring himself to give up work entirely, though. With his zeal for making something out of unlikely materials – a sort of honest man's gambling instinct – he continued to hear of painting jobs for 'the men' to do, and often he went with them. Railway stations neglected through the war could be painted by the still new spraying method, old buildings could be renovated and resold. Fiji had faded like a colourful and unlikely dream.

More than they realised, they were re-creating the life they had evolved together in Greenmeadows. The essentials of their shared beliefs remained the same – most obviously, the faith in healthy living, natural food, a positive outlook. Books about the Ulric Williams programme, the Dr Hay Diet, treatises by Harry Benjamin *(Your Diet in Health and Disease, Better Sight Without Glasses)* lay about the house along with copies of the English journal *Health for All*, which Lewis ordered through the Williams clinic in Wanganui. I had bought my own copy of Williams' *Hints on Healthy Living* before we left for Dunedin, partly because it contained recipes and I wanted to be able to make wholemeal scones and vegetable soup in my own kitchen.

The verandah on the north side of the Pyes Pa house was open and sunny. It gave onto a lawn that sloped down to the edge of the few acres of bush which, with the citrus orchard, made up the small farmlet. Lewis extended and widened this verandah and at one end built a half wall – rather like the one he'd made in Greenmeadows years before – the top open to good weather, covered with a canvas shutter when it rained. Here Fanny lived. Her bed took up a great deal of the space, and she was mostly in bed. Around her were shelves which gradually filled up with her daily paraphernalia of books, letters, notes, photos, fruit and the flowers she picked herself on slow careful walks round the garden every morning.

She said almost nothing about her illness. She coughed, and we knew the phlegm was infectious, also that her temperature rose during the day and about five o'clock she was likely to be tired and flushed. She ate separately from us. On the whole, however, the clean open air was to deal with the problem of infection. She was, in fact, a remarkably tactful invalid, eager as ever to know what we did and thought, excellent company, subtly compelling in her opinions. The mixture of excitement, challenge and slightly anxious obligation which she had always induced in us was still there, though it took some new forms. If Lindsay and I talked too long in the kitchen while cooking a meal, we suffered spasms of guilt that sent us running out to the verandah with some excuse to consult her. She would be sitting up reading or writing and waiting, poignantly eager to be interrupted.

We accepted the positive outlook principle so unreservedly that we felt no real alarm for her or ourselves. This was a time when tuberculosis was a major infectious disease without a known cure. Every sanatorium in the country was full, wards for contagious patients in hospitals were kept strictly segregated, half of those diagnosed as TB sufferers died within five years. At the same time, fresh air, good food and isolation seemed to be the staple treatment – and Fanny had the first two in abundance. As for the question of quarantine, she believed absolutely that incarceration in the 'sickness environment' of a hospital ward would make her worse. Over the next few years she grew very gradually worse anyway, but none of us could know that, since she refused to have X-rays or visits from a doctor. For all that, my parents weren't acting without authority of any kind. Other people, some they knew as Social Crediters, shared their views; they wrote letters, and swapped books about enlightenment in health as well as in the already familiar field of monetary reform.

There was much we didn't know, or try to find out, about the disease. According to a nurse in Tauranga Hospital, a curative drug had been discovered only a few years before, in 1944. Its name was streptomycin. However, even if Fanny had considered accepting such 'unnatural' treatment, it had already proved less effective than doctors had hoped. It killed the TB bacillus, but other organisms quickly grew and resisted it. This seemed a kind of vindication of the 'natural good health' approach. I knew that if there had been a drug or anything else that really worked I would have tried it, but I was a long way from saying so to Fanny. Our alternative was 'positive reassurance' and this we could all administer.

Clive taught John to play chess and they both became fixated on the maddening game; you couldn't talk to them for hours at a time. I boasted about my own prowess but was eventually beaten by each of them in turn. John was in the fifth form at Tauranga Boys' High, a tall leggy boy, drily amusing in conversation, given to obsessive enthusiasm. Not chess alone, but cricket, tennis and most of all table tennis (on the enlarged table top Lewis made to fit over the living room table). He practised with a steady rhythmic devotion.

But he spent long times on the verandah with Fanny, too. They were alike in rather the same ways that she and I were, they laughed at the same absurdities. She never wanted him to leave, once he had come out to sit on the old seagrass chair that stood at the corner of the verandah near the foot of her bed.

A great deal went on as before. Friends came to stay, on hot afternoons we went swimming, on New Year's Eve to a dance at the Mount, dancing till midnight and beyond. Slowly the summer passed, the first term of the year drew close and with it our working lives. Yet again Pyes Pa surprised us by proving that it was not, after all, for ever.

Wellington. February. Blazing hot by day, the smell of the heat all night in small rooms built of old timbers; a small street in Kilbirnie. The morning tram came down the open valley of Island Bay and clanked to a stop at the terminus at 8.30 each day. From there I set out to walk along the beach and up into the next break in the hills, known as Happy Valley; this, in 1947, was the only way to get to the little sole-charge Ohiro Bay school before 9 am when classes were supposed to begin. By the time I, their teacher for the first term, arrived at the door it had been unlocked by the caretaker, though the children – all twelve of them – had to play outside till I rang the first bell at five to nine.

From then on the day was a tight knot of planning, like a piece of knitting in which I did not dare to drop a single stitch. From Primer 1 to Standard 6, every class, even if it had only one pupil, must know the day's programme, since most of their work would have to be done without the benefit of teaching. The one exception was Standard 3 because that year there was nobody in it at all. There was one girl in Standard 6, two boys in Standard 5, and all three, as country children are, were matter of fact in their maturity; they were used to 'hearing' spelling and tables performed by the juniors, and were kindly and sensible in keeping an eye on them – indeed they seemed like half parents, half teachers themselves. I relied on them with the sincere gratitude of the helpless, and was never betrayed.

The four infants I liked, too, for their eager acceptance of the family hierarchy that the school really rested on. In between there were 'the Standards' – 1, 2, and 4 – five children who largely pleased themselves. One fat, studious boy finished his daily programme long before anyone else and simply read, hour after hour; when we all went out to play 'minor games' for Phys Ed he always had a sore foot. The two girls in Standard 2 also finished quickly, got most answers wrong, marked each other's work and, apparently satisfied with their awful results, settled down to draw ladies for the rest of the time. I, having written the complete programme on the blackboard the afternoon before, made frantic efforts to teach these two, as well as hearing everyone read, and play instructive games with the primers, which usually turned out to be my main occupation. Each day disappeared in a puff of frenzied activity; at home I fell asleep as soon as I sat down, was woken by Trevor, and fell asleep again, right through the evening.

At 10.30, twelve, two (for five minutes, little play) and three o'clock, Joseph the bell monitor went out and pulled its long rope.

Each time the classroom was instantly plunged into silence, the sounds of children's play outside close yet thin against the huge stillness of that quiet valley. After the last bell everyone disappeared within moments and then the silence became enormous, spectral; it filled the little classroom and seemed to enter me too, so that when Mr Stevens from the school committee occasionally knocked at the door as I stood writing the next day's work on the board, I nearly fainted with fright. At four o'clock a bus on its way from Brooklyn and back came past the school gate and I locked the door and left this shadowy place. There was often mist in the hollows, and even on clear days the little settlement seemed to crouch between close dark hills on either side, within sound of the sea and the forlorn crying of the gulls. Happy Valley indeed; an unlikely name. Was it a joke?

However that may be, I was happy there. I worked hard, rather pleased at the odd location which relieving teaching in Wellington had found for me, wanting to keep this small buzzing enterprise running well if I could. In March we decided to try and have a baby, studied the facts about fertile and 'safe' phases in the menstrual cycle and acted in accordance with them. Nothing happened. I went to the doctor and asked for a check-up. While she was talking on the phone I leaned over and read her pad; the note said 'sterile?' I went home checked-up but depressed. The next month we mixed up the dates by mistake but pregnancy ensued anyway, so for most of the time I was at my little country school I felt sick and easily tired. For all that, I was secretly in my glory; my view of the whole world changed with the knowledge that I carried a miraculous second life with me wherever I went.

Returned men whose university study had been interrupted by the war were granted some subjects on 'wartime concession' and enabled to take others on rehabilitation bursaries, especially if their courses related to particular occupations, as Trevor's did. He was in no doubt about his dedication to teaching, and the rehab bursary he applied for when we came back to Wellington was to do an MA in Education. He went to a few lectures, mostly he read, wrote essays and swotted at home. One of the chief consequences for me was that he was always there when I came home from school. We developed amiable little routines – he would have the kettle boiling at the proper moment, I would arrive with a paper bag containing two muffins, or two custard squares, or lamingtons, or whatever else I might spy on my forays into the small shops in Island Bay, Brooklyn or Kilbirnie.

When it came to the second term this system acquired refinements. I taught Standard 3 at Miramar South and it took less than half an hour for a boy or girl with a bike to take a note to Salek Street where we lived, and return with the reply. Such emissaries were of course eager – indeed the practice could be used as an aid to scholarly advancement: 'Can I go, Miz Edmonds?' 'Only if you've finished your comprehension . . . when your spelling's all correct . . . ' We took great pleasure in this half clandestine correspondence. 'Dear Miss Prudence Prim . . . ' (Trevor thought my way of talking, my choice of words, pedantic); and as the term wore on and my body swelled, 'Round and Beautiful Miss Prim . . . ' He was the lad, the student swot, the lurker behind doors, while I went out and did battle with the rough world; my innocent reward was the prepared afternoon tea. It did not occur to either of us that he might reasonably do cooking, washing, ironing as well. Everyone knew that a woman did those things.

In these months of shared anticipation – our baby was due at the end of the year, in November – our interest in each other grew so much that we seemed to be falling in love for the first time. Yet it was not exactly 'love' for the other person as an individual; rather, a new and surprising pleasure in the fact (and the consequences) of our being so uniquely combined. Whatever happened to me, how I felt, what changes my body made, were as much Trevor's business as mine. Well, almost. Every detail of my bodily condition I eagerly described – a stretch mark, the minute flutter of the baby's first movement, a swelling varicose vein. In the last few months we could both watch the rolls and humps of the unknown little creature crossing the hill of my belly as I lay in the bath or in bed; he could feel the enclosed but sturdy bumps and thrusts with his hand. It was our little fish, our frog, our hidden swimmer dog-paddling round its pool, our octopus all arms and legs; our slug, torpid for hours, usually at night, in its bed of water.

My manual of instruction was the Plunket book *Modern Mothercraft*; I read and re-read it, knew by heart its momentous list; everything that must be ready by the seventh month in case of premature birth. Three gowns, three petticoats, three cellular cotton singlets made to the Plunket pattern with ties not buttons. Viyella was the best material, a mixture of wool and cotton; clydella was cheaper and poorer quality – that is, it contained less wool. Babies stayed in bed for the first three months of their lives so whatever their sex they needed only nighties. There were of course nappies, cotton and flannel, on the list, a chaff pillow (so your baby wouldn't suffocate if it lay face downwards), an aircell blanket . . . The list also featured items for the mother, nightgowns (bed seemed to loom large here too) and things called breast-binders, which you had to make to a given pattern. They were broad bandages which you were to lace up tightly to keep under control the milk-filled breasts you expected to have. You pasted the list on the inside of your suitcase lid and checked in anxiously from time to time in case you'd left something out. If that happened, would you be allowed into the hospital at all? There was no knowing. Everyone knew stories of women having their babies in taxis or on the hospital steps or in the toilet; it was as well to be careful.

I stopped smoking and walked the four miles a day that the book advised. Often that winter I battled my way in wild winds or cold sleety rain along the Evans Bay foreshore, through Kilbirnie and up the hill towards Newtown, or past the Miramar cutting and along Shelly Bay Road, the sea storming over the rocks. Sustained by a virtuous pride in making perfect conditions for my baby, and at the same time guarding it from the tumult of the weather and the world, I sailed through these hard conditions in the late afternoons after school, unswervingly committed to my task.

In the third term I moved again, to Worser Bay, a small school on the top of a hill, high up among the soughing pine trees and pohutukawa, and overlooking the Miramar plain on one side and the steep slope down to the sea on the other. It was a remote, windy place and the school, appropriately enough, seemed outside the system that bound other city schools. This was perhaps because the headmaster, a retired sea captain, had come to teaching late and with an unusually casual attitude to the job. He was a fanatical bowls and golf player. He spent every afternoon, and some whole days, at the bowling club or golf course or, if the weather was disappointing, dozing on the staff-room couch. He was a genial, whiskery old chap, adroit at easing his way through differences of opinion with his teachers – indeed at morning tea, or on his rare visits to my Standard 2 class, he didn't show a great interest in educational matters at all. He talked of his days at sea, or in the Old Country, asked how we were. It was as though only by chance did he find himself in the company of people who spent their days shut in rooms talking to young children arranged in rows before them. He himself did no such thing, and after lunch appeared not to concern himself with whether we continued to do it either. There was much getting out early at Worser Bay.

The house in Salek Street was a low-browed, snub-nosed cottage, all wood and old cream paint; it had been built in the 1920s, had the routine front-to-back passage of the period, two bedrooms opening off it on one side, a kitchen-living room at the far end and a small glassed-in porch near the street. The square patch of garden at the back, like the house itself in its essentials, was identical to all others in the street. You could stand on the back doorstep on a Saturday afternoon and look along one way (a hedge prevented this on the other) and see all the backyards, with men in shirtsleeves gardening or women at washing lines, a wooden fence exactly like ours dividing each from its neighbours.

But an impenetrable psychological barrier divided us all the same; in the eighteen months we lived there, not one of our neighbours spoke to us beyond an occasional mumbled 'good morning' if we emerged from our gates at the same moment to go to the tram stop. We were surprised, but since we ourselves were supremely self-engrossed, did nothing to change it. This was what living in a city suburb was like, I supposed.

I adored that shabby little house. The smell of the sun on wood when I sat on the front porch that first hot February went straight into my blood, a sort of ecstatic pulse. I daresay it mingled with the remembered hot smells of Hawke's Bay summers and the wooden verandah where I'd for so long crouched over the pages of whatever book I was reading – as I did now, when there was time. The tiny garden might have been acres of parkland, so great was our pride in it. It was bounded at the back by a higher wooden fence and stacks of timber above that, the back end of a timber yard and small mill. Even these shapeless grey heaps pleased me; and the rows of rather depressed silver beet and seeding lettuces we'd inherited from the owners seemed merely hopeful signs that our own crops would in time burgeon around us. I planted ranunculus corms to come up in the spring.

During our year in Dunedin Clive had been teaching at the opposite end of the country. News of him had been sparse; he seemed to drink a lot, lead a 'wild' life, fall in love constantly as usual. He didn't care greatly for teaching, except for music and singing which he liked and was good at doing. When we saw him at Pyes Pa in the summer holidays he told me that sometimes, living by himself in a cottage near the school, he forgot to do the shopping and ate fruit cake (sent from home) for breakfast.

Then we came to Salek Street and suddenly he was with us all the time, staying in our house or visiting us regularly. And he fell in love in a new way. In his ravings about women, the qualities he found appealing, thrilling, bloody fantastic in fact, was included a regular one about their size. They must be tall. Now he'd found a girl who was as tall as himself, about six feet. She was also beautiful, fair-haired, Nordic-looking; intelligent and charming, full of laughter, not in the least pretentious like some earlier girlfriends. Most satisfactory of all, she was someone I already knew. She had come to Victoria House in my second year, was known to be a talented artist and eventually became an art specialist. Her name was Dorothy Peebles.

It had been rather a habit of Clive's to ask me to intercede for him when he quarrelled with his girls, or make instant friends with new ones I'd never met. I was now released from this burden. Dorothy and I were already friends; I was frightfully pleased with him. For the last six months of that year they were formally engaged and Clive increasingly anxious about his new responsibilities; he took on not one but two extra jobs, teaching till three, then working a late shift at a battery factory, finally a night shift for the Milk Department. The family obsessiveness. He had a few snatched hours of sleep, ate erratically if at all, was tired and cross (he was staying with us) but insisted on taking Dorothy out in his rare free spells. I thought it would kill him and began to worry and fuss, but of course it didn't. The worst that happened was that we quarrelled a bit. He told me later that he didn't make much money anyway.

Lewis also came to stay in the dim little establishment I thought such a paradise. Going to Fiji had discovered in him a thirst to wander, and he now allowed it a careful indulgence, as he once had his taste for buying and restoring unwanted and decrepit buildings. He built a cottage at Pyes Pa and installed an elderly couple, Mr and Mrs Eastlake, as caretakers and family help when needed. Fanny would thus be looked after while he continued to go on working trips with 'the men' – though whether this was because he needed the money or was part of his natural desire for action I didn't know.

Visiting us on his own, after a painting job in Feilding, seemed to induce in him a mood of quiet triumph. He was my little-known parent; at times I had connected with him so seldom that I'd even spoken to him through Fanny – I wanted a driving lesson, would he lend Clive the car . . . She had always been a useful advocate because he found it hard to refuse her anything.

He was unshakeably loyal to her, he truly adored her all his life, and caring for her now that she was ill was his central preoccupation. Nevertheless I think there was a distinct wry pleasure for him, the shy one, in visiting us on his own. It was Easter. The weather was still hot; we had beans and lettuces in the sandy little patch we called our vegetable garden. Lewis weeded, dug up an untidy corner and planted winter cabbages, mowed the minute lawn, fixed a hinge, replaced a board in the ancient verandah. In his reticent, gentle way he became briefly indispensable; he was our steward, our resident overseer. He was easy to like. Perhaps he asked a shade too little of us, of Fanny, of life itself, and as he said goodbye, forgot some trifle, came back, said it again, I wondered if he felt something of this himself. My father. A modest, honourable man.

Chapter 23

Trevor's bursary and some saved earnings of mine paid our rent, and covered food and clothes. We had neither car nor telephone; our house was furnished with the nondescript chairs, cupboards, brown lino, speckly carpet of furnished flats and houses everywhere, the squeaky wirewoves and lumpy kapok of their beds, the ancient cream and green painting of their kitchens, the confused floral cretonnes of their curtains. It didn't cost much to live there. We knew the bursary would end with the exams, but already, with a couple of other students, Trevor had organised a job for the summer, painting wharf gates for the Harbour Board.

We didn't think much about money, being apparently sustained, like others before us, by love in a cottage. Moreover there was a convention, acknowledged by both our mothers, that they should provide many of the basic items of baby equipment. White embroidered viyella gowns and petticoats for instance, three of each, that Trevor's mother gave me on one of our Sunday afternoon pilgrimages to their apartment. I decided to be better tempered about the Edmond ménage. Then we went for one of their Sunday drives, and sat with them in their parked car gazing at the sea across one of the Wellington beaches, and by the time we went home all my habitual intolerance had returned.

I went to antenatal classes, practised my exercises, read Grantly Dick Read on natural childbirth and was convinced that it could be painless. Not that I knew what sort of pain to expect; I'd once fallen off a seesaw, leaving one leg stuck, and had been 'split' . . . I'd had broken and festered chilblains on my hands, bleeding feet after walking out of the Tararuas in boots that were too large . . . What was a pain too great to bear, and if you couldn't bear it, what did you do? I was curious rather than apprehensive. As for relaxation, Dr Read's key, well I was surely not a novice there – after all, I'd *studied* the stuff.

Read said: 'What manner of thing is this love that leads its most natural and perfect children to the green pastures of all that is beautiful in life and urges them on by a series of ever-increasing delights until their ultimate goal is in sight, then suddenly and without mercy, chastises and terrifies them before hurling them unconscious, injured and resentful into the new world of motherhood. I strongly suggest there is only one answer – this is not the course of the Power of Love. This is not the purposeful design of creation.' I was of course quite used to books in which love-making was spoken of as green pastures and ever-increasing delights and so on, but I was sceptical about the Power of Love – not the words, the capital letters. I used them when I wanted to be funny, but clearly the doctor was no satirist. I decided he wrote like that because he Passionately Believed in his Theory. So, without doubt, did I. I wrote to Fanny:

Saturday. It has started! Or it had. Yesterday at lunchtime I produced a blood discharge and woke up about one o'clock this morning with real pains, which was very thrilling; we spent the rest of the night whispering (I don't know who we were keeping quiet for) and giggling and timing the contractions, but they were disappointingly irregular. About 3.30 we made another cup of tea and decided to try and sleep; but quite suddenly it seemed they got stronger and regular, every ten minutes. So we got dressed and went round to the phone box in Coutts Street to tell the hospital. A soft, warm night, cloudy, no stars, no moon,; we hurried along in the dark as excited as children going to a party. Trevor spoke to the nurse on duty and said, 'My wife's got pains', whereupon she held the phone away and repeated to someone else in a really smart mimicking voice, 'Oh, my wife's got pains!' Then she came back and said we were to go home to bed and try again in the morning if they were still going on. But – and this is the awful thing – they weren't! Not a tremor, not a flicker; I was all one big fat body, just as I've been for months and months – for ever.

December 15. My dearest-mother-of-great-standing-and-experience, I suppose after twenty-five years you get over the complete surprise and wonder at being able to produce a completely new person, do you? It seems fantastic and impossible and very wonderful indeed to me – every time they bring me my little girl to be fed I feel incredulous all over again. I know Trevor can't have told you what a beautiful and far-above-normal little creature she is, because he's only had the briefest glimpse of her – I feel enormously proud of her all the time, and nurses and other mothers are constantly remarking on how lovely she is, how amazing that she knows how to suck, never having done it before. And really I am surprised at her appearance; after expecting all the time she was my little frog, and entirely internal, that she would be wrinkly and red at first, she has a plump smooth face and the most perfect skin, soft pink and white and no ruffles anywhere. Also as yet no eyebrows or eyelashes – will they grow?

What had actually happened the night of my baby's arrival I didn't tell Fanny or anyone. I couldn't have explained what kept me silent – it was as though some racial memory, a lesson I had learned countless generations before, instructed me; it was an instinct, I obeyed it. My labour had in fact shocked and horrified me all the time it was going on; it was an interminable nightmare, with myself at the centre roaring and shrieking to an array of busy yet impassive spectres who acted upon me as though I was a joint of meat, to be turned this way and that and carved to the bone.

The puerile idea that if I relaxed all would be well lasted no time at all. Once the pains became strong and frequent, I could do nothing. I would try to relax as each began, but quite soon it would grow larger, deeper, more gripping, more savage and mountainous, till I lost all vestiges of sense or control and yelled and yelled. I'd never done such a thing before, or ever imagined doing it, but equally odd, the nurses seemed not at all surprised – as far as I could think about them, which wasn't much.

Then I opened my eyes, realised I'd been asleep, and was given to lie beside me the most beautiful baby in the world, dressed in one of the new gowns, and also asleep. 'It's a girl,' they said, 'isn't she a prize?' Then the doctor arrived and said, 'You did very well.' What on earth were people like who did badly?

I settled down to pursue a course of sustained adoration of my personal miracle, either in silence, or by prattling to the nurses and other mothers, or by writing to Fanny. Quite soon I couldn't remember very clearly what my labour had been like, and began to say to visitors that I would certainly have another baby soon.

There was no limit to my child's perfections. She had a wide beautiful mouth, big dark blue eyes, curly black hair, ears like the best of our family, small and close to the head, infinitesimally tiny feet which I could find underneath her blankets and hold in my hand, opening and closing it as though to convince myself again and again of their microcosmic wholeness. What's more, I could chronicle a series of sensations of my own, probably never known by the human race before – the tickle and shiver of newly chewed nipples, the sting of healing stitches, a daily flood of gloating which had, however, to be distinguished from the maternal instinct. It didn't seem to be that, more an enchanted (but entirely unpossessive) delight in the separateness of this newest of the world's persons. My baby was also the healthiest ever known, and after a few days the most amazingly mature. It was also true that after a time my over-exposed nipples developed cracks which were excruciatingly painful, my flawless baby turned yellow with jaundice and a young nurse inadvertently told me that when she was extra sleepy it was because she'd cried for hours in the nursery before it was 'time' for a meal – none of this reduced my euphoria, or not for long.

The hospital was Bethany, owned and staffed by the Salvation Army, and specialising in offering refuge to mothers of illegitimate children. They worked as kitchen staff during their pregnancy and sometimes stayed on after their babies had been taken away for adoption. A wall of silence separated these sad creatures from us, the 'legitimate' mothers. I never saw them, and it would have seemed bad manners to put questions to the nurses. They remained forlorn wraiths at the edge of consciousness, impossible to reconcile with my own joyous fulfilment.

Bethany itself seemed so remarkable that it demanded detailed descriptions in letters to Fanny:

There is much rushing about and opening and shutting doors this morning because there've been two inductions (something they do to you to make you 'come on' – one woman says it's just castor oil) and a sudden birth. We were woken as usual at 4.40 am, when our babies arrive on a big tea trolley, rows of them, and a nurse picks yours off the top and gives it to you as though it's a cup of tea and a scone. Mine was wide-awake and hungry, the little pet, and then afterwards she performed some amazing feats – yawning, sneezing, blinking (I know sucking is an instinct, but all this too!). We were allowed to go back to sleep till six, then had the first of seven meals (or in-betweens) of the day, then babies again, morning tea, sleep, dinner, babies, afternoon tea, visiting hour, bedpans, babies, tea, visitors, supper, wash, babies (have I left anything out?) finally a prayer and Bible reading by one of the nurses. Lights out, and we fall instantly to sleep like exhausted workmen. We have not, I might add, put a foot to the floor because this is an absolute embargo. All through the day we sit bolt upright with six pillows behind us (for the surplus blood to drain out of us) and at bed-making time we crouch on the end. Feet go to the floor on the eighth day.

Now I must tell you about our name decision. You know in that list you sent you put 'Victoria Anne' – well we thought you probably meant Virginia Anne, because we all talked of that, and liked it, do you remember? Anyway it had faded away (perhaps partly because the only name we were really sure of at the end was Christopher); suddenly the other day we thought of it again and it's beautiful. It's good enough for this astounding baby, already it seems to fit her. It is dignified, but musical too.

I didn't tell you – and now it doesn't matter – that one day before I was allowed up I got rather a fright; I suddenly felt very faint and sick, sitting there against my six pillows; I lolled about, apparently went white and someone called a nurse. Her solution was to get a bedpan, into which I discharged several enormous blood clots – it was as though the afterbirth had only half come away before. I was quite all right afterwards, but did wonder if this would have happened if I'd been allowed to walk about a bit. What do you think?

One morning Clive, breaking all the rules, had come to show me his wedding clothes – well, socks and tie; he just described the suit. Since I'd heard a dozen conversations between him and Trevor on the subject of weddings (how unimportant they were, what a lot of fuss, best to endure and then forget them), it was funny and touching to find him in this state. His hair was cut and brushed, his smile stretched from ear to ear; he told the nurses that since I couldn't be there I had to see what he was wearing, and they seemed to have melted at his touch. 'He's so young to be getting married!' they kept saying – and indeed he did look boyish and eager as he strode in with his special clothes in his hand. After he'd gone I found my eyes wet with unexpected tears. Mercifully I didn't know till later that the wedding was riotous in the manner of country festivities (Dorothy came from Woodville and had rural relations), the bride and groom, and many others, weaving drunkenly in and out of the treacherous turns of the Manawatu Gorge, laughing in abandonment at the marvel of marriage and paying no attention at all to their driving, or the road.

Lewis and John were there (Lindsay stayed with Fanny in Tauranga) but I had no way of guessing what they thought of all this. Perhaps they had simply looked on, shyly. Clive was a hero to John, I knew: he often talked and gestured like him, learning from his older brother how to grow up and be a man.

As often before, there were marriages on all sides. The most remarkable one by far was one I didn't in the least expect. I first heard from Molly that she and Gordon were seeing a lot of each other – both taught in Hawke's Bay, nothing could be more likely than a renewed friendship. But had they especially liked each other before? I couldn't remember. My picture of him had such a cast of doubtful grey over it (I had after all tried very hard to fall in love with him – until my excitement about Trevor wiped out the possibility). In fact I'd thought so much about how I liked each of them that I hadn't paid the slightest attention to them as separate beings. Now they were together, without me . . . talking of new lives nothing like mine . . . it was a strange, not quite comfortable, idea. Then in no time I heard they were to be married.

Almost at once, it seemed, the photos arrived and I saw Molly in cream hat and short cream dress walking down the path from the clean wood and stone Napier cathedral that had risen from the ashes and rubble of the old brick one, destroyed by the earthquake. Gordon was holding the cream-gloved hand she'd put through his arm, and I had a rush of happiness for them. He was a splendid, dignified, intelligent man, she was the dearest friend I could ever have – and look how she had seen this splendour in him, where I simply had not. He need never have bothered with me, I'd done nothing but make him wretched. I stared and stared at the small, poised, pleased smiles they wore: they were beautiful, both of them. I sent a telegram, not the usual abrupt kind leaving out 'and' or 'the' (because each cost an extra penny), but long and expensive, costing far more than I could afford.

Closer to home, and more intriguing still, was the news that Lindsay was 'always out' with the same person. When she asked to have her probationary year in Tauranga, she had been given a Standard 2 class ('large but more or less bearable') under an elderly headmaster who, like my Worser Bay sea captain, took an afternoon doze on the staff room couch. Also on the staff was Doug Audley, 'this marvellous man', she said, 'tall, handsome, clever, witty, and outrageously attentive to me'. They danced at Hayman's Hall every Saturday night to the Hawaiian band, they swam and went for picnics. When she began bringing him to Pyes Pa he was seen by our parents to be amazing, brilliant, compelling, truly original . . . He and Fanny, and occasionally John, wrote smart verses about Lewis's rural experiments – excessive pigshit in the compost, a failed soya bean crop; Fanny kept on quoting his *bons mots* in letters. His father wrote novels and Doug himself had a taste for composing witty sketches which made him and Fanny like blood relations from the start. I too was very impressed. What would one say to this marvel, I wondered nervously, when we met on our next visit to Pyes Pa?

Events moved very fast. Not only did Lindsay and Doug shortly declare themselves madly, exhilaratingly in love; in no time they were secretly, then openly engaged. Our next visit, scheduled for the May holidays, would coincide with their wedding.

Fanny was still a huge figure on my landscape. Her conflicts remained my own, in particular a profound ambivalence about truth-telling, 'plain-speaking', being honest – whatever you called it. This was an article of faith. But I had come to see that unadmitted lies lay beneath this creditable surface. We had learnt long ago to take extreme care of Fanny's sensitivities – her touchiness in fact – and this had induced in me too a kind of deviousness that fitted very well with the broader lessons that all women unconsciously absorbed. Be nice, not rude or angry. If there are faults and misunderstandings, blame yourself . . . or appear to do so.

In other words, I had brought with me as part of my family inheritance a habit of concealing 'unsuitable' behaviour, often even from myself. The disease of noble dishonesty. I think I had it in quite an advanced form.

Chapter 24

Ours became a famous baby. No one else seemed to have one, or no one we knew. All through that hot summer and the mild, windy autumn that followed, our little house was crowded with visitors. It wasn't, of course, just Virginia, miraculous as she was, that they came to see; it was the visible proof that such a leap into the very heart of adult experience could be made, and apparently without too much trouble.

But the changes were immense. Each came as a discovery, and was upon us before we knew how to be ready for it. From the first Saturday I came home from the hospital and the three of us began to live together, the entire chemistry of my body altered. I had been a heavy sleeper; suddenly I woke if there was the lightest sigh or sniff from the next room. Through the previous nine months I had come to see my body as capable of plurality, but now I was really separate from someone who had nevertheless become more to me than I was to myself. I didn't, then or at any time, have to choose her life in preference to mine, but in those first months it slowly dawned on me that I would be capable of such a choice. Certainly I wanted her to be warm, comfortable, well fed, happy, far more than I wanted these things for myself. The enormity of my responsibility, to provide the total world in which all this could happen, fortunately came into focus only gradually.

Still, one morning when Virginia was several months old I woke up early – even earlier than she did – and was suddenly appalled at the casual way I had come into this stunning and terrifying inheritance. I looked back and saw that something like this had happened quite often before. Experience arrived like a train stopping at my personal station; again and again I'd thought, 'No, I'm not ready, I don't know enough', yet each time I'd felt the excitement of trying, and so after only a small hesitation I jumped aboard and it carried me on to places I had never known existed. Acting in those training college plays, writing my first sketch, editing *Ako Pai*, taking the third year in speech therapy, that unknown field of enterprise, going on the *Hamlet* and *Othello* tour, even getting married. And now this, momentous in a way none of them had been, because this was truly a question of life or death. How many times in those first weeks had I bent over the pale sleeping face of my baby, in panic, because she was so still and silent I had to put a finger below her nose to make sure she was breathing. How often had I dragged myself out of heavy sleep at her first cry at two or three in the morning, gone at once, stumbling into her room to sit with her on the low stool I kept there for us, aching with weariness but willing to wait for her to drink the very last drop she wanted. Changing her, whispering and laughing at the sudden crowing she would do which seemed so to surprise her as it came out, I'd already forgotten my own body's claims and desires.

Because I had to rub dirty nappies on a wooden washing board and then wash them by hand in the tub every day, my hands grew red and sore; constantly woken up, I came to have a craving for sleep; the unending crowds of visitors meant my time, apart from Virginia's meals, was always scrambled and hectic. But if these unfamiliar hardships were greater than I'd expected, so too were the compensations. On hot days

. . . in the morning before her bath and again in the afternoon Virginia kicks in the sun on this baking little verandah, soaking Vitamin D into her small fat tummy and busy bottom and legs – she stretches her legs out quite straight, then thrusts them up so high she's almost airborne, only her shoulders on the floor. And at the same time her arms are going frantically and she's breathing in that quick urgent way babies do, and looking about her as well.

Clive and Dorothy knocked at the door the other night, I opened it and there they were, smiling radiantly and hand in hand (they dropped them as I appeared). Dorothy shows more signs of changes wrought by marriage than Clive, but they are both looking very bright and assured. Dorothy was more talkative and more emphatic than before; she said she still remembers feeling junior to me when we were at Training College, it made her quite nervous. But even while she was saying this I was thinking that her whole manner tells you something else – 'I'm married now. I'm equal to anyone.'

Like hundreds of other young couples, Clive and Dorothy couldn't find a flat, so for most of that year they lived in rooms at the Lopdells' house. This was Frank Lopdell – Loppy, the revered creator of the liberal and civilised training college in Wellington, so vastly superior to all others in the country. I was still so in awe of him that I could hardly believe that an ordinary household and family could be attached to him in the usual way. Yet I had sat by Margaret, his daughter, at Education lectures at Victoria, liked her and admired her stately carriage and craggily handsome features. She and Dorothy were friends and contemporaries, and Clive called Mr Lopdell 'Frank'. Such boldness, such aplomb.

Peg and George were often there too and she, in her open-hearted way, was delighted by my natural child and eager to practise handling, bathing, dressing and undressing her, since she would have no hospital preliminaries for her own baby. They expected the adoption in March. Molly and Gordon, quietly happy and at ease, came to lunch or dinner a few times. On such occasions I was amazed at how completely we all seemed able to 'do' this new life; how, like old skins, we had shed other earlier existences. Trevor and Gordon talked amiably about teaching, Molly and I about everything – yet almost without our noticing, the intense intimacy had leaked away. Once we had confided every sensation, the emotional nuances of every experience. Now we were shy of mentioning our marriages at all. Still, she did tell me that Brenda and Paul lived not far from us and had a baby about the same age as ours.

Brenda. Fancy that, my old enemy, the thief who stole away my beloved Beetles. We laughed, and marvelled at how benign we felt towards her, now that she posed no threat to anyone. As for Beetles himself, he had vanished to the South Island, to a school on the West Coast; Neville had gone to England; Trixie to Hawera where she had married her old English teacher. We remembered her wondrous account of him sitting at his classroom table with a shotgun and taking pot shots at birds as they flew past the window, and we laughed even more. He and Trixie now led an eccentric life, though Molly did not know what form it took. Strange, here I was hearing bits of news of those people who'd once been giants, as though they were no more than names picked out of the daily paper.

Sandy too came on occasional visits. He no longer made innocently amorous suggestions to me, but otherwise seemed much the same, voluble as ever in his jumpy way and inclined to know everything and everybody, though I thought his face fell into rather melancholy lines when he was not talking, which happened occasionally. Bruce Mason had married Diana Shaw, a young doctor who was brilliant and imposing. It had all dispersed, that old life, those friendships I'd been so sure would remain unchanged for ever. They were no more than a flock of starlings that take off at some unseen signal and land far away, in places of their own separate choosing. Did Molly feel strange about it? Not particularly; neither did I – that was the *really* strange thing. Would she like to give Virginia her orange juice? Yes, she would – and we slipped easily back into the present.

Once the long summer vacation was over I had more time alone, or alone with my new companion. 'We are never lonely,' I told Fanny, 'we talk to each other all day.' But I began to keep a diary again, though my letters to Fanny were, as usual, such a complete record of every event that I was rather half-hearted by the time I came to the green notebook (I frugally used the spare pages in a book of speech therapy notes). It was useful all the same for my very secret thoughts – such as that there was plenty of time to become a real New Zealand poet because there had been hardly any women since Katherine Mansfield, so the field was wide open. It seemed not to occur to me that a) this was not the point, b) it wasn't true about the other women not being there, and anyway c) it could change. Bits of poems and stories I scrawled between the green covers too.

Since Virginia's arrival Trevor and I had not had time for the reading of poems to each other which had been such a pleasure before. It was always the thirties poets, Auden, Spender, Day Lewis, MacNeice, and we had favourites we read again and again. Like *I Think Continually of Those Who Were Truly Great* – 'Born of the sun they travelled a short while towards the sun, / And left the vivid air signed with their honour' and Day Lewis's *Conflict*, which we saw as a heroic call to young men in England to fight against Franco in the Spanish Civil War – '. . . only ghosts can live / Between two fires'. And there was MacNeice's 'The sunlight on the garden / Hardens and grows cold', which could make me almost cry, and his *Bagpipe Music* – 'It's no go the merry-go-round, it's no go the rickshaw / All we want is a limousine and a ticket for the peepshow'. But the poem we returned to most often and came to know by heart was Auden's love lyric 'Lay your sleeping head'. Those beautiful lines we possessed as our own, there was no finer declaration we wanted to make to each other. 'Mortal, guilty, but to me /

The entirely beautiful . . . / Beauty, midnight, vision dies; / Let the winds of dawn that blow / Softly round your dreaming head . . . '

But we were too tired and busy to read aloud any more. At the end of the holidays Trevor took a relieving job at South Wellington Intermediate, then at Te Aro School; if there weren't visitors I spent evenings working as hard as he did, helping to prepare work for his next day's classes. Only during the day, after the washing was done and Virginia was sleeping, could there be small islands of time for me. Then I got out the old green notebook and wrote and wrote. When I ran out of time I squeezed it into the bottom compartment of a chest of drawers where I kept paper and envelopes and unanswered letters. It would no more have occurred to me to tell Trevor about it than to describe how I'd cleaned my teeth, or washed my face. It was a completely private act.

In writing these fragments I unconsciously chose the Hawke's Bay hills and hazy summer air, the long-familiar grassy places, when I needed 'country'. So, in the same way, Salek Street became 'town'. The dim little house, our quiet repetitive neighbourhood, the sandy garden and the faint growl of the sea coming up from Evans Bay (we were only a few houses from the foreshore), all became the natural place for city people to live. It was as though beginning to write about this place, and the new life it contained, showed it as another kind of childhood. It was so vivid, so immediate, that, like a small child, I took in at every pore the look and feel and sound and smell of the world I had come to inhabit.

I tried to put Janet, one of the speech therapy students, into this milieu. 'The clear light in her eyes was deceptive . . . behind it she was constantly watching for slights and insults, something to be angry about.' But away from that small group of students jostling for places, I couldn't get her to come to life. If she was constantly looking for insults, I had to produce some situations where she might find them. The next time I opened the notebook I crossed it all out and wrote instead a poem that was to glimpse her deceptiveness, and I was much better pleased with that.

On my now rare visits to town I occasionally called in to Modern Books, intensely aware of its poignant associations – the visits with Beetles . . . the day of his birthday when he bought the violets . . . the long meditative browsing. But my centre of concentration had shifted entirely; I had only the interval between baby feeds, perhaps on a

Friday night when Trevor was at home, and there was no time to linger. However, I did notice that there was a new literary journal, a small chunky volume which published poems and stories written by New Zealanders. Its name was *Landfall*. Who were these people? They weren't, like Katherine Mansfield, dead; they were close by, alive and well and making themselves heard. An interesting discovery; curiously uncomfortable, too. My secret desire to be a writer mostly concerned the act of writing, catching experience and pinning it down. But clearly there was something else – a tiny, barely awake worm in the brain that dreamed about being read, known, recognised. The ambition factor. Well, it had better stay asleep; its time had certainly not arrived.

In the meantime, family concentration was given to Lindsay's wedding preparations. Clothes, to begin with. Wartime austerity had allowed, indeed compelled us to wear the same short skirts, barely to the knee, year after year – the whole time, in fact, that I had been wearing grown-up clothes. Suddenly there was a New Look. The Butterick, McCalls, Simplicity and Vogue pattern books that I raced through on my quick dashes into town featured strange creatures in long swathing dresses, trailing not merely below the knee but nearly to the ankles, some right to the floor. I was highly sceptical. A return to Victorian inhibitions, I scoffed; I would never change out of my short skirts, the brief casual clothes I liked, I didn't care in the least about fashion. It was a silly trumped-up business. Scotty had taught us at training college that it was the conscious creation of the bosses of big firms, who were nothing more than corrupt commercial manipulators.

It was odd, though, how gawky my long bare legs began to feel, how I unaccountably found myself tugging at my hems, as though they were growing shorter by the minute. I had some money Fanny had given me on my birthday, I'd saved a little more. I bought a Butterick pattern for a dress with a fitted bodice and gathered skirt falling to mid-calf, and a length of dull pink wool crepe. Feeling secretly adventurous, I took them home to make a new dress for Lindsay's wedding; it was only fair to her to look my best.

I wrote to her, congratulating my little sister on arriving at the threshold of maturity, responsibility, total womanhood; I said I knew I'd love Doug on sight, I couldn't wait to meet him. But they arranged the wedding on the first day of the May holidays when we couldn't go. Telegrams flew, there was much rushing round to the phone box on the corner, letters explaining with mounting emphasis that Clive and Dorothy wouldn't be able to get there either because Dorothy was being capped the night before, and they were to hitchhike the next day, while we took their luggage in a borrowed car. They would surely consider changing the day to Monday – we couldn't bear not to be there, there was no way to alter our arrangements . . . and so on. They could change; they did. We went.

The surprise for me on the wedding day was that I felt excluded, and minded a good deal. However severely I instructed myself as to my sister's necessary separateness, I found it hurt to meet Wendy, her bridesmaid, and to see that theirs was a closer friendship than any I could now claim. Lindsay was happy and excited, eagerly responsive to her stylish young husband, slightly preoccupied when he wasn't close by. But that wasn't often – he hovered near her, in visibly intense adoration. Did I envy them this enveloping passion? Perhaps. But of course we all behaved decently, and if I felt tearful, as occasionally I did, there was always Virginia, five months old, an infallible distraction for me and everyone else as I carried her about in the crowd.

They both had teaching jobs in Rotorua and even a cottage to live in; after the wedding they whirled away, all smiles, to their shared destiny. Lindsay told me afterwards that not only had she modelled her wedding on mine, but that her problem as a younger sister had always been how to devise a method for anything at all that did not closely imitate and parallel mine.

However, as we each moved more securely into our separate lives, this residue of a closely interlocked childhood disappeared quite naturally. We came to show greater differences in temperament and outlook than I, at any rate, had realised were there, and there was a curious parallel to this in the men we had married. Both had the same altruistic and obsessive dedication to teaching, both were already looking towards jobs in high schools, where their university qualifications would be acknowledged, both liked the idea of living and working in small towns. For all that, they were men of a different stamp, and as time went on they evolved in very different ways. Lindsay and I had to begin to 'learn' each other as friends, a new state that replaced the seemingly automatic knowledge we'd always possessed as sisters.

Chapter 25

During the winter of 1948 we made a great many decisions about how and where we would live – and then unmade almost all of them. We were offered a state house which we could keep as long as we liked, and that meant in effect deciding to live in Wellington after we left Salek Street. Certainly, I found it hard to imagine that we ever would leave, so strongly attached was I to my suburban haven. We had grown fine vegetables – carrots, leeks, cabbages, beans, lettuce – in its enclosed and unpromising-looking garden; also – though this was my preserve and not of interest to Trevor – marigolds, asters, sweet peas, delphiniums, ranunculus, almost everything except sunflowers and that was only because I didn't have the nerve to try.

There was by now a ghostly population that inhabited the house. I liked to think of them wandering about at night, passing the time in inconsequential chat while we slept, ruminating at leisure upon the events of the day. They made a large crowd for so small a space; all my family except Fanny, and Doug, the latest arrival in it; all of Trevor's – both the brothers with their wives had paid us visits, Don and Rae bringing their own baby, a dark handsome little boy eighteen months older than Virginia. Most of my old friends, those who had so powerfully filled my time and fed my imagination during the two years at training college, had come too, Molly and Gordon several times, Peg and George over and over, as though they were family themselves, Sandy from time to time, occasionally Paul, even Brenda. Beetles? Alas, no. When Virginia was a few months old he'd written me a long, funny, affectionate letter (with a reference to the direction of squirts of milk at the wrong moment as 'nor'-nor'-west of the Pole'), but for the time being that was the last I heard of him. The South Island, especially the West Coast, was another planet.

There were others, too, friends of Trevor's from an earlier time, new people we met teaching in our Wellington schools. Bruce Mason reappeared too – glittering old Bruce, whose new wife Diana I liked a great deal; she was firm and sensible, not twittery as some women were when husbands you knew produced them for the first time. Everyone was making plans of some sort; the war was over, we were all married, first babies were arriving or, like ours, had already done so. These friends had come into our little house, and they remained as invisible presences that populated our rooms.

But whoever occupied it, the house was not to be ours much longer. The owners were returning to claim it; we too must get on with our decisions. We didn't take the state house because we found we'd have to forge the papers to get far enough up the list of the needy and were repelled by this idea. We didn't think we'd stay in Wellington either. Trevor, who had not lived in the country, wanted to try it; indeed he said if he had the money he'd like to leave teaching and become a farmer. I was sceptical. I remembered Uncle Bert's sustained rage when feed was short at Patoka and wool prices down, and he belonged to a family that knew the land in all its moods and vagaries. Trevor, like his parents, had always lived in cities. However, it didn't matter because it was not a dream to be readily realised, and I was quite pleased to agree to applications for jobs in country schools.

District high schools were primary schools with a secondary department attached; when they grew big enough they separated into two. Trevor applied for a job in the high school section of Ohakune District High School, and got it.

Ohakune? Somewhere in the middle of the island, wasn't it? High country . . . wasn't there a mountain? We peered at the atlas. Our conversations became all wild surmise, we looked at everything in a newly dramatic way. We had become a family with a future; we too had plans, a destiny waiting to take us up like a magic carpet and whirl us into a shimmering distance. There was an all-electric three-bedroomed house. And high school teaching – it might be rather interesting. We agreed that at the end of the August holidays I should come back with Ada and Charlie in their car – they were to be in Hamilton, where the family had bought a motor car business which Don managed. They would pick me up at Pyes Pa, with Virginia, basket, baby paraphernalia, and drive down the island, stopping at Ohakune to investigate its prospects.

All at once, my sense of possession of Salek Street weakened. I began to look at it as someone else's after all – the fruitful little garden, the rooms crowded with the shadowy characters of my own life, the bed where we'd lain and watched the inscrutable jumpings of my unborn baby move across my body; where, enveloped by clouds of sleep, I'd staggered out to feed and comfort her, where we'd laughed and whispered and made love, and where I'd often lately gone to sleep alone, discontented with Trevor's sometimes surly obsession with school work, as he went on reworking some plan for the next day or rewriting a class test.

Virginia had lived more than half of the first year of her life here. On dozens of windy days she'd lain outside in her pram watching the stubby ngaio tree flicking its leaves above her; here she had been hot and cold and miserable, she'd squirmed about on the baking little front verandah, discovering her hands, her feet, and the expanding world as it opened out round her; she had been dim and secret in the unreachable dreamworld of a baby's first weeks, and had gradually come to chatting and laughing and telling me her news – though not yet with words – as she did now. And she'd learnt us, our separateness; that Trevor was not some sort of rude intruder into the closed world she and I occupied, but a proper member of it. At eight months she was alert and chubby with enormous eyes, grey now, and fair hair beginning to curl.

And there'd been all those visits from friends, the shared meals, my running along the Evans Bay foreshore to get extra food from Kilbirnie while someone minded my baby; even the visits to Oriental Bay on Sundays, perhaps to drive with Ada and Charlie in the afternoon as they liked to do: that was part of the Wellington life, and I had to admit I'd come to recognise the steady kindness behind the monotonous conversation of my parents-in-law, whatever I might think of that. I began to sort and pack.

Quite soon I came to the drawer of letters, my writing notebook, a few scraps of poems; next to the sewing drawer with carefully rolled up pieces of spare material and used patterns. Then the bookshelf made of lengths of wood supported by bricks that held our collection of red-covered Left Book Club books, favourite poets, my old copies of *The Mill on the Floss* and *The Cloister and the Hearth* together with Marie Stopes and *Birth Control for Modern Couples*, a *Yates' Garden Guide* Lewis had given us. These would come with us, of course, yet I left something of myself behind here all the same. This was the place where I'd come to my first great adult realisation, in the birth of my child; I'd given more of myself away here than anywhere before, yet paradoxically I felt more sure, more in charge of myself. Was it a natural destiny, then, not to be a certain sort of person, but to arrange different kinds of fulfilment to take place around me? Yes, I thought it was. And indeed growing up in Greenmeadows had been full of awareness of the push and pull of family personalities. Now I was at home again, for the first time since those years in Osier Road. That had been a system of dextrous management, with its overflow in drama and conversation; so was this. My own life of coping had begun.

I saw the town first, as we'd agreed, coming from Hamilton by car. It was early September, a perfect spring day, clear and sunny; everything was lit by a vivid, powerful light of a kind I'd never seen before. The mountain was enormous, so close you could almost reach out and touch it, a vast glistening presence, white to the very bottom, where the dark blue-greens of the bush banked against it. The air was so sharp and cold I had to breathe in a new way to take it in – were we high enough for it to be more sparse than the lowland air I was used to? We stood about in the road – small and stony, rather like Osier Road in Greenmeadows – and gazed at the house where I would live. A neat, undistinguished, three-bedroomed wooden bungalow, probably built to an Education Department plan, and much the same as thousands of other school houses. Flat oblong section, a few straggly bushes, no trees. But as I could see at once, the open spaces of the country, houses here and there widely dispersed among the fenced paddocks, made a kind of privacy in themselves. If the air had to be taken in heady gasps, so did the whole sense of being out in the open, surrounded only by endless green distances, the overshadowing bulk of Ruapehu, and a new kind of silence.

Once our daily lives there had begun, it was this silence that struck me with the greatest force. It was a new element, almost as unlike the apparent quiet of a city suburb as if we'd moved from air to water. Any day in Salek Street happened against a background of buzzing, clattering, humming, a muted jumble of tram clankings, car horns, rasping chainsaws from the timber mill, footsteps, children's voices. Here, especially at night, there was a hush that seemed to go all the way up to the stars, a million miles above us.

On the other hand this sparse little settlement, scattered about the countryside miles beyond the township itself, was occupied by a community that was not silent in the least. It was instantly sociable, neighbourly, pointedly interested in new arrivals, extraordinarily active in offering its gestures of welcome. Kindling arrived ready cut for our coal range, bottles of preserved fruit for our dinners, garden produce, invitations to join clubs and committees, offers to drive me to Taihape or Wanganui to shop. This mountain village clearly felt itself to be some sort of outpost; indeed in those first weeks I felt almost as though I'd been brought to a station at the South Pole or a depot in the Himalayas sealed off by avalanche, so emphatically did the Ohakune population – or the part of it I saw – impress upon me that I could be at home here and not need the outside world – which presumably I would never see again.

The most helpful visitor, and the most frequent by far, was a woman about my own age, colourful and exuberant in style and looks. Marie had a mass of wavy auburn hair, she laughed loudly and often, she talked constantly, was profusely inventive with proposals for my entertainment, and in short elected herself an instant best friend.

She had a little boy too, slightly older than Virginia, not much interest in domestic routine, and a car. With her I visited other local people – some, like her sister-in-law, miles away down Lakes Road on the way to Raetihi; I went to 'town', to a flower show, a Pony Club demonstration day and several fund-raising shop days, for which I soon learned to have my own fresh-baked cakes ready, whatever the cause might be. It was a sudden and comprehensive initiation; and, of course, she overdid it. Her car seemed always to be pulling up at the gate and she would be upon me with a scheme for the day or, if there was none to be found, all the time in the world to stay and chatter. I grew restive, morose, over-fussy about Virginia's regular requirements for meals, clean clothes, sleep (in fact I *was* fussy and precise about these things). Eventually another teacher's family, more recently arrived, attracted her, and the hectic temperature of our association mercifully cooled.

Although I was much occupied by the lively social networks that obviously held the town together, I found I had sudden attacks of forlornness. The space about us was wide and silent enough to make me shiver, however busily its other occupants filled it with friendly reverberations. Besides, there were patches of strange living that I was not invited to approach. Maori kids made up about a third of the school population, but I met none of their parents, nor did I find out where they lived, though there was a conglomeration of shacks far back from the road a few streets – or roads – from our house, and from these untidy brown urchins emerged each morning. There was a pa on the other side of town and a flourishing Maori community at Makaranui on the way to Raetihi; many of these people became Trevor's friends when he taught their kids, but they were always shy with me – and I, equally, with them.

There were wild goings-on, I was told, in 'Kune on Saturday nights, but these too, were strictly outside my scope. Boozy fights in the darkness round the dance hall, brawls in the street or the backyard of someone's house. Because the King Country was 'dry' there were no pubs, but the clubs – the Sunbeam, Pioneer, RSA – had many ways of distributing bottles, or indeed whole crates of beer, to those who wanted to use it off the premises. It could, for instance, be left under a bush or behind a fence outside, where it would be appropriately 'found' by those who'd already paid more than the market price for it.

There was a furniture shop at the edge of the township, one I passed every time I made the ten-minute walk, with my little girl in her pushchair, to the post office or one of the handful of shops. It always looked very seedy – which was not surprising once you knew it belonged to one of the sly-groggers, and the dusty tables and chairs were the merest mask for its main operation. It was odd to reflect on a night several years before, when Trevor and I had driven one of the cars ordered by the Edmond motor firm in Hamilton from the Todd factory in Wellington, and because of engine trouble had to spend a night in Raetihi. I remembered now our walking up and down the silent, lost-looking little main street on a Saturday night, and a car charging down the centre of the road, stopping to open its doors to a couple of youths who appeared from nowhere: 'Come to 'Kune,' the driver yelled, 'the crowd's over there!', and they roared off.

Well, the main street of 'Kune, once the shops shut, looked much the same as that one in Raetihi, so the crowd wasn't here either. And I of course would never come within miles of where it was. I thought a bit about this; in so small a place, the same separate worlds seemed to exist side by side as they did everywhere else.

The headmaster of the school was, for everyone except himself, a problem. He was a big stout man, cheerful and bossy, generally indifferent to the problems of his teachers who wrestled with large classes, scrappy equipment, an ancient freezing building in which the rooms were grouped round the assembly hall, and no staffroom. The water heating broke down often and there were plenty of sub-zero days when the frost had burst the pipes and there was no heat at all. But there was one school activity George McCullough was fanatically interested in – school banking. This he promoted with all the energy and enthusiasm he saved from more educationally useful matters.

However, the enterprise that George was really devoted to was his own small farm, a mile or two from the school near the Junction. He ran dry stock there, and let the house to teaching families – ours among them – a year or two after we arrived. He was as insensitive a landlord as he was headmaster; largely, I suppose, because he never listened to anyone. If there was anything you'd done that hadn't worked, at school or elsewhere, George would find out and remark on it; your triumphs passed him by. When I had more than one child and we were established as his tenants, he told me one day that I did too much for the children, didn't leave them to fend for themselves enough. I took umbrage, as everyone did at his interfering ways, though with the acumen of tactless people he was saying something I should probably have listened to.

His wife, who became quite a friend of mine, was a mild and, perhaps predictably, sweet-tempered creature. She had a stately figure with the large bosom I believed was the mark of a singer – and sure enough she turned out to be a distinguished contralto, who not only sang at local concerts but also went to Wellington or Auckland for broadcast performances.

In my first few months in Ohakune I had a miscarriage, and Mrs McCullough became a character in the drama. For years I'd been sure I wanted to have a lot of children – a million, I'd said to Trevor in the halcyon days when we were first engaged; four at least, I'd decided while falling in love with the speech clinic waifs and the charming (if wrong-headed) demoiselles of St Margaret's. I so enjoyed my one baby, two would surely be even better. We confidently initiated a second pregnancy. Summer came, we joined the Tennis Club – I was so spectacularly healthy I need take no notice of the conventional cautions about violent exercise.

Trevor was good at all games, and did play, but I gambolled about actively enough, noting with satisfaction that I felt no signs of sickness

– one grew out of such things, apparently. But at three months, and indeed after one sunny Saturday afternoon at the Tennis Club, I began to bleed. Just a little, but it was instantly necessary to consult Dr Jordan. This wasn't easy by phone; he was a large, impenetrably silent man – so silent that once you'd breathlessly described your problem to him the line seemed to go dead. The silence stretched into minutes – hours, surely. 'Dr Jordan . . . ?' you squeaked. There was the faintest sound of vocal chords, a phantom of a grunt; eventually he articulated in very slow syllables, 'Go to bed. At once.' Our next door neighbour, and a friend, was Kay Ross, the district nurse; when consulted she too said, 'Don't move, and it will probably be all right.'

It wasn't. I stayed in bed for several days while the bleeding grew steadily worse, and this is how I came to know Mrs McCullough of the statuesque figure and gentle smile. She insisted on coming to my house each morning to look after Virginia, who at a year was half baby, half toddler, and to manage my household. Mrs McCullough was much older than me, and grand; it was a case of noblesse oblige. I was overcome with an apologetic gratitude as she pushed the carpet sweeper round my room. 'You must lie still, Mrs Edmond,' she said, as everyone else had. 'Call me Lauris,' I asked earnestly; but she explained that much as she would like such intimacy and casualness, she had been brought up differently, and would be quite incapable of speaking my Christian name. She did say her own was Una – but what could I do with that? I smiled respectfully and she went on with the housework.

In the long hours I was left alone I read *War and Peace*. It drew me into a theatre of reality vastly larger and more splendid than my own, which was just as well because as the bleeding thickened and grew I realised I would lose my baby, and this made me very miserable. In the end there was a painful internal cataclysm, a sort of small-scale labour, and engulfed in a lake of blood the little lump of a thing came away from my body. Kay, who had come over to help, directed Trevor to bury it in the garden. My sense of loss was terrible. I was very weepy. He said as we mourned together afterwards that he was sure it had been a boy.

Dr Jordan was a local representative on the Education Board, so knew about the 'problem' of our house, or rather its section. The land had once been swamp and was still inadequately drained, so from time to time inspections by solemn board members took place. They came one morning when Virginia was waiting on the front porch for the milkman, a genial fellow who made a point of bringing her a half-size bottle of milk each day. When three dark-suited men came through the gate and down the path she was horrified and ran inside, though all they did was poke about in some muddy places and leave, ignoring us.

A few months later, when I was successfully pregnant and stretched out on my back on the bed in Dr Jordan's surgery, with my bulging body rising palely above me and silence enveloping us as usual, he suddenly said, 'You've got a dry section.' His tone was ominous; I thought wildly of passages through which my poor baby would be unable to pass and, once dryness began, who knew where it would end? I waited for further bad news.

Finally he said, in the same slow voice, 'The Education Board decided to put the drains under your house.'

'Ah,' I gasped. Really, his dumbness was infectious.

We were by that time in our second year in Ohakune, and John had been living with us since school opened in February. I now knew a good deal more of the true facts of the family move to Pyes Pa. The idyllic holidays, the garden weddings, the charmed gatherings of friends and family on Fanny's verandah, the magical conversations, were temporary and intermittent interludes. When no one was there Fanny was desperately lonely. Lewis continued his trips away, perhaps from necessity, perhaps because he could not give up the idea of himself as faithful provider; the two elderly stewards he had installed in their cottage were useful but hardly companionable. John was at school, the neighbouring families were homely, stodgy people, gossipy in a way Fanny could not tolerate, not remotely interested in the reading and speculating which were her central occupations. No doubt they thought her snobbish and unbending.

Deprived of all companionship, she became frightened, suspicious, ignorant of the most ordinary facts of other people's lives. At least in Greenmeadows, however 'outside' she had felt, there were groups in which she belonged and held some authority – the drama and garden circles, the other women with whom she exchanged visits. Here she was alone, truly on the outside, despite the physical beauty of the Pyes Pa farm and orchard. It's true that she took great pleasure in the life of the garden and its creatures, and wrote us lyrical and often funny letters about such characters as her friends the two bellbirds who came up the valley and hopped about where they could sip the nectar of the red hot pokers. Nevertheless, in crucial ways the vision of a fresh start among new people had proved impossible to grasp. The move must often have seemed a catastrophic mistake.

However the person she worried about most acutely was not herself, but John. She clung to him as a companion, and flew into panics because she did so. She went on walks with him to escape from too intense solitude, and then was alarmed to find her temperature going up and her strength diminishing. Probably she tried to persuade Lewis to stay home more, but nobody thought him especially sociable, even at home. When John's best friend Percy left school at the end of 1948 a crisis developed, and the solution eventually decided upon was to send John to live with us for his last year at school. Trevor had the common touch, he would be just the person to offer him a normal boyhood, or early manhood; a passion for sport suddenly seemed an advantage.

These theories were sound. Trevor was indeed a stable, highly masculine, middle-brow, educationally thoughtful but tolerant older relative. He didn't suffer from the Scott anxieties about being 'different'; he was not, and gave no thought to the problem. John's year at Ohakune District High School was a success. At school, and in our family, he became a star. A quiet luminary, of course – it was not in him to strut and perform – but everyone seemed to have some reason to like and admire him. He fitted in by never being too close to anyone, I think. The school's sporting fanatics recognised his prowess, and his enthusiasm, at cricket – and even forgave him for preferring table tennis to rugby in the winter. I liked him because he was patient and gentle with Virginia; he would take her over to the paddock opposite our house and play ball games that made her laugh and squeal as she ran after it and him. He obligingly took her for walks, talking to her more like a friend than a baby-minder – and what does a child want but that?

He really was an almost faultless visitor. He dug all of Trevor's vegetable garden, chopped wood and brought in coal for our incessant fires. Moreover he was a first-class student, unselfconscious about taking school work seriously. To top it all off, he captured the attention of every senior girl and was secured in a kind of partnership with one of the prettiest, a girl from Karioi. Trevor, who saw more of him than I did, said he acquiesced rather passively in this and was actually bored by the girl's chatter. John told Percy when they were both home in Tauranga for the holidays – and Percy later told me – that the big argument among the Ohakune lads was whether a fellow took his trousers off when coupling. Neither of them could answer this perplexing question.

Fanny's solitude was now complete. But for John the first taste of independence was visibly nourishing. He was well served by the very qualities I had recognised in Trevor's family and seen as a relief from the singularity and crankiness of the Scotts – a plain acceptance of the conventions, an unspoken belief that the world gave you its rules and it was normal and proper to keep them. Trevor and John took everything that happened at school seriously, their jokes were jolly and companionable; they were mates. At the end of the year John got distinguished marks in the bursary exam, which Trevor said was remarkable from a 6A class of four in a small country high school. He went off to enrol at Victoria University for the first year of a BSc. His future was full of promise.

The science teacher, and senior assistant in charge of the secondary department, was a likeable eccentric called Varna Cook. He lived, before we did, in the McCullough farmhouse where he used the barn and other outhouses to store his specimens – he was said to be a notable authority on sedges and swamp grasses. And indeed he quite fitted the image I had from my childhood reading of the preoccupied scholar with spectacles on the end of his nose and his clothes on back to front. His most spectacular act of absent-mindedness was to walk to school one day, pausing at his gate – a long way from the house – to put his lunch in the milk box and carry the family milk bottle all the way to school. He sometimes said John was exceptional, which pleased me, though I could never be quite sure he remembered which one of his students John was.

Whatever their eccentricities, it became more and more obvious as time passed that the other teachers were our natural companions, mine as well as Trevor's. Some invisible barrier lay between the 'locals' and the 'itinerants' – the farmers, timber workers, market gardeners, shopkeepers whose town it really was, and people like us who, with varying degrees of surprise, found ourselves in what still felt like a frontier town. Not all the local teachers lived in 'Kune though. More than half the pupils in both parts of the school came in buses from Waiouru, Rangataua and Karioi to the south, or Pokaka and Horopito, milling settlements further up the line to the north, or from Raetihi, the neighbouring town about the same size as Ohakune and seven miles west. They arrived every morning in school buses driven by teacher-drivers who lived at the other end of the route. The teaching community spanned the district almost as widely as farmers and timber workers.

But for the first two or three years we didn't have a car, so our friends were mostly within walking distance. They made up a smaller community which grew close, almost tender; it seemed at times to have an enchantment cast over it, a spell that gave us size, glamour and authority, at least in our own eyes. Wherever we'd come from, here we were in this odd little high-country town, depended upon, asked for advice, expected to run its clubs and committees, yet free to do anything of our own that we could imagine and carry out. It was a bit like going up the mountain as far as the bushline – you came out into a high open place where you felt you could stride easily about the world, with nothing getting in your way.

The thing that appealed to us first was putting on a play. There was a defunct local drama club, a church hall for performance, a cause to support by holding a charity show. It was a project that suited us all; every teacher had the experience of dismal classrooms, no books or blackboards to speak of, no school library, no musical instruments, no pictures – and children bursting with eagerness to learn. Any extra funds we could offer could do nothing but good. We would enjoy the satisfaction of being benefactors along with the pleasures of self-display. The children we hoped to serve were a mixture of Chinese, Maori and European, bus children and walkers, many from large families which linked classes at every level: there was even a Maori girl who had two nieces in the class above her own.

As a preliminary skirmish we put on *The Long Weekend*, a smooth English farce which amused us so much that we suffered, as Lindsay and I had done in the Taradale Town Hall long ago, from a violent need to join the audience when it roared with laughter.

Once we had the scent of adventure in our nostrils we thought we'd do a bigger, better play and stage it in more commanding surroundings. The Majestic at the Junction was the aristocrat of the local halls – although rats had been seen running on its rafters (and once, to be honest, along the top of the piano). It was of huge size, had a stage and two dressing rooms, and seats which could be added to by borrowing blocks of old velveteen-backed seats from the picture theatre round the corner. It was mostly used for Friday and Saturday night dances but could be hired for shows. The cast took it for three nights in a row – a bold decision – in August. We'd been a year or two in the town, and had thoroughly learned the principle of belonging by enthusiastic detachment. The play we chose was Priestley's *Dangerous Corner* and the person we thought should produce it was Colin Hardie.

Colin was a teacher who'd come about the same time as we had, a fair-haired, stylish young man with an air of authority and a flair for impersonations and story-telling. He said he'd never acted nor had anything to do with play production, but nobody thought that mattered. He turned out to be capable and shrewd – and just authoritative enough to allow a headstrong cast to shape most of its own performances. The subdued elation that pervaded everything we did carried us through endless hours of evening rehearsals, even when we had all been up since before first light, and worked hard all day. Sometimes we met at our house, but for the later, stage rehearsals we found baby-sitters from among the teachers who, oddly, I thought, lacked my own consuming passion for the stage.

They all lived at Kings Court, an ancient, capacious barn of a boarding house set on a hill overlooking the railway station and the huddle of shops that constituted 'Junction' as distinct from 'Town'. They talked of Ma and Bert, the elderly couple who ran 'the Court', with a protective kindness, as though with the permanents, shivering in their freezing rooms in temperatures of 10 or even 20 below, they had common cause against the others, the casuals, who often sneaked out before breakfast to avoid paying their bill. In the evenings before the open fire in a tiny downstairs sitting room, Ma would chronicle their crimes to her friends, the teachers. There was an enormous coal range in the kitchen which everyone was sure would one day burn the whole place down (and one day, years later, it did).

As we had found in Dunedin, people who live in institutions in a cold climate are glad of friends with houses and fireplaces. Most of our wood was slab from one of the mills, delivered at the gate in truckloads, but we could also buy (or be given) 'real' wood from one of the outlying farms. This meant matai or, better still, maire, a dense grey timber that burned like coal. Sometimes on a clear night in those first winters I would go to the front door, stand for a moment on the front porch and look at the mountain, standing there beside me like a great menacing presence beneath a sky brilliant with stars. I almost believed it waited only for my back to be turned to move in and devour me. I would shudder and go inside, tempted, absurdly, to lock the door. The only predator was winter itself.

The play proceeded to its final stages. We began to try out costumes; someone went to Wanganui and bought stage make-up, so for the dress rehearsal we smeared ourselves with Number 5 or Number 9, greasy sticks smelling of sweat and dressing rooms. Then Colin announced he wasn't satisfied with the scream: this uttered in total darkness, was supposed to come out of the radio around which the characters were grouped when the curtain went up. He said we'd all better do one, and he'd choose the most bloodcurdling. This, it turned out, was mine. So, inflated with an unexpected and equivocal pride, from then on I screamed each night at eight o'clock. The play was a riotous success. That is to say, it had full houses all three nights, which had never been known before.

Chapter 26

My second baby was a girl. Raetihi Hospital was a very different proposition from the systematic Bethany, geared to the naming of days, almost of hours, according to their place in a faultless routine. This was a country hospital, small but comprehensive; all but the most serious cases (which were sent to Wanganui) it dealt with in its operating theatre, its 'general end' or its 'maternity end', so named because of the long thin shape of the building. It was a row of rooms, with the entrance, office and reception in the middle. When I lumbered in about nine o'clock on a hot Saturday night in February I found that the nurse who was to admit me was a plump and smiling Maori girl who'd turned fifteen and left school in December to do 'nurse-aiding'. Shy but firm, she told Trevor he need not stay, took me into the office and began to fill in my admission form. In the space for occupation she wrote 'housemaid'.

Reading it upside down, I took a moment to prepare a protest, and in that interval the grip of a labour pain put everything else out of my mind. I agreed readily to the bath and pubic shave that came next; indeed, I felt so knowledgeable about the whole experience after one experience of it that I was hardly even frightened, at least at first. As the pains grew in ferocity, however, it was impossible not to panic, and the night nurse's examination for 'dilation' – a word which sounded like ecstasy but was not – threw me into despair. How could my baby hope to emerge through an exit described as 'sixpence', or, after hours of effort, 'a shilling'? To make matters worse, I knew Dr Jordan was away on holiday; and that there were alarming rumours about the Raetihi man; it was said he was sometimes so drunk that the Sister on duty had to put him to bed for a few hours before he could perform an operation. I imagined my baby imprisoned for ever in its dark and slithery tunnel with the merest dot of light at the end, while I groaned and shrieked and the doctor snored on in the day room next door.

Instead, the sister on duty reprimanded me for making a noise and knocked me into silence with an ether mask, after which the doctor – a young locum – successfully delivered my baby. I woke up to a fine early Sunday morning and a little girl with a red face, an enormous mouth, beautifully shaped, and a loud and assertive cry. She had been born with a caul, part of the birth membrane, over her head, which nurses said was lucky, especially as a protection against drowning.

She was, I soon found, an insatiably hungry baby, much more restless than Virginia, more given to protest than to pondering. In her initial response, at least, to becoming a breathing waking sleeping organism, she was also a fighting one. I was utterly charmed by the stunning newness of her, the extraordinary actuality, the something-from-nothing miracle of her, all over again. A second child was every bit as magical as a first, and this was itself an amazing discovery. I did, however, have a slightly breathless sense, even in those first few days, of the enormity of introducing this rumbustious little creature into a household that fitted perfectly round the requirements of the three of us already there.

This hospital didn't care much when you got out of bed, so I did it straight away. They didn't think you had to stay with them for two weeks either, moving at a stately pace through every step of your recovery – indeed, they didn't think you'd been sick to start with. Neither did I, and within a week I was at the hospital door, Trevor was getting out of a borrowed car with a half-shy, half-eager small girl in a green gingham dress. 'That,' I said proudly to the sister holding the shawled bundle of my baby, 'is my daughter.' Delicious. It was true that I could have a million babies, cope with them all, love them all.

In the car Virginia said, 'Who is it?' 'Frances,' I told her. Naming had been easy; this name seemed always to have been there, as the graceful version of Fanny's much disliked 'Fanny'. Sometimes she'd asked us to change hers to Frances, at others she became Eliza, which we were embarrassed by, but used. Now Frances had that too, in its proper form, Elizabeth. We rode home exulting. The world outside the hospital, even after one week, looked startlingly fresh and alive, the mountain blue and bare for summer, except for the white streaks of its glaciers; the farms along the Raetihi were a good green, their rows of stumps like streets of small dark buildings across them. Even the grey unpainted shacks of the Pakahi mill looked picturesque that fine morning.

Our own house formed the nucleus of this whole, a central cell in the body of the land, charged for us now with the meanings of familiarity. The pattern of our lives came vividly into my mind as we drove towards it down our quiet, shingly road. There was Trevor who concentrated on the History and English he taught to everyone from Form 3 to 6A; he had several units of English in his degree and no History, but it was History he liked. Most of his evenings were spent marking or planning or 'reading round' the subject. On Friday afternoons he and his friend Murray went to the Pioneer Club for what they called a few end-of-the-week beers. No one was used to drinking, and there was a good deal of fuss about this ritual; Murray made self-conscious jokes, Trevor pretended he didn't really want to go but thought it good for 'colleague relations'. I considered this a laughable lie and said so. However, fuss or not, they continued to go with unshakeable regularity, and gradually attracted Colin and Leo and some others to what I crossly called their boys' party.

My days were spent in the washing, cleaning, ironing, sewing, cooking that my household demanded. Virginia was a clever and talkative two-year-old who explained most of her games to me as she played them – indeed we played them together, though I drew the line at squatting in the sandpit. (We had furnished this with bags of sand from the Wangaehu, or sulphur stream, at Tangiwai, halfway to Karioi; it smelt of sulphur still.)

Occasionally in the afternoons I had tea with a group of women who also had small children. I regarded these events wryly – I was pleased to have friends, but their visits were alarmingly like Fanny's ladies' afternoons long ago in Greenmeadows. I remembered the knocks at the door, the formal smiles – 'Good afternoon Mrs Scott, Good afternoon Mrs . . . ' – the unashamed competitiveness of the conversations about children. I worried that I too had become a routine housewife, who simply reproduced predictable habits in a later generation.

Surely I had different purposes, a more modern outlook and principles? I was, for instance, fanatically opposed to Virginia eating a crumb of the cakes and sweet food these afternoon tea visits produced. The peanut brownies, lamingtons, iced orange cake and so on that we had prepared and eaten at Greenmeadows I now knew were bad for children's teeth and health. Other children out to afternoon tea might gorge and wallow, mine would not. Only after a long spell of this enforced austerity did I notice one day that as the time to eat approached Virginia began to whimper forlornly. I was suddenly horrified to see that the only effect of my scruples was to make her feel unjustly excluded from the normal pleasures of other children. I hastily changed the rules.

Sometimes I went to meetings. I learned from Kay, who was Plunket and district nurse all in one, of the frustration of visiting families who knew nothing of child health and nutrition and cared less, and were resistant to all advice. She told me hair-raising tales of babies nourished by (or at least fed on) beer and fish and chips, kept up in smoky rooms till parents went to bed, sharing food with dogs and cats and even sheep. The more money her committee of parents raised, the more books, pamphlets and pictures for teaching parents she could provide. I joined the Plunket committee, and while Trevor marked essays and Virginia slept I went to the Plunket Rooms, five minutes walk away, for serious and even momentous deliberations. Policy, salaries, care for frail babies, worried mothers. I found instead that almost the entire evening was spent in loving concentration upon the question of sandwich fillings for the jumble sale on an approaching Saturday. Back and forth the urgent assertions snapped and rattled. Cucumber . . . too slippery . . . egg . . . smelly if hard-boiled . . . ham, too tame . . . what about mincing? It couldn't stop, I gradually realised, because a night out is a Night Out when Dad minds the kids, and these end (as Dad had often proved) around midnight.

I went home and wrote a story about small-town life; the next day I typed it on a borrowed school typewriter and sent it to the *Listener*, which published it a few weeks later. In one swoop my vague and uncertain literary ambitions cohered, became a solid, accomplished fact. Yet this was not somehow good enough; was the story too close to reality to count as genuine fiction? Or was it that funny? Did funniness not count? There was something unrealised about this first success which prevented my exulting as I might have expected.

But in any case there it was, our Ohakune life. And I was about to change it by introducing a tiny but already vociferous new person. I began a series of elaborate games designed to satisfy the urgent hungers of a new baby and convince a two-year-old that this was no more than an exciting extension of the fantasy play that already filled her days. I probably (and characteristically) went to so much trouble to prove that the arrival of an outsider made no difference that the real changes took an unnecessarily long time. But of course they occurred. We became a family of four. I increased my speed through the necessary daily work; sometimes I ran out to the clothesline, ran back again; I devised games to lure Virginia away from the sleeping baby; I bought a cane seat in which she could ride on the end of the pram when we went out. I learned to grab a scrap of sleep, wake, grab another. In the afternoons when both children slept I brought out my folder of untidy pages and wrote bits of poems or stories; sometimes I too fell asleep in the middle. Then friends would call in and I'd make tea, answer the phone. At night I sewed, making clothes for all four of us, though I didn't get beyond shirts and pyjamas for Trevor.

One afternoon I came home from town with my cargo of shopping and children to find Fanny and Lewis waiting at the gate. I was dismayed, disbelieving – was this their caravan parked on the road? When had they . . . how was it that . . . why did they not tell us? They said coolly that they'd booked in at the camping ground – a charming place – and would come and spend each day with me. Fanny smiled, innocently proud of their subterfuge; Lewis looked a little more subdued. And I – well, for the first time in my life I was so absolutely furious with my mother I could not speak. I stared at them as at alien creatures; they might have been standing upside down, for all I recognised the habits of normal human beings. 'Come inside,' I said finally, with a pinched formality, and Frances mercifully began to cry.

We survived the visit, naturally. Fanny thought I should not put rubbish in a carton in the kitchen, that I didn't look after myself; she bought me a towel for my exclusive use, and especially not for the children's baths. I continued to seethe. A lifetime's training in not allowing her to become hurt or upset kept me from quarrelling with her – but only just. This was the first time we'd met at my house, not hers; it was a revelation. I saw an unexpected and disturbing image of her – a woman encompassed about by protections and privilege, a wall which I myself had helped to construct. On the morning they left I mumbled something about warning me of future visits, but Lewis quickly broke in 'Are you comfortable dear?' as he helped her into the car.

Why had they come? I supposed that with John at university and Lewis often away, Fanny had reconsidered her own survival and decided she too must take to the road. Later in the year they did so more dramatically and went to Australia.

You had to admit they were an enterprising pair. Ever since Fiji, Lewis's programme of duties and desires had been 'care for Fanny, work, make enough money to travel, find a new place . . . ' After Australia it was to be Africa. Their method of travelling was unconventional but perfectly suited to their requirements – they carried their own food, bought a cheap van in which they could sleep, and moved or stopped exactly as it suited Fanny's condition and their neatly matched enthusiasm for the new and strange.

Long and compelling letters began to arrive. For Fanny herself these were half-conscious writing practice. With greater solitude she had become more serious and systematic about her recording, speculating, fabricating on paper. She and I had begun to exchange 'bits' and to agree in letters that one must work carefully on each, looking out for the 'creeping paralysis of sentimentality'.

At the end of the year, as we prepared as usual to go to Pyes Pa for Christmas, I felt an obscure discomfort. Fanny's unheralded visit had left me with a sense of injustice, of something out of balance. She had entered my territory, the place where my authority counted, and she had failed to recognise or understand it. It was a question of sovereignty – that which had always been unquestionably hers and now, in my newer, younger household, was mine. I was not used to criticising my mother, and did not like the jangling effect of breaking old loyalties; but there was no way back to the simple, single vision of her I had for so long preserved.

However, Pyes Pa was still the best place to go for the holidays, and Fanny was still excellent company. It was possible to put aside for the time being the new complexities in my view of her. By Christmas we were all there. In mid-December it was already a perfect summer. Day after day the mist in the valley rose slowly to clear the Mount, its blue triangle framed in nearer trees, the young birches Lewis had planted at the edge of the lawn by Fanny's red hot pokers. We sat on her verandah or on the grass, we picked early plums in the orchard, talked, joked, laughed, slightly performing ourselves as we had done so many times before.

Everything in its moment of fullest flowering promises to live for ever. Fanny had broken the tie of her illness by proving she could travel and master at least one of the arts of solitude, in her writing (and it was an art – she still didn't think seriously of trying to get her work published). Lewis, after reading and dreaming of his utopia for years, was actually building it in this ripe land, the first he had ever chosen; all the other addresses, even the Greenmeadows house which he'd taken over from his parents, had been accidental. Fulfilment for both of them meant having their children at home, with the wives, husbands, friends they cared to bring with them. I don't think either of them really believed that we might come to have other homes, more important to us than the one we'd grown up in. At the same time it was extra proof, if any were needed, of the fruitfulness of the family, that we had acquired partners who came with us. In his heart Lewis was an ancient tribal patriarch still, self-effacing and tentative though he might be when faced with the concentrated volubility of the crowd.

One by one – or two by two, and in our case four together – we left to go home for the beginning of the school year. Even John had to leave in January because Alison, the pretty girlfriend he had brought with him, had to go back to Wellington for a summer course at her dental nurse school and he had lab work to do. Our departures marked the end, though we didn't know it, of that young, complete, exquisitely optimistic and internally fragile family we had all helped to fashion. Within weeks of our going Lewis, sitting on the verandah one afternoon, was gripped by a violent pain in the stomach. It went away, and he did not ask the reason for a long time (what would orthodox doctors know anyway?). By the time he did, the diagnosis was cancer of the bowel too far advanced for an operation to be possible, though there was an almost certain cure for cases identified early enough.

Would he have agreed to an operation? Clive, who went with him to see the surgeon, said yes. It was one of the tragedies of their blind faith in unorthodoxy, his and Fanny's, that it kept them from other useful knowledge. Both were inclined by taste and temperament towards extremes, but they also lacked a milieu which might have encouraged a broader view. In 1951 'natural living' was still the pursuit of eccentrics or cranks.

Towards the end of the year Lindsay and Doug moved, as we had, from the city to a small town – in their case Wairoa and a job at Wairoa College. Fanny and Lewis visited them and Lewis painted and renovated a temporary shack for them so they could sell it and move into a house, necessary because Lindsay was pregnant. He 'didn't feel worth a tin of fish' and could work only slowly; a local doctor advised him about a special diet, consisting mainly of grapes, which was said to have miraculous effects in arresting cancer. In our usual way, we all went on believing that this, or something else, would succeed and he would recover. We had by then lived with Fanny's illness for several years, and maintained our high morale by a mixture of 'positive thinking', evasiveness, the peculiarly convincing (through frail) optimism our family specialised in. To the extent that our confidence rested on principle, it wasn't changed by the threat of a different disease – though I, at least, had moments of being shaken by a more acute fear than I had ever felt about tuberculosis.

In the meantime, we had a modest crisis of our own. At the end of 1951 the wayward and abstracted Mr Cook decided to leave Ohakune and take a job in a larger Auckland school.

The chief consequence for us was that the new man wanted the school house rather than George McCullough's farmhouse, which we would now have to move into. In some ways this was tempting. It stood on a hill far back from the Miro Hill road, and connected to it by a long curving track. It was close to the Junction, within sound of its noisy night trains, and had a wide view of the surrounding country. It was the 'real country' aspect I liked – all those hills to wander about on, the whole recovered world of grassy places and high quiet sky which had slipped away from me with my childhood.

The reality was, of course, not at all like that. The drive, as we euphemistically called it, was made of rough metal, some stones almost boulder size, and pushing my pram with its double load through the loose piles of stones and patches of puddly mud, always uphill (it managed to have hills at both ends, with a dip in the middle), was a grunting, shoving struggle. Once out of the gate I had to walk a mile to town, less to the Junction, but that hill was so steep it didn't seem worth it. Anyway, one corner dairy and Chan's fruit shop could hardly serve all our needs. The hills rising about the house, which was fenced in on a section of flat land to keep the stock out, were indeed grassy and pleasant, but this wasn't a rustic idyll either. Our lavatory, a tin can in a little outhouse, emptied by the night-cart man, was a hundred yards from the house round the shoulder of a spur. George McCullough had a bouncy young bull, and although it wasn't supposed to be there, sometimes it was, and I had to run for my life – or thought I did – to get back to the house. It would have butted not killed me – but butting was bad enough.

Frances continued to be a turbulent baby. She began to crawl months earlier than my books about 'normal' development said she would, shooting about the floor on her stomach in a sort of swimming action, much faster than the usual baby. I made all her clothes with stout patches of drill or calico covering the front. She ate everything in sight but seemed scarcely to sleep at all; when she was displeased she made the most dramatic scenes I had ever witnessed, throwing herself about with an abandonment that looked like flying. When she cried hard she went down and down the scale till she lost her breath, went deadly pale and actually became unconscious for a moment before she took an instinctive breath and began to revive. Other mothers told me that this recovering breath had to happen, and she would always be safe, but each time I was in mortal terror that she would disappear out the end of this fatal spiral and never breathe again.

At the same time, and perhaps for the same temperamental reasons, she was a little clown. She and Virginia shaped and lived in a magical make-believe world which, changing as they grew, nourished, taught and entertained them for most of their childhood. They 'were' everyone in turn – Trevor putting his books and lunch on the back of his bike and pedalling off to school; George McCullough, stout and peremptory, lecturing us from the fence on Saturdays; Margaret, the tall, gentle, auburn-haired girl Murray brought to see us just before he married her; most mortifyingly, me on the phone talking and laughing ('ho, ho, ho,') or scolding them with a noise like an enraged dragon. Virginia often began the game or the character, Frances picked it up and made it melodrama. One day Frances on her own conceived and performed the voice and walk of a woman we hardly knew, a Mrs Murdie. She was tall and angular with big feet and a gravelly voice; Frances' act was so exact and so funny that Virginia, sitting at their small table – we were out in the sun by the back door – laughed so hard she fell right off her chair. Another day Frances, chasing flies, as she was not supposed to do, climbed on to the table by the window in the kitchen-dining room, took a leap and crashed through the glass, landing bruised and bleeding on the concrete path below. There was no denying she had a flair for crises.

As for parenthood, that pungent experience, it seemed I couldn't have enough of it. For most of Frances' second year I was pregnant again. There were other events, too, new friends, changed habits. The farmhouse was much further away from the school, not so many people dropped in, there were afternoons when I could write, even for short spells. I always put my papers away when the children reappeared after a sleep or rest, and I did not of course consider talking to Trevor about an urge that felt even to me like a secret vice. Not that he would have disapproved – I could do what I liked in any spaces I could find in the mother-housekeeper routine – but after all what was there to say? 'I want to become a real writer and these snatches are a kind of practice . . . ' Oh? Harbouring a secret ambition? He would have been pleasant, and missed the point. Fanny was the only one who loved doing it for itself, as I did, and so was easy to talk to.

And ambition? Nobody would or could disagree that my main occupation was fully formed; I liked it, the career ambitions in the family were Trevor's entirely. If I had suggested these left me out – which I didn't for a moment think of doing – he would have been shocked. Of course it was all for me too, for us all, the long hours spent talking to the teachers, the weekends coaching sports teams and taking them on trips, the evenings of marking. And the work was valuable. For his own pleasure? No, no, not that; for everyone's, for the family's.

In the time we managed to spend together we mostly swapped news – the children, school – or we sorted out practicalities, money (there was never enough), a broken tap washer, rats from the barn appearing in the kitchen. A new school was being built to house the secondary department of the district high school and prepare it to translate, as they called it, into a full high school. The new senior assistant was a small man with a sharp intelligence, a lined, frowning face and a talent for creating tensions, problems and arguments out of the simplest situations. We began to have 'Friday nights' at our house when the men leaving the club gathered up their wives, if they had them, and came to fulminate about the catastrophes that proliferated round Mr Perry. At first these gatherings were occasional and casual, but they gradually became institutionalised; I would make bacon and egg pies or 'cheese and onion' (a dish traditional in the Scott family). It was part of the system that we ate predictable food as the group settled down to its litanies of indignation. The children had a part in it too; they ate 'Friday dinner', a wholesome concoction of vegetables in cheese sauce, and went to bed early.

As these evenings became more heavily conditioned by teachers' rage and their urge for more recognition and better jobs, I came to feel a great boredom with this single inescapable topic. But at first having a crowd was a pleasure, and some individuals became my real friends. Murray's companion Margaret I found fresh and surprising to talk to. Murray travelled to Ohakune by driving the school bus and Margaret and I began to exchange long and companionable visits of our own. She, in her angular, unexpected, often amusing way, admitted that the Friday celebrations by the men at the club were not to her taste either – as though it was only men who 'worked' and so must have such weekly release. Well, evenings at home would help (neither of us thought we had the slightest power to change the thing itself); she began to come early so we were in it together.

She had class too, my new friend. We might enjoy these tart exchanges, but she would no more have embarked on mere gossip about our husbands than my fastidious mother, who had taught me such a precise (not to say prissy) distinction between 'analytical' talk and malice. This interesting subject, the subtle juggling of loyalty and self-interest in conversation about friends, was not one I could explore with Trevor. His distinctions were quite different from mine. In talking about 'the boss', the unfortunate Mr Perry, every excess was justified, indeed was part of a code connecting teachers who were banded together in being under his authority. Minute observations about other members of the human race did not greatly interest him; his friends were teachers, divided into camps of 'us' or 'them' according to their loyalty and co-operativeness on the job. Not that he didn't look for fun and flavour in the personalities round him, as I did, but his group were mates because they worked together, hated the boss, supported one another, knew the same pupils, planned the same projects.

Friendship for me was something else. I had learnt it early in a family that quite extravagantly laid itself open to the scrutiny of its own members. We had really shared one another, felt a passionate responsibility to know 'how it was' for the others in the family. My urgent anxieties about Clive in the period of his early experimental love affairs, his own desire to draw me into them, the copious revelations I had sent to Fanny in my student letters, the equally detailed accounts she in turn wrote for me, now she travelled to new places, indeed the casual assumption that we might all read one another's letters whoever they were from; all this was part of a pattern of intense personal awareness I had grown up with. It had been the basis of my first important friendship, the glowing partnership of my two years with Molly in our

191

beastly little student hostel room; now I transferred it to new relationships.

Where was my marriage in all this? I didn't know. The adult solitude and small-child companionship that made up the main part of my days I usually found no fault with. My little girls were a delicious pair, my pregnancy burdensome but bearable; I had some time to do my precious writing, though this was small, and diminished as Virginia and even Frances outgrew a daytime sleep. Trevor and I continued to be partners, lovers, parental colleagues; we were, as our friends said, a happy couple.

But there were undoubtedly shifts and alterations, subterranean changes of emphasis in our shared lives that showed so little on the surface that it was easy not to recognise them. I had occasional spells of deep melancholy that seemed to have no cause. There were things to worry about, of course – Frances when she began to walk was so bandy-legged that I, and even the doctor, thought she had a bone defect (till an X-ray proved otherwise); Lewis, despite the resolute cheerfulness of Fanny's letters, and their undimmed faith in natural healing with the right diet, seemed no better; Trevor's unwritten thesis hung over us, a vague malaise. But my periods of misery seemed not to be connected with any of these. I talked to Trevor who tried as always to be helpful and kind: I should do more, join the newly revived Drama Club, the Parent Teacher Association, better still the Community Arts Service . . . It's true we were both willing to take our part in the ubiquitous club and committee life of the town, and I wasn't against such advice, indeed I took it. But the dark spells recurred all the same. Sometimes at night I cried long and silently, without relief.

Was there a kind of loneliness in spending almost all one's time with small children, delightful as they were? Or, underneath my eagerness to belong, did I actually find Ohakune an isolated, dull, cramping place? Was my marriage doing what good marriages should do – whatever that was? Who could tell. Certainly I had tried, unsuccessfully of course, to persuade Trevor to move back to Wellington, and had once taken a day or two to stay with Clive and Dorothy and look at possible houses. And I did know there was something I obscurely wanted and could not expect from my school-obsessed husband, with his cheerfully unsubtle distinctions about the good and bad in the way human creatures behaved. Even our physical intimacy, enjoyable though it was, sometimes left me feeling stranded and alone. At the same time, he was wonderfully interesting and well informed when it came to more public affairs. My knowledge of political events, their history and significance, was always vague; his was precise, packed with revealing facts, authoritative. He was becoming a specially admired History teacher, and I could see why.

Contradictions. Mixtures. A room full of ill-matched furniture, but drawn together, for me, as if through fine muslin at its window, by my lifelong training in 'positive thinking'. I admitted nothing. On the contrary, I was always keen to defend the domestic vocation. One of the pleasant consequences of Mr Perry's arrival was that his wife turned out to be funny, shrewd, likeable. She was a good actress and largely responsible for the resurgence of the Drama Club; she was more forthright than anyone else I'd known about the sacrifice women were expected to make. 'You give everything up for the kids, and then when they get older and don't need you, everyone complains you don't have enough interests of you own to keep you from being neurotic.' I liked the savour of that, but thought her different from me. Years older, anyway.

There was a younger friend, though, with the same idea, and on her I urged a resolute and if possible cheerful acceptance of the dilemma. This was Shannon, new girlfriend and then wife of Leo, one of our friends among the teachers. She had come to work in the school dental clinic, boarded at Kings Court like everyone else, met Leo and in no time they were engaged. She was slight, dark-eyed and had a nervous, intelligent refinement that I found very appealing. I also enjoyed the sensation she gave me of being depended on for the insights of my greater experience, and this took on a thrilling dimension when she asked me if they could hold their wedding party at our house. She had fallen out with her mother, largely because Leo was neither a Catholic nor of a satisfactory social class. I was overcome. Such grandeur, such august responsibility!

And the party? It could be said to be a success. The bride and groom, both darkly beautiful, discreetly radiant, talked and laughed among their celebrating friends. Children, fed forbidden delicacies, hovered about on the fringes. All as it should be, merry as a marriage bell. The farmhouse living-room, not a spacious place, somehow fitted everyone in among its flowers and ashtrays (of course we all smoked). But there was one guest as ill-fitting as a wolf among teddy bears. Shannon's mother. Talking to her, even seeing her there in my room, made me frantically uncomfortable, yet I admired her spirit in coming at all. It was the more remarkable in that I knew how conventional she was. Submitting to being my guest when by every rule she knew I should be hers, she looked miserable, stiff. But she stuck it out. I didn't know anything about the pains of being an older parent, but I thought hers a performance to be remembered.

There was a rather flimsy little cottage about halfway down our drive; Leo and Shannon negotiated the rent with George McCullough and decided to live there. She and I, it turned out, were good at being both friends and neighbours. She looked after my little girls, I lent her all our books (she read much faster than I did); we amused each other in talk on many subjects. Sometimes we sat together on the top of the hill at the back of the farm while the children played in the sun, and considered the state of being married but without either a job or children – she did not yet have any – and what made it so unexpectedly difficult.

Another summer came, Christmas, January, long hot days to carry my fat body through. Then in the middle of that quiet month, when all duty and obligation was in abeyance and everyone we knew was away at the beach, I had my baby, and it was a boy. Enormous (over nine pounds), healthy, beautiful – and a boy, a boy! So Trevor greeted him – I had had no idea he so distinguished between fatherhood of daughters and sons, and was dismayed by it, though I too was exuberant at having achieved both sexes in the same family. Our son, if we had one, was to be Christopher, but by now we were tired of that idea and called him Martin. And John, after John.

He was a baby on the Virginia model rather than the more vocal and obstreperous Frances one. Plump and peaceful, he ate and slept as if, I sometimes remarked to the others, he was already used to being a baby and knew how to do it. All the pride and excitement at the new existence of a still unknown little creature flooded through me again – the astonishment that a human being there had never been before was now in the world, breathing its air, beginning to focus eyes, ears and brain on the limitless range of its possibilities. However, I no longer marvelled quite as I had that this could happen to me, that this incredible force could work through my body, use my blood and cells and nerve tissues and bones. I knew it could.

Confirmation was sweet, though, and with it came something else

– the discovery that a baby born into a family is everyone's. In their way Virginia and Frances were as delighted as I – Trevor too, with the extra dash of male posturing he didn't try to hide. That summer we had a very good vegetable garden – late of course, in a place of interminable winters and short hot summers – and a row of broad beans was still yielding its crop of furry green pods. I would spread a rug on my small lawn and in the homely shade cast by the bean plants Martin waved his minute arms and legs, while I did sporadic weeding and the two little girls made up the universe with their inexhaustible pretending games.

At my post-natal check-up Dr Jordan said my large baby had caused an abdominal rupture and I would have to go back to hospital to have it repaired. And so when Martin was six months old we were installed, the pair of us, in the 'general end' at Raetihi Hospital, and my permanently smiling baby commenced a week's programme of charming the nurses. Not wanting to have breast feeding disrupted by a general anaesthetic, I asked for 'the needle' and was given several. Not enough, though, to prevent the surgeon's knife sending a shiver of shock and pain through me as it whistled down my middle. From then on I watched the action reflected in a large gleaming light suspended above the operating table. A messy business it looked too, as blood was mopped up from time to time as though with an old dishrag. 'Do you want your navel?' Dr Jordan had asked at the beginning. 'Yes please,' I'd humbly replied, and so, somewhat crumpled, it was put back in place when the stitching up was done.

It was the August holidays and Trevor, who had a reputation among our friends for being able to take over household and children when needed, came and brought the two shy and shining little girls to visit me. They were dressed in their matching blue cotton tunics and red and white striped blouses that I had recently finished making, and my heart stopped when I saw these two little creatures, so inextricably woven into everything I thought and did. I suddenly couldn't bear to stay away from home for another minute.

We had our first car by then, a small second-hand Hillman bought on easy terms from the Edmond motor showroom in Hamilton. Home again, I learned to drive. We would ask Leo or Shannon or one of our friends from 'the Court' to baby-sit for an hour or so while I weaved up and down the roads between town and Junction in the dusk, then in full darkness, and Trevor sitting beside me tried (and failed), to be patient with my ineptness. 'For Godsake watch the paint!' he'd shout as I careered along, scraping into blackberry bushes at the side of the road. Mostly I mumbled apologies, but in the end there was a kind of reckoning. 'I won't do any more,' I declared, 'or if I do, someone else can teach me.' But that would be worse – what might a stranger allow to happen to the new treasure? He promised to be more forbearing. When I went to get my licence I drove a mile or two along Lakes Road, turned a corner, answered a question about the right hand rule, paid five shillings, and was henceforth a legal driver.

But going abroad in daylight was an alarming business, not because I couldn't drive, but because the world on both sides of the road, instead of being a wall of silent darkness, was full of distractions – animals, houses, people, noises, not to mention the cars that loomed and roared on the road itself. Of course we were lucky to own a car at all – many of our friends could not afford such a luxury. We could do so because the Edmond family business in Hamilton permitted cars to be sold to family members at special prices. Visiting Trevor's family, we would drive to Hamilton where his two brothers and his parents, now retired, all lived. My favourite among these Edmond relatives was Don's wife, who seemed to share something of my view of the world; but we were all parents of young families – there was much to talk about.

All three families lived in comfortable, carpeted houses adorned with domestic conveniences like clothes driers and refrigerators. Business was clearly the life, materially speaking. Coming back to Ohakune after holidays in Pyes Pa and Hamilton, I was struck by the comparative primitiveness of our mountain village circumstances. The weather was always colder (it could snow even in summer, and rain could gather and fall round the mountain when the whole of the rest of the country was having a heat wave), the farmhouse was old and small, our furniture cheap and in some cases rudimentary. Some of the cupboards were forty-pound apple boxes which Trevor had nailed together and I had covered with gingham, including a gathered curtain to provide a door. But of course it was home, and I was glad to be there.

Money. Ah, money, that pervasive pest. Ours was like a pallid and lugubrious guest, always hanging about the house looking miserable, chronically hungry but never strong enough to do anything useful. We kept making plans to liven it up, and some of them worked. The *Wanganui Chronicle* for instance. Trevor knew several borough councillors, and indeed was interested in practical politics at that level himself. One had told him that the *Chronicle* wanted more coverage of events in Ohakune and asked if one or both of us might like to write for them. We would, by God we would. We could hardly wait to start. A pound a column represented riches indeed. Bad for literary style, I told Trevor because the more we puffed up our reports with useless words the more we earned. As it turned out I, who cared more about this hazard, proved the better puffer-up; I was sometimes ashamed of my over-decorated effusions about the Tennis Club's annual meeting, or the Council Works Committee meeting, each extending satisfyingly far down its column and rich in pointless and irrelevant speculation.

The *Chronicle* car delivered the papers at the corner dairy at the Junction every morning at about six o'clock, and the driver then picked up our copy, which at some time during the night one of us had delivered. You had to slip it into the crack where a metal plate advertising AMP Insurance didn't quite connect with the verandah post at the corner of the pavement. Finishing a report late at night and then walking over the hill in the quiet dark, lights out in the few houses and the only sound a muffled shunting from the station, was one of my pleasures. I always wanted to be the one to go.

Chapter 27

'The Latest T.B. Miracle Drugs: New Hope for T.B. Sufferers . . . Since the disappointments of streptomycin therapy, the discovery of new drugs brings fresh hope . . . The latest drugs are derivatives of the B vitamin family – iso-nicotinic acid . . . '

In July 1952 a four-page article, carefully documented, appeared in the *Mirror*; Fanny and Lewis had taken the journal for years because its editor was a Social Crediter, or at least a monetary reformer. When the article appeared we devoured it as eagerly as if we had always subscribed to conventional medical principles. Fanny too. Did Lewis's illness raise doubts in her mind about her own independence from hospitals and doctors? It must have, surely – but for the time being she said only that a cure was wonderful to think about. She would find out more. There was less joy, I thought, a bit less conviction, in the way they had begun to talk of the natural life as the key to perfect health. Even when Fanny had first talked of the grape cure for cancer, she cried. They were staying with us, a planned and welcome visit this time, and were installed in 'the annexe', a furnished Army hut set up near the farmhouse back door. I put my arms round her, murmured he'd be 'all right', but we were both very frightened.

Perhaps that was where it began, the habit of doubting our own optimism, the positive thinking (talking, anyway), though we could not give it up, it had been there too long. Lindsay and I, at Pyes Pa for the summer, asked each other wonderingly if one diet or another was really making Lewis 'stronger all the time', but since he didn't complain and continued to garden and cook, though perhaps more slowly, it was hard to know.

John was home with the graceful Alison, apparently more securely his girlfriend than ever; Lindsay and Doug had their first baby, Evan, with them. He was already a year old; so was Clive and Dorothy's Karen. Every day so much happened that was newly remarkable in the assembled families that it was easy to suppose that nothing could really be wrong. Nothing serious, you'd tell yourself, as tumbling babies and busy and excitable parents dashed about everywhere. John had finished his BSc with his usual brilliant marks, and had a scholarship to go on to a Masters degree; he was talking about extracting and studying the poison tutu, the native plant you were never allowed to touch, though it grew freely on banks and hillsides. Alison had brought photos of them both, taken at balls and parties with groups of friends, laughing; John playing billiards with other students, the two of them on a farm somewhere, staying with friends. John's shyness, that old worry about him as the late rather frail, lonely child – all was dissipated by this picture of vigorous normality in a friendly student crowd. We took photos of them ourselves, in the garden, picking plums and feijoas in the orchard, playing tennikoit.

Anyone coming to visit us – Percy for instance, who like John was home for the holidays – could only be reassured that we were as healthy and happy as always before. But this was the last summer we were ever to spend in that house of the open windows and wide verandahs, that enchanted garden. By the end of the following year the Eastlakes were looking after Pyes Pa, John had been diagnosed as having TB too, and Lewis was dead.

During the last eight or nine months of his life we – and he – slowly came to terms with the realities of his condition and in the end talked openly about it, though I could never do this without helpless tears. I was pregnant again for most of 1953, and in July Lewis came alone to Ohakune. He wanted to make a last bid for help from one of the natural health experts, Ulric Williams, who ran his own hospital in Wanganui. The first evening he spent in our house was extraordinarily poignant. He was thin, quite shrunken, yet everything he said was alight with the mild kindliness he'd always shown; he sat with his square hands in his lap and asked questions about the children. He found it hard to eat, even a Chinese gooseberry I sliced, and could swallow only a mouthful. He had an obvious swelling in the lower part of his body.

'We're alike,' he said to me with his crooked smile, 'you're bulging too.' I sat still and willed myself not to cry.

The next morning Trevor drove him down the Parapara road to Wanganui. 'The poplars will be over,' I said as they left. When we took that road in late autumn the poplars were wonderful, marching over the hills like golden battalions. Now it was winter, on the way to Wanganui it rained, mist obscured the spurs. But it was the journey back that was really grim. Dr Williams had said he could not admit Lewis because he was 'too close to being a bed-patient', and driving north with Trevor at the end of that day Lewis came at last to the end of his optimism. He arrived pale and drawn.

'It's a long way,' he said, and told me over and over, as though it would make sense of things. 'He would have taken me, but he doesn't take bed-patients.'

In August that year I went to Pyes Pa on my own. One day Fanny came into my room to put his washed brush and comb on the window-sill to dry.

'It's all I can do for him,' she said despairingly, 'this, and learn about bills and money. We say I'm his secretary, as though it's funny.'

In the bed on the big verandah, round the corner from Fanny, and their shared bed, he talked to me, saying at last what must have been in his mind for a whole lifetime. That he wished he'd known us better, hadn't worked so hard and missed so much of what happened at home, hadn't been so shy. He said sixty was too young to die; he couldn't understand why this should happen to him when he'd been so careful about his health. (One question nobody could ask was about his long exposure to lead in his home-mixed and, more recently, hand-sprayed paint.) We would have to look after Fanny; we were not to be sad, he would stay with us, in our minds, in our dreams.

Bowed down too by regret for time and opportunity not under-stood, not grasped, and now lost for ever, I could make no answer.

On the way home I failed to recognise Ohakune station and was carried, ridiculously, on to Waiouru, where I had to wait for a midday goods train to take me back. Lewis, who had painted so many railway stations that he had accumulated a comprehensive lore about them, would have enjoyed my dilemma, but it was already too late to tell him. I had said goodbye.

He died in October. Clive and Dorothy stayed with him for the last week, and Trevor and Doug went for the funeral. Lindsay and I were both pregnant, and Fanny insisted it would be too distressing for us. Through that day I worked as usual, played when necessary, but later I lay awake in the dark and struggled to grasp the remorseless finality of my father's death. The months, indeed years, of illness were, I saw, no preparation at all. The shock of the event itself was as great as if I'd had no warning. Lewis, dead, was so inexpressibly different from Lewis alive, even if ill, that I could not make my mind take it in.

There was one eccentricity of my father's that, even in our grief, we all found truly bizarre. Not wanting to leave the money he'd earned, and kept for us, to be diminished by death duties or other taxes, he had sealed in tins, then buried, a large amount of cash – several thousand pounds. Fanny alone knew where HT (Hidden Treasure) was, and when Clive had brought it inside (musty-smelling but otherwise undamaged), together they counted the notes and banked them. Each of us was given our share. We made a great many jokes about HT, I suppose to express, or conceal, our embarrassment at such a legacy – so affectionately planned, so queerly executed. I spent mine on a piano.

John had graduated in May; he and Alison had been to Graduation Ball, got mildly drunk, danced, romped about at parties for most of the night (student couples drank together, it seemed, but did not go home to the same address after a night out). Not long afterwards, having a routine X-ray, John discovered he had 'a shadow' on one lung. He was boarding with Clive and Dorothy, having finished the three years allowed in Weir House. Already he kept stricter rules about healthy eating than anyone else in the family; now he decided to go on an all-milk diet, recommended in a book he'd read. Alison approved, so did Dorothy. But he was still not satisfied, and took leave from his MSc work to go to Pyes Pa and embark on a total health programme. During the last months of Lewis's illness he lived at home, reading a great deal, especially on the subject of new approaches to TB. He meditated, ate alone, began a long correspondence with a Dr Benjamin, an American expert on natural cures. He seemed curiously remote and silent. He had always had the irrepressible laugh I associated with the Price uncles, that wonderful helpless cascade of joyful shouts. Not now. He barely smiled. He was like a person who'd buried his real self so deeply nobody could find it, not even himself.

Alison had finished her training at the dental school and taken a job in Taumarunui. She visited the family in August but left early, looking puzzled and sad. During 1954 the Pyes Pa house was sold. Fanny bought a large house in Lower Hutt, had it altered to make a flat for herself and John, and Clive and Dorothy and their family moved into the rest. Clive had become a skilled and imaginative photographer, and when the chance came he left teaching and bought a school photographer's business. He had Lewis's canniness and flair, also his limitless capacity for work; he set about building a lucrative business.

John improved; an X-ray plate showed his 'shadow' had all but disappeared. His spirits lifted too, he went back, part-time, to his work on 'toot', as everyone called his poisonous plant. With no one to help her, Fanny decided at long last that the time had come to try the new drugs. She went into Ewart, the TB ward of Wellington Public Hospital.

At home we had other preoccupations. In February 1953 Virginia started school and Frances had her third birthday party. I noted in an intermittently kept diary that she was 'utterly overcome' to discover that every parcel was for her. 'She quite rends my heart at times, she's such a radiant little creature when happy, but so many things upset her beyond words.' Virginia loved school. She learned to read . . . 'throws herself about in a paroxysm of pleasure when it comes home to her that HERE COMES JOHN really *means* here comes John . . . '

We went to Wanganui for a day . . . 'Marty is a little nugget far too heavy to carry'. Back home he 'spends hours creeping up and down steps, having just learned to do so . . . appears smiling in doorways . . . Yesterday when Virginia came home from school Frances and Martin were in the sandpit and their two faces radiant with greeting would have warmed the heart of any home-comer – certainly V was pleased, and dropped her raincoat and hopped in with them with only a passing reference to food (usually the first topic). Such scenes make up for a lot of thumps and smacks . . . '

The Community Arts Service was beginning to send its currents of sweetness and light through isolated parts of the country, including Ohakune, and I of course took part in the action. For teachers and other educated outsiders in the town, working on committees, often running them, was inescapable. I was always resolving not to – not, that is, to go to meetings, take office, catch the infection, the unhealthy euphoria that glued you to the phone all day, plotting before meetings, patching up afterwards. Alone among these terrible committees CAS stood untarnished, wholesome in my mind. We had to raise money to make a local guarantee to travelling artists, we held dances, shop days, cake stalls; I took part in them all, then exulted when the performers came – Ralph Woodcock, Janetta McStay, David Farquhar, the rudimentary Opera and Ballet Companies, Poul Gnatt's Dance Group . . . And then it was Bruce Mason, my old friend, on the first of his tours with *The End of the Golden Weather*. He stayed with us, of course, slept in a room already crowded with children and charmed them, and us. Our vastly changed circumstances, his and mine, seemed curiously natural, we didn't exclaim about it. Nor did I tell him that I too struggled to write in an undercover fashion. I didn't feel the slightest envy, either, of the glittering consummation of his powers I saw in his performance. I suppose one of the advantages in entirely accepting the hand fate has dealt you is that you do not imagine changing it.

It was the end of 1953. During the night on Christmas Eve we were woken by a phone call from a friend who was the correspondent for the other local newspaper, the *Taranaki Daily News*; he sometimes did our reports for us, if we were too busy or away. He told us that the bridge at Tangiwai was down and the express from Wellington had gone into the flooded river. But it was the merest creek, we protested; we'd forded it that very day going to Taihape for Christmas shopping. The sulphur stream – it was so small a trickle that nobody thought a road bridge necessary at all. The rail bridge, spanning the valley higher up, was another matter, but it was still impossible to believe in a flood big enough to engulf bridge and train – especially since it wasn't even raining. Trevor went to investigate these wild rumours. Certainly neither the north- nor the south-bound express had come through – you could hear the trains easily from our house.

Morning came, the children and I had breakfast, there was no word from Trevor, nothing at first on the radio. About nine he arrived, white-faced with shock and exhaustion. The incredible tales were all true. The sulphur stream had become, briefly, a towering flood that swept the train, the bridge and its huge concrete supports downstream, tumbling everything over and over like toys. And in the appalling wreckage floated real toys, Christmas gifts, teddy bears, carry-cots, the paraphernalia of countless family Christmas celebrations.

All day we listened to radio reports, including the message from the Queen who had arrived for a royal visit. Reporters from all the national dailies gathered to photograph and describe the fearful event; the *Chronicle* for the moment did not need our services. A hundred and fifty-one people had died.

The crisis that began for us a few miles down a familiar road echoed round the world and became linked, by a bizarre chance, with the other event of that summer which had New Zealanders at its centre – the first ascent of Everest by Edmund Hillary. The sonorous platitudes of the Queen's traditional Christmas message had never been so compelling. In our small farmhouse kitchen we crouched over the radio; even the children felt the vibrations. Martin, not quite two, made himself famous in the family by pointing to a royal photo in the paper and announcing with satisfaction, 'Dat Dook!'

Just over a fortnight later my fourth baby was born. Everything about her advent went very smoothly. I was weeding the garden one afternoon, judged there was time to cook the family dinner (so nonchalant had I become), we installed a friendly sixth former as babysitter – teachers being away in January – and as darkness fell on a warm summer evening Trevor and I drove to Raetihi, slowing down when I writhed and groaned, as at regular intervals I did. He left at once, as he was expected to do; I went through the usual procedures, the bathing, shaving, the awful recurring examining, and soon after midnight my baby was born. I was unconscious, as usual, but ecstatic upon wakening, also as usual. She was black-haired, beautiful, very sleepy. We called her Rachel Mary, and because the young locum managing Dr Jordan's practice was 'modern' I could get up and walk about at once, visit her in the nursery and go home after three days.

If sleeping soundly and making no fuss constitutes being 'good', as parents believe, Rachel was a perfect baby. Except for her four-hourly meals she caused so little disruption in our lives that when she was only two weeks old we decided we could go on holiday. The most enduring of my old intimacies from training college was, it turned out, with Peg and George. We had visited them in several remote places where they taught in tiny schools and lived in ancient tumbledown school houses. Now they had advanced into the relative sophistication of Pohangina, a green valley a few miles from Palmerston North. With our four children and an inclination to show off our parental prowess, we went to stay with them for a week. Peg had a remarkable reproductive history – her near-fatal ectopic pregnancy, the tying of tubes, the verdict of sterility, two adopted children and then, miraculously, two natural pregnancies. She now had four boys. It was an easy-going household, and we had a busy, scrambling, loud, laughing week of it.

How separate and different all the truths one holds to at the same moment. I was still in my twenties (and these currents broaden with age) but even then I was amazed that my life could contain, at one instant, the sorrow of Lewis's death, my worry about John, the nameless dread that increasingly hung about him, my delight in my new baby, the frivolities of the holiday at Pohangina . . . trifles, crises and climaxes, all tangled together. As my reproductive system gradually and invisibly expanded, did my psychic muscles also loosen – did everyone's – so you grew by a slow complication, a subtle expansion?

Coming home from Pohangina to my house on the hill reminded me of a regrettable change: Leo and Shannon had left. Shannon had been the perfect neighbour; placed halfway down that frightful drive, she was at any time ready to suggest I pause at the cottage to be restored by conversation. When Virginia started school she ran down to show Shannon her school bag, her new shoes; when Shannon had her baby, a boy, we took our prams and battled together up the track, grumbling satisfyingly.

There is a special quality to friendship in a place that feels itself beleaguered. We fiercely challenged the usual opinion of friends in the city – that Ohakune was the bleakest hole on earth, nobody in their right mind would get off the Limited Express on a dark night, walk off under the pale lights of the Junction and actually stay there, to live. But inside the family, as it were, we acknowledged the thinness of the air we breathed and our need to draw together. We were shaken by departures.

And Shannon had not only left Ohakune, she had gone 'to town' in the shape of Palmerston North. We weren't quite so sensitive if people went to another country place, but of course they seldom did. Colin too was ready to leave; he had a job in Napier (nearly as bad as Palmerston North). What is more, he fell in love, married, moved into a cottage with his bride, out again, and then they too were gone.

John's improvement did not last. He was well enough to help with the move to Lower Hutt, and indeed worked hard painting new rooms and constructing bookshelves. He even seemed to recover some of his enjoyment of the incidental absurdities of existence. (Clive and Dorothy, visited by the landlord of the unstoppable stories . . . all doors and windows closed . . . everyone looking trapped . . . John suddenly caught by laughter so overwhelming that he had to stand with shaking back at the window while the visitor droned on . . .) But gradually he seemed less well, less interested, less in touch with the new household, which by now included two children, the second a baby, Rachel's age. By the time an X-ray again showed signs of infection in his lung he was altogether in poorer condition, though it never seemed possible to say exactly what was wrong. Certainly at a family party in Ohakune that summer he had worried both Lindsay and me; he stood always on the fringe, wrapped in silence and some terrible unhappiness that we had no idea how to penetrate.

Now, in Dorothy's rather complicated ménage he asked, gently but with a kind of urgency, for special rarefied conditions – raw food, hours of meditation behind locked doors, a troubling seclusion. Early in 1955 he too went into hospital. A local doctor suggested psychiatric treatment, but it seemed that nobody – not John himself, nor any Wellington Hospital authority, nor any of us – really knew how to go about getting such help. He was put in the men's TB ward.

There Lindsay and I visited him, the first time rather pleasantly. Rachel was a year old, an engaging little creature, a black-haired, blue-grey-eyed infant beauty, content to toddle about the hospital lawn while we sat on seats in the sun, talking to John. The second visit was at Easter; this was a much grimmer day. He was 'nice' to us in a way that suggested an outline, a silhouette, an impression drawn by a pen without ink. He wasn't really there. We found this deeply disturbing, yet the thought that we might say so, brush aside the flimsy shell of conversation, dry as a sloughed-off snake skin, was almost equally distressing. Even our long familiar habits of family intimacy stopped far short of that. Helplessly we burbled on about the arrangements for doing washing in the ward, how interesting that he'd got to know Eric Heath the cartoonist, another patient, what a sweet face Denise had – she was the pretty nurse with whom he appeared to have a special closeness.

A male nurse followed us out and told us that John had made a suicide attempt the day before. Lindsay and I walked across the lawn and down the hill distracted by shock and fear – a sharp intensification, I realised, of the dread that had clung to my image of John for a long time, though I had never been able to give it a name. The only thing that had been real in the fearful artificiality of that visit had been the moment when he'd said he'd tried everything, helping Fanny, being such friends with her, making his health perfect, studying hard – nothing (and here there was an unexpected rush of vehemence) nothing worked. We had found no answer. 'Oh John – ', I began, but he'd 'shut off' again already.

I went home, wrote to him more often than usual, and in fact he wrote back, amusing friendly letters much in the old style. Perhaps the bad time had passed. We moved house again, this time because George

McCullough sold the farm. I had several times tried to persuade Trevor we had spent long enough in Ohakune, but now I argued in favour of buying our own house, and for once he agreed. Reluctantly, dubiously, and with maddening slowness – but still, he agreed. It was a fine house, big and plain and solid, set in a quite wonderful long-cultivated garden, a section of nearly an acre running down to the Mangawhero River at the back.

We had been there for several months, it was June, freezing cold but fine; the mountain, less visible from here, still showed a noble white shoulder through the trees. I was pegging out the mid-morning washing, while the children played inside in the commodious kitchen, warmed by its coal range. Trevor came round the corner of the house. I stared as he came quickly towards me, put his arm around me and began to lead me inside. 'I will just have to tell you straight away,' he said, 'John is dead. He did do it, in the end.'

Even at such a time there are snatches of merciful ordinariness. Stupefied as I was, I could still arrange for friends to look after the children while we went to Wellington. They – as children do – responded to my state of shock with an instinctive gentleness. We prepared to drive through the night and arrive early the next morning. As I opened the front gate in the darkness to go to the car which Trevor had already started, I looked in the letterbox. Yesterday's uncollected mail was there, a letter from John, warm and easy, beginning with talk of a plan Denise was making for them to go on a winter picnic. I felt it as truly beyond belief that even the harshest Fate could have quite so cruel an act as this, lying in wait for me, as the letter had done for the last twelve hours of that day and evening.

A kind of limbo followed. As we drove I stared unsleeping into the darkness hour after hour, seeing John's thin sensitive face and long bony body, hearing his helpless laugh, but all floating in and out of a miasma of shock and fear. It takes time for the mind to believe the impossible fact of death; through that endless dark drive, over roads I did not recognise, in fact hardly saw, I did not come to 'know' that John was dead. I was filled instead with an agonising confusion in which that most terrible idea could find no place.

Lindsay and I spent the next day with Fanny in her hospital cubicle. John had been able to visit her, by taxi, from his building at the other end of the hospital, and had several times done so. The visits had gone well. She was as unprepared as the rest of us for this nightmare.

The devastation was in fact far more profound for her than it could be for any of us and caring for her, in whatever ways we could find, came quickly to seem our main task. We stumbled through old reassurances, made clumsy attempts to extract a kind of sense out of the facts of John's brilliant intelligence, and his fears, his frailty, but again and again we found ourselves reduced to uncomprehending tears. At such times you act as you must; there is no deciding. I came to think that anxiety for Fanny, while it drew us close, also delayed my own realisation of loss. Only long afterwards could I begin to tell myself the unbearable truth of my young brother's death.

As for Fanny, she was caught in the most difficult circumstances she had ever known. The hospital ward confirmed all her fears of being alone among strangers who shared none of her tastes or interests, and induced in her that stiffness which looked so like condescension. We knew how incapable she was of crossing the gap she unwittingly established round her, but while John could visit her it had been bearable; Clive of course came too, Dorothy sent fruit and flowers, Lindsay and I wrote letters; she was sufficiently in touch with the family that was so precious to her not to feel the pinch of trivial malice too sharply. But cast into this maelstrom of pain and despair she lost all her defences. The practice of writing down what she saw, thought and felt was, however, still with her and she turned to it like a drowning swimmer.

In a private journal – not shared at the time even with us – she articulated the extremities of her anguish, and over the next year worked her way towards some sort of new beginning. She learned first to tolerate, then to respect the other patients, her unlikely (and perhaps equally unwilling) companions. And her health improved – by the middle of the following year she was strong enough to leave hospital and go to an open sanatorium in Otaki, a village by the sea not far from Wellington.

She expected not to live much longer, and in the same journal wrote a moving farewell to us all. However the erratic course of her life had not yet by any means come to its end. My embattled yet heroic parent was about to embark on further journeys. Mid-life, mid-century – a difficult terrain; she would need all her courage to navigate it.

Chapter 28

The question of what life is for or, more exactly perhaps, how something beautiful, or even sound, can be built out of it when one is given such confused and imperfect materials – John's question, unanswered – is urgent at some times, quite forgotten at others. One of the best ways to forget – though you don't realise it at the time – is to hand your life over to others who seem to need it more than you do. Your life, I say; well, your energy, concentration, purpose, time – most of all, time – and imagination, intellectual struggle, the bouquet of yourself called personality . . . I'm thinking of course of parents and children, and myself in particular: four children, a house in the country, a time when women's most sensitive pleasure was to serve. In 1955 my daily work (and long, busy days they were) was, simply, my children. They held it, the outer life of cooking and cleaning, washing, dressing, fixing things, because they needed it. But they also had the largest part of my inner life, the thinking, planning, wondering, imagining, the mind that like a back-room committee prepares the visible action. They needed that too – or I thought they did. Natural obsessiveness made me the most thorough parent alive (the soaking of barley for nourishing soups, the endless seams on dresses and shorts and crawlers and jackets, the sewing of hems and plackets long after midnight, the nightly story reading, no matter how sleep-numbed my voice and brain).

There was little else to demand my full attention. Trevor's absorption with his work continued to intensify; Ohakune had long since defined its limits. Friends were precious, but friendship itself had become an aspect of child management, since all the women I knew were mothers too.

And so, shocked as I was by John's death, I was a long way from asking, as he had, if life was worth having. I did not know what depth of darkness he had fallen into, nor understand how his life could be lost to him before it seemed it had properly begun – and I did not find out. The days followed one another, busy bright beads on a continuous thread, and I ran after them, trying to catch each one. At night I dreamed of him, strangely not in sadness but as a reassuring, even comforting presence, or warm and laughing as I'd so often seen him.

One morning two or three weeks after his death, I had an unexpected visit from Archdeacon Young, the local vicar. He was much admired in the district for his powerful personality and reputation as a writer and broadcaster; he had put us on the map by telling amusing stories about fishing – the genial cleric capable of enjoying secular pleasures. Now, sitting at my kitchen table, he began to talk about the life after death which is the true fulfilment.

I could say nothing. I was unwilling to talk of John to a stranger, but he felt no such compunction and asked me outright if I believed my brother had gone to his everlasting glory in heaven. I could not say I did. He set out to prove it, stopping every now and then to demand with growing insistence if I understood and was ready to change my mind. The more he pressed me, the greater my distress became. My awareness of loss was still raw, and this militant onslaught uncovered something almost too painful to contemplate: my deeply hidden outrage, even horror, at the thought that John had wished this death for himself. Among ourselves this bleak fact aroused much greater compassion towards him; faced with an aggressive outsider who insisted I must be taught how to think about him, I completely lost my defences and began to weep helplessly.

Archdeacon Young saw this as the beginnings of capitulation and redoubled his efforts. I cried even more, I was engulfed by tears. It was an appalling scene. Somehow, at last, I managed to ask him to leave, and eventually he did.

I never quite recovered from this disaster. Far from bringing heaven – for John or anyone else – closer to me, it hardened the conviction, already quite strong in my mind, that whatever was to be known or understood about this most inscrutable event, it had nothing to do with eternal bliss and the Kingdom of God set up in a tangible heaven. Archdeacon Young had succeeded in making that prospect look not only unconvincing but hostile as well.

Obscure and troubling fears remained, questions I did not even know how to ask myself, let alone talk to anyone else about. Unresolved, they formed a kind of paralysis within me, and for nearly a year

I was unable to make love at all. Trevor's lightest approach took me to the verge of tears. He was kind, but mystified, and hurt. Our mutual absorption in work grew stronger, and slowly more habitual.

The time we took away from necessary work was in fact an extension of it – Trevor's coaching of teams and trips with them to other schools, my evenings at meetings of parents, the Parent Teacher Association, an embryonic Playcentre group. We sometimes remarked, with a kind of wry satisfaction, that where other people organised their lives around their pleasures, we devoted ours to work. We felt useful and productive, and so we were.

The buying of the house oddly confirmed a growing separateness in what concerned each of us most closely. I became more confidently established on my territory of house and garden, friends and children, Trevor more secure in his authority as a strong and popular teacher with a passion for sport. Ownership itself turned out to be an intermittently compelling occupation. It worried Trevor because it meant a mortgage, problems with paying bills, the need to attend to gutterings and drainpipes, paintwork and rust in the tanks. I, being of a more optimistic temperament, thought the immense amount of gardening I had to do, and the fairly regular painting of rooms, not to mention the general upkeep of my vast and sprawling establishment, all worthwhile because it was so beautiful. However, I too was depressed by the monthly bill-paying (or bill-postponing) during glum evenings at the kitchen table. A ponga tree grew outside and brushed the window with its splendid green swathes, but this was not much comfort as we decided that Virginia and Frances, also now at school, must wait for new sandals or a bigger raincoat, the items I could not make on the sewing machine.

But we had made a gesture of belonging. We weren't 'doing country service' nor even 'having the country experience' – we *lived* in Ohakune. One consequence was that we found ourselves approved of by local farmers; no doubt they saw us crossing the line from 'temporary, outside' to 'inside by choice'; and were gratified. The owners with whom we negotiated our purchase were themselves solid members of a semi-rural hierarchy and had lived in the house for forty years, planted its trees, built the outbuildings, harvested the raspberries and gooseberries, established and nurtured the spacious garden. My historical awareness was not equal to theirs, but I did feel this house as a particular inheritance, and expanded in the presence of the capacious rooms, the expansive but shapely garden, the big verandahs, even the high style of the polished wood columns of the fireplace in the living room.

The street outside was also a pleasure to the eye and the senses: it was not really a street but a road, a country road. To the left was the local pa, forbidden ground, and a row of houses far back in their sections; to the right the 'Maori Bush' and a quarry. Bush was close in every direction; to walk to town I had to cross a bridge over a stream that ran straight under the overhanging trees and into the bush reserve that at its far end contained tennis courts and club pavilions. Burns Street between us and the post office, my most regular point of call, was a struggle of houses and paddocks with windy, overgrown footpaths.

We were almost in the country, and quite close to the main highways through the North Island, to Waiouru in the south – or southwest – and Taumarunui and Te Kuiti to the north. Taking to the road in our car was natural and frequent. I made occasional trips to Taihape or Wanganui, once or twice we drove to Taupo and back, a distance of seventy miles, to spend the day by the lake, and every January we chose a beach to camp beside for ten days or a fortnight. Ohakune is far from the sea, and I sometimes felt a sort of sea-homesickness, a state perhaps natural to island people. We had a commodious tent, bedding and box cupboards, a canvas floor – modest but comprehensive equipment. Napier, Mahia, Te Kaha, Taupo (lake water was different, but would do) – all were memorable. Hard work for me if there happened to be a young baby, but exhilarating too, a re-creation of the trips I'd so loved as a child.

Some of our journeys were to make connection with the other Scott families – to Wairoa, for instance, where we camped on the lawn beside Lindsay and Doug's house and spent all day cavorting with our children in the swimming baths or by the river. In the evenings, after a certain amount of swapping children between house and tent, the four parents settled down to talk their heads off, till we were so drugged by exhaustion that there was nothing for it but to stagger off to bed. Mornings would begin at first light, however we might hope or pretend otherwise.

Holidays with Clive and Dorothy followed much the same pattern. Sometimes we met them at a camping ground in Taupo or Napier; they had more money than us and could afford a cabin, so this served as an adult evening retreat. They were successful ventures, all of them. Children played well together, or if they did not there was usually someone, adult or older child, to administer a snub of a cuff over the ears or some other sort of offhand justice, in keeping with our casual summer cohabiting.

Nothing like this would have been remotely possible with Trevor's family. For one thing, their holiday trips to lakes or beaches were to rented houses, where they seemed to live rather as they did at home; and they would no more have thought of squeezing double the number of children and parents into those than we would have thought of going. Likewise exchanges of birthday presents did not matter to them in the same way; for the Scotts these were rituals scrupulously honoured and lovingly carried out. Presents that 'worked' would be chosen for cousins – like the spangly high-heel dress-up shoes Father Christmas had given Rachel, in the last year of his authenticity for her, which had to be reproduced for Lindsay's Jane.

It occurred to me at some time in those years that there was a strange irony in my having linked my fate and future with a clan so alien in its outlook and habits to my own. The very conservatism of the Edmond household, the quality I'd thought of as 'essential bourgeois', had been what I liked best, because it appeared to offer me a certainty and confidence that my own shy and cranky family could not give. Yet as time passed it became more and more obvious that the Scott family model produced far more affection, vitality and action – a lively humanity which could and did grow by shared experience. Observing these contrasts I had a first inkling that my choice of conventional security had been part of a twenty-one-year-old immaturity, and something I would leave behind as I grew older. The developing life of the families, expressed in letters, gifts and shared expeditions, was part of that process.

But every holiday ended with the beginning of school, and 'Trevor's school' could still encroach largely on life at home, detached though the Burns Street locality might be. In 1954 it ceased its existence as a district high school and became Ruapehu College. There was much ceremony about the opening. Buildings, teachers and children were all the same, yet each acquired a new lustre by recognising a motto, a crest, a principal (more august than a headmaster) and most of all the status of 'college'. And Mr Nigel Barclay, the stylish gentleman who inherited this magnificence as first principal, was perfectly designed to exploit its possibilities. He had a handsome leonine head, a polished manner, an air of slightly confiding condescension. He believed intensely in his own powers and that the greatest of these was to be the kind of headmaster (the old name stuck after all) who groomed others for high office. He was a natural kingmaker.

His staff reacted in characteristic ways. Murray's irony sharpened; he greeted his friends with 'Good-morning-you'll-be-a headmaster', all in one breath, holding out his hand and giving a wide magisterial smile. Paul Jones, a new clever science teacher who had bought the house next door to us, began to kiss his wife with elaborate public devotion when she appeared in the staffroom after school with their two small girls. Clearly he knew how to combine the tenderness of the family man with the erudition of a dedicated scientist. Vera his wife lovingly co-operated. Trevor laughed with Murray, scoffed at Paul, but found himself troubled by the lure of advancement all the same. He began to spend more time on his thesis, and to talk of the need to make his mark as a teacher and organiser, because he didn't have 'subject qualifications', only Education as theory – and, of course, practice. Mr Barclay's wife was appropriately gracious. They brought a new style to Ohakune; they held dinner parties, they went to restaurants, we believed, though this was not actually possible in Ohakune or Raetihi. Mr Barclay was said to drink a lot and flirt with waitresses.

But having dinner parties, and drinking wine at them too, soon came closer than hearsay. It emerged as part of our new habits as 'real' Ohakune residents. Buying a house meant not only that we paid rates instead of rent, and had an attitude to roads and water supply. We also met new and, as it turned out, very satisfying friends, people who like us had come from the city, bought houses and decided to stay, at least for the time being. They were *au fait* with as fine a style of living as Mr Barclay's. We too began to attend, and hold a species of dinner party, Always before we had exchanged evening visits, for which you arrived at eight, talked till eleven, were given supper of tea and cakes and left for home at twelve.

Going to dinner was quite different; there were new codes, a new ritual, almost a new language to learn. Sherry wasn't the same as wine, for instance (Trevor had won a bottle of sherry at the Sunbeam Club and since then we'd sometimes had a glass before our own dinner, or tea, as we still called it.) White wine had to be cold, red did not; red tasted nasty, but once I'd learnt to say, 'New Zealand is good at whites, just finding out about reds,' I felt better about that. 'Dry', I found, meant much the same as 'sour', but it was smarter all the same to prefer dry to sweet. This was in another sphere altogether from the 'grog' ordered for teachers' parties. I was not the only one to be struck by the new ways. Our hosts in one of the local farming families seemed not to have learned the distinction between wine and liqueur. When we arrived we'd be given tumblers of benedictine which he topped up as we swallowed the ferocious liquid, a treacherous accompaniment to conversation.

The most significant of our new friends were Ken and Pat Lawn. Ken had worked in an accountant's office in Wellington, decided there was money to be made in small-town business and bought a book shop in Raetihi. He and Pat lived in a small house on the edge of town, with a bosky garden shadowed by rhododendron trees and large clumps of bamboo. They had a girl, Barbara, exactly the same age as Frances, and, when I first met Pat, a new baby. Pat was lively and talkative, full of ready laughter; at once and as a matter of course she treated me as a close friend. I soon saw that she generated an aura of friendliness which took in even her own marriage; Ken had a flair for getting into absurd situations and giving accounts of them which made Pat and everyone else – including Ken himself – speechless with laughter.

Pat's way of serving dinner brought back Fanny's long-ago dream of an elegance she couldn't achieve at the family kitchen table – a white linen or lace tablecloth, vegetable dishes, napkins, slender wine glasses, a tray with cream and sugar for coffee afterwards. The first Christmas after the Lawns became our friends Pat asked us to spend with them the day that all my life had been given over to the celebration of family intimacy, and in recent years had always taken place at Pyes Pa. This year Fanny was in hospital, Pyes Pa no longer existed for us, the other families were encompassed about with small children, as we were. The Lawns as friends suddenly became, and remained, a new kind of family. The constant sharing of plans and projects I embarked on with them, their natural hospitality, an understood taste for the daily absurdities of living – all this I associated with growing up in the Scott family. A good deal of it had been recreated in my years with Molly; now I had it again, although in a new form, since so much of it was connected with our children. The Lawns were more enterprising than we were, and knowing them changed us.

Their children and ours embroiled us in the demanding drama of girls' horse riding; together we went regularly into the country around Ohakune to attend the local gymkhanas. These began before dawn on summer Saturdays and ended long after dark, when both riders and parents were dazed by exhaustion. We acquired two lumbering old nags and encouraged Virginia and Frances, the family's committed riders, to save up for better gear – riding boots instead of gumboots, for instance. For several years they embraced, while we hovered on its edge, the cult of the Pony Club.

There was laughter in everything we did with the Lawns. And it wasn't long before we met other friends of theirs who had come to these high-country towns with the same post-war adventurousness and enterprise. There were special reductions in the price of a medical practice in some country districts, and Raetihi was one. As it happened, a commodious house went with the practice, and Bill and Ruth Young arrived to occupy it. Rumours of drunkenness had clouded the career of the doctor Bill replaced, culminating in the accidental death of a local farmer hit by the doctor's car. Bill, by contrast, was sober, also quiet, intelligent, unfussy; he was quickly liked. He worked even longer hours than Trevor, but had a much more expansive attitude to what leisure could be squeezed out of busy weeks and on-and-off-duty weekends. With them I sometimes went to Taihape or Wanganui to see films or plays, and once, memorably, to Wellington for a performance of Madame Rambert's ballet. Bill gave me a benzedrine tablet to keep me awake on the exhausting drive home. It did too, even while I did the mountainous family washing at home in the late afternoon. By that time, however, I had the kind of headache that made me want to lie down and die.

I had a good many headaches, in fact, but though each one temporarily crippled me, I did not see how I could live differently and so perhaps prevent their onset. On the contrary, the charge that drove my daily life, and dictated its speed, seemed to grow stronger and fiercer all the time. I no longer had time to write – or only very occasionally, late at night when everyone was in bed, the lunches cut, clothes ironed and set out for the morning, and Trevor at a meeting or away on a school trip. In those spells of brief and confined solitude I didn't write stories but poems, or parts of poems, fragments, lines that rushed urgently down the page. A glimpse of John in a moment of intense and now terribly poignant shyness; a snatch of Fanny, ladylike while bereft and frightened; the whispering of the million tiny leaves of the beech tree that stood by the gate and brooded darkly over everything we did. I stuffed these scraps into folders, and shoved them into drawers; there was never time to look at them again or revise. My daylight self was altogether more active and external, my head full of planning, conversations tense with news and stories.

Virginia had emerged from being a spectacularly beautiful baby into a plainer, purposeful, concentrated childhood. In the rapid propulsion of the days I was often impatient with her, inclined to pull her sharply into line. One night I went out through the verandah room (the small, hot, space-heated room where we gathered in the winter, if the fire in the big living-room wasn't lit), along the side verandah and into the 'outside room' where she and Frances slept. I came to tell her that although I was often cross it wasn't because I didn't love her; I did, a great deal. She gazed at me in silence. I remembered other things I'd wanted to explain – the traditional mystery of where babies come from; at that, too, she'd listened politely and then asked, 'Can I have an apple?' More recently there had been a matter she herself brought up: 'Mr Marks said to us girls that we aren't to play in the pine trees with the boys, because boys have got lots of things to do, they go to work and make money, girls have only one thing, and it's their secret and nobody's to know. But,' my young daughter assured me, 'I tell all my secrets to Jenny. Isn't that all right?' Mr Marks was an anxious, severe man with a faintly military style; what was one to say to him?

Out of a tempestuous infancy Frances emerged an active, rebellious, inventive child, capable of violent conflicts and extravagant enthusiasms. She appeared to have inherited Trevor's physical prowess, and ran, climbed, swam with zest. By contrast with Virginia's orderliness, she was always torn and dirty, her hems came down, threads pulled from her jerseys, her shoes and sandals got lost. When we played Frog Jumps she leapt and tumbled with high abandon. Frog Jumps had evolved gradually as an entertainment: soon after Lewis's HT bequest had rather oddly provided my piano, I bought two books of words and music – action songs for young children. There were also short pieces labelled *Walking, Jumping, Rabbit Hops* and so on, so you could change the music, the time, the rhythm and volume, without explaining first. We all joined in, and the children could go on for ages, adapting their antics to the music, especially if it postponed someone's bedtime. We learned the songs, too, and sang them with a sort of thin verve – *Jimmy Monkey, The Elephant Song* – performing the actions and teaching the younger ones. As the children grew more sophisticated they began to make up plays, as I had once done, and perform them using the Mexican curtains with which I had divided the enormous draughty hall, front from back.

All this had its parallel in adult parties where, in our innocent way, we reached the highest pitch of excitement by singing loudly together. There was always someone to play by ear, and at times I did it myself. Our schooling had left us all with a secure knowledge of an enormous number of traditional songs, English, Scottish, Irish and Maori, also some American, especially Stephen Foster and the Negro spirituals. But anything would do, even hymns – in fact hymns and carols were a sort of mainstay of these nights of singing yourself hoarse; they were still there to be done when you'd been through everything else. After hours of singing there was a release of something in the brain – energy, fire – that must have been like the euphoria long-distance runners speak of. It was certainly better than the amiable confusions of alcohol, though we didn't know much about that anyway.

Martin too was emerging from babyhood, becoming a family character; in fact he had always been that, could command a captivating charm from his earliest days as a fat and smiling baby who made funny faces. I wondered if a family full of impressionable females – not to mention the one man who was so struck by the re-creation of maleness in his son – had taught him that he had some natural authority over us. He was a shrewdly intelligent little boy and easy-tempered too, though slightly elusive. He was the only one of my children who could make me laugh so hard in the middle of delivering some reproof that I forgot what it was. When he was still quite small Trevor began to take him on incidental trips to school or to watch teams playing their matches, and of course as he grew older he made friends with other boys with whom he went off playing, fishing, exploring the country. His days became slightly separated from ours. The girls, it seemed, played at home, 'here'; Martin and other boys played away 'there', wherever that was.

But he was in the family action too. Even in the capacious Burns Street house we had at first only one children's room, which like an enormous dormitory bedded them all. He usually solved the privacy problem by reading with blind (and deaf) absorption, beginning as a small boy with the Reverend Awdry's train books. So great was his love for the trains-with-personalities that he sometimes took one of the books tightly locked in his hand into the sea on summer holidays.

Into this close population Rachel brought her gentle, serious presence. The perfect baby who had allowed us to go on holiday when she was barely a fortnight old, she continued to live among us quietly, often playing by herself, talking to her dolls and to other characters we couldn't see. And she too rode a horse – a painted wooden head on a stick, with wheels at the other end – with quite as much absorption as the older riders, indeed with all their equestrian talk and manner perfectly reproduced. A dear little girl, easy to love, impossible to fight with; beautiful too, with that black hair and pale skin, and rather delicate gestures. Friends and visitors often declared her their favourite in the family.

In 1957 I had another baby, and two years after that yet another: two more girls. Catholics traditionally had big families, so did our Maori and Chinese neighbours, but we just seemed to go on as though we couldn't think how to stop. In a way this was true – both conceptions were technically 'accidental' in that I grew very casual in the use of the 'highly spermicidal' cream which accompanied my supposedly faithful diaphragm; I ran out of the stuff, I forgot to buy more – but of course such carelessness is not really an accident.

I had once said that with my first child I took on 'the life of coping'. Now it was a decade later – Virginia was almost ten when Stephanie was born. Ten years of a life of action and planning, of management, watchfulness, the organising of systems that constantly loosened, expanded, teetered, finally fell and then had to be re-formed, differently. A slowly deepening habit of alertness for cries in the night, signs of sickness or distress, for too sharp a tenor in family squabbling, too many tears and tantrums (and how did one recognise 'too many' or 'too few' of anything?). Ten years too of the quaint innocence of each child's first encounters with the world, their first language – partial, wonky and brilliant as it is – their staggering physical beauty, their abandonment to the moment – a bumble bee on a pane, a sore knee, the newly discovered power to put ears and shoes on a drawing of a person, a snowfall. And, perhaps most compelling, their absolute and artless acceptance of everything you say and do. 'The world is . . .', you explain, 'We know that . . .', 'It is right to . . .', and reality, some shape of it, forms about them, you putting the pieces in here and there, and imagining you have built a temple, a cathedral, in which they will always find a commanding faith.

This isn't true, of course; much of what you tell them will be disproved, or shown to be illusory, as they expand into worlds you can neither enter nor comprehend. But when they are very young that doesn't occur to you, nor does it matter. I lived richly and fully in those years, and scarcely even noticed the absence of any separate adult life I might have had up till then – I was thirty-two when Stephanie was born. Nor did I observe that marriage itself, the adult relationship that after all formed a major part of the family system, was not now a particularly vital enterprise. It no longer had the inner momentum of the first few years; instead we put almost all of ourselves into our separate occupations.

The children, of course, were indisputably Trevor's as well as mine, and I was conscious that his work provided us all with house, car, clothes, everything we had; also that it was his ambitions that could change our course. However, the sharing of a family began gradually to show different facets to each of us. After a week or ten days of our summer holidays Trevor would become restless, want a newspaper to see the School Certificate results, to talk about school. It was the beginning of a new tension, or the deepening of an old one, which cast me in the role of suppliant, for time and attention he was often reluctant to give.

As if to confirm the decision that underlay my lack of decision about the size of my family, the birth of my fifth baby was spectacularly more satisfying than any of the others. It was a hospital error, oddly enough, that made the difference. I lay in bed in the 'maternity end' trying to read, interrupted by increasingly ferocious labour pains and, occasionally, one of the monstrous intrusions of an examination for cervical dilation. On the last of these the nurse dismissed my case quite peremptorily. 'Nothing doing here,' she announced, and went off to attend to more important matters in the 'general end'. It was about nine o'clock in the evening. Left to themselves, my as yet invisible baby and my experienced and businesslike muscular system went quickly through the pains-that-expand and began the pains-that-expel. There were three or four of these cataclysmic seizures. I had never before been conscious when they occurred and was amazed – they went beyond pain; that had become irrelevant. They were instead a huge natural surge of the force of life itself. It took over my whole body, shook and contorted it, split it open, and my baby burst out onto the bed and lay there, half curled up still, grey with sticky vernix, taking seconds (hours, I thought) to gasp and cry. I held up an edge of the blanket to protect her from the cold air at the open window, I hung on the bell. And a nurse did appear at the door, gazed horrified at the pair of us and rushed out again shouting, 'My God! My God!' Bill, who was my doctor by that time, told me afterwards that they were inclined to think it all his fault, even though nobody had told him to come. I and my clever baby heard these speculations and privately gloated.

I had come to spend a good deal of time with Bill and Ruth, and relished their company almost more than any other. I thought I recognised in Bill someone so like me that we might have been of one blood; indeed I was sure I was a little in love with them both. Certainly they represented a new kind of adventurousness – their New Year's Eve party for instance, when we all dressed in the style of the twenties, finding in Urwin and Drury's Draper's Emporium in Raetihi the buttoned shoes and wide lace trimmings we needed, still on sale in boxes on high shelves. In this finery we danced for hours; on the way home I said to Trevor, 'What's that funny light in the sky?' 'The dawn,' he laconically replied.

Bill and I discovered that our birthdays were on the same day, so we began, and continued, to write poems for each other on that day.

When it came to the birth of my sixth and last child, less than two years later, I was full of confidence. Clearly all would be as before, only more so. It wasn't. By one of the paradoxes of reproduction, this was a long, slow labour, a conservative nurse insisted on 'managing' it (which meant administering early and obliterating drugs), and Bill had gone, as the hospital agreed he should, to Wanganui to see a play. There were other changes too: 'rooming in' had been discovered, so had the H-Bug. One allowed mothers and babies to share a room, as a way of developing a secure relationship; the other compelled them to stay in hospital for ten days or longer. The 'Hospital Bug' had been found to flourish in carefully sterilised environments and turned out to be a new organism resistant to penicillin.

I called my daughter Katherine, spelt like Katherine Mansfield, and Lindsay after my cherished sister, and we pleasurably occupied our little island of protected time in the hospital making friends with each other. Then I took her home to my truly vast household.

Chapter 29

She was, again, a beautiful child, with dark eyes and a creamy skin. People we knew began to exclaim at the amplitude of our good fortune in having not one or two well-endowed children but six, and not a weak link among them; on the contrary, all had quick intelligence, all were fine looking, all appeared to have a future full of promise.

They became, my two little girls, 'the babies', everyone's favourite entertainment, the news they most wanted to hear. By another paradox, Stephanie, who had slid into the world so simply, was a restless, impatient little creature, full of changes of mood that made her withdraw and advance by sudden impulse. Katherine, on the other hand, seemed to have been in the world already, she was so smilingly assured, so friendly and affectionate. Actually I learned as she grew older that her external calm was often deceptive and she suffered a good deal of concealed turmoil.

I was myself developing an apparently unruffled style which I used to keep a kind of control of the burgeoning complexities of my household. The process began in a strange sickness that beset me when Katherine was a few months old. I had a choking sensation, a sense of suffocating constriction as though I had too tight a collar round my throat; I developed an anxious habit of loosening something that wasn't there. 'Strain,' said Bill briefly, 'you have to go away for a while, take a break.' So taking my baby in the carry-cot I'd made for the purpose, I caught a train to Wairoa to spend a week with Lindsay. It was a long time to be away, but my sister was welcoming and sensible, insisted that I not spend the time worrying about those I'd left behind. Naturally restless and excitable, I had been threatened with obliteration by the force of my devouring days, and now had to devise a weapon of self-protection. I tried to practise calmness. I succeeded, too, with my new accomplishment; I returned home to enter a period of high activity, more dense and sustained than any I had known, and survived it. I did not for some years realise how superficial this managerial equilibrium really was, nor how damaging in that it induced a kind of internal paralysis from which eventually I must consciously recover.

In the meantime, it served me well. In these years, the last of the fifties (though nobody thought in decades; time was continuous then), everything in my daily life intensified, became more so. More children, all growing bigger by the minute, larger platefuls at meals, bigger shoes to buy, more questions to answer (and more still to push aside as unanswerable), more school lunches to cut, teachers to get to know, homework to watch over; more panic at high temperatures or sudden falls (subdue it how I might) and relief at peaceful bed times, at safe returns from a swim, a long ride, a bush or mountain expedition; more laughter, labour, terror, exhaustion . . . We bought a wallowing old station wagon, filled it with kids and camping gear and saddles and sheet music; gumboots and garbage . . . sometimes when I gathered my children and their friends from the school gate I counted wrongly and had to go back for one forlorn straggler. I fell asleep in the middle of reading a story and woke to hear the valiant listener continuing the tale by heart. The winter of the deep snow we rolled up thick white strips and made them into snow furniture and sat on it and tumbled over as we broke it; in a winter drought we had to make tea out of hot-water bottle water. The night Virginia didn't come home from the Maori Bush I sat by the fire breast-feeding the baby – Katherine – mindlessly for hours, for ever, till I heard the clink of a bridle at the door and we could ring the police and tell them to stop looking. Rachel in Standard 2 strapping the bed with hysterical cries of 'Take *that* and *that* and *that* you *wicked* boy . . . ' Stephanie waking a thousand times a night from terrible dreams of black dogs with barks like bombs exploding. Every noise was a roar, every note a chorus, every detail an all-over repeating pattern. A dense, pulsing, stampeding jungle of a life.

In the middle of it, we went into politics. That is to say Trevor and I, who had made friends with a lively young eccentric who was town clerk, helped him to stand for parliament, a Labour challenge to the Waimarino seat held by a cliché-ridden conservative called Roy Jack, a man I would in student parlance have called a 'hearty'. Ben Winchcombe, by contrast, was an eager intellectual, so interested in questioning every orthodoxy that he might have been trained to it in the same school as I – the Scott family. He was in a sense more authentic than I, in that he later left his job to experiment with organically grown crops and natural food, and on family land at Karioi tried to create a self-supporting agricultural unit.

As a candidate he was almost too good, so energetic and honourable that by election day his lacerated throat would not allow him to utter a sound, and he had spent so much of his own money that he was almost destitute. And after all that he didn't get in. We had a very good time nonetheless, planning his publicity, writing brochures, making up speeches. Ben had a taste for florid prose; my main job was to concoct plainer phrases than 'the rosy dawn of a new age of enlightenment' or 'a well of happiness and fulfilment for the parched human spirit', and persuade him to accept my duller style. If writing for the *Wanganui Chronicle* had encouraged me to puff up a few skinny facts to make a story, my political adventure taught me the opposite: conciseness, even terseness with (I hoped) the throb of conviction beating within it.

My secret urge to write was directed into another channel too. We celebrated birthdays, along with other occasions, with the Lawns, the Youngs and a few friends, mostly of theirs (Ohakune seemed to contain only teachers, and our favourites among them had come and gone). One year I decided to write a play, a comic farce, for Ken's birthday. I lightly distorted our names, parodied songs we knew, incorporated known idiosyncrasies and made up an absurd plot connected with Ken's craze for fishing. We rehearsed in secret, even made costumes to fit our parts, and gloriously we performed, savouring our own brilliance every bit as much as his surprise.

Trevor too made a foray into light entertainment, but where mine was private and individual his was public and collective – he produced *Trial by Jury* with Ruapehu College students, using the school music teacher as musical director. It was a famous event, and probably changed for ever local perceptions of what high school children could do. Sporting boys at the school especially admired him and he used this hold to persuade them that singing and clowning successfully on stage was an achievement comparable with getting into the First XV. A remarkable feat.

As they grew into little-girlhood Stephanie and Katherine increasingly operated as a pair; they played together with utter absorption, they faced the rest of the family, and outsiders even more, as a team of two. Katherine, being less shy and in fact gifted with great charm, was usually charged with delivering their message, but Stephanie was purposeful and shrewd in private about what it was. They fitted together as friends much more readily than Virginia and Frances had done, perhaps because they were far more often left to fend for themselves. They grew up with multiple parents, reserving a special adoration for 'the big kids', especially Virginia as the oldest and grandest, and Martin, the only boy.

And then everything stopped. Trevor suddenly got a job, as first assistant at Kuranui College in Greytown. Dismayed, we stared at one another, trying to take it in. 'We can't *shift!*' cried Frances, 'this is where we *live.*' Even I agreed, though of course I'd known of the application, and indeed helped to write it. Now it could not be reversed; Ohakune was suddenly not for ever, it was a phase.

We had an enormous number of farewells – parents, teachers, board of governors, pupils, old pupils . . . even the Sunbeam Club had a ladies' night, dreadfully burdened with speechifying about 'better halves' and the use of the rolling pin. We acquired a pile of ornamental crystal, glasses, other shiny stuff, which prompted our friends, when they said goodbye, to outdo all the committees by choosing the ugliest present ever known. It was a thick plaster wall plaque, bulging with the leaves and petals of a bunch of grotesque flowers, painted with colours never seen in nature and encrusted with gold glitter along their frizzled edges. On the back of this monstrosity they wrote that they hoped we would Feed Well on Pastures New, and signed their names.

The last public event we attended was the primary school swimming sports, in which the four older children took part. We had spent most of the time on our yearly camping holidays in the seas or rivers of the North Island; Trevor was a strong swimmer and had taught the children poise and confidence in the water. As we watched Frances swimming her lengths of what I'd thought of as 'overarm' (but now learned was 'freestyle'), another parent watching from the edge said, 'Watch that girl!' There she was, shooting through the water, scarcely breaking its surface with the smooth economical action of her arms and body. I stared, unable to help smiling; I was overcome by a rush of pride.

I wrote to Fanny, the only person, apart from Trevor, to whom I could openly boast. During the years since John's death she had passed into an entirely new phase, which gradually revealed itself as a series of attempts to make whatever sense she could of her new solitariness. She had left Otaki Sanatorium after six months, free at last of the disease that had dictated her every action, dominated every experience for ten years. The 'miracle' drugs, once she agreed to take them, cured her as they had cured thousands of others. She would never be strong, a good deal of natural lung tissue having been permanently eroded, but she was free to live as she chose.

It seemed that despite the terrible losses that lay behind her, she was capable of optimism, of purpose. She went to the house in Lower Hutt to plan her next move. Dorothy, who had always enjoyed Fanny's vitality, was glad to help. Fanny, she confided to me, was in a better condition than she'd ever seen her, energetic, almost plump (which meant not startlingly thin) and, even more than before, well groomed and elegant.

So it was that as our lives, Clive's, Lindsay's and mine, grew more populated, more enveloping, hers began to look for a single channel through which it might again begin to move. She had no adult experience of being alone, without her husband and family, and indeed she had depended on them more than most women. Despite her recovered health she was quite unfitted to embark, in middle age, on a single life.

She was bound to make mistakes, to encounter disappointments and failures, but mercifully neither she nor any of us anticipated the inevitable problems. In any case we were all so preoccupied with our young families that our links with her – and thus our patience with her mistakes – steadily declined. It was just the time when she needed our goodwill most, and knew least how to get it. She didn't give up wanting to be helpful, but this too could be a problem.

We had the six weeks of summer holidays to gather ourselves for departure, and after the frantic whirl of those hot days I sometimes went and sat on the cool steps of the front verandah and looked up into the shifting shadows of the beech tree, as I had done a hundred times in the years this house had been home. More truly home, I realised, since Lewis's death and John's, and the end of the Pyes Pa holidays.

My own family now filled almost every part of me; like a full tide it had come in, spread over and through me, widened me into shapes I had not known I could take. Sitting there in the cool summer dark I thought with a sudden flash of knowledge: my children will grow up with the memory of this house in their bones. All their lives it will be these cabbage trees rattling in the wind, this hill where the old nags browse and knock over the fences, this hot little winter room where we've so often huddled in the smell of coal smoke to dress and undress, read the nightly stories, cram in homework and sewing and books and even saddles and bridles being oiled for a ride the next morning. When they have grown old and feel their way back to the unconscious residue of sensations and shapes in their minds, the deeply laid layers of childhood experience, this will be what they find. It will be for them what the house in Osier Road has been for me, the willow tree and its swing, the plum tree, the paddocks of long grass, the dreaming verandah, the place furthest back in my mind and imagination, always waiting.

A pattern of temporariness and experiment lay behind us, a gradual coalescing into a family. As each child was born and began to live with us, we had become the kind of group we were, living in the way we'd fashioned together. And this had come to its richest fruition in this spreading old house; here we had come to believe in ourselves and our powers, to establish a coherent image, in our own eyes and those of a familiar community.

I had a conviction, too, that more than ever before, at this moment of leaving, my home was something I took with me wherever I went. I had become so intimately and profoundly connected with my children, and Trevor, their father (which was how I now most often thought of him), that I existed more significantly with them than by myself. I didn't think much about how this would change, though in small ways changes had already begun – Virginia had new friends, rebellious girls who seemed alarmingly not like her, not like us. But we were together still; the other families, Clive's and Lindsay's, with their children, stood at a distance; we couldn't even spend holidays with them now, there were too many of us, and of them.

Thirteen years I'd lived in this little mountain town, all my children but one had been born here; I was moving into the middle of my life – soon I would be forty. And I was not, so far, a writer of poems or stories, a known recorder of New Zealand experience; instead I was a mother of six children, a woman who had taken up the familiar pattern of my generation. Certainly I had expanded it – no family I knew had so many children (except Clive, with seven) – but I hadn't otherwise changed or challenged the conventions I'd inherited. I didn't think of this regretfully, I simply observed it with a small detached surprise, and went back to reflections about what it was we were leaving.

'Aren't you ever coming in?' Trevor demanded from the front door. Oh yes, I would come soon . . .

I'd had no choice in where, when, or indeed if we moved – I'd badly wanted to, and we'd stayed; now I didn't care and we were going. But I could sit on in that caressing dark, alone, and think about it. The residue of the years, what I would take with me – some shadow, colour, whiff of sound or smell that would always bring this place back – what was there?

The Aubrey girls, of course, Tut and Pet, singing in their throaty Maori voices to guitars as they lolled in the long grass next door on warm Sunday mornings; Mrs Aubrey their mother, thin, brown, toothless and elusive, though their cottage was only a few yards through the hedge from our back door; the cottage itself, papered with newspapers, impeccably tidy while they cooked on bricks outside. Charlie Herkt, the veteran mountain guide who lived with them as stepfather, husband, grandfather, patron, adviser, all in one, and who baby-sat for us, reading the *Reader's Digest* through glasses held to his ears by black wool, and refused to answer that new-fangled contraption, the telephone. The terrible night when Virginia's horse Quickstep, left to graze the Aubreys' grass, was frightened in the dark by local larrikins and, in panic, ran round and round the tree we'd tethered her to till she was strangled, and nobody knew till it was too late.

Noeline Bruning, the painter who advertised for a teacher's house for the holidays so she could paint the amazing high-country light, and in the end stayed with us a dozen times as a friend; the person in fact, who'd taught me to be myself when I answered difficult questions ('Where has she gone, that girl who was supposed to be having a baby . . . '), not the voice of morality approved by the town. Vera, my neighbour on the other side, with two children to my six, insisting I must want morning tea every day and when I refused bringing it anyway on a tray, to my suppressed and un-neighbourly fury . . . Rachel plump with mumps playing contentedly in the garden and coming in to tell me she needed 'a dear little filly' of her own. Rachel in Primer 4 bringing home the spelling list beginning ANT NEAT COTTAGE CORNFIELD PATAPON SWEPT, which made me laugh so much I began to chant it, just as it was (nobody ever found out who or what Patapon was), and so it became a family incantation . . . The Book Group – Ruth and Pat and me, and Margaret Watson who had maintained a steady, humorous, intelligent presence through all the Ohakune years (I could never forget her standing by the living room fire and ironing for me all through an afternoon of desperate misery after John died). We'd begun by doing a WEA course on children's reading, spent evenings at one another's fireside through an interesting winter, then proceeded to literature (the novel) and music (the concerto), when we listened systematically to the records that came with the lecture notes, and as systematically fell asleep, one by one, weakened by warmth and ease after the fourteen- or fifteen-hour day we'd already worked.

The reliable *Chronicle* whose filled columns paid so many bills, and its representative, the encroacher – a little man who inched forward as he talked, so you had to keep backing away while he eagerly spouted, 'You keep sendn' it we'll keep printn' it!' Bill and the tree; not my friend Bill Young, but Bill Sellars, Fanny's Bill, who had usually appeared with her the last few years – and been greeted with universal (if secret) disapproval. We were mean about Bill, we didn't think he was good enough for our mother, we didn't like their jokes, and when he called her 'Fay' intimately and tenderly (a name we had never thought of in all the years of trying to improve on 'Fanny'), we hated him. And then they came to stay and he destroyed our tree – got up early one morning and cut nearly all the branches off the dark amethyst conifer that spread most beautifully over the lawn. We couldn't bear him after that. What on earth would have happened if we'd known then that he also used to corner Frances when no one was about and try to kiss her? Nobody knew till after he died, a year or two before we had to leave. Just as well: poor man, he gave Fanny a kind of freedom none of us could offer, partly because he had a car and was entirely at the disposal of his superior friend – and why should she, both of them, not have this late friendship? I was ashamed we'd been so heartless.

I remembered how many we'd known of the newly married who had, like us, moved away from the city after the war, to leave behind earlier plans and ambitions – Bill Young's city practice, the law office Trevor's father had wanted him to prepare for. We weren't the only young family to look for a quiet place in the country. Other women too had wanted large families, though mostly they hadn't gone as far as I had.

Well, we'd done it, and so completely that now I hardly remembered that we'd considered any other life. Politics had become borough council affairs, the new town water supply, for instance, which in the last year had replaced our rusting old tanks. There had been the year we tried to get Ben elected to parliament, of course, and our disgust over the waterfront strike in 1951, not long after we'd come to Ohakune. Country dwellers or not, we'd raged about the National government calling out the Army to break the strike, and when we read an admiring comment in *Time* magazine about 'tough, hardhitting Sidney Holland' we'd cancelled our subscription in protest (though we renewed it, to read about McCarthy and his Un-American Activities witch hunts). Living in Ohakune didn't cut you off from events in the rest of the country, or the world, we had many times insisted, to ourselves and to our friends who'd stayed in town.

    I had another sudden glimpse, an afternoon when we still lived in the farmhouse, a Friday, Trevor home after his weekly visit with other teachers to the Pioneer Club, the children temporarily out in town with Margaret, and the two of us laughing, leaning . . . and then with a half guilty delight finding ourselves locked together on the bed. I remembered thinking, 'This is one of the things marriage is for, that a moment like this is there for the taking' – well, occasionally. It wouldn't happen now; the same flare would simply heat up Trevor's chronic rage against the incompetent Mr Perry, his headmaster – the real reason we were leaving. Ah, days of our lives, looming up, trembling in focus, slowly dissolving . . . I went inside at last and put coffee on the stove.

Chapter 30

Greytown was about the same size as Ohakune but worlds away from it: a self-conscious, educated village, filled not with civic defensiveness but civic pride (not to say complacency), in touch with city people, some of whom lived there and worked in Wellington. A charming, tree-shaded township where the old buildings were carefully preserved and even old trees defended by public protest if threatened by someone's axe. A small town tingling with committee activity, but this time the Beautifying Society, the Settlers' Museum, the mobile library were the aristocratic centres, not footballing and drinking. The Wairarapa, unlike the King Country, was 'wet' and the pubs were substantial old wooden piles, quite grand in their way, and entirely fitting the wooden shopfronts with upstairs quarters where families still lived. Their high sash windows looked out over their verandahs as they had for a hundred years in a settlement begun in 1860 and named after Governor Grey. Ohakune was raw, tough, sketchy in its communal life, Greytown old and proud and conservative; a few of its larger houses were mansions, its orchards and farms had 'homesteads' (the name, in fact of one apple orchard); there was a life of refinement and sophistication there, of cocktail parties and soirées. As well, and in some ways associated with this local grandeur, there were artists – potters, weavers chose to live there for the ambience, painters who liked the light on the hills, the old buildings, the trees; parties of friends drove over the Rimutakas to concerts and exhibitions in Wellington, others sang in choirs in Masterton. 'Take care on the roads,' Noeline Bruning had advised, 'there's a lot of money in the Wairarapa, and long straight roads for fast cars to get up speed.'

Greytown had been the natural choice for a secondary school to serve the small Wairarapa towns, and busloads of students came from Martinborough, Carterton and Featherston to Kuranui College which stood, still self-consciously new, at the southern end of the town. Its first principal, Sam Meads, had learnt his craft in the old-fashioned boys' school tradition of Wellington College. He was immensely chauvinistic, proud, competitive, a fomentor of that ancient institutional virtue *esprit de corps*, though by 1962 when we arrived this was simply called 'school spirit'. He had invited Trevor to be his first assistant because he knew him – a highly respectable way of choosing staff. He was bluff and hearty, with a footballer's physique (and a family name made famous by football), an old-style Kiwi joker's suspicion of women, and a good heart. A grown-up schoolboy and a small-scale imperialist. 'His' teachers lived in a cluster of new houses near the school and locally known as 'Meadsville', but there was not a place there (or perhaps a house large enough) for us, so Sam had arranged for us to live above the chemist's shop in the middle of the main street. In the four years we were to remain there I continually tried to persuade Trevor to move to one of the houses I was always finding for us, but had no more success than I'd had when I wanted to leave Ohakune.

Trevor had a capacity for passive resistance ('inertia' was my word) at which I sometimes marvelled, occasionally laughed, often – and more as time passed – raged. None of these reactions made the slightest difference. He agreed to make changes if forced to, and every year we lived together made it more obvious that there was only one power that could do this – the school, its expectations of him, its rewards in better jobs and the honourable gratitude of parents and other teachers. I saw him, in rare moments of detachment, as a deeply conservative man, caught in the grip of an all-but-consuming ambition. I detested that house. It was cramped and ugly and dark and noisy, and its backyard was abominable, a patch of concrete and grass bounded by a wire fence and an alleyway, a carpark and the wall of Wright Stephenson's liquor store. The back door took you into this open cage, the front door onto the street at the side of the shop. The windows of our bedroom looked over the shop-verandah roof and onto the passing traffic and the butcher's opposite. My first visitor was the teacher's wife who'd lived there before me and had hated it as much as I now did; this was some solace, and in fact Renée and I established an enduring friendship that was built at first on a shared indignation that in Sam's mind (and he was all-powerful), teachers' wives were poor creatures, necessary servants of the great enterprise of the college, but of no interest in themselves – unless they spoke up, in which case they were queer, unsuitable, perhaps radical, rather frightening. I told Renée after a while that I had only one ambition regarding Sam; it was to have a conversation with him in which one sentence, just one, was spoken by me and listened to and answered by him. It never happened.

We came to Greytown as to a summer holiday, stopping to picnic and swim, and spending a few hours with Peg and George and their children. When we drew up at the chemist's shop in full regalia – station-wagon with heads sticking out everywhere, roof-rack with flapping tarpaulin tied over it, bulging trailer – we met our landlord. A tense, good-looking, fussy man, he looked with distaste on this vast caravan, and as he handed us the key visibly (if wordlessly) began making lists of the new rules that would be necessary for occupancy on this scale. The stairs, he confined himself to saying, were noisy if used during shop hours.

He also handed us a letter, which turned out to be a note from Fanny. She had decided she would help us move in, advertised for a room in the town for a few weeks, gave the address and invited us to visit her that very day. Without telling us? Just like that, out of the blue? I felt a surge of rage – it was like the time she and Lewis had arrived unannounced in Ohakune. Fanny never seemed to get anything right these days. I knew she tried – goodness, she was always trying, as though each time she changed places, moved to another house, made a fresh proposal for staying with one of us, she would find what she was looking for, whatever it was.

I could see she'd lost her old secure foundations and thus her bearings, and I admired the way she made a point of not complaining (though that too could be irritating). All the same, she was like a child learning new lessons and almost always getting them wrong – look at how she turned our household upside down by making new rules for everyone when she came to stay. She must have an outdoor room – there was only the big tent; Trevor, the least handy of men, must fix up the connections for light, heat, her radio. All reasonable enough, yet these demands had a way of becoming a crisis just as a child was ready to leave for a school trip, or one of the small girls had brought the sky down on her head by scraping the skin off a knee or elbow, or Trevor was late coming home and everyone was quarrelsome, starving, and I'd forgotten the stove so the soup or stew had gone off the boil. I always repented afterwards, resolved not to be exasperated next time, remembered that she was alone and felt precarious and was getting old. And then she would send children on messages – Frances, say, and Martin – and give one of them sixpence as a reward and not the other, and I'd be furious all over again. She was often rather unyielding towards Martin anyway; charming child as he was, he perhaps reminded her painfully of her own young son, especially since he had an obvious physical likeness to John.

When Clive and Lindsay and I met, as occasionally we did, we grumbled about our mother – a new and querulous habit, so long had she been adored by us all. Clearly in need of our affection too, and our reassurance. Had we now lost (or perhaps never had) a view of her as a separate, suffering human being, not merely our parent? On this occasion she had come to be helpful and succeeded only in being a nuisance. Right at the end of her stay, and for just a short time, she and I managed to talk frankly, as we had once done so satisfyingly. I drove her to the Masterton station to catch the Hawke's Bay railcar, and as I embraced her, felt her thin arms and shoulders, I found I was crying, for all the losses and sorrows a life has to hold and the knowledge that I could not now comfort her, nor she me. We had a separate present and a different future, and mine, I saw, was richer and stronger than hers.

Driving home I thought of how many places she'd tried to make herself a home in since she'd left hospital five years before. There had been the rest-home in Havelock North with its emphasis, appropriately, on health food and exercise; then two attempts to live with other families – Clive Price, and Lindsay and Doug – and her bitter disappointment at each refusal; the time in the Wanganui boarding house. Enterprising in its way, and fruitful in that she'd met there the problematical but useful Bill, who went to stay with her in the apartment in Clive and Dorothy's house she'd built for herself and John. It was bearable, she said, because now so changed by the tenants (they were away at the time). As for having her new friend there, she'd said, quaintly, to Dorothy, 'It's all right at our age, isn't it?'

This was followed by a valiant, sometimes funny and sometimes touching struggle to live with him in Napier and preserve the decencies by installing a caravan in the garden which he was supposed to occupy. Quite revolutionary really, in 1958. Then there was another house, one I did not see; Lindsay, closer to Napier and not quite as overrun by children as I, was more in touch with these movements, though Fanny's visits to Clive and me continued. What a mixture it all was; her letters were still charming, often amusing, gracious in their concern for whatever concerned us (but this too had a faintly irritating side – she had taken to writing with carbons so we all got the same letter, the top and the lower dimmer copies evenly distributed). Despite the acts of discrimination with the children she could still be great fun, inventive and full of games and stories; often they liked her. Did I? Oh yes; she hadn't stopped being a compelling personality, and of course I would never give up feeling responsible for her. We (the Scotts) all did that for one another, however disconnected our lives and habits, however sharp our impatience. (I noted in passing that this was not true for all families, as I'd once thought; Trevor's, for instance, maintained much slighter, less personal links.)

After Bill died, Fanny moved into the last and best of the Napier houses, a pleasant wooden bungalow with an old-fashioned peaked and gabled roof and finials; it was on the waterfront at the port, she could walk by the sea, ships came and went. She made the house elegant and was happy there; lonely too, but more resigned to her solitariness than anyone would have thought possible a few years before. Furiously regretting my earlier impatience, I decided that we must visit her at Hardinge Road at . . . at . . . Easter, yes, that would do. And I drove on home.

The pattern of life in Greytown came into focus. For all that it was a small village, to live right in its main street was to live 'in town'. I felt less private, less free to think my own thoughts and considerably less independent than I had ever before. This sense of being at the mercy of my community, almost possessed by it, was strongly reinforced by my membership, unwanted as it might be, of Sam's patriarchy: he was the headman, and teachers and their families the tribe. At least, I could reflect, I didn't have to live in the Meadsville compound. There, it was not unknown for Sam himself to be seen (if you looked out a window) working in your vegetable garden and sometimes harvesting its crops.

Everything was close, intertwined. The camping ground, bush reserve and swimming baths were round the corner, ten minutes' walk away, and all four of the older children were at once drawn into the swimming club, so that in no time it came to assume the place in our lives that horse riding had held. This was partly because Frances was instantly recognised as a good swimmer and snapped up by the club coach. Her friend Claudia, who came to college by bus from Featherston, was a girl with a witty tongue and as much taste as Frances for self-dramatisation (the mature fruit of the childhood scenes and tantrums). These girls, though maddening at times, were a constant source of entertainment for me: in the next few years when the worldwide Beatles craze rolled into our town, to our door, Frances and Claudia learned all their songs and would come down the stairs singing with a florid grandeur, flinging their arms around each other as Beatles substitutes.

Everyone fell in love with Virginia, all the more, it seemed, because she responded coolly. She had had boyfriends in Ohakune, but everything in Greytown was more refined, more confident, and so were her admirers, poised young men who made quite polished conversation when they brought their fathers' cars to collect her for an outing. When she was late home, and indeed when any of the others didn't arrive at the very moment I expected, I worried. Worry became for a time a sort of disease. I had monstrous fantasies about cars in ditches, dead bodies strewn over the road, swimmers drowned, children lost or kidnapped or unaccountably mutilated. Trevor did his best to dismiss these nightmares by making fun of them, but one night, goaded by my distraught ravings, he did take dramatic action. It was a scene which could take place nowhere except at an upstairs bedroom window looking out over a street, and it assumed at once the quality of a Jacques Tati farce. Father in striped pyjamas pushing up the window and leaning out to shout at embarrassed daughter and amazed young man gazing up from their goodnights beside motor car drawn up to the kerb in a silent village street in the small hours of the morning ... Virginia, naturally, was furious; I was secretly entertained, and cured, I think, of some of my terrors.

Trevor could also give sage advice about how to jolly difficult teenagers along, ease them through their traumas without caring too much oneself. I was grateful for this advice, and often asked for it, but I was completely unable to follow the last bit about not caring. I saw him as a professional and admired his skill; it did not occur to either of us that there could be anything professional about my own job as a parent. In fact in the heady atmosphere of his new authority, Trevor seemed to take on some of the colour of Sam's view of the world – that is, of the school and those insufficient creatures, the wives of teachers, who nourished and supported the front line. He spent longer times than ever at school and when, quite soon, he began to produce Gilbert and Sullivan operas, his whole location, the very base of his existence, seemed to move from home to school.

The effects of all this I felt most strongly at teachers' parties. These had quite a different character anyway from the more homely gatherings I'd known in Ohakune; they were larger, smarter, more glittering, more tense. They had an undercurrent of competitiveness that I found menacing, as though this was a social courtroom in which everyone knew and obeyed the law, and I alone was condemned for ignorance or inferiority.

The teachers talked shop. I didn't know how to stop them and saw hardly any evidence that other wives tried. They laughed at jokes I did not understand, they were intimate and gay with one another, sometimes flirtatious, out of patience with anyone who couldn't 'join in', especially, I thought, my unfortunate self. I supposed my awkwardness made for them a particularly sharp contrast with Trevor's popularity and ease. Whether this was so or not, Trevor himself thought me exasperating, recalcitrant: why couldn't I enjoy these dos? What the hell was the matter? They were all nice people, weren't they? You just had to relax. It wasn't as though I was left out; he always took me, didn't he? If he'd been playing around with one of the other wives, as Bob or Fred or someone was, I'd have something to complain about; he *wanted* me there, needed me in fact, I was part of the show.

Impossible to explain that I had become wracked with jealousies about school, the other teachers, the whole enterprise that so stunningly enclosed him and left me out – in fact I hardly realised myself that jealousy was the name for the horrible dread that took hold of me when he went off to dance, laugh, joke, flirt with Mona or Doreen or Stella. I only knew that my smile became stiffer than ever, my conversation more jerky and irrelevant, my urge to go home (which began almost from the moment of arrival) more insistent.

Later in our Greytown years one of the other men began to make a great fuss of me, and this I had to admit I enjoyed, but by then I was beyond the hope of safety or comfort on the risky carousel of aging marriages. Several we knew had begun to look shaky: the music teacher ignored his wife and flirted openly with a senior student, a mixture of affairs hopelessly tangled two other couples. Even our old friends, Peg and George, whom we still often saw, had each fallen in love with other people and were on the point of separation. The world of the married was a much more unstable place than I had imagined.

In any case by then a major calamity of a quite different kind had overtaken us and was, as it turned out, about to change the whole course of our lives together. From the day of our arrival Trevor had thought of moving on – not because he didn't like Greytown; he manifestly did. It was because the promotion to deputy principal (which he felt to have been long delayed) led naturally to the next step up, a principalship. Mr Barclay's 'Good-morning-you'll-be-a-headmaster' had done its work, but the fact was that the whole secondary school system was one of success for some linked to the failure of others, a fiercely competitive hierarchy. Teachers talked constantly of interviews, short lists, and school boards' idiosyncrasies in choosing from them men all over the country (there were no women, except in girls' schools) who had 'made it', or 'missed out', 'got stuck' without a principal's job. The smallest school in the most unlikely district was better than nothing.

Trevor too began to apply for jobs. He brought the *Gazette* home and we scanned it, then the map, for towns we didn't know, before filling in the elaborate form which we hoped would produce a summons to an interview. Several times it did, but he came home again still unchosen. Then he went to Greymouth. We had never been to the West Coast but agreed it was worth a try, and the board almost offered him the job. He promised to consider it, but came home very disturbed; the place was remote, grim, unprepossessing, he disliked it on sight and had decided to take the proposition no further.

He was called next to Opunake, a small town in Taranaki, and I went with him to the interview in the Education Board office in New Plymouth. On the journey we had great fun; it was exciting to be away for a whole day and a night without any children, and we were both exhilarated by the knowledge that the success so longed for was on its way. After dinner at the little Opunake pub (a night at a hotel was like an orgy), we walked about the town and made up stories about its inhabitants, including the triumphant new arrivals, ourselves.

The next afternoon I waited in the car for the conquering hero to emerge from the dull but portentous portals of the board office. When he came out and walked across the road I scarcely recognised him. His face was grey and set; as he approached the car he looked at me but could not smile – indeed he could hardly speak. When he did, his voice was a dry croak: 'I've got it'. I set about offering him congratulations and assuring him that success at last would be a wonderful thing, it was terrific news. Nothing made any impression. We drove home almost in silence; when we got there he did not want to see anyone, least of all Sam or the other teachers, though the phone kept ringing with their congratulations.

It was a strange time. For several weeks he behaved as if he had moved into a kind of darkness where nobody could follow. He would go to school, and appeared to perform there much as usual – except that he smoked far more heavily and came home earlier. Then he would simply sit upstairs in our room in a state of black terror, and I would talk to him, on and on, trying to make the new job and all that went with it seem easy and manageable. Was there something else causing this extraordinary upheaval in him? If so, I had no idea what it could be, and supposed that constant reassurance would in the end bring him out of his dark tunnel. Not so. As pressure mounted for him to talk to the new school board, make decisions about the house we were offered, plan courses for the next term, it slowly became clear that he had no real intention of going. It was simply not possible. Finally I could not support the inexplicably slippery situation alone any more: I rang Sam.

About the same time Noeline Bruning visited us; after only a few minutes of talking to Trevor and observing the lost look on his face, she said, 'He must see a psychiatrist – I know the right person.' A psychiatrist? 'This is a breakdown,' said Noeline briefly. She knew an elderly Jungian therapist, a Mrs Christeller, who was no longer in practice but would take occasional cases for friends. Trevor must go to her – and in due course he did.

More pressingly, Sam, Doug Banks, the local doctor, and I worked out a formula for Trevor to be relieved of the immediate nightmares that shrouded him so suddenly and mystifyingly – a letter which explained his withdrawal from the new job on medical grounds, and agreed in advance that he would not apply for another for two years. We began to make regular visits to Wellington. Trevor would go to Mrs Christeller, the children and I would visit Pat and Ken Lawn who had left Raetihi and lived in the city. They were rather pleasant visits, Trevor's spirits lifted, Mrs Christeller was perceptive and kind. She saw him as a scholarly, thoughtful person who would be better to stay away from the urgent pressures of institutional authority. We would eat with our friends and drive home over the long Rimutaka Hill road late at night, children asleep in the back of the car. A settled pattern emerged, a future: Trevor would get well, and the wretched secondary school promotion system which demanded such constant homage from its teachers, so relentlessly kept their ambitions aflame, would for a while leave us in peace.

He turned to teachers' union politics instead. The Post-Primary Teachers' Association offered expansion without danger, and he took to it as though born for committees, negotiations, meetings, chairmanship. He moved upwards quickly and before long was spending a good many weekends at regional or national meetings, staying in hotels in various towns with other teachers, discussing policy, convincing the indolent or ignorant of the importance of political action.

I had myself been excited by a whiff of political power in Ben Winchcombe's campaign to become a Labour MP, but this new enthusiasm for teacher politics made me cross, bored and unco-operative. I detested PPTA parties, when I had to go to them, almost more than the local staff jollifications. Here, I thought nastily, was another closed circle, ripe with complacency. I could do no more than hover uselessly about its edges, trying to crack the codes of its secret language, and was irked to see that other wives smilingly formed a chorus line of praise and encouragement for their more venturesome partners. I worried a good deal about these incapacities of mine, but at the same time a sort of slow indignation began to take shape in my mind. Not merely that Trevor now spent almost all his time, and certainly his best energies, on projects that kept him away from our big busy household, which I thus managed alone. As well, I had a growing sense that I had spent a great deal of my time and thought on helping him regain his peace of mind (or trying to), and each time he emerged encouraged and cheerful from a black spell he redoubled his efforts at school, in the ubiquitous operas, with rugby and cricket teams, or for the PPTA. None of the benefit, I savagely – though silently – observed, came my way.

I did not in the least understand why such a morass of rage and pain should roll about inside me like slowly heating lava. I admonished myself: Trevor had suffered a kind of hidden terror I had never known, he must have whatever experience restored his balance, his forward momentum. I redoubled my efforts, I was sympathetic to the last degree when he felt morose, then the same cycle would reappear: he would vanish, comforted, into his separate world. My hateful feelings returned.

Only very gradually did I come to suspect that my own eager helpfulness might have been part of the cause of this dislocation. Nobody had ever said to me 'Keep out of this,' or 'You are not a therapist,' or perhaps 'Let the experts do it,' and it never occurred to me that it might be wise to do so. My response to Trevor's trouble had been simple, childlike, naive: I loved him, I must do everything I could for him in his distress. In those years I learned a whole new knowledge, a new vocabulary, a new cynicism. In dealing with depressive illness, helpfulness was often a delusion, loving observation misplaced egotism, generosity a trap. Everything had the wrong names, an evil underside; to give was to lose, hope bred despair, love came back as cruelty, and was perhaps half cruelty itself. They were bad days and, when I woke up and couldn't go back to sleep, black and fearful nights.

I came to think of illness as a predatory monster. Having found lodging in one person, it then looked about for whoever was nearest, and willingly available, and reached out to fasten its tentacles around them. I was first in line. Had I not developed in childhood, and practised ever since, the habit of sustaining my own family, feeling their woes as mine? Had I not gloried in my prowess as supporter, sympathetic listener, patient friend? The extreme thanklessness of Trevor's response felt at first like an undeserved punishment; I slowly discovered that this is the character of this kind of illness, this greedy and heartless monster, and that if I didn't learn to put myself at a distance I would remain part of its inexorable cycle of despair, recovery, relapse.

Through all this, my children, and apparently the rest of the world, ate, slept, played, lived what are called normal lives, had pleasures and adventures, grew older, changed. Virginia, I reported to Fanny in my still regular letters, was becoming quite an intellectual, liked to discuss serious subjects, led the school debating team. Frances was full of zest and energy, came top of her class, was still doing homework at 11 pm if I didn't intervene, went to swimming championships and won places and prizes. Martin was beginning to want to devour facts and make discoveries about the great world; he read piles of books to nourish each obsession as it came – insects, battleships, aeroplanes, cricketers, ancient cities. Rachel danced and sang at school and Sunday school, liked still to dream but easily joined the rest of the clever Edmond kids in being top of the class. She swam too, a junior in the shadow of an illustrious older sister in a star-conscious swimming club. And the two little girls played and made up the world, populating it with paper dolls and other less visible characters. Then Stephanie started school and Katherine had to find compensation for the wonders we all heard about. She soon did so. The Queen visited Greytown kindergarten, and Katherine described for us how she got out of her coach at the gate and walked in among the children, speaking, it appeared, only to her.

As for their awareness of the difficulties that beset their parents, this seemed not to matter too much, at least on the surface of things. We were used to carrying on through lesser crises – having no money to pay half the bills, month after month postponing buying new shoes, raincoats, suitcases, camping gear, blankets; the recurring battles and minor hysterics when Fanny came to stay; my frequent eruptions of hatred for our narrow boxed-in living quarters; sporadic tears and quarrels, which of course were kept for late at night. I believed in protecting my children, even though several of them were well on the way to being grown up themselves, from the unlovely aspects of adult behaviour.

Chapter 31

The summer before the Opunake crisis something else had occurred which was hardly recognisable as a major event, yet as time passed proved to have been the beginning of a profound and enduring change. It happened, however, only to me, and affected me most deeply. We were in Napier for our summer camping holiday, installed in our big tent in the grassy expanses of Kennedy Park. It was the last year of the full-scale family holidays, and everyone was there.

One afternoon I sat in the tent alone and watched the family out on the grass playing cricket with their father. I often elected to stay in or about the tent instead of romping about with bats and balls because it was a chance to feed, even temporarily, my permanently unsatisfied craving to read; it was also the only time in the year when Trevor, a natural sportsman, was completely at his children's disposal. All was well. I turned my pages peacefully, then at a sudden shout looked up, and as I watched a kind of somersault took place in my mind. The figures moving about on that green background suddenly changed, took on a new angle, almost a new dimension. I saw them as I never had before – they were my dearest people in all the world, almost everything I thought and did was directed towards their welfare, their happiness and fulfilment. And I saw with blinding clarity that not one of them thought there was a single thing to be done for me, in my turn. I didn't have a turn. I didn't exist, except as I helped them to exist. Without them I was nothing, and so they perceived me – theirs, useful, indeed necessary, loved of course, depended upon; but as a person with possible separate requirements of my own, not there. And nobody, not even I, thought this unbalanced or wrong. I shook all over, that moment in a hot afternoon, I was so struck by the momentousness of the discovery. It must have happened gradually – was that why I had seen nothing of it till this instant? It was not even as though a major cathartic event had shed light on it; this was a peaceful day with everything perfectly in order. Perhaps it was an idea, a little nub of knowledge, that had been waiting just outside consciousness for a very long time and, catching me off guard, quickly and quietly entered.

Trevor, when I talked to him, saw that I felt strongly about some lack of my own occupations, though not that this was really any concern of his. However, he made the quite sensible suggestion that as I'd always regretted not finishing my degree I should enrol as an extramural student at Massey University. I was interested at once, and keen to begin. English was the obvious first choice, related as it was to my twin passions of writing and reading; and I was tempted to complete the Education II course I'd begun as part of my speech therapy training. Letters came and went with great urgency (at least on my part), I ordered the English II and Education II books through interloan at the Greytown library since I couldn't afford to buy them. I simmered with anticipation.

Another project appeared too – the teaching of Playcentre mothers in the Wairarapa. I would drive to Martinborough in the evening, once a week, and for two hours discuss child-rearing with young mothers less experienced than I. The course was based on a series of printed lectures, part of the same adult education scheme that had supplied the books and music I'd studied in Ohakune, but I was now a paid tutor. I hadn't earned any money to speak of (a few pounds for rare days of relieving in the primary school, nothing more) since I'd taught at Worser Bay school the year my first baby was born. *Wanganui Chronicle* cheques had been ours, not mine. The tiny tutor's fee was absurdly pleasing.

As well, I liked talking to women whose lives were quite unlike mine, though we were all equally aware of our parenthood. The narrowness of some of their experience horrified me, the isolation when husbands worked from early morning to late at night, and even when they were home thought children's learning nothing to do with them unless a beating was called for. Some were actually hostile to the women's attempt to educate themselves, and the classes had to be kept a secret. What should you do, one woman asked, if your six-year-old son wets the bed, sets fire to his room, runs away? The other women were ready with ideas, we spent almost a whole evening on that one case, but I came away feeling depressed. I had thought my child care lonely and unsupported, but here was a whole bleak territory of struggle, ignorance, despair, and women wrestling with it alone.

We had a visit from another tutor who happened to ask me if I'd read *The Feminine Mystique* by Betty Friedan, and lent me her copy. At once I was in the middle of a whole series of mental somersaults, a carnival of sudden new views and changed ideas – a revolution. I could hardly believe it. Thousands of women all over America were saying in interviews again and again that their families were well, happy, busy fulfilling their ambitions, their husbands likewise, and yet beneath this apparently perfect façade they themselves suffered a profound and inexplicable malaise. Extraordinary as it was, it seemed that at the same moment women thousands of miles apart were coming to exactly the same conclusion. Years of patient dedication to one's husband and children, the best and happiest kind of life, appeared to have an unpleasant secret hidden within it, and like parallel inventors we had unknowingly come upon it at the same time.

Oddly enough, nothing changed much at first. Or, more exactly, becoming a student again was so enormously interesting that I didn't have time to think of what other changes might be possible. Then Trevor's illness engulfed me, and with it the urgent desire to maintain family equilibrium and reduce shocks and uncertainties to a minimum. I had long since forgotten George McCullough's reproof that I protected my children too much; my instinct was to save them if I could, from turbulence they had done nothing to cause, and I followed it.

I worked while they were at school, did washing and housework and cooking after they came home, when I could talk as I worked. I sat upstairs in our room, hunched over *Tess of the D'Urbervilles* at nine o'clock in the morning after everyone had left, ignoring even the breakfast dishes. I'd read it before, but found ten times the pleasure in it now, and some of that came from the heady experience of turning upside down the domestic routine that had dominated my days for fifteen years. Reading for Education was rather less intoxicating, requiring as it did the absorption of huge textbooks, mostly written in America in a new and hateful language – my first encounter with the new social science jargons. I used to fall asleep over these wretched tomes every afternoon; one day I woke to hear the children coming up the stairs and Virginia's voice saying, 'She'll be in my room in the sun, asleep with her book.' This made me laugh, but it didn't stop it happening.

I went to vacation courses, alone, wonderfully alone. Trevor agreed to stay home, friends helped; it seemed hardly possible that everyone would survive my absence, but they did, quite easily. The lectures were like bombs going off in my head. By the end of the afternoons my head hurt, not with a headache, rather a feeling that the brain was expanding so fast that its stiff joints hurt as they were rushed into action. Every word was an illumination. A writer's shaping of fictional characters, as these dazzlingly perceptive lecturers described it, was so filled with currents and eddies of the real life and real people I knew that I felt constant little stabs of recognition; my whole body tingled with them. At night, in the students' Pink Hostel, I dozed lightly and fitfully, too excited to sleep.

There were others like me, women – and a few men – who had left school early or in some way neglected their education the first time. That was a surprise too, and pleasant, but the real electricity was generated by the lectures and discussions. A young Irishman called J. O'Gorman so stirred me with his analysis of *Middlemarch* that I had to go and talk to him after the lecture. 'It's all to do with the questions you ask,' he said. A remark with a wider application, I thought, life and literature stunningly coming together at every turn.

The next year I took French. Perhaps the ghost of Miss Moncrieff, the French teacher I'd adored in the third form, touched my elbow. But French had changed too. You had to speak the wretched language, not just recite verbs; make conversation, say ordinary casual things. Plays were performed (at the vacation course) without introduction or explanation in English – like Sartre's *Huis Clos*. I was fascinated and appalled at the idea of hell being a cycle of constant small cruelties inflicted by one person on another and repeated through all eternity. This was part of another revolution in my mind and outlook, prompted not by reflection on my own experience, or not that alone, but by my first encounter with one of the great intellectual and philosophical movements of the century – existentialism.

Initiated by a young lecturer with a wonderful guttural French 'r' (from somewhere near the German border, I imagined, but he turned out to be a New Zealander from Pukekohe), I read Jean-Paul Sartre and Albert Camus, and a great deal about how they arrived at their by then famous idea. 'L'absurde', I discovered, was a name for the anguish of modern man who wants to live for ever but can no longer believe he will go to heaven when he dies. From there I followed them to 'moi, c'est mon projet': my life is my own, it is all I have; mine – since God will no longer take it for me – is the responsibility to find its meaning, to become (as they put it), 'authentic'. It appealed to me that part of the 'projet' for French thinkers was to be found in the wartime Resistance.

I knew of Kierkegaard, the Christian existentialist who apparently had a way of modernising God, but I did not read him, largely because I ran out of time – as I was always doing, no matter how I contorted my daily routine, or how late I managed to stay awake at night. Television burst upon our household that year (it had already entered a good many others), and this worked to my advantage because I could vanish upstairs well before the older children were in bed, knowing they would have nothing to say, ask, demand, object to, discuss, while their thrilling personal picture show flickered in a corner of the living room.

Exams were held in a church hall in Masterton, and at the end of that year, in preparation, I pinned the exam timetable on the wall above the table where I worked. There too were various other notices about notable events, one of which was the primary school Calf Club Day. No one in the family had a pet animal to show (though we had tasted this experience in Ohakune with Sam the Lamb) but Rachel and Stephanie and Katherine and Martin all had drawings, stories, projects on display; naturally I must be there. I was too, but since the Calf Club details had somehow obscured the French exam, I set about going to that the next morning, twenty-four hours late. I made a panic-stricken phone call to the French Department at Massey, explained breathlessly that I'd seen no one, could know nothing of the paper, begged to be allowed to sit. Sorry, impossible; never allowed. 'There's one every year,' said the laconic voice. I squirmed. Useless to trumpet my excuses, my good intentions. I sat the horrible thing the next year, and passed. Extramural students do well.

Reading and learning, constructing essays, took over from the writing of stories and poems as my secret life, to be cherished but not talked about. However, I had friends among the Kuranui teachers who had long since completed their degrees, and to them there was nothing odd about my new occupation. Just along the street, with a front door even more directly onto the pavement than mine, lived Margaret Lopdell, daughter of my old training college hero Frank Lopdell. I visited her, sometimes with Pat Patterson, a Home Economics teacher I also liked; occasionally we shared her front entrance, the only one she had, with the grocery boy, a postman or, in winter, the coal man, who had to take his dusty sack along her carpeted passage to the back regions of her flat. 'Living on the street' took on new meanings in our neighbourhood.

I also went to afternoon tea parties for teachers' wives given by Betty Meads, and had to admit that, however objectionable Sam's hierarchies, she was a model of grace and tact as a hostess. If one had to be a headmaster's wife – and I supposed one day this fate would overtake me – hers was the example to hold up to one's apprehensive gaze. One of these tea parties produced an unexpected phenomenon, a new arrival who was not a teacher, not even married to one.

'This is – ' began Betty, 'Barbara . . . look, I'm sorry, I've forgotten your other name.'

'Oh . . . well . . . my goodness, I've almost forgotten it myself,' said an elegant grey-haired woman with a very English voice. I laughed, and of course wanted to talk to this surprising new person. It was the beginning of a profoundly sustaining friendship. When Trevor was so mysteriously ill, lost to himself and to me, it was Barbara I went to with my perplexities; wiser than I, she listened but offered no explanations, developed no theories, conceived no advice.

Renée Turner, the friend who so well understood the miseries of residence above the chemist's shop, also embarked on journeys of the mind that took her a long way from her origins, though these were different from mine. She and Trev were South Islanders and had lived and worked at Medbury in Christchurch, a small church school which prepared pupils for Christ's College. They and their children, a little younger than ours, were active members of the Anglican church. The vicar was a genial individual known as Whisky Bill who ran the parish like a club; we too took some part in its affairs, though I felt uneasy about my lack of conviction.

My adolescent fervour for Anglican doctrine and observance had, I believed, been fully extinguished by Archdeacon Young's crude evangelising after John's death, but about this time it produced another flicker. When Trevor's distress was at its deepest, I went to church and truly prayed – for what? Wisdom? Enlightenment? Relief? Whatever it was, I didn't receive it. The following year I began to read the existentialists and gave up for ever supposing that God (whatever I meant by that) awaited me in the Anglican service, beautiful as its sonorous cadences still were.

I once asked a friend who, like Renée, was an active church participant, if she believed in God. 'I don't know,' she replied. 'That's not exactly the point.' Renée's religion, or perhaps her temperament, was of a different order. When she began to question her faith she read widely, considered other doctrines different from Christianity, and in the end detached herself from Anglicanism – but not from the study of religion, which took her, too, back to university, to a degree in Religious Studies and later a lectureship. Adult study led women like us out of our wife-and-mother occupations (though these of course continued) and along new tracks whose end we could not possibly foresee.

Times were changing, and not just for women. A year after we left Greytown, Lloyd Geering became a national figure by challenging the more conservative tenets of Presbyterian doctrine and being accused of heresy. And my old reforming conviction, carried more or less intact from my student days at the 'political university', also received its death blow.

The *Listener* carried a small boxed feature called 'I Know What I Think' (I myself, with unusual boldness, occasionally contributed to it); one week James K. Baxter recorded there the collapse of his own political faith, learned like mine before and during the war, when young men and women all over the world were star-struck by the Marxist experiment in Russia. We had believed, said Baxter, that poverty was the greatest evil; if you gave a poor man enough to eat, he became good. But the war had been followed by boom times, the Depression had faded from people's minds, and the lamentable fact was that being well off made nobody any better. Marx's connection between money and morals was not one of the great absolute truths, after all, and this was a sharp disappointment to him. I realised I knew it too, and minded in the same way.

My first year of extramural study had ended with calamities at home and abroad. In November John F. Kennedy had been assassinated; Trevor was still too ill to pay much attention, and for the first time in nearly twenty years of marriage I pondered alone the causes and implications of an international crisis. Public and private torments haunted me as I frowned over my exam revision.

I turned forty, and though I hadn't taken much account of such landmarks – even twenty-one had not seemed especially significant –

I did find, in the years of the early forties, that again and again I looked at my life more consciously and critically. For the first time it occurred to me that I would not after all do everything – become the good pianist I'd not managed to be, compose piano music, take up drawing, neglected since my teens, be a scholar instead of the dilettante I felt I was, even become a brilliant conversationalist, not someone seized by vagueness and confusion at crucial moments. And, of course, be a writer. Write poems. Even that had slipped away, and I'd never done it so it mattered anyway. I had not in fact published a single poem, ever.

I talked to Trevor about some of these realisations, and found he had them too, though the details were different. We did still, though less often now, have peaceful, engrossed conversations that weren't about school or headmastering or PPTA or problems. Was it, we asked aloud, that for the first part of your life you were a sort of receiver, the beneficiary of older people's plans, care, support, and then in the middle – if turning forty was the middle (Trevor had already got there a few years before) – this changed? You began to see you'd had your share of their preparations for you, and now had to attend to your own life and its direction, as well as working and planning for those younger than you, especially your children. In the larger sense, was it that you'd been busy absorbing the ideas, books, theories, educational and otherwise, the intellectual and material provender that the world had for you, and now it was your job to help provide that for other people? A moralistic view, but then we were a moralistic generation; one that didn't precisely fit the facts either, since I was setting out to be a student again, to start at the bottom. Perhaps it had something to do with the retreat of parents, the decline of the old family. Trevor's father had died while we were in Ohakune, his mother a few years later; and Fanny, though she was sprightly enough in the way she talked and wrote, had now moved from her house in Napier to a wing in Wairoa Hospital.

Our relationship with the Edmonds had always seemed sparse and formal compared with the vigorous and sometimes exasperating intimacy of the Scotts. Trevor's family had no tradition of the close, voluble, sometimes chaotic conversation of mine, nor was it as practised as we were in the mutual exposure of the self, especially the secret aspirations, fears and regrets of parenthood, as well as its poignant entertainments. I probably relished this old habit more than Clive and Lindsay. My life-long conversations with Fanny had been most fundamentally about the mysteries of people's lives, their motives, the cause and effect of every kind of behaviour. It was a passion that could only grow with my absorption in my own young family.

Remarkably, Fanny was better able to conduct her single life in Wairoa than she had been at any time during the nomadic period of the Napier houses. Of course in Elinor Harvey Ward she was not alone, and this was probably a relief, though a geriatric community cannot have been any easier to live in than the TB ward where she'd suffered such nightmares of alienation years before. But Fanny had made good use of her mistakes, and had learnt some at least of the rough lessons of loneliness. The real advantage of living in Wairoa – apart from the fact that her breathing was now so impaired that she lacked the strength to manage her own household – was that she was in daily contact with one of the families, Lindsay's. And she'd found out at last how to be a courteous and undemanding grandparent, affectionate yet detached.

She was a woman with a long history of being cherished and protected, and had acquired all the dependencies that this engenders, not to mention the innate dependency of the chronically frail. Her mastery of the difficulties she'd faced, when left alone, brought her back to me, in a sense, as someone I could again love and respect. As she completed her journey towards maturity I was just beginning to glimpse the direction of my own, though we did not ever have the chance (how we would have enjoyed it!) to realise this by talking together.

Although Trevor and I could still occasionally find a shared point of view, there were more and more currents and fluctuations in my mind, and undoubtedly in Trevor's, which we kept to ourselves. For one thing, the deep discontent I had felt during his recovery from his illness remained unresolved. More significantly, perhaps, the Greytown years represented for me some loss of ground: if marriage is a bargain, a tension, a constructive mechanism to contain the 'battle of the sexes', ours had begun to shift its axis. The two poles between which we moved in orbit were 'home' and 'school' as separate enterprises. In the four years we'd lived above the chemist's shop, 'school' had captured a good deal of territory, which I had been powerless to hold. Partly of course this was because the older children actually joined that camp, if camp it was. Trevor was a highly popular teacher; their talking to him about school affairs took over a great many dinner tables and evenings. The adult conversation we had with friends and visitors also tended to move in his direction, and become a sort of background to the news, where, as a History teacher, he had a special knowledge. I, with scarcely time to read the newspaper, had none.

At the same time, whether anyone knew it or not, I was making intellectual journeys of my own. In those years I entered a larger world, though I wouldn't have claimed I had any sort of foothold in it. I went on reading feminist writers, so knew that my lowly status in the family was one that millions of women shared with me. My literature study in both English and French had opened up new philosophical vistas, and in an odd way I felt at home with these discoveries – I had after all grown up in a family which habitually examined the meanings and purposes of human life.

But the world had become insistent news anyway, and not only for women. Early in 1965 the American bombing of Vietnam began, and Keith Holyoake's prevarications about sending New Zealand troops; the social upheaval which came to be known as 'the sixties revolution' was well advanced in America. Flower Power and the hippie movement, the Counter Culture, student riots in Europe and the States – all these were reverberating in our minds, though Greytown couldn't quite be said to be changing its style, yet. There was also that wonder of science, the contraceptive pill, and nobody knew what its effects might be.

But considering how much was changing, it is remarkable how much stayed the same. A family, like any institution, grows a core of conviction out of which its forward momentum keeps flowing, no matter how its patterns are disturbed. In obvious ways 1965 was a year of achievement for the Edmond family. At Christmas I compiled for Fanny a scrapbook of family artifacts, newspaper cuttings and photos: Martin in a junior football team, Poshy Edmond (that was Rachel) in the top maths group, Stephanie with a Mona Lisa smile, 'S. and K. the family's best friends', Virginia was dux of Kuranui College, Frances proved herself the fastest swimmer in the country, doing freestyle over a 100-metre distance at national championships in Dunedin. She and the others were all top of their classes, or nearly, a recognisable triumph in a competitive school system. I passed my subjects, Trevor's production of *The Yeomen of the Guard* (in which Virginia and Frances took part) was spectacular, and we had our first teenage party to mark its final night.

In January, having for two years avoided applying for headmasters' jobs, Trevor returned to the race and was appointed principal of Huntly College in the Waikato. I had tried hard to persuade him to consider other possibilities, especially lectureships at teachers' colleges, an option chosen by talented teachers who did not like the headmastering hierarchy or could not rise in it. He actually completed one application, and I offered to take it to the post office, a couple of doors along the street, but at the very moment of reaching towards the box I found Trevor beside me, seizing the letter to take it home again. I remained much more wary than he about the warning inherent in the Opunake crisis. We left Greytown in the May holidays.

Evidence of the elevated status we were to enjoy in Huntly came as soon as we arrived. We were installed in the town's chief hotel while our house was being freshly painted. We had never stayed in a hotel before and were enchanted with everything, from a waitress offering Martin a Coke at dinner time, to the manager taking Trevor's hand with proper obsequiousness and welcoming him as a new-found local dignitary. We laughed a lot, we fancied ourselves; apparently there was advantage for everyone in this dreaded headmastering. When we moved it was to a blue house on a hill overlooking the town, and set at the top of a long sloping section, a sort of mown paddock. The house had been built by an Education Board architect who afterwards got the sack for introducing more stylish designs than the education system could afford, and, though small, it did have considerable style and originality, especially in the addition of a study, an extra room built at the top of a steep little staircase of its own, giving the house three levels and a view out over the river, the town and part of the lake, so that they became almost beautiful.

The truth is that it was an ugly town, with a crabbed and ill-tempered image of itself; mining villages surrounded it and provided some of its money – it was quite a wealthy place – but it had failed to develop the civic pride we had grown used to in Greytown. There we had been received with congratulations for having chosen our location so well; here, characteristically, people we met began with, 'Did you have to come?' or 'We're only here for a while' or, more concisely, 'The money's good.' Business firms, banks, insurance companies, commercial networks of various kinds seemed to send their employees here as though it was a kind of occupational obstacle you had to get past to rise further. Although the population was three times that of Greytown, the main street wasn't much longer. There was a proliferation of small clothing shops, as though this was a community that didn't bother to sew, or was too busy, but had money in its pocket. Wages were good in the mines but leisure circumscribed because of odd shift hours.

The small Huntly house was such a squeeze that almost at once the Education Department agreed to provide a caravan to stand beside the house and serve as an extra bedroom. This was occupied by Martin and, quite soon, the labrador pointer puppy he brought home one day from school, explaining that a single boy among five sisters needed a surrogate brother. And Mungo did begin at once to serve his interests – he charmed the household, but also learned how to terrorise it. When Martin made trips to town in my car (which Trevor's higher salary allowed me to have) he would install Mungo in the front seat beside him while Stephanie and Katherine, his little sisters, sat humbly in the back.

After our move to Greytown I'd taken six months or more to establish even the most rudimentary sense that I belonged. Every new person, every occasion or event, seemed to have nothing to do with me, even if I was publicly welcomed and officially included. I joined in, of course, smiled, thanked people, assured them I liked being there (the ubiquitous New Zealand question), but my spirit, my real self, wasn't there. It floated in a forlorn limbo between some lost region and a landing not yet made. In Huntly I found the same dissociation – a greater one, in fact, because this community was much less coherent than Greytown and therefore colder, less spontaneous.

There was no question of Fanny, invited or not, coming to help us settle this time. Her visits to Greytown, after the first unfortunate one, were shorter, and marked for me by a new poignancy, a concern for her which was easier to feel, and to show, because she herself seemed gentler, less demanding. She was also visibly more frail, and alarmingly thin – that was not new, but her increased slowness was. The old energy and spirit burned there still, but her body seemed less and less able to follow their lead. These damnable lungs, we would both grumble, and she would laugh and shrug; one day she remarked, 'I am the sort of cracked pitcher that lasts a long time', and I was willing to be convinced this was true. There was a new, or returned, affection between us; I sometimes felt a quite desperate desire to help her, not, now, to unravel the emotional tangles that had caused so much of the turbulence in her life, but simply to breathe. Watching her struggle for enough breath to speak, I'd find myself, after a few minutes, breathing for her in helpless sympathy; and when she clung to the bannister on the stairs in the Greytown house, fighting for enough air to take her a few steps further up, I could hardly bear to stand by and do nothing.

She had been ill too – a cold, then flu, pneumonia, which took her to Masterton Hospital for several weeks. My visits to her, conducted while the two little girls played on the lawn and we sat at her window, were friendly, even fun. Was it because of her physical weakness that she seemed at last to acknowledge that the next act of the family drama belonged to another generation, in which she could be only a minor character? Lindsay spoke of her unassuming kindness to her and her children in the years she'd lived in Wairoa.

In January 1967, staying with Clive, she was ill again and had a spell in hospital. We had been in Huntly for two terms, and had decided to try the fresh territory of North Auckland for summer camping; we inspected North Cape, the Bay of Spirits, the Ninety Mile Beach, we gazed in wonder at kauri forests, then set up camp near the sea at Rawene. One morning when we were still stretched out in our sleeping bags like a row of dull green caterpillars, someone came to the door; he'd had a phone message from Clive to say Fanny was in Hutt Hospital. Not serious, but we ought to know. We packed up and left, but it was late in the evening before we and our loads of children and gear were home in Huntly. We would ring Clive in the morning and probably leave again in a day or so to visit her. During that night she died in her sleep.

I was wrenched by shock and dismay. At first I could not take it in that Fanny, who had always been so indestructibly there, through the growing up of my own family, was not there nor ever would be again. I even felt an absurd kind of betrayal at the sudden and silent way of her going – as though it simply could not happen that she would not have told me of it. We had for so long – for ever – talked of everything in the world, understood it in similar ways. Well, no; there had been these recent years of my running irritation with her – but what, actually, had she done, for me to be so often angry? In my sudden desolation I couldn't remember why there had been trouble between us at all.

We left at once. The next day I stood with my old friend and uncle Clive Price beside the grave where John was already laid and Fanny had said she wished to be too. Trying through tears for a touch of the lightness Fanny herself could produce out of even her deepest anguish, I said to him, 'The trouble with being dead is that people were so terribly recently alive – ' He held my arm.

Ah Fanny, what a restless search her life had been: I thought of all the conflicts, the amazing generosity, the profound suffering, and that overpowering laughter, the thrust and sparkle of intelligence, the abiding satisfaction of all the talking – those hours, days, years of the shared inquiring that talking was with her. Standing there, teeming with my awareness of her, I saw that there would never be a time when I would give up wanting to tell her whatever mattered, was funny or absurd, perplexing, frightening; she was the person in all the world it had always been best to tell.

Chapter 32

In his first year at Huntly Trevor established himself as a liberally minded, sympathetic high school head. There was a a large Maori community and 1966 as it happened was a year of crisis for the Waikato people: King Koroki died and was buried with ceremonial honours on the sacred mountain that looms up beside the road, with the river on the other side, when you drive to Taupiri and Ngaruawahia on the way to Hamilton.

This I began regularly to do soon after we arrived. I had been so engrossed in my extramural studies that I was in no mind to wait a whole year, or even part of one to make my approaches to the new university at Waikato. Besides, I had heard that it had a revolutionary new structure – Schools of Humanities, Social Science, Administration, rather than individual subjects and departments – but that people like me with part of an old-style subject degree could still do 'unit courses' in 1966. It might be the last time. I hastened to address myself to the university officials; the first term was over, I had the remaining two to cover a full year's work. I was sure I could manage this easily and begged to be admitted, Stage III English my particular goal.

'Professor Sewell is not here today,' I was told; could anyone else help? They could not. I must make an appointment for the next day.

Eagerly I drove the twenty miles from Huntly the following afternoon; it would not do to keep the professor of English, the first in the new university, waiting a single moment. Alas, I didn't. Once more, Professor Sewell wasn't there. I made another appointment, again dashed across the farmlands of the rural end of River Road, turning off at Ngaruawahia, cleverly I thought, but then I was held up by a herd of swaying, ruminating cows. There! Just in time – but once more he hadn't appeared. The expressionless secretary gave me his home address.

I knocked at the door of a small prefab in a settlement of such places, gathered together for the new university staff. It was a fine morning. The ground was bare, the whole suburb (as it was called) was like a refugee camp; it could have been put down by helicopter the day before. The person who opened the door was a slight, elderly man with the most enormous luminous eyes I had ever seen. Intelligence, prescience floated in their blue depths. He drew me in and began to talk of philosophers – Whitehead interested him very much, so did Andreas Papandreou: did I know his work? No? He was a contemporary Greek thinker Professor Sewell had known at the University of Athens. I must read *Man's Freedom*.

As for the courses at Waikato, yes, yes, naturally I must be enrolled; he would tell the Board of Studies to waive the late fee. The question of getting the work done – no, I must not be tiresome, he could see I'd be able to do the work in two terms . . . the only thing was, it was clearly difficult to come to lectures from Huntly: I must attend only his. No others. He would arrange it. Eventually we had to have lunch. But we had drunk several glasses of gin and, according to the bottle, tonic water; something must be found to eat. I opened a cupboard. Empty bottles. Another, the same. Finally I found a tin of toheroa soup and heated it in a small saucepan; there was no bread or anything, so we just ate the soup.

I left about three o'clock, horribly aware that Frances would be foraging for biscuits and drinks for the younger kids home from school before I got there. I drove home fast, full of turmoil, full of glee.

I did go to Arthur's lectures, racing into town in the afternoons (they were held late to accommodate teachers who were finishing 'old' degrees). They were thrilling in the way some at Massey had been, but there was a new ingredient, an emotional undertow that I'd never encountered before, yet with which matched perfectly my own response to what I read. Great writing didn't merely send the horizons of your mind shooting off into the distance, it could break your heart as well. When Professor Sewell lectured on John Donne's poetry I wept, and, incredibly, so did he, at the vastness of the tremulous new world opened up by the Elizabethan giant. And also, he told me later, at his own eloquence. I'd never met anyone the least like this before; he brought a cultivated European sensibility to his scholarship, but there was a quick tenderness in him too; and with all this he was a show-off, a clown, a rogue. An unholy delight of a man.

I would go and talk to him in his room before and after the

lectures; I could not get enough of his delectable, fastidious talk, extraordinarily funny but deeply serious at the same time. He knew and practised a kind of truth-telling, both flippant and adventurous, that I had never met in conversation before (except perhaps with Fanny). Eventually he came to Huntly on a family visit. He caught a bus, he talked to Trevor about football with every bit of the commitment he used for a Shakespeare play; he was charming in a slightly arch way with each of the children, flattering and cajoling Frances and Rachel. Stephanie's name he could not remember, he told her; he preferred Iphigenia, and that is what he always used. The next year when I enrolled in Stage II French he sent me an enormous two-volume dictionary. He explained afterwards that while I was a student in one of his classes it would not have done at all to give me presents. When I graduated – the English and French courses were the final pieces in the mosaic of my BA – I went to dress, in the robes one hired from the Federation of University Women, in the newly established Founders Theatre. Arthur came downstairs, wearing his own august regalia, pressed through the crowd in the women's dressing room, and kissed me. My first congratulations, too precious to speak of to anyone. Others behaved correctly and waited till the degrees were actually conferred.

Alcohol played a part in our taking increasingly separate directions, Trevor and I, in the short, sharply eventful time we spent in Huntly. It was a businessman's town, and its prominent citizens – those who controlled such bodies as the college board of governors – were commercially thrusting; they lived well, some of them drank heavily and in their company so did he. What cultural appetites there were could be satisfied by a short trip to Hamilton, where the Founders Theatre attracted visits from orchestras and theatre companies from larger places, and housed local performances as well. Remembering the much greater isolation of the other two small towns I knew, I thought closeness to a big provincial city acted as a kind of impoverishment to Huntly, perched as it was beside a road that stretched only twenty miles to Hamilton, and about sixty to Auckland, the great glittering city to the north.

Hamilton itself was said to be a centre of commerce rather than culture but – and this was my special luck – there was the university. There I began to explore the possibilities of a life that I might choose for myself, independently of my family; there too I made the only friends who mattered in the time I lived in the Waikato. I too learned to drink in a different way; wine was served at occasions engineered for the practice, halting and often infantile as it was, of our French conversation, and at occasional parties given by my new friends.

That year Trevor needed a teacher of senior English and junior French – staffing was often difficult in provincial high schools – and he offered me the job, ten hours a week. The most onerous duty I'd ever done in a secondary school was to supervise School Certificate, when I'd sat in a big hot room full of frowning students and written letters, in between regular perambulations up and down the rows. I was terrified at this new prospect, and tempted.

Mornings became desperate affairs. Long too, because I woke about 5 am and began a frantic rehearsal of what I would say to the nonchalant (but as it turned out quite kindly) young men and women who would slouch into the room and turn to face me in a few hours' time. There wasn't a simple transition from learning to teaching; I had to do hours of extra work to teach what I already knew. Country kids, however mature – and some of the boys had led a man's life on their parents' farms for years – had little background for *The Importance of Being Earnest*, less for *Pride and Prejudice*, least of all for *Measure for Measure*, the most problematical of Shakespeare's 'dark comedies'. With a colossal effort that play could be made to reflect and dramatise conflicts Huntly College seventh formers had experienced . . . yes, it could. But it's a wonder I only woke at five; probably I should have stayed awake all night.

In any case, by afternoon when I was driving towards Ngaruawahia on the stinging highway, with trucks lumbering past and the tar melting beneath my wheels – or, in winter, a cold gleam in the river, and the car heater turned on – I had a terrible time staying awake. I would sing, shout, take my shoes off, open the windows; even then I usually had to stop four or five times on the twenty-mile journey, and walk round and round the car before I could get back in and set off again.

It was Frances who coped with the household on those afternoons. Life in Huntly was hard for her – not because I was sometimes not at home after school, but because this was for her, as for us all, a step back into a less sophisticated, less cultivated community than she had known in Greytown and it came at a sensitive time for her. Virginia had gone to university and had the beginnings of an adult life, adult friendships; Frances was still preparing for hers. She was unhappy too in sensing disruption at home and even 'ran away' (though not very far) on one occasion. The disturbances that wracked Trevor and me affected everyone.

What had happened was no less remarkable than the transformation in him that day in New Plymouth when he got the job in Opunake. The illness that took hold of him with such extraordinary suddenness had remained with me as an evil ghost, though on one level his acceptance of a new job seemed to mark its final demise. Other men we knew of, who had been similarly caught and hurt by the secondary school system and its fanatical pressure towards the top, were better for having stepped aside. Trevor's was a different outcome. If I'd thought that the predatory monster of illness had reached out to grab me before, it was nothing to what it did now. It – whatever 'it' meant – now took over Trevor's whole personality, at least when he was not at school. Instead of the gentle, affectionate (if preoccupied) person I'd known, the man who came home in the evening was angry, peremptory, abusive. At the dinner table he talked insistently, scoffing at what I produced as opinions, even turning to Frances or Martin with a condescending smile as though I was too stupid to be answered at all. This was inconceivable – and, I found, unmanageable. I raged at myself as much as at him, but nothing seemed to dislodge the alien creature that had taken possession of his personality, nor give me any authority to counter it.

Everywhere I turned hurt and disappointment seemed to lie in wait. Following an old habit, I begged him to take some time off, to relax, ease the pressure, but in his mind I had become the real problem because I failed to provide the relief other headmasters could expect from their wives; instead, I thought about myself. What was happening, of course, was that both of us were changing, and neither could forgive the betrayal implicit in the change. Nor could we understand the process. Trevor's presence at home was more often than not an incomprehensible punishment; I irritated and disappointed him at every turn. Some such puzzlement and pain must have been enacted in a thousand other households, at a time when women were looking for opportunities and occupations they had never been allowed to have, or even to hope for. There must have been men everywhere who, like Trevor, expected in their most successful years an unquestioning and increasingly deferential loyalty from their wives and found instead that even what they had was slipping away from them.

It wasn't merely the question of whether women worked at jobs that took them away from home. The tensions lay far deeper, in the very bones of the shared body of marriage – and ours, like many others no doubt, was stiff with old habits. Changes hurt. When I said I wanted to look for achievements of my own, Trevor's reply was probably typical: 'Your satisfaction is in what I do'. Yet when I did begin my paid work as a teacher, he was pleased with the results; he didn't particularly oppose my university work nor the trips to Hamilton. Had we been able to see it, our separate lives, of action and experiment and challenge, worked for us both. It was what we shared that had gone badly astray, and neither of us could understand why. I sometimes said to him in a kind of anguished entreaty, 'We should have three lives – yours, mine, and ours', but this, like so much else, he heard as a threat, a gesture of disloyalty.

We were, I suppose, at the very axis of one of the great social changes of the century; the revolution of 'the sixties', the new women's movement, the liberation that we knew of from a distance had arrived at our own doorstep and come in. And all we found in it was grief, struggle, a sense of loss. I seemed to have lost a whole person, one I'd loved and depended on for almost all my adult life; home itself, the place where I'd always so intensely belonged, was no longer the haven that kept me safe, nor the adventure that gave me my direction. It had become hostile, even dangerous, a place where I was abused for wrongs I had no idea I'd committed.

But women had an immense advantage. They had their noses to the wind, scenting change, and were excited by it, moved by an unexpected feeling that we had been waiting for this for a long time, without knowing we were. Men, by contrast, were defending a system that not only looked increasingly conservative, but depended for its stability on a kind of self-denial in women that they were less and less inclined to give. Sensing the threat, men like Trevor, in the full flower of their careers, acted like beleaguered persons anywhere: they hit out. The wife of a primary school headmaster in the district came to see me one day out of her own desperation. She too was afraid of her husband's rages, but a greater problem was that she could not bring herself to sleep with him, and as a consequence he had stopped her allowance our of his salary. She had no money and several children; she was understandably frantic. As my Playcentre mothers had taught me, there were women with more intractable dilemmas than mine.

I reflected on the wider question of how people decided the direction of their lives when (in their forties, as we'd said) it became entirely their own affair. I remembered the phrase 'reverting to type' that I'd learnt at training college: in the middle of your life you tend to become the person you most fundamentally were, however this had been disguised or overlaid in your youth. I began to think of myself as not naturally submissive: the habit of wifely accommodation which I had taken for granted seemed after all to be a thing of the times; history now encouraged me to throw it off. Perhaps – a stunning idea – we had both been betrayed by the old conventions, Trevor into a kind of authority he didn't like or want, I into a humility that didn't fit my inclinations. My new urge to choose for myself took me back to my childhood, and the conviction that had so consistently informed it, that whatever was conventional ('orthodox') must be wrong; one must stand out against it.

When I did, I saw an entirely different way of looking at the world, freer, more truthful, more demanding, but also more pleasurable. It came with knowing Arthur and others at the university, and through my explorations in English and French literature, and the glimpses they gave me of a humane European tradition. Recurring bitterness at home made a painful contrast. Perhaps if we'd lived at an earlier time I would have accepted the hardships of my situation more readily; at a later one we might have expected less of each other. But your life is when it is; you manoeuvre the rough reefs of history, or you break on them.

Certainly it was true – well, widely believed, and documented by Kate Millett and other feminist writers – that in the fifties there had been a worldwide movement of women back to the home after the relative independence they'd been given by the war. Was it one of the invisible gestures of history, a sort of signal from the sleeping giant of survival, that women found themselves wanting large families, a settled parental existence, after the mass slaughter of a world war? Occasionally I saw with painful clarity how much I had helped to construct the system of beliefs which now imprisoned Trevor, and from which I could escape. Then I'd lose that quick glimpse and think: now is now. If I fitted that mould, I fit this one too.

I joined some women's groups. I gave talks about self-determination, harnessed my knowledge of existentialism, the philosophy of personal responsibility, I held forth. This made some women very angry. At a gathering of Country Women's Institute members at which I was asked to speak I was accosted by a woman who hated what I said: 'What was good enough for my grandmother is good enough for me,' she spat at me. But another woman, a Scottish immigrant, told me she had taken for granted all I said for years, and was amazed at the backwardness of New Zealand's women.

Backwardness of a different kind was talked of among Playcentre workers and officials, too, when I again began to teach young mothers. This was a community with few leaders, they said, and a low educational level. I observed for myself, when I began to work in the Huntly West Playcentre, that Maori mothers were sometimes illiterate in English; a few were suspicious of me because I was Pakeha. Another tutor, herself a Maori, became a good friend, and told me something of the King Movement and the lingering enmity towards white settlers. When we talked of a possible playcentre at Turangawaewae in Ngaruawahia, she avoided the question of whether I might go there to do a workshop; it was clear I could not. It was here, in my encounters with Maori families, that I saw from the outside the fruits of Trevor's work with Maori kids who were not at home in the 'Pakeha system', as I heard it called for the first time. I found that he often supplied uniforms, made medical and dental appointments, organised lunches; I spent a day with him at Waaihi, the Huntly marae, and met parents and elders who wanted their children to learn Pakeha ways and do well in Pakeha terms; I moved with the slow line of guests, was welcomed by the lined, inscrutable, grand old women in front of the meeting house, and for once was glad of the status, a reflection of Trevor's, that allowed me to be there.

There were few enough occasions when the privileges given to people like me, wives of public figures, could be said to be a pleasure. I presented prizes, of course; I attended official afternoon teas at school and parties given by board members; I organised staff parties myself. I made conversation, I dressed decently in suits and pleated skirts . . . but my heart was not in it. The place where I was saying what I really thought was quite different, and known to nobody, not even my new friends at the university.

In the early afternoons, with Mungo the dog in the car, I drove to a place by the lake where there was quiet water, trees, no people. Mungo ran about and snuffled in the grass, and I, for the first time with absolute seriousness, wrote poems. On and on, a great many of them. It was as though some voice in me said, at last, 'To hell with it all, this is what I want to do' – and I did it. Many of them had careful rhyme schemes, formal structures, all were dense, tightly packed, full of meanings. They were not in the least 'confessional' (not that I knew the word), but I was aware that my very real unhappiness had a good deal to do with the urgency with which I wrote.

I bought an ancient typewriter, tiered like a grandstand, and typed them out. Some I sent to Pat Lawn, who was by now the secretary of the English Department at Victoria University in Wellington, and asked her to type them decently. Perhaps I secretly hoped she would do more than that; anyway, without asking, she did show them to Don McKenzie, a lecturer on the staff. I was overwhelmed, and ecstatic, to get the poems back with detailed comments written in that august hand. If he praised poems – and he did – I saw them thereafter in letters of gold; if he criticised (and he did so intelligently – 'echoes of Eliot') I was at once prepared to read an entire literature to understand my flaw. This was the first time, since I'd shown poems to Lindsay and Fanny when I was about ten years old, that I'd admitted my secret occupation. It was a mark of my new seriousness.

I did not meet my distinguished critic, but I did go to Wellington for several days early in 1968, for the Peace, Power and Politics Conference. It was a notable gathering of academics and historians who were critics of American action in the Vietnam War and New Zealand's association with it. Politics were in the air, even Huntly, remote and parochial though it might be, could not ignore the rising tide of protest against the brutalities of the war. Young authors in my English classes wrote poems about the use of napalm and the plight of Asian orphans.

For me the political movements of the time were beginning to coalesce into a general perception that personal freedom was always at the heart of political action. I had embraced principles all my life – Social Credit, diet reform, the labour movement – but only now, when the onset of my own middle age coincided, miraculously enough, with some sort of growing up of the world at large, did I realise that liberal theory was to do with how you actually lived. It was a matter of choosing for yourself, as the teaching of the women's movement was telling me I could, and I must.

The conference, every speech, every paper, was riveting. I had especially wanted to go because Sartre, whose writings had shaped so much of my personal revolution, was to be there. Alas, he was not, but

I eventually read his paper, 'On Genocide', and I did listen to Conor Cruise O'Brien, Felix Green and the New Zealander John Male; I saw in a way I never had that important ideas needed knowledge as well as humanity, industry as much as vision. These were men of action; the utopian dreams I'd shared with my father long ago seemed now the merest preparation for this comprehensiveness.

I, of course, could have nothing to do with the Vietnam War, beyond marching in the street (which, tingling with the adventure of it, I did). But there were other things I could do. Another noisy public argument was about abortion, and women's 'right to choose'. In Huntly I was asked to take part in a debate on the subject; Professor Lilley of the Auckland Medical School was to lead the team advocating the foetus's 'right to life'; I and a local lawyer spoke on the other side. This too seemed to take me back to an earlier, younger time; I had last debated when I was a training college student more than twenty years before. Virginia by this time was engaged to a young Wellington lawyer and they were home for the holidays; Fraser gave me useful legal facts to support my case. The next day the *Waikato Times* ran a headline, 'Mother of Six Favours Abortion', which made me shudder. A woman in town rang me and said, 'Even if nobody else will speak to you, I will still be your friend.' Politics, it seemed, had come home.

The normal processes of promotion took a new headmaster to a country school as to a kind of apprenticeship, then to a bigger city school as the fulfilment of their career. This meant that, despite Trevor's natural reluctance to move, he was willing to apply for city jobs. I had for years wanted to return to Wellington, and certainly I could not imagine staying in Huntly longer than necessary. It was the only place I'd ever lived in that I truly disliked. Admittedly, out of the pain and confusion of that time had come my first glimpse of a new direction, but I could follow that anywhere, and perhaps more fruitfully, away from this cramped little town.

Frances left school and went to Auckland University, where she and Murray, one of Don's sons, formed an adult friendship, as Virginia had with Rod, his older brother, at Victoria. I drove to Auckland occasionally to see Frances, and sitting in Albert Park with her and other students I had a distinct sense of the dislocation, the excitement, the risky adventurousness of being students at that time. I had thought my own student experiences remarkable, and so they were, after my sheltered country childhood, but these young people were quite different. They drank, experimented with drugs, walked about all night on various expeditions, went to bed with one another, wore clothes like rags: a friend of Frances and Murray had tried to commit suicide, and they talked of this as 'making a choice'. Anything and everything was making a choice, it appeared. It was exciting being with them, but alarming too.

Closer to home, we paid a visit to another high school headmaster and his family who lived at Ngatea, in the marshy country of the Hauraki Plains on the eastern edge of the Waikato. He was none other than my long-lost friend, Beetles. He had married in the South Island and lived for years on the West Coast; now the random choreography of the teaching system, which directed the prance of teachers about the country, had delivered him and us to the same neighbourhood. We spent a Sunday with them. Beetles talked to Trevor about school and football, especially football; he was, in dismaying but inescapable fact, a bore. I enjoyed talking to his wife far more. The world was a changed place, indeed.

Trevor's advancement followed the proper course. He had made a success of a difficult country school, stood well with teachers and inspectors; when Heretaunga College, one of the big city schools in the Hutt Valley, advertised for a new principal, he applied and was appointed. When he rang to tell us after the interview he sounded resigned rather than triumphant; unlike me, he would have liked to stay in small towns. However, there it was. I was delighted, nobody else objected; we were, after all, a family of teachers and teachers' kids. After the move from Ohakune, all others seemed minor.

The first thing we had to do in Upper Hutt was find our own house. Despite the turmoil of the last couple of years, I didn't consider living anywhere but at home with my family. Even at the worst of times it hadn't occurred to me that I could go elsewhere. *Leave? Leave home?* Where would I live – and on what? We looked at houses.

Upper Hutt was a city; Trevor would be head of one of several large secondary schools; he would have money and position (land agents were deferential). Otherwise we could fend for ourselves. We had left behind the affectionate, inquisitive concern country people feel for their public figures; here nobody took much interest in us, which suited me because it released me from public duties as the headmaster's wife. We were better able to establish ourselves too because we had some money from Trevor's parents' estate and we could look for a presentable house. In fact it was more than that, it was elegant, spacious, shapely, by far the most beautiful house we'd ever occupied.

And in certain ways we lived gracefully there. Martin and Rachel finished their high school years at Heretaunga and left to go to university; friends of the two older girls, already there, came to visit us. There were often groups of eager, talkative young men and women sprawled about the terrace (we now had one) or the lawn, or in the rooms full of windows looking out over a pleasant garden enclosed by hedges.

I enjoyed these visits, talked too, listened a great deal to new theories, unexpected ideas. Architecture creates shapes and spaces that condition the way people think and feel . . . technology has produced mindless mass production and the death of aesthetic sensibility . . . individual choice – almost always it came down to that. Individual choice. The very air tingled with it. Yet, in a diary that by now I consistently kept, I grieved endlessly at the limitations of my life, acknowledged the ruin of my marriage.

Last night we saw Staircase, *a beautiful, sad, appealing film – a study in how two aging and unattractive people (both men) manage to live together. It was through their weaknesses not their strengths – when one survived the childish and vicious attacks of the other, and in understanding the other's need lost none of his own identity, he showed us one of the achievements in relationships. We talked a little of it – Trevor thought it sleazy, empty, could not see anything in it. Later we had a row and he reminded me that my ideas of living together were all theoretical. Perhaps, but I often wish his were more so. He fights bitterly for what he wants – (usually that I will admit I'm in the wrong over something) and so there will be no irritating mopping-up, forgets all he's said – or pretends to. Am I 'too good' and afraid not to be, as he says? I'm not any good at all at his sort of living.*

All power has left me. Any good mental ferment acting on the words, faces, ideas that float in the pool of daily living has vanished. My interior life is thick and sluggish, composed of futile arguments about the hopelessness of fitting both myself and Trevor into the mean little territory our marriage has become. We dwindle in each other's company till we are like two wary little dogs circling round each other waiting for the moment of attack. The dust lies under our feet and the gay and beautiful world round us fades into a dull blur beyond the ends of vision. We stare and growl and tremble with fear and dislike. If only we could stand up to full height and be good, calm and compassionate people, as once we seemed to be.

Coleridge writes 'No sound is dissonant which tells of Life'. In the sort of hopeful despair in which I live, I see this writing everything down as it comes into my mind as a new chance. But how is it that Coleridge, a very unhappy man, writes so much of joy? It is not important where one's passion leads I suppose – it is the strength and quality of it that matters. The pleasure in a new idea that I can never share with Trevor is probably not so different from his excitement, mostly kept hidden from me, in participation in his teachers' meetings. Perhaps passions are solitary – but no, they are not. Ours just have to be.

Frances asks me to understand all she means by her own declaration of faith, which means she asks me to feel it as she does. She sees the organised, materially comfortable but spiritually impoverished life of older people like ourselves as death to all she hopes for from life – freedom to be honest and spontaneous, opportunity to follow the calls of emotion and friendship, time to experience the living world of real feelings. How could I not understand, and agree – such desires are of the greatest possible importance. What I can't do is feel this as she does. In a crisis the need to compromise, to contemplate enduring the unendurable (and doing so alone), is so pressing that it takes precedence over everything else. If one is not to lose everything one must accept the bitterest disappointments, love becoming selfishness and greed, honesty a door to bitterness and rage, loyalty a policy. You emerge from all this crashing down of the illusions of years to find that all your most precious dreams have been ground to powder. Frances' dreams are strong and real – and that makes me both happy and sad. I hope they will satisfy while they last, and not require more courage than she finds she has, when she faces their collapse.

My own worst mistake has been to protect myself for too long from the pain of this realisation. Somehow it has to be faced, allowed to happen and flow. Otherwise there is the death of more than the capacity to be hurt; all true and living feeling is frozen and the whole of life seems to withdraw. You are left in a small dry place alone, doing nothing, knowing nothing. This happened to me at the end of last term when I was sick – those weeks in bed reduced me to a sort of non-existence. No matter what pain I have to suffer, I will never again shut myself away from it in the wretched terrified coma I did then.

I want quite desperately at times to break out of the killing routine of polite self-control. Trevor is away and I feel this most strongly then, because it seems momentarily possible. I could imagine myself walking alone in strange streets at night, neglecting everyone and reading and dreaming for whole days somewhere – not here, where the boundary of the garden is so close I can almost touch it from the window, and the very air, sweet and full of birdsong as it is, is heavy with duty and virtue. But my protest is as timorous as it has always been – I cannot even give it a name. And yet Frances said she and Murray both were greatly moved by my letters. I am moved myself by my own eloquence – or self-pity!

Perhaps it is habit that kills in the end. More and more it seems Trevor and I do less and less because we keep to what has been tried, and are afraid of everything else. So, we go out – one night to dinner with the Aitkens; everyone showing off though with different ways of doing it.

I have voices shouting in my head – mostly protests, violent ones, at never being listened to or understood or assessed fairly. Today Trevor and I actually did talk like real people for once. I'd got a letter from Wolfgang Rosenberg saying the Monthly Review would accept my 'little story' (actually it's an article criticising some middle-aged attitudes). Trevor poured us a drink as a kind of celebration, and when I explained why I'd used his initials – because I think there's a prejudice against women writers – he understood and didn't deride the idea. Once I've had a few acceptances I won't care; I'll have defeated prejudice by foul means if not fair.

A very different prospect the following night – a disastrous evening with the Rotarians. They ate and drank together, wore paper hats and were oppressively gay. Then a feeble and inconclusive speaker, a young policeman, addressed us on the subject of narcotics. I cannot imagine a less suitable audience or occasion – they seemed determined to make light of the subject by asking frivolous questions. The only useful one was 'Is this a social trend?' and to my incredulous ears came the sound of Trevor's voice saying 'unfair, unfair'; then there was a loud, aggressive, not very sober argument, followed by an almighty row at home because I queried his idea that the social consequences must not be examined. How degrading it all is – I really think he has a view of outings as show pieces, like concerts. Or competitions, your performance vying with others, you hope surpassing theirs. I suppose there is an element of this for everyone, but surely there is a communal possibility, a new something, a mood or an idea or a memory that is created by the mixing of personalities on the occasion.

Sometimes I think I will yell aloud if I have to endure any more of these hours of selling the school, which is all Trevor's conversation is lately – very loud, very insistent, very much in the manner of an auctioneer. Of course I think the issues important but so many lies are twisted in with the truth, and so much showing off with informing, that I cannot want to take part – and yet eventually I am sorry for myself if I am left entirely out. There's no solution. He's a politician, and I'm not. I must give way about this because it matters to him, and if I want another, subtler, more truthful and sensitive kind of talk I must get it elsewhere. Anyway I'm not above showing off myself when I get the right atmosphere, but it isn't Trevor's kind, and they can never be combined. In fact it is amazing that we ever talk at all, our methods of doing it are so unlike.

Last night was the much discussed and planned-for staff party. The evening began disastrously, at home. I suggested we should try to perform jointly this time – at least to remain aware of each other, without struggling. This brought on a fit of temper which made Trevor abuse me violently for ruining the evening before it began by putting him in his place. I am constantly amazed at this process: I produce an idea, a statement, and hand it to him, but when he receives it something has happened to it in transit and it is entirely unlike what left me. It's like a parcel wrapped up and sent, and when it is opened it proves not to be the boxed handkerchiefs of the giver, but a nest of scorpions, cunningly concealed in gift wrapping.

 I wept, and made us so late that Tony came to get us, perhaps mindful of his position as head of English. Control of my tears and my face proved so difficult that even after a long preparation in the bathroom, when I sat down to have a drink with him (Trevor had gone on), I almost wept again at his first kind word. He knew of course and said with great gentleness, You aren't really all right at all, are you?

 Me: No of course not. Him: We'll look after you. Me: Just don't be nice to me – whatever you do, don't be nice. Be as nasty as you can, and I'll manage the party. I can't do that, he said. I can only be nasty to nasty people.

But it was all right. I talked to Percy – John's friend – for a long time and we talked of him. I wish I could write John's story, although it's as much a part of me as my hands and eyes, I am afraid of distorting it. It's an indication of my amateurism that I cannot yet control what I write – it almost at once begins to control me. So much vital experience must vanish, unrecorded (Socrates' idea of the unexamined life) – or does it just flow into other parts of a life? I am stronger today. Last night's bitter weeping, and the solace for it, unexpectedly sweet because from a casual source – Tony is not even a very close friend – has left me more resolute. I could find the firmness today to say I would not go to the PPTA dinner party. I always make a mess of them and have never been able to stir any sympathy in Trevor, only hostility. Suddenly I am not willing to put myself in that painful and degrading situation any more and he will have to go alone. I think at last he sees that to abuse me for my failures is the wrong thing to do, and always has been, but it is too late now. He never sees things till I am beyond the point of endurance. If I had handled this with more firmness and finality at the start perhaps all would have been well. But to do that I needed not to be weak – and then there would have been no problem anyway.

Trevor says Martin should take a law unit as well as his social science arts units, 'just to keep the door open'. I came into this conversation and fortunately had enough sense to shut up instead of openly disagreeing. But disagree I do, and at another time I shall say so. The tension in our family comes from the fact that Trevor and I compete for our children's favour, for our friend's attention. Listening from the next room to his 'man's talk' with Martin and thinking, 'This is something I can't do, and it's better that I'm right out of it', at the same time, I thought, 'He's so marvellous when he's got it all to himself. If I come into the room he'll fear perhaps he hasn't, something may have to be conceded to me, so the performance will have to stop.' Is it years of teaching, bloody teaching, that's done this to him? He's acted for so long on the principle that to be good and successful you have to get rid of the opposition – and now that's me. I'm necessary, as a failure, for him to succeed. What an awful statement – I hope it isn't true, yet I believe it is.

Yesterday I met Maurice Gee, and we talked of teaching. It expands, then *limits*, he said. I said people used children to complete their personalities; he agreed, added that this is why people are damaged by teaching – they can't grow as separate adult individuals. None of this sounded momentous – just gentle, rather mumbling talk, but it contained that good thing, a sense of looking together for something sound – 'the feel of truth'. I met his wife, a smiling, direct person; I think he wanted her to be there to be part of talk that interested him. This is so far from the desert of misunderstanding and suspicion in which we live that I cannot bear to think of the two together. I suppose neither Trevor nor I is in the least fair to the other – we have come to occupy different worlds that do not touch. He says I want only 'my way', not 'our way', and I suppose that's true. We would be better people if we didn't have to live together. I can respect what he does because it's useful and he does it with devotion, but as a person I have no happiness with him, only pain and wretchedness. Marriage should become a steady friendship, not this terrible war.

Virginia has been talking to me: she says Trevor too is unhappy. I can feel sorry that he has to endure his disappointment, but at least he only has to look round and see the devastation when he stops work. I think he really hates the sort of person I am; I have imagined him with the quiet, agreeable, submissive wife who would make him happy – perhaps that's what I used to be!

Chapter 33

My teaching of senior students for part of the week at Heretaunga College did not draw Trevor and me closer together – far from it. For the first time I had a 'form' of my own and when they, the seventh form, wanted to wear mufti instead of school uniforms I supported them (over angry lunches at home) against Trevor's more traditional view. It was stupid of me to teach in his school at all at just that time, but that didn't occur to either of us.

For all that, some benefits did accrue – to the students, and to me. For one thing, I did really learn how to teach in that school; I came to understand the rewards of teaching and to accept its discipline. I didn't ever think I was a naturally good teacher, as Trevor was, but I was glad to master some of the secrets of the game. And one at least of my schemes worked famously; it was a weekly afternoon of discussion on topics of current interest known as the Friday Forum. The students invited visitors to speak and then argued (or agreed) with them – Patricia Bartlett on pornography; Carol Shand on abortion, the pill and contraception; someone from the Russian Embassy to defend, if he could, the 1968 invasion of Czechoslovakia, and a Czech diplomat (the following week) to tell his version of the story. In the event the Russian talked movingly of his faith in collective rather than competitive systems, but the occasion ended catastrophically all the same. A Czech girl who spoke fluent Russian was in the class and agreed to welcome the visitor. This she did to our great pride and gratification, but when the time came to farewell him she was suddenly overcome with the enormity of the disaster for her country, and ran from the room in a storm of tears.

Seventh form students are naturally conservative, I found, but Patricia Bartlett, when she came to testify in the cause of strict censorship, managed in a single afternoon to turn a whole class into liberals of the deepest conviction. But even when the issue was not so clear, or the speaker more competent, they, and I, enjoyed flexing our rhetorical muscles, and the incisiveness of our debates sharpened as the year went on. And in July we gathered in the school hall with everyone else – indeed with millions of others in such assemblies all round the world – to hear a radio broadcast announce that an American astronaut called Neil Armstrong had taken the first step by a human being on the surface of the moon.

For all the rewards, I grew discontented with teaching, and decided to go back to university – Victoria this time – to do an MA. The excitement, the expansion, of my experience at Waikato were all repeated, but without Arthur. Not that Arthur himself disappeared, or my friendship with him; on the contrary, both flourished.

They also required me to make a crucial decision. Some months after our move to Heretaunga, Barbara Green, a friend from the French classes at Waikato, invited me to spend a weekend with her in Hamilton. This was wonderfully tempting. I had no close friends near where we now lived, and was all the more imprisoned in my unhappiness at home because I had to keep up an infallible pretence of harmony. Trevor was making his way in a new milieu; to talk openly to anyone he knew would be an act of betrayal (though Tony had hinted that he guessed how things were, I had not elaborated on the drama of the staff party). Barbara would see my problem in the light of larger philosophies; she would intellectualise it. She lived, moreover, at a great distance from Trevor and his public. The children – as children do – had made friends far more quickly than I, absence was possible. I accepted, and went.

Barbara and I did indeed luxuriate in our theorising. 'Right action . . . is determined by her by a regard for absolute values as laid down by God' (I wrote in my diary), 'for me it's to do with human dignity, that's the basic value . . . ' We talked and talked. Then I went to visit Arthur. He was alone, very pleased to see me; he opened a bottle of wine. It was a clear evening in late October and the light beautifully faded as we sat near a window and talked, laughed, not of theories but using the stylish and profound nonsense I so enjoyed in his company. Nothing could have been a greater contrast with the harshness I'd left behind. I did not want it to end.

Then suddenly events took a new turn. Arthur too wanted me to stay, and for the first time I realised he wanted us to make love – a possibility which I saw had been with us ever since our first meeting, but which I'd been too naive, or too inexperienced, or too conventional to recognise or admit. And too married? That also. I had never seriously considered that such a thing could happen to me; now it had, and I was filled with excitement and dread. Most of all, I was simply frightened out of my wits. I insisted I must leave, I struggled to go; and in the end, foolishly and ingloriously, I ran out.

That evening Barbara took me to Frankton station to catch the night express. Arthur was there standing on the platform and proposed coming too, travelling through the night and returning to Hamilton in the morning. Again I panicked and rushed onto the train alone – then spent the entire journey restless and awake in an agony of doubt and confusion. For several weeks I wrestled with the question, looked at it in every way I could; and slowly, in a state of shocked, yet profoundly serious resolution, I decided to accept Arthur's poignant proposition.

He began to come and stay, a few days at a time, in the Heretaunga house, and was affectionately received by everyone. The long times I spent with him alone after the others had gone to school (on the days when I didn't have to) had a particularly luminous quality. He was no ordinary friend and family visitor, nor did he pretend to be. What he could do was have natural friendships with everyone else in the family; he told me he liked them, his warmth wasn't policy.

He died a year or so later, after a crushingly painful cancer illness. I stayed a few days with him not long before his death, a time for quiet, searching conversations in what seemed, all day, to be a glow of evening light. Afterwards I missed him greatly. He was the first person to show me that the real truth about the world contained its most disgraceful parts as well as its most beautiful; he taught me not to be afraid of folly and egotism and greed, even cruelty – he himself could be cruel – because these taught you the courage without which love, the ultimate good, cannot survive. To love what was beautiful was nothing, you had to learn to love what was harsh and ugly and incomplete. Arthur didn't say any of these things, yet I came to understand them through talking to him, being with him.

He made me read too – Hardy, Donne, even Milton, and of course Yeats, on the joy beyond tragedy, for instance – 'gaiety transfiguring all that dread / . . . all things fall and are built again . . . '. He read like an angel, at a time when reading poetry aloud was to me an unknown art. He visited my seventh form once, and his reading of Hardy's *A Broken Appointment* – quite a short poem – moved me so greatly I could not stop my tears, even before the sharp eyes of my students.

After my work at the university came to an end, I didn't really want to stay at school. I was sick of school, I'd seen too much competitiveness, too much artificial authority, heard too many hours of dull, spiteful, claustrophobic staff-room conversation. The very air of school seemed stale, shut in; outside was the real world, or so I believed. As well, I had a low-stream fourth form class that I simply could not control – they barely concealed their fights in the classroom, made no pretence of doing what I said was to be done.

A job was advertised in the *Education Gazette* for the editorship of the *Post-Primary Teachers Journal*; I applied, prepared for the interview as for an exam, and got it.

For the next six months I had so much energy I hardly knew what to do with it. This new job made me feel as I'd felt as a child when we stood in a doorway and pressed the backs of our hands outwards. We'd step out, and our hands would rise right above our heads entirely by themselves. My hands, my whole self, did that. If I was tired of teachers, I *loved* journalists; they were real, ordinary, direct; I as editor needed them, they equally needed me for the typesetting and processing I gave them, or to publish their articles. There was no unnatural authority anywhere, it was simply an exchange of work, effort, results. I liked the way they talked, too; many of them were openly left-wing and often very knowledgeable about politics. Nobody had to prepare a subject for classroom consumption or please educators who might fuss about the effect on the family, the school . . . We said what we liked.

I was writing a good deal myself, and was also for the first time in touch with New Zealand writing, partly because writers sent poems and stories to the *Journal*. I encouraged them; I wanted the magazine to be read by others outside the teaching profession, even though the PPTA general secretary grumbled that I was making it into 'another *Landfall*'. I found a brilliant illustrator called Jim Gorman who worked in School Publications and had a quirky, original style. With him I published a poem a month (one per person, no more) for years. I also met Denis Glover. The previous editor of the *Journal*, Alister Taylor, had established a new journal called *Affairs*. It was for sale in schools, it gave voice to the 'counter-culture' that arose out of the sixties revolution. Of special interest to me was a series of articles about New

Zealand writers, which he invited me to write. I seemed to think if I couldn't be one, at least I could talk about them, and I accepted.

Some time after the article about Denis Glover was published, I met the old gentleman at a party at Alister Taylor's house, and he decided, apparently, to 'take me up'. What that meant was that he invited me to edit the letters of A.R.D. Fairburn, having waited, he claimed, seventeen years for the right person to turn up. He was Fairburn's literary executor.

This was extraordinary and terrifying enough, but he also, as time went on, talked about poetry itself. I read his own, of course, and Fairburn's, and the work of other New Zealanders, especially R.A.K. Mason and Robin Hyde, noting the prejudice against her that Fairburn and Glover had felt – and Denis still expressed. I also embarked on Frost and Emily Dickinson and William Carlos Williams. And I wrote my own, dozens of poems all the time; two I actually sent away to the editor of a literary quarterly, *Islands*, rather like *Landfall* but a breakaway venture. When Robin Dudding accepted them for his next issue, I felt a deep, resonating pleasure.

I gave one of my finished pieces to Denis. It was a half-nonsensical address to 'Mister Dog', my reliable companion during forays to Trentham Park, the secret place in which I now did most of my writing. Working with him on the Fairburn letters entailed listening to many hours of tales about the two poets' shared past; we spent a great deal of time together. Sometimes he visited me at home, made friends with my family, and had once remarked that he loved each one, but Mungo most.

Denis's response to the poem was yet another surprise. He said that if I had others like this he would help me to publish a volume of poems.

I could hardly wait. I took my battered manila folders to the office and as soon as the day's work was done I fell upon them, sifting, criticising, re-writing, trying various combinations of phrases and words, wondering what shaping idea might make thirty or forty poems into a collection. Sometimes I took the train from Upper Hutt and used the hour's journey morning and afternoon in the same way.

There were poems about my children, including two about Stephanie's remarkable unattended birth; one about John; another addressed to an old miner in Huntly; glimpses from every corner of my life that had crystallised into words. As I shuffled pages with fragments, reflections, whole poems, many about Ohakune, the phrase 'bonfires on the hillsides' struck me strangely. Yes, there were bonfires blazing on the hills. But weather changes; now they seemed more like bonfires in the rain. When I had a tentative collection, I took it to Denis. He would look at my manuscript, he said. (So it wasn't a book yet?)

He treated it with the respect due to any other writer. The idea made me shiver. I looked in my Yeats *Collected Poems* for a title, and found a poem that said, 'Find in middle air / An eagle on the wing' – and chose *In Middle Air* for its power to suggest that poetry is to be found close by, in the familiar things. Albion Wright, the publisher at Pegasus Press and the person to whom Denis had recommended the manuscript, designed a cover in a hard bright blue. The colour, presumably, that he saw as 'middle air'.

'Can't have that,' said Denis, and redesigned it himself much more subtly, in a soft blue-green with white lettering. He was the elder statesman of printing and design in New Zealand, as well as of poetry; this was a wonderful bit of luck.

But every day ended with going home. The miseries of my conflict there continued, though as time went on its character changed. For one thing Trevor began to feel more acutely the effects of my withdrawal from the support and scapegoat role we had together somehow shaped for me. One day when the house was full of young holiday visitors he asked me to go to his room and talk to him alone. I saw then that behind the bursts of rage he was himself badly shaken and as miserable as I. He had come to hate going to school, he said. We talked a little of his family history.

The conventional bourgeois confidence of his family, which I had once so admired, had contained within it, as all families do, a particular psychological and social structure. A fiercely dominating father, a kindly mother sharing her weakness with a sensitive young son. We had talked of this before, but had not seen that it was likely to create for him an insoluble conflict about authority itself – that he could become a person who was driven towards authority and at the same time longed to be protected from it. This moment of rational speculation didn't really help us; rather it induced, in me at any rate, a forlorn sense that there was no way back to that good time, now irretrievably lost, before we had begun to damage everything we touched together, as we now did.

As for my children, I had no such illuminations. Because my love for them did not diminish, I could easily imagine that all was well, that they wanted my life to expand, and were pleased to take a lesser place. Not so. There were disturbances I had never known before and could not explain, but in the end had to see as expressions of a deep disquiet, a sense of betrayal, of loss. The two youngest girls joined in escapades with rebellious kids who at their worst stole a car and drove it about Upper Hutt; it belonged to the mother of one of the boys and on the scale of teenage delinquent acts this was quite minor.

Nevertheless, it did highlight a new rootlessness in the family, a dislocation in once stable loyalties. So tightly knit together had we been, my children and I, that it took them a very long time to recognise my unaccustomed eagerness for myself, my new ambitions, and still longer to accept them. Some did not manage to do it at all, but preserved a sense of grievance and betrayal which I in turn failed to recognise as the complex distress which the disintegration of a family causes. For that is what it was. Stephanie told me later that she was afraid to bring friends home in case they heard her parents quarrelling. One Christmas Virginia cried almost all day; Martin told me, with a despairing peremptoriness that only the young can have, that I *had* to go back to loving my husband, his father.

So we rocketed through those difficult years. I loved my editor's job and the time given to work and friends of my own choosing. I must at times have seemed to Trevor and the children, at home and away, like Nero fiddling while the city burned. Nobody thought about the larger questions raised by Trevor's (and now my) devotion to work, though the new science of sociology was beginning to associate our generation with something called 'the work ethic'. We were puritans, we held to the secular morality of hard work and tangible success. In our children we had failed to allow for differences, other values, room for individual happiness without overt achievement. I also began to come across the idea that after the war there had been a period of settled values, for men devotion to 'getting on' within whatever system they knew, for women home and children. Now that it was all breaking up, it seemed analysts could see it as a pattern.

But these were ideas. Historical change is a huge unwieldy beast, slow to move, devastating in its threshing about after new directions. I did not seriously apply the new theories to my own case, or to the family that Trevor and I had created without knowing our rules would become discredited. I didn't see that 'the drive to achieve' (as one now knew to call it) had run right through the shaping of our family – nor that we had denied our children the chance to be ordinary, different, 'non-achieving'. We began to hear of drop-outs. The turbulence in my family did not produce that, or not at first; yet, had I thought to apply the term, I must have looked myself like one of them, an adult drop-out from a system I'd been wholly loyal to only a few years before.

Women's ambitions, I (and others) believed, were different from the old destructive drives that had so controlled the lives of men; we were broader, more humane, more likely to include family and personal claims in our schemes and policies. This was partly true too, but undeniably I was competitive myself in some of the old ways. I wanted my new self, but could not bear to leave the old, and neither I not anyone else in the family could see the faintest glimmer of where we might be going. Or if, in fact, the lifelong 'we' of ourselves, so deeply embedded in our consciousness, would survive at all. Virginia gave me a book called *The Death of the Family* which talked of a disintegrating economic unit, a Marxist view. I thought it interesting to read, but the realities of change were messy and miserable. We were all in some way permanently scarred by them.

I had formed the habit of going off somewhere in the car, not merely to write but simply to think and recover my balance when the house was unbearable. Such trips had been harmless, wholesome, at first . . . I had taken the two small girls to buy vegetables, to see a furniture repairer. One day Katherine had written a note for the 'older kids' and left it on the dining room table.

Dear People (it said)

We have to go to Whiteman's Valley. I know it's boring but Mum says we have to go. She says we'll be back for dinner but I know we won't because its 100 miles there and 100 miles back.

Love Katherine

My later trips were of a different order. Then I looked over the no man's land of our present lives. Marriage and my life within it had for many years been a complete whole, each person, each act, each mood and change simply an aspect of a single operation held together by love, conviction, certainty, a sense of being responsible, and dedicated to the good health of the whole; it was a complex contract that had grown denser as years passed, but did not loosen its grasp. Now everything was breaking into fragments; there were attitudes and beliefs that belonged in one part of my life but not in another: I no longer wanted to be the kind of wife I'd been. I certainly couldn't be the same kind of parent: my children were leaving home, one every two years (as they'd arrived). By the time I went to Victoria as an MA student, only Stephanie and Katherine were still at school.

As for Martin (I wrote in my diary, that essential recourse) – *last Sunday a wet chilly day. He felt too I think a sense of things passing beyond recall (though his consciousness of adventure and expansion ahead is much greater than mine) and kept saying, 'This is like last winter.' And indeed we had a stable homely day with tea to drink and the ironing for Monday shared out in the evening and a funny clever play on TV. Every person who leaves home grows at the end so big, uses up so much of the time, space, noise, scope, attention and fuss, that one feels the womb must burst and of course it does. With Martin there's little tension though, and much cheerful nonsense. After each departure there's a shadow somewhere in the house.*

As children grew away from home some parents did of course find they still 'had each other', but it was clear that we had not made the common life that would survive the end of the family years. The quarrels we now had were a way of saying, 'You've turned into someone I didn't expect, and I don't like', as though strangers (our real selves perhaps) had all the time been lying in wait to take us over when our children stopped holding us together. 'Who were the guardians . . . ' (I asked in a poem I called *The Reckoning*) 'and who . . . the guarded?' While we were taking care of our children, how much were they protecting us from the selves we would eventually have to become? And, further, how much in all this was history, how much the inexorable processes in ourselves? We could not know.

I often felt a kind of grief, not only for a person lost, and not only for the loss of the love and comfort of a partnership, but for the defeat of faith. I had entered my marriage lightly enough, yet it had developed into my greatest act of faith, continually made. I would almost have preferred to lose what I still admired and believed in, to walk away as if from a house that still stood, rather than to know it was fallen and could never be built again.

There are times in people's lives when the distance between visible surfaces and tumultuous realities within grows so wide that a break has to occur, and for us this happened with unexpected and appalling suddenness. Rachel had been at university for a year and a half, having chosen Auckland because it offered Art History. She'd taken a strictly academic course at school but was very interested in art and did small elegant drawings of her own. She lived there in a variety of flats with groups that formed, changed, dissolved, moved on; she appeared to spend a good deal of time with the older members of the Edmond family, all living in Auckland. The only time I felt any particular concern about her was when friends of Virginia's said on a holiday visit that Rachel was moving too quickly, taking shallow root in the more sophisticated milieu of older students, could lose touch with herself.

And this, apparently, she did. One night Virginia rang to say that Rachel had taken an overdose of sleeping pills and been taken to hospital. I was so unprepared for such an event that at first I could make no sense of it, and when, with the help of friends and family, she seemed restored, I wondered if it had actually taken place.

This sense of unreality persisted throughout her illness, for that is what I gradually came to see it was. At the same time, a current of fear began to move through all my thinking, a rising apprehension as each move – and she moved often – looked like the search for a secure niche that could not be found. At home she seemed much the same gentle creature we'd always known, rather elusive (her 'secret quality') but also responsive to the troubles in the family in a typically tactful way; she tried hard to understand Trevor's conflicts and to help solve them. From Auckland she wrote him long letters full of advice. 'Dearest Father . . . '

Virginia, by now with an MA in History and a Teacher's Certificate, began to feel oppressed by the closeness of a large family in a small community of the young, mostly students past or present. Having worked at home for a while to save money, she joined a group of travellers going through Africa and on to Europe. She was the first of us to travel anywhere, except for Trevor's wartime journeys in the Pacific. Not long after she left, Rachel had another crisis, and so it was with Frances that I stood in the intensive care unit in Auckland Hospital as she came back to consciousness after another overdose. It was a terrible moment. She opened her eyes, looked at us and realised what had happened, turned away; her eyes filled with tears. She murmured, 'I don't want to be here.'

She was by then established in a fairly stable household in a pleasant old house in Ponsonby, and several times I stayed with her there. She came home too, she brought friends – Gerard, with whom she'd had a passionate love affair, and on whom she'd come to depend a good deal; Max, who also lived in the Jervois Road house and was the partner in a new relationship. Indeed she was surrounded by friends, but as I stood among a group of them round her bed as she recovered in hospital, I had a troubling glimpse of her not quite concentrating, of being adrift at the heart of her own networks, however affectionate they were.

Should she have come home to live? Was she actually ready for the perilous cross-currents of Auckland student life at that time of risk and upheaval? I asked such questions in a recurring confusion, helpless to answer them, continually reminding myself that neither I nor anyone else could decide for her, though her own decisions continued to be disturbing ones. An A-grade student, she decided to leave university, to 'explore her own creativity' untrammelled by 'the system'. It was a common idea, part of the search for freedom of choice, for 'alternative lifestyles' that was everywhere in the air in that young community. Max had left too; students spent long times talking, listening to music – in Rachel's case writing and drawing. It was a life that bred introspection; indeed exploring the self was a major part of it.

A good deal of this 'youth culture' was second-hand. One of the motivating forces of the hippie movement had been a reaction against the growth of technology, mass production, the soullessness of American urban life. New Zealand students (and no doubt many Americans too) must have absorbed the ideas without really knowing much of the cause, and this probably increased the rootlessness of their world. At the same time, as I had found in my own explorations, the principle of independence was unquestionably attractive. I sat with Rachel on the back doorstep of her house one Sunday morning, and agreed with her that there were creative possibilities to be found outside organisations like the university, and that the quest was exciting.

I think I did not recognise her frailty, or her obsessiveness – her way of becoming lost in what happened to her. I also came to think that if we had been, say, a Polynesian family we might have dealt with her recurring crises more easily, by simply taking her back home. But we did not live on a marae or in any other group, and home as a unit, even for those of us still there, was beginning to disintegrate. The future, even the next single step into it, was not a settled path, but an amorphous whirl of dark or glittering fragments.

Rachel turned twenty-one, moved house again, quarrelled with Max, appeared to be reconciled. Then she entered a far more serious, truly terrifying phase and was taken to Ward Ten, the psychiatric unit in Auckland Hospital, in a state described as catatonic. I went to Auckland, stayed with a friend who drove me, on the first morning of a visit of indeterminate length, to the hospital. A block from the gate we saw Rachel herself, in the familiar black and pink woollen coat she'd made, walking quickly along the footpath. Günter stopped the car for me to jump out and go with her. It was a day of nightmare. She had 'escaped' from the hospital with some idea that she would find Gerard (she had lived with him in the Coromandel, where he still was). I walked with her, in her distracted state, round the Domain, hour after hour, talking urgently. I couldn't have said afterwards what it was I'd said – some sort of appeal to come back with me, to let the hospital, her family, everyone who cared for her, try again and draw her in among us . . . In the end she did come; we walked back, and into the hospital.

I stayed for a week, spending every day with her. At first she would not eat or speak or acknowledge me or anyone else. This was a state recognisable in schizophrenic patients, doctors told me: she was listening to voices within her that drew her away from the external world. In long talks with the Ward Ten psychiatrists I asked about R.D. Laing and his new psychiatry, the idea that madness was to be respected as another reality. 'No known cures for this condition have come out of Laing's experiments,' I was told.

But slowly, slowly, Rachel did emerge from her frozen state, from the 'otherness' that had made her seem, and even look, as though she was listening to some message that came from outside the tangible world – the ward, and I and the others moving about it. Among the other patients was Rewi, son of Hone Tuwhare, whose poems I knew and liked; Hone himself, like me, was there day after day to try and help his son, and we became friends within this sad, perplexed milieu. He told me one day that he'd gone to a group therapy session at which a counsellor tried – and failed – to get Rachel to talk; then, 'Is there anyone here you feel is a friend?', and she had stood up silently and gone to sit beside Hone. I too felt that to stand beside him was to receive warm emanations, as from some radiator of the emotions.

By the end of my visit Rachel would both talk and eat; it seemed she had come back from that cold presence that in an almost physical sense was 'fighting to get her'. She then wanted to abandon the drugs she was being given, leave hospital at once, come home. The most difficult thing was to persuade her (in apparent contradiction of all I had been saying) to stay a while longer, though I myself would leave and go home.

There were daily phone calls, she continued to improve; eventually she came home, properly discharged though under the supervision of a Wellington psychiatrist. It was a fragilely beautiful three months. We talked about possible jobs of a manageable kind: she knew hospitals well by now, the offer of a ward clerk's job in the TB ward at Wellington Hospital made some sense. So I took her to work each day; she shared a room with Katherine, she began to laugh again, cooked sometimes, arranged flowers as she always had, took to reading again. A wave of relief passed through us all.

And then it happened again. She had a cold, spent a day at home, and when I came in from my day in the *Journal* office (which of course I wished I hadn't gone to) she was pale and silent, and had again the terrible hollow look in her eyes. 'I have to tell you it's come back, I can't help it,' she whispered. The next day I did stay home; we talked – unbelievably, and terrifyingly – of her wish to die. We even took Mungo in the car to the river bank behind Upper Hutt, and he ran about while we talked in the car. I cried hopelessly. She said it was right for her to do this. 'I have a good life,' she said, with the strange, rarefied certainty she had in this state, 'friends, a family that loves me – a much better life than Father, who has troubles at school and is miserable at home. The difference is, he wants his, and I don't want mine.'

At the end of that day of desperate struggle she slipped out and bought some lethal stuff and took it; then she wandered, cold and distracted about the park where we'd so often walked. Someone searching for her brought her home. In the ambulance I sat with my arms round the shivering person she'd become, wrapped in a blanket and still very far away from me. She died slowly in hospital over the next day and night. A young house surgeon, a friend of Frances, talked to her after any of us, and said, 'I think you have really done it this time – are you sorry?' and Rachel had said no, she was glad.

By the time I knew that, I also knew that suicide attempts made after an apparent recovery almost always succeed. The patient has greater strength and uses it to follow the dictates of the inner voice that Rachel had heard, and wanted to obey, so many times before.

Perhaps she was simply tired of having to make yet another struggle to 'come back' to the world we all said was real and inviting. All I read about the disease called schizophrenia said there was no known cure, but this did not stop me, then or later, asking the most painful of all the questions – 'If only . . . '

This was a greater loss than any I had known, and a greater defeat. It had the effect, in some ways permanently, of detaching me from all other experience; as though I said – and I did – that if something so precious could be swept away in a moment, what value could anything have? Every person, every moment, carried within itself its own temporariness, and the source of its own destruction.

Grief was work, I found, the hardest work I had ever done. Rules emerged, and once I understood each one I had to keep it. One was that I must never say, 'Why us? Why me?' because that led on to self-pity and turned me aside from the truth of this terrible event, and from Rachel herself. I came to believe that what I had to do, working from day to day, was to learn the truth, take it into myself, possess it, live with it, keep it in me. I thought of it sometimes as a large, black, sharp-edged rock that would never change and never move. It stood between me and everything that was living and hopeful and happy; somehow I had to change, enlarge my understanding of the world to make room for it, so that living could go on with me in it, and Rachel, and her death. She herself, all my memories of her, and the fact of her short life, her loss, must become part of everything I thought and did.

This wasn't fanciful. Others in the family felt a need to keep her qualities alive in us, not as someone we remembered and talked about, but as a presence in the new things we did. In the six months or so afterwards it seemed to me that in different ways each person in the family, shocked and shaken as they were, gathered themselves together and moved into their next phase with more resolution. We all seemed to acknowledge that if fate (or whatever we called it) could do something as appalling as this, it was, or could be, an enemy one needed all one's strength to contend with. Nothing could ever again be 'given', ours as of right.

The reasoning, the thinking and shaping of these ideas – and my constant writing about it – was my occupation in the most central way. Every time I finished a poem about Rachel, or the experience of her death (and I wrote an enormous number), this had the effect of briefly – but only briefly – ordering the chaos in my mind. There was also the question, the task, of bringing her into focus, gathering all I knew of her to keep with me, since this was now all I had. Part of that was the new and painful acknowledgement of how much of her I had not known anything about at all. I said over and over again to myself, 'I don't know, I don't know.'

Talking to some people helped. Katherine in particular had a wonderful patient tact, and time and again she was willing to come with me 'down Moonshine' with Mungo. There we would walk along the river bank and go over and over things Rachel had done and said, searching all the time for every scrap we might have let fall, so nothing should be missing from what was now to be our whole view of her. There was also of course a search for the reasons we wanted, but never found, the 'why' of it. I knew already that it is impossible to disentangle 'the person' from 'the illness', but I could not help continually trying. Sharing a room with Rachel for that last three months, Katherine had seen more of her than anyone. They had been good friends, but looking back she thought there had been some part of Rachel that never came close, never entered at all into their daily exchanges.

A few other people were good to talk to – the poet Alistair Campbell, for instance, was a mixture of compassion and astringency that often helped; we had become friends and he worked near my PPTA office. I rang him one day to say I simply could not go on sitting at my desk and working; he quickly understood and took me to the pub at the corner where we drank a slow beer and talked about Rachel, and how to learn a new way of being that accepted her death – though he said, wisely, that I would never be reconciled to it any more than I was now, and I found this was so. I could learn new accommodations, but nothing ever changed my repudiation of the death of someone so precious to me, and so young.

I had long and wonderfully perceptive letters from Alan Roddick, another new friend, also a poet; they were exactly the kind of sinewy examination of the truth of loss and impermanence that I could grasp, and work on. Because we were friends, he said, this was his experience too of the death of a daughter, and he wrestled with it accordingly.

But there were times of absolute blackness, waves of unimaginable misery when I simply did not know what to do. The first and perhaps the worst of these came in the first few weeks; I woke up one morning with the full realisation burning right through me; I stood up, and it was as though my whole body was a sheet of pain; I stumbled into Trevor's room in some sort of reaching for someone to touch or tell. But he could do nothing. Of course he could do nothing, as I, now, could do nothing for him when he was in extremity; we had moved too far away from each other for there to be more than a generalised kindness for each to give. I was truly on my own – and came eventually to be surprised that I could have lived so long without fully knowing this before.

I thought endlessly too about what she had herself said to me on that last day. It's not what you have in your life, she said, beautiful or ugly, rich or plain, it's simply whether you want it, whether it's worth fighting for. Was this the fundamental question? Not 'making something beautiful' but fighting for what you have – is it the fight that gives life its quality, the struggle, not the prize? And if so, was this something you learned, or was it in you, almost organic, as she seemed to suggest? Or was this simply the voice of illness? All I knew was that I must struggle with these questions, and I must do it alone.

And then, slowly, I began to find that I was not alone, not entirely. Help in the form of some insight, some new way of thinking and seeing, came from unexpected sources, but it came. Alan Roddick sent me Rilke's poems, which were full of momentous discoveries: 'In the end, those who were carried off early no longer need us . . . But we, who do need / such great mysteries . . . could we exist without *them*?' Rachel Wallace, a friend of Martin's and of Rachel's, wrote to me with a kind of courageous sternness: I must not possess Rachel's death, she said, or her choice of it; everyone has this right, and if she believed in it for herself, I must respect even this. It was a point made again and again in the Rilke poems, and it often led me to larger views of life and time: 'Angels (they say) don't know whether it is the living / they are moving among, or the dead. The eternal current / whirls all ages along in it, through both realms / forever . . . '

Clive, with whom I'd had many sharp arguments – as we grew older our ideas more and more diverged – now showed me a steady and faithful kindness. It was as though beyond all opinions he saw himself as the 'elder of the tribe', and so he behaved. He visited me again and again, never for long, never with much to say, but I was always glad of his sturdy rather inarticulate presence, as though I couldn't see ahead and he gave me his arm.

It took a very long time for the usual protections, the masks, to grow back; in the meantime I could be hurt by the simplest remark or gesture. And yet, surprisingly, quite miraculously, I usually felt safe; it seemed I was a naked creature in a world full of weapons, and the restraint and compassion of people I knew well (I mostly avoided others) took thought for me. This sustaining care operated most strongly inside my own family. We wanted to be together a good deal, and were nourished by our shared understanding. In a poem I didn't try to publish I spoke of this.

> But let us remember that death
> did not dishonour us; think how
> we drew together as if in a savage
> place without protection, how we
> felt there the stirring of a new
> power, some knowledge that had
> slept in us and woke then
> to a hasty blossoming; each
> beyond cure, we began at once
> to care for one another, practising
> as though by nature the perfect
> courtesy of the helpless.

Rachel's friends were often at our house; they had a freshness and openness in their talk of her, and kindness to me, that seemed a kind of gift. Max, unremittingly generous of his time and himself, came to stay for weeks together, to help – without exactly saying so – in the reconstruction we were all intent upon. And my own writing and reading gave me a sense of wider networks in which I could have some place. More and more I could at least come within sight of a new knowledge, that my loss was part of something much greater than myself. The more I felt the reality of this greater milieu, the better able I was to understand the impaired life I now had. At times I felt there was something miraculous about this realisation, as if I stood in a vast chamber filled with echoes of every human experience: there I was nothing, or close to nothing, and greatly at risk – and yet somehow in the right place, and at home.

At the end of the year Virginia, who had been working in London, came home, and helped us to move to another house. It was right in Wellington; Trevor too worked in town by then, none of us belonged, or wanted to belong, in Upper Hutt. The new house was perched on a hill, exposed to wind and weather, standing on a small piece of rough ground. The lower part was only half built, there were weeks and months of hard labour. Somehow in physically putting together a place we could call home – though most of the family lived in it only intermittently – we all began to piece together something new in ourselves.

In Middle Air came out towards the end of the year. Fiona Kidman, a new and already important friend, had a first book too and we launched them together. At a party afterwards, at her house, the heightened emotions of the moment plunged me into hopeless tears; nevertheless I knew that however damaged, however incomplete I felt myself to be, this new work, my own writing, was the beginning of my next journey.

Part Three

The Quick World

Chapter 34

I came to Kingsford-Smith Airport in Sydney on the day the first commercial flight in history left for the South Pole; it was boarding at Gate 9 while I roamed the gift shops in search of postcards to send home. I was fifty-two, and I had never left New Zealand before. During the nomadic fifties and sixties, when everyone supposed you had to leave these islands to breathe as a free person, neither I nor anyone in my family had ventured further from home than the South Island.

Everything about a first journey is miraculous. Planes on the tarmac were the biggest in the world; they towered over me like dinosaurial monsters, glittering in the February heat against the milky haze of the Sydney skyline. In my lifetime, I thought, dazed, Kingsford-Smith had flown the Tasman in a single-engine Tiger Moth with room for one in the cockpit.

I flew over Australia in everlasting daylight, eternal sunshine: heaven as proven fact. Darkness which had reliably divided one day from the next since the world began now crowded into a diminishing heap behind us as we forged ahead. As long as we kept up our speed, I speculated, we could keep ahead of it right round the earth, finally being overtaken by the night we were fleeing from when metal fatigue caused us to explode or melt. I put my watch back three times, in the recurring illusion that it was lunchtime. If days and nights were to be abandoned like this, had I indeed jumped off the edge of the known world? Yes, very likely I had.

But evening, or some hopeful shading of the light, did come eventually; the huge plane went to ground, and I stepped outside into air that flew at me like a blast from a furnace. Small dark boys jumped and shouted for luggage to carry; the noise and stink and brightness burst over me like a shower of fireworks. So this was foreign travel. It was Mauritius.

A small island in the Indian Ocean may seem the least likely place in the world for a New Zealand traveller to choose as an introduction to the great civilisations that flourish, we know, beyond our horizons. Indeed I wondered myself what queer route I was taking to my OE, the overseas experience New Zealanders honour like a household god they dare not neglect. Sticky heat, jungles of sugar cane, black crowds chattering incomprehensibly in the streets of funny dirty villages with French street names on their signs . . . what had all this to do with me? I wandered and stared; peered briefly through the gates of a convent and was laughed at by a crowd of unkempt little black girls for doing so. I bought a book about the island and read it in French – the language I'd learnt so thoroughly but had never used, and now could do no more than mumble.

The truth was that I'd left home knowing almost nothing about where I was going. Undoubtedly by 1977 I had advanced quite a long way along the risky path to independence; I constantly experimented with separate occupations, rather than remain the cog in family machinery I'd always been. All the same, this plan to travel had less to do with the expansion of my world view than with some half-conscious desire to strengthen and care for family connections, including those that were not close at hand. I was on my way to visit Miranda, a young niece and the one family member I knew well who lived outside New Zealand. In Africa, in fact, on Lamu Island off the coast of Kenya.

With her I crossed that country in a night train, watching from the windows for the gazelles, wildebeests, even lions, I knew were there – and in the early light seeing them too, though most turned out to be thorn bushes that put up their branches and galloped off into the distance. I rode in a killingly uncomfortable bus full of livestock, and an open barge loaded up with luggage, athletic looking black youths and ourselves, the English ladies. I learned to haggle in the market, to take my bedding on hot nights up onto the roof (a curious re-creation of scenes from the Sunday school cards of my childhood); there I could sleep, stretched out under the African stars. I saw groups of Moslem women, black-veiled, coming out of hiding in the evening, to run about the streets of Lamu town, giggling and shy.

It was all improbable – beautiful, and bizarre. But wherever we went, the heat was an overpowering physical presence. We were the Jonah in its belly. To make matters worse I was horribly dressed in the wrong clothes – dress, petticoat, shoes, stockings. Could I really not have understood this most basic requirement of a tropical climate, that you shed the appurtenances of temperate living? Would it not have been quite simple to avoid the ridiculous incongruity of these layers of garments that each day threatened to liquefy me altogether? It became clear to me that I had embarked on my great adventure without considering the facts of its conditions much at all.

It was nearly two years since Rachel's death. This crushing event, the greatest loss I could ever have to sustain, had broken into fragments every habit, every pattern of thinking by which I'd lived. Nothing that made up my view of the world had been able to survive that absolute defeat, my daughter's willed death. And the disintegration of my marriage, which was still going on, simply added to the disarray in which I lived and thought. Nothing held; my loyalties, my old faith in family and parenthood, all I'd believed in, lay about me like rubble at a bomb site. 'Death's an explosion in the mine / of love' I'd written in a poem I kept going back to, trying to find a way of speaking to Rachel about the new world her death had compelled me to search for.

It was this new world and its entirely unfamiliar ground that I now occupied. From here had shot up, like random fireworks, the idea of foreign travel; Miranda had been my close friend in the family for many years, so I had a ready destination. The fact that I'd made only rudimentary preparations was not really strange, since everything was rash and sudden in this new life. I didn't plan, I just did things. And I watched, observed; that faculty, at least, was not diminished. On the contrary, it had grown sharper with lack of forethought. The world quivered with a vivid unexpectedness.

My increasingly separate selves seemed for the moment to be dispersing even more actively than usual. I was not one person but many – writer, parent, woman experimenting with independence, editor – and now, traveller. Each seemed not to know how to connect itself to the others, and my lack of preparation or policy must have been part of this dispersal. I lost myself in the moment, as one concentrates, willy-nilly, on recurring and deafening explosions.

In Lamu, everything I heard was an instruction in an encyclopaedic new lore and language. I listened earnestly, trying to swell up fast enough to have room in myself for all the discoveries. This, as much as the heat, gave me headaches. I wanted to go away and think, write in my notebook – it alone could confer a kind of order on the vast confusion of unfamiliarities that beat about me. Sometimes in the afternoons I did go to the 'office', a room off the courtyard which, in a traditional Moslem household, would have been used for prayer and meditation. There I could write, and reflect. Perhaps, by a curious association, I did fulfil the traditional Islamic purposes of this small dusty refuge, set in its enclosed garden with an ancient pomegranate tree growing over the window.

After I left Lamu, I returned to Mombasa in the terrible bus. Each time we crossed a river we had to climb out and stand beside the bus on a shaky-looking platform while a team of men pulled us slowly across the water, now thick and red with dust from the road. As we waited on the bank for the last of these crossings, a tall woman, very black, wearing a pink patterned khanga and a high-piled pink head cloth, caught my eye and gave me a wide and beautiful smile. Later, on the raft, she came up to me and took my hand and elbow in a firm grasp. Her smile was followed by a long searching look, full of intimacy and some discovered understanding that in a moment leaped across all the barriers that divided us. I did not know what she had said to me – and yet perhaps I did. After the gay but pitiful little Lamu women, the sheer power of this splendid creature was deeply stirring.

During the hours when I was shut up alone in the office I wrote about every encounter in letters home and in the journal that existed, apparently, to receive the overflow of my alarms and perplexities. Perhaps its function really was to represent some of the other voices that jarred and jangled about the echoing chamber of my divided self. If this was so, it was a voice that exclaimed, gushed, rioted, stormed, agonised, cried for clarity but seemed never to achieve it – in short, a *young* voice. The voice of someone fluctuating between childish ignorance, nostalgia for past securities and an eager leaping forward; sane and silly judgement jostling each other in the same sentence. However, I emerged from these occasional retreats somewhat calmed, ready to jump again into the electrifying present, shallow though my immersion might be.

Before I left Africa, Miranda and I went to Dar es Salaam, that tarnished city, steaming in the tropical heat. Half-finished roads, derelict buildings, shortages of food, rumours of vast corruption – it was my glimpse of a desperately beleaguered, heroically determined new Africa, in which I was, clearly, an unwanted outsider. Soberly, we travelled back to Nairobi – and beyond: I, to Europe. Miranda, the experienced traveller, had prepared me as well as she could for fabulous places she already knew – Florence, Assisi, Paris, London. The plane rose in the hot midnight air. I went to sleep, and woke up in Italy.

Florence. Fabled city, heart of Renaissance culture . . . and so stunning a contrast to the fierce, raw African towns I had come from that I could not at first take hold of my spinning imagination. Miranda's kindness had extended to the address of a pensione where I would be clean and comfortable; inside, I went upstairs and stood for a long time at the window of my small room. I had bought a blood orange in the street and, eating it, I looked down on a scene like a set for a Verdi opera. The characters, ordinary people – a young man in a cloth cap, a smart woman in knee-high black boots, a couple closely entwined in a long embrace, a businessman reading a newspaper. I could see, to the left and high above them, the richly dominating tower of what my guidebook said was the Cathedral Santa Maria del Fiora, the splendid Basilica.

It was evening. Here too it seemed the life of the street did not end with darkness or the shutting of shops; many seemed not to shut at all, and cafés and the clusters of tables and chairs outside them were all crowded. I thought of the critics who said New Zealand shut down for evenings and weekends, and stared all the harder. Of course I *did* know this place – travelling through Tuscany and the Umbrian countryside to get to Florence I'd seen the picturebook country of childhood – the ordered rows of vineyards and olive groves, all strictly rounded by pruning, the cypresses marching in formation up the slopes, the shuttered houses with tiled roofs, curved medieval stone bridges arching across every stream. Outside Perugia I'd also seen, to my delight, the old woman driving her pig to market, just as my mother's long-ago tale had told me, a thousand times. Grey hump-backed oxen had ruminated and stared as the train passed, and in one paddock, all by itself, I had looked out at an ordinary, munching, lackadaisical New Zealand sheep. Well, an Italian sheep.

I didn't want to move away from that window. Indifferent as they were, the crowds below made me less alone, and aloneness was by now rolling through my mind like bushfire smoke. Leaving New Zealand, I had been taken in by my niece, who had treated me with the steady familiarity of a daughter; Africa's thunderous reverberations had reached me in her reassuring presence. Familiar with the old milieu as well as the new, she had made my first journey imaginatively possible – and physically bearable. I would never forget standing with her, one human dot beside another, on the ledge above the Great Rift Valley that swept away as far as we could see, dividing Kenya east from west, but to me striding through the entire world. I had lived my whole life in small islands; even more than the journey through night and day on the plane, these huge slopes and limitless horizons brought the scope of the world to me, the world I'd known – or thought I had – through books and pictures and maps.

Now, in a small pensione, managed by a cross, watchful and avaricious signora, I realised for the first time that I had to make my way among people who, like her, had no interest in my welfare, or even my survival, so long as my bill was paid. I might live or die, nobody here would care which. I decided to look for something more than an orange to eat (found you could buy pieces of pizza at any hour, day or night) and then sat down to the only occupation I had carried across the world with me: I wrote. For page after detailed, confiding page, my notebook received my excesses with the willing tolerance of a family dog. But, like him – the one I knew – it didn't reply: for that I had to write letters just as copiously to all those at home who might. I began sending in advance the poste restante addresses for every place I intended to visit; found, the next morning, the post office – in Florence a noble palace, arched and pillared like a cathedral. I bought stationery, postcards, stamps; how else could I be sure, amid these rapidly changing realities, that my own, the one I hoped to return to, still existed?

Through the next few weeks poste restante enquiries in European cities were deeply, consistently disappointing. I was by turns hurt, mystified, alarmed; I wrote twice as often, letters two or three times as long. Only afterwards did I realise the absolute impossibility of arranging that letters from New Zealand should arrive at European addresses that change every few days. But by then my perceptions of home had changed in many other ways; by the time I returned to New Zealand in early May, three months after my tentative and tearful departure, I felt myself to be a sophisticated cosmopolitan, altered in every cell of mind and body by a massive new knowledge of Europe and the world.

In the meantime I went to bed and dreamed of home, a disturbing kaleidoscope of images that dissolved and re-formed – Greenmeadows was there, and the first of the Ohakune houses I'd lived in; and then, with a shaft of pain that woke me up, the terrace of the Heretaunga house and Rachel sitting on the step, turning to me, about to speak, though I had no idea what she would say. That was how it always was. I had learnt, over and over, that however often I relived the last part of her life, questioned every moment I could remember, I would come back to this, the fact of her silence, her death. The implacable, unchanging fact. Learning this, in the two years I'd so far had to do it, had begun a process of detachment from every other experience, and this, I realised, was still going on. Being where I was, alone on the other side of the world, was part of it, a logical next step after the changes and departures there had already been.

By the end of 1975 I had acutely wanted to move from the Heretaunga house and the community where we had lived; I had looked for new projects, new struggles; quiescence was the hardest condition to bear. And in practical terms the move to Wellington had made sense for us all. Trevor now worked in the Department of Education, I had for years travelled more than twenty miles to my PPTA editor's office in the centre of the city. The only person officially connected with Upper Hutt was Katherine, still at school, and she was willing to spend her seventh form year at Wellington High School.

She had been, as often before, the person who most helped me through the transition. She would look through the 'For Sale' columns in every day's newspaper and put a ring around possibilities; I would sift them and visit the most promising. At the best of those we would all assemble for judgement. 'All' meant Frances, Stephanie and Katherine, Trevor sometimes, Martin usually, with his new young girlfriend Jan Preston. I said I wanted hills and sea because this was the essence of Wellington living. Hills and sea, however, cost money, so we found ourselves looking at oddities of houses offering sea views but not much else. Many were queerly renovated – a house in Seatoun Heights with elaborate marbled archways and a huge bar; a Hataitai villa done up by a retired sailor to look like the state rooms and cabins of an ocean liner, an elegant Wadestown bungalow that never got the sun.

A land agent, despairing of my difficult taste and shortage of cash, drove me one day along Oriental Parade and pointed up the hill to a house that was to 'come on the market tomorrow'. I was tired and indifferent, but agreed to look at it. In the late afternoon the empty house was full of light; a boomerang shape (an open right angle), it was neither large nor distinguished, but it sat in a niche in the hillside so that it caught every ray of sun a changeable climate could provide. On that cold spring afternoon it had a warm and mellow glow; the sea shone below, even the city sparkled. It was reached by walking up or down a thousand steps, and this terrible access made it cheap. I wanted at once to live there, and although there were a few crises to follow, I succeeded.

When we moved into the house, it was only half formed – the lower part remained a block of raw clay, enclosed by walls. In gouging out this earth floor to make a legal level for rooms to be built, we exhausted ourselves again and again. Frances sweated on the rowdy kanga drill, Martin wheeled endless barrows of clay to the bank and tipped them over, Stephanie and Katherine wielded spades; everyone grunted and sweated and heaved. This hard and dirty work, and the sense of a new shared enterprise, drew us together; we laughed and talked and planned. A young architect friend of Rachel's designed the new rooms, and Max, the lover and partner who had shared her last years, came to stay, built, among other things, an archway over the gate, and designed a garden. My 'letters home' were addressed to this house on a sharp, sudden hill overlooking Wellington Harbour.

Chapter 35

While I travelled the world Frances went to live at home with her father to 'look after' him. Though not ill, he was often depressed and, like most other people, we assumed he could not manage a household without a woman's help. In the event her presence was intermittent because she partly lived, and usually slept, with her newest young man, a musician and photographer who, like her, worked at Downstage Theatre – she had trained several years before at the New Zealand Drama School. Her letters to me, and Trevor's, were full of the daily detail of work and home, the garden, the animals, Mungo the dog and two white cats she had added to the ménage. I read every word with a devouring attention.

When Frances had a theatrical triumph in *The Constant Wife*, Trevor was so proud he wanted to send all the reviews to me, Mungo had given up wandering the neighbourhood to look for me, Trevor could make soup, tomatoes ripened in the garden, they missed me, Martin had come to lunch, Steph and Kath were well . . . Frances found it hard to imagine her mother walking the streets of foreign cities; she could tell a lot of things were 'happening in my head'. Indeed they were. Each time one of these rushes of warm air from home blew in through a foreign post office, my sense of distance grew and solidified. With me again, close enough to touch, were the living room looking out over the sea, the new rooms downstairs smelling of fresh timber, Mungo's snuffling nudges, the sharp light of a Wellington day. Everything had a strange poignancy as I sat on beds in furnished rooms or at café tables, on benches in huge museums and galleries, in crowded compartments of European trains.

Distinctions between 'here' and 'there' had so far been local and familiar. On camping trips up and down the country I had seen the remarkable mountains and lakes of the South Island, East Coast towns where electric power had not arrived and telephones often didn't work, where horses were tethered to posts in the main street. In camping grounds, or on visits to schools as editor of the *PPTA Journal*, I had talked to Southland farmers whose families had owned the same land since the arrival of the first European settlers, to Poms who scoffed at the emptiness of the countryside and the early closing of bars; I knew distance and its contrasts perfectly well – or thought I did. Now everything was wrenched into unexpected shapes and dimensions; the muscles of the mind creaked, stretched, quivered. Distance? I was learning it for the first time in my life.

Each night when I lay down in a (usually) hard and narrow bed in some small foreign hotel I closed my eyes and tried to assemble a map of familiar things, in order to span, in some rudimentary way, the windy spaces of the mind where I wandered whenever I found myself not busy, and alone. There were – ah yes, Frances and Trevor securely occupying the house on the hill which now marked for me the central point of my dispersing family; like my own parents before me, I wanted to hold to this centre, to keep it as a living manifestation of home, even as 'home' was being re-invented and re-interpreted by each of my grown-up children. And, whatever grown-upness meant, all those young things seemed to have attained it. Kathy and Stephanie, the two youngest girls, lived in the mixed flats that had now become commonplace for students, one of them in Wellington and one in Dunedin. Martin did too, in Wellington; each was embarking on adventures I scarcely understood, though I hadn't in the least given up wanting to know and if possible be a part of their discoveries. Perhaps the profound sorrow of Rachel's death kept this desire strong in me after its due time had passed; perhaps so for them too. I didn't know, but certainly once my map of love and longing was in place I could stretch out and go to sleep in my corner of the nameless foreign expanses I had decided to traverse.

I went to the Uffizi, and with thousands of others jostled for places before more paintings than I could possibly assimilate or remember. In a way this didn't matter, because there were two so overwhelming that I returned to them for a part of every day I spent in Florence – the famous Botticellis, 'Birth of Venus' and 'Spring'. Rachel had for years given me an unofficial artistic education through books, prints and her own enthusiasm, and my old friend Arthur Sewell had also talked lyrically of paintings he loved; indeed he had instructed me years before that I must one day visit the San Marco monastery in Florence and see the Fra Angelico panels there.

This had the force of a secret mission. Arthur had been dead for five years, but the glow of his expansive vision and subtle tenderness had stayed with me. The panels were exquisite, some surprisingly funny, and that too seemed like a private message he had lodged with me, to be revealed at its due time. 'The Last Judgement' showed me the beatific but rather bored faces of the virtuous, correctly haloed and dancing in Paradise, and at the other end the damned, writhing and shrieking in Hell, some even leaning out of a sort of cooking pot with flames licking round its base, their faces ten times more alive and expressive than the others. Perfect. I stood there grinning; it was as though Arthur's impious shadow leaned close, and whispered of sin.

I went to London, and found, as every traveller from my country must do, the long-familiar world of childhood – London Bridge (is falling down . . .), the Tower where kings were executed and little princes incarcerated, the River Thames-that-ran-softly-e'er-I-end-my-song, and far along it Greenwich, where time began; Westminster and the poets sleeping there as I'd always known they did, stone knights dead in St Paul's. And, of course, The Strand and Mayfair (Becky Sharp, lurking) and Islington and Old Kent Road of the Monopoly board – and oh, Bloomsbury, Russell Square, Virginia and Leonard Woolf, Katherine Mansfield, Lytton Strachey, the Bells . . . there was no end to it. My imagination reeled; this was where I'd grown up, learnt all I first knew, and yet each tangible moment, each act of physical recognition, came with a shock of disbelief.

There was another quite different sense of homecoming in London – two, in fact. One was that I stayed at William Goodenough House in Mecklenburgh Square, a sort of hostel/hotel for Commonwealth graduates working in London, and the other that, being there, I re-discovered a project of my own that I could dignify with the name of 'research'. The place itself reminded me powerfully of St Margaret's, the Christchurch private school which I had thought all along was modelled exactly on English institutions. The difference was that this time I was a real resident, not an outsider, so had to keep the rules myself – not, now, about homework and prayers, but about mail and keys and laundry.

As for the company I kept, men and women from all over the world lived at William Goodenough while they worked at the British

Library, or conducted other kinds of scholarly investigation in London or Europe. Many were on sabbatical leave from their universities. If I saw myself as a 'working' traveller at all, it was in a more general, more sporadic way, as the writing of poetry dictates. However, it was time now to bring out my own research – editing the Fairburn *Letters*.

I had for several years had Denis Glover as a benign and expansive tutor. Also, much of the material was already in the Turnbull Library archives in Wellington, and together we collected a good deal more. His method was to introduce me to everyone in Fairburn's personal network and actively promote the friendships thus made possible. This, presumably, would persuade those reluctant to relinquish their letters to do so. It was an approach that had worked well so far, but there was one large body of letters which nobody had been able to secure. They were held by the author, an expatriate New Zealander who lived partly in London and partly in the south of France. His name was Geoffrey de Montalk, or Count Potocki de Montalk or, as it seemed he most liked to be known, the King of Poland; he asked a high price for his treasure.

The problem until now had been that he quickly turned against everyone who approached him with a proposition, complaining bitterly that he was himself a far greater poet than Fairburn, but that Pig Islanders refused to recognise his worth (not to mention his present need for cash). Denis arranged with the Turnbull Library that if I could find him I should be authorised to offer him $1,000 – an improvement on previous offers – and try hard to persuade him to sell. Spreading out the contents of the Fairburn file in my meagrely furnished room at William Goodenough, I felt another rush of familiarity, a reassuring connection with my working life at home.

I found the royal eccentric in London. He turned out to be a rather charming beslippered old gentleman, who served me a terrible dinner in his London apartment (burnt parsnip, burnt chop) and nearly froze me to death by economising on money for the gas heater. He talked volubly, indeed impenetrably, about himself, his place in the cosmos, the power of astrology, his writing, printing and publishing (he had edited a periodical called *The Right Review*, which had supported the Nazi cause during the war). I managed to get through the evening without arousing his anger or his suspicions, and late at night, after much nervous reconnoitring, I brought up the subject of the letters. Then, flattering and cajoling (I told myself I would make every sacrifice except one, to gain my end), I extracted from him a promise that he would sell the letters, for the 'paltry sum' his wretched little country was willing to pay. Then he drove me home, weaving erratically through wet London streets, with the lights of the car turned off, presumably for economy reasons.

As I climbed out, it occurred to me that I would one day be able to tell my grandchildren that I had once sat at midnight in a London square in an ancient Citroen and allowed the King of Poland to hold my hand and whisper to me of the stars.

Chapter 36

If my colourful final scene with the Count made me think of grandchildren that was because they were already in my mind, a nameless company which had always lurked in a twilight of future time, my attitude to them benign but vague. However, six months before my departure from New Zealand a surprising new turn of events had altered this comfortable stance.

In 1976 Stephanie had left school and elected to go to Otago University. I had visited her there and seen her shaping a daily programme full of experiment, in friendships and in ways of working. Yet it was very different from the atmosphere of hectic anarchy that had swirled round Auckland students when I had visited Frances there nearly ten years before. Stephanie and her friends had inherited a flat-dwelling, free-roaming way of life; earlier students had wrenched it out of the conventions of hostels and parental supervision.

Stephanie was a bright and perceptive student, rather irked by the artificiality of academic language and its abstract theorising. She spent a lot of time with Barry, who visited her from Christchurch where he was a student at the School of Fine Arts. I had taught Barry at Heretaunga College, I liked and admired him, and we had all been aware of the intimacy between them because he had come often to see her when we moved to Grass Street. He was attractive, energetic, intelligent, and very talented. In the August holidays of her Dunedin year, Stephanie stunned us all by announcing that she and Barry wanted to have a baby. She said that it was obvious to her that women did things in a different order these days – so would she. Deciding her occupation, career, training – all that could come later. I, eagerly pursuing my own late career, could hardly disagree, and indeed I thought the two of them wonderfully adventurous, and said so. At the end of the year they both came to live in Wellington, and when I left in February Stephanie was within three months of the birth of her child.

I intended to return home just in time for this magnetic event, and as I bounced and shivered through my own adventures I often thought of the startling fact that my young daughter, resolute and full of purpose, but after all only recently out of high school, was about to change the shape of the family in the most dramatic way possible.

I went to the Midlands, streaking through the English countryside eating English breakfast all the way; I viewed Countesthorpe College and took notes for the *Journal*. I stayed a night in a stately-home-turned-hotel, and went to Birmingham in a train as small and homely as James or Edward in the Reverend Awdry's books that Martin had so loved as a child. I marvelled at Coventry Cathedral, at Midland speech, at English bobbies and English pubs. Then it was Easter; I packed most of my luggage and gave it to my old friend Neville, who lived in London with his English wife and two children.

I went to 'the Continent', taking the boat train for Paris. I learned the French for 'Easter' but did not wonder if others would also visit that legendary city just then. In fact there were (one taxi driver said) four million others besides me, roaming about through an interminable, freezing night looking for hotel beds. Despite my mounting panic, I found that frail, desperate, intense travellers' camaraderie that is all one has of human aid in the midst of disasters in foreign countries. My taxis, as they drifted from one *complet* sign to another, were occupied by others as helpless as I. One young man decided to settle for an all-night discotheque where he would at least be warm, another begged a couch in the tiny street-level salon of one of the thousands of cheap hotels that didn't want us in its bedrooms.

I too at that point decided that even a chair, inside, would keep me from dying in the street, and pleaded with the same concierge. Scowling fiercely, he led me up seven flights of narrow stairs and unlocked the door of a single room at the very top. It had a cracked and dirty wash basin, a rusty nail as a window catch, a bed made up with ragged blankets and filthy sheets, and floor space that looked about two square feet. 'Merci beaucoup, merci bien . . . Formidable – ' my textbook French was preparing to mumble, but the fellow had shut the door and was gone.

Despite my mismanaged arrival (I moved the next morning to better quarters), coming to Paris crystallised for me another literary shadow, beautiful but remote, of a great city. Did not English school-girls go to Paris on vacation – and after them almost every character in English fiction? I had just read Henry James' *The Ambassadors* and its Parisian setting was still sharp and clear in my mind. Is it possible, though, to know or imagine too much, before encountering the fact? I felt a strange resistance to what sometimes felt like a prescribed perfection.

But then I took a train to Chartres Cathedral where I stood overawed for hours before the most beautiful stained glass in the world, as I'd heard it called. And in the Louvre I felt again, as in Florence, the wonder of recognition of a tradition I could claim as mine simply by sharing an old knowledge. My real discovery was of the continuity of time and experience, and thus of the art that expresses its quality.

Denis, the patient introducer, had given me a letter for Anton Vogt, a New Zealander living in Menton, and before leaving Paris I posted it to him. The name was familiar – a young poet in the thirties and forties, a teachers' college lecturer encouraging to young students who aspired to write; a charming man, said Denis. In my covering note I asked if I might stay a night at his house (the train from Paris arrived about midnight) and find a hotel the next morning.

When the taxi put me down at his gate – iron railings, locked – I found a note attached to one of the prongs. Directions to an obscure entrance, no doubt. I paid the taxi driver a vast number of francs and opened the letter. You are rude and thoughtless, it said, to invite yourself like this with so little warning. Tony is old and sick and has had too many New Zealand visitors already. You are not welcome. I moved from the street lamp under which I could read this crushing rebuke, and was staggered to see, as I turned round, that further along the row of iron stakes yet another note was impaled. At least it isn't raining, I thought, as though this might help me to meet the next onslaught.

'Don't take too much notice of whatever it is they've said to you. Go to Garavan, following the railway line – map attached – and sleep in the KM Room, here's the key. We're not supposed to do this, but the bed's OK, and anyway I don't care. Hope you're warm enough; we'll come in the morning and bring more blankets if you need them. See you then. Love, Barry Mitcalfe'.

I had never met Barry Mitcalfe, but knew he was the holder that year of the Katherine Mansfield Fellowship and so was living and working in Menton, in the south of France. All he could know of me was that I was a fellow New Zealander and, however modestly, a fellow writer. Floundering through the back streets of that midnight city, keeping close to the railway line, I thought of him as a shining knight, my chevalier, my great-hearted saviour. When he knocked on my door next morning I saw that he was a middle-sized man with an open face, rather hairy, and a warm, wide smile – all entirely consistent with my ecstatic vision.

In the couple of days I spent in Menton we picnicked together on the beach – he had his wife and three children with him – talked of home, of being poverty-stricken in Europe, of writers and writing. After I left, I found the money I'd given him for our last bottle of wine tucked into my raincoat pocket. He knew no French, had to pay for lessons, and on the tiny income then provided for the fellowship somehow had to keep five Mitcalfes alive. I saw him once more, years afterwards in New Zealand; we laughed over the wine, the raincoat, the angry Vogts. And then suddenly, a day or so later, he died. A beautiful, gallant man.

In 1976 New Zealand PEN had decided to offer membership to one of the Czech writers denied free association in their own country. The novelist Ludvik Vaculik had written, 'art must continue to criticise governments, because it is culture which makes governments what they are'; I was to meet him, if I could, and express our support for him and his friends in their struggle for freedom of speech. It was the year of Charter 77, the Czech Human Rights Declaration.

I had a useful contact, George Mucha, son of the famous painter Alphonse Mucha, but explaining my request to him brought a painful surprise. Beleaguered writers were in hiding and searching out one of them, even for kindly reasons, could do nothing but harm. Everything I said to George had to be written down and destroyed, in case we were overheard. Even Ian Milner, the famous New Zealand expatriate, would only talk about my mission as we drove about in his car, away from walls that could have ears.

I was mortified that we in our safe little country had not understood the true nature of the dilemma facing these people and for the rest of my visit left the subject severely alone. But I had another, immensely privileged, glimpse of life under occupation; Ian took me to lunch with the Czech poet Miroslav Holub, who talked of the enforced secrecy of their own writing, and their dependence on Ian, translator and conduit to other countries in Europe where their poems might be read.

On my last evening I walked with the Milners over Charles Bridge and through that heartbreakingly beautiful city glowing in the mist. Then I left in a train that took me across the heavily guarded border and into 'legitimate' Europe.

Prague had been the most taxing of my arrival ordeals (except for that unforgettably frightful night in Paris), the most uncertain in its outcome and the only place in which I could be in actual danger – apart from the normal hazards of falling planes, derailing expresses and randomly violent strangers. Yet it became a kind of consummation of all my travel experiences, the place where I felt I most truly belonged, without, for those few days, losing any of my natural connections with New Zealand and home.

Perhaps only there, almost at the end of my journeying, had I discovered the stillness that lies at the heart of journeys: the need to wait, passive but wary, ready for events you cannot know or anticipate. This had been induced in me by long hours in European trains, confusing delays in railway stations, the pervasive European indifference to wandering foreigners.

I am [I wrote in my by now battered notebook] *peculiarly free here. I am alone yet feel cared for by these good Milners who take the responsibility of New Zealand visitors very keenly. This morning I have a good strong sense of the future, feel the energy and purpose to go back and work on the endless Fairburn job and* finish it. *The working routine – can I do that? – work, work, leave a bit of time each day to talk, drink, be at leisure, keep Denis and his interminable stories and booze at a distance without causing trouble – this balancing act – and so finish the bloody thing. It's very tempting. At the same time I know that poetry writing has got in the way more than anything else, and I can't give that up . . .*

I am ready to go home, I've suddenly realised it here. I think it's because I really have learnt at last how to be away. Not only how to do all this moving and settling without getting too desperate, ill or exhausted, but how to use my own common sense and pleasure – yes, that – in living the life. At first I could only make things real by telling people – family, friends – about them in letters. Now it's different; I can tell myself, or write it, and feel satisfied. Yes, imperceptibly it's happened – or it's begun. What's the effect of such an experience, what carries over into the life one returns to? I can't say yet – perhaps just another dimension, another layer, to your thinking, made up of what you've seen and remember, what lodges in you and stays there. Like that little videoscope thing we had as children into which you put two flat pictures, and looked through the glass and they'd become three-dimensional, alive, with distance in them. Is travel a glass like that over the retina of the mind?

In London a telegram awaited me. It had lodged in the 'E' pigeon-hole in the New Zealand House mail department for two days, keeping its momentous secret. I was so shaken by the very sight of it that I could not open it at once. I went downstairs to the washroom, the loo, and there, trembling, I broke its gummed edge open. It said, GIRL BORN TUESDAY ALL WELL LOVE TREVOR. All by myself in that infinitely prosaic, but securely private corner of the most public of buildings, I cried. Secret, tumultuous, joyful tears. My first grandchild. The world turned over, rearranged itself, sent out sparks and rockets. I cancelled my American stop-over and caught a plane for home.

As I drove to the airport, daffodils were coming out in the London parks, though the trees were still bare. The sunlight was clear and cool – the spring of all the English poets, going back as far as the language itself, and certainly encompassing the stirrings of poetic wonder in my own earliest reading, my first childish writing.

Half an hour from Auckland I looked out; we were between skies, one above and one below, with all the clouds in the bottom one. After nearly thirty-six hours in an aeroplane, every tissue in my body felt swollen, clogged with weight and weariness. Auckland Airport was like a little country station, and suddenly, stepping out into it, I had my first realisation that New Zealand is indeed a small and far-off group of islands. When other travellers had said this I had always wondered, 'far off from what?' Now, at last, I knew.

Stephanie's baby was a black-haired, black-eyed little creature, in features resembling her father far more than any of us. Her presence revived in me the powerful magic of the birth of my own children, yet there were interesting differences. I had imagined that my already vast family experience would make me a little lacklustre in contemplating another generation; I would be pleased to pay compliments and depart, thankfully going back to my increasingly engrossing separate life. Not at all. If motherhood had once blown my young woman's habits into a shower of starry fragments, grandmotherhood did the same to my sense of my place in the world.

My daily life, it's true, was not greatly changed by Ruth's appearance, though I often visited her and her mother; but my interior life darted about in a thousand thrilling directions, making room for her entry.

In the two years since Rachel's death I had been continually aware of a need to widen and strengthen the whole shape of my consciousness to accommodate the fact of her loss, and to learn the ways in which I could keep my knowledge of her fresh and untarnished by bitterness. It had been a long and gruelling process, and it was still going on. This birth, with its opposite prompting, was breathtakingly sudden. Each time I watched, touched, held this small perfect creature I felt a rush of happiness, I couldn't stop smiling, exclaiming. I am like every other grandmother there's ever been, I thought in dismay; what delusions of difference had I suffered from, then?

The fact that my closest attention was every day fixed on my new literary occupations, rather than my old domestic ones, was beside the point. The birth of a new person was on a grander scale than anything else except a death, the other absolute alteration. Life, not art, would always sweep in and grab the prizes.

Several others of the family were in Wellington that year. Katherine was a student at Victoria University and shared with other students a house in the Aro Valley; Frances handed the Grass Street household back to me, extended now by the addition of Brian and Valencia, her two white kittens, and went to live with her friend Stephen. By a charming curiosity of circumstance, this dark-eyed young man, with his artistic flair and mercurial intelligence, turned out to be the son of friends from our long-ago Dunedin sojourn, Alan and Shirley McCurdy – she who had given me my first glimpse of the glistening pathways taken by stretchmarks on the pregnant woman's belly.

And Martin, the first of the family to marry, lived in Kelburn with Jan, also a musician, beautiful and talented and with an unstoppable vitality. I found all these partnerships marvellously interesting to observe. If I was proud of my grown-up children, their manifest abilities and maturing individuality, I was more impressed than ever by their acumen in choosing just such people as these with whom to fall in love. And I was permitted a considerable knowledge of the inner workings of their lives and aspirations.

During my time away they had written with an eager affection, they wanted to know what I thought. 'I'll be glad when you're back,' said Kathy in one letter. I knew, and they often reminded me, that I was a highly favoured parent. Most of their friends had mothers who had not 'broken out' as I had, did not have fulfilling independent occupations, least of all were publicly known for what they did. However modest my reputation might be, they took pleasure in it; moreover they thought me 'in touch', 'modern', 'with it', and it seemed that many of their friends did too. I knew perfectly well that I was one of a vast company of women who had been freed from old patterns of living, but for some reason the changes didn't show in the lives of these other mothers as clearly as they did in mine.

I accepted, indeed gloried in my new status, taking it for granted that my own thrust towards independence made me my children's natural ally and confidante. I knew too that in the whirl of social change we called 'the sixties' (though in New Zealand it was rather more the seventies) women retained an unnoticed advantage. The old conventions had kept them in touch with their growing children, while fathers were habitually away at work, preoccupied when they came home, irritable. The 'big learning steps' these young people talked of were usually taken (if parents were involved at all) in the company of mothers, in odd moments after school, in letters, in a sudden burst of tears about 'nothing much', and the conversation that followed, while dinner was being prepared in the kitchen. Mothers were first to understand and tolerate mixed flatting, experiments with drugs, sexual permissiveness, girls wanting to 'do anything'.

I now had the benefits of this traditional access to my children's confidence and, as well, those of having broken out of the mould. It was a time of marvellous expansion of powers, without, it seemed, any loss of my existing advantages. Trevor's situation was as different as possible. As much as any man of his generation he had staked everything on success in his career, and the massing of obstacles and difficulties before him now dismayed him quite as much as my expanding opportunities delighted me. Conservative by nature, and deeply enmeshed in his sustaining networks in which home and school were themselves tightly bound together, he must have felt it as a major betrayal that I could so celebrate my own occupations and denigrate or ignore those we had once shared.

And school itself had changed. When we moved to Heretaunga

he found conditions for which his long spell of country teaching had not prepared him. There were senior teachers wedded to old-style methods – caning, the minor militarism of school cadets, authoritarian discipline – who fiercely opposed his more relaxed style. He felt alone, beleaguered; eventually, in miserable frustration, he had resigned and gone to work in the Education Department. When I left to go to Africa and Europe he was lonely and full of a sense of grievance.

Beneath our pleasant exchange of letters, with 'love' always at the end, I knew this pain and turmoil boiled away – if 'to know' is to be vaguely sorry but not at all responsible for another person's torment. Did I berate myself for not sharing more fully in his frustration? Should I, again, have gone into the river and accepted an equal chance of drowning? This had happened once, and we had both been profoundly misled by it; I was still hurt and angry at the consequences. Besides, I so greatly relished the hastening pace of the action in my own life, that I could not contemplate leaving what was 'mine' to re-enter and live again within 'ours'. And so, encouraged by my children's affection and enthusiasm, I could persuade myself that we had achieved – or would soon achieve – a new balance and detachment out of the old marital forces that had locked us so tightly together and damaged us both.

I supposed we would not go on living together indefinitely, but had no notion of how we might break apart. A mountain far ahead when one is driving through flat countryside requires no effort; it will have to be surmounted eventually, but for the moment there are trees and flowers and sky and weather to take in with a postponing pleasure. And so for a long time I barely noticed that, while my days were full of adventures, his marked time, were darkened by resentment. A mutual ignorance was actually quite easy to maintain, because we talked to each other now as scarcely more than acquaintances.

Chapter 37

Three months of world travel detached me from home in a way I had never known. On my return, it presented me with a sharper outline of the reality of what I had always called 'home', and a new sense of how widely dispersed it had become, how broken and separated into fragments. Home had always been the starting point and final destination for every journey, but what I now saw, with the quickly fading insight of the traveller, was a centre which already was not central at all; not one thing but many, parallel rivers into which I plunged, taking quick intermittent runs from one to another and back again. They never came together, and I never tried to make them do so. Indeed, connecting the strands of a complicated experience is a matter of confidence in oneself which I was a long way from achieving.

Most days I went to the office, talked to journalists, teachers and bureaucrats; I became, simply by going up the dim concrete stairway in Westbrook House to the PPTA floor, the *Journal* editor. It was like stepping onto a stage with my costume intact and my lines (more or less) in my head. At morning tea people talked of events at home – a party, a power cut – but I never did. If anyone asked how Trevor was I said 'fine' and changed the subject. Nobody asked about my other equally separate, and even more private, lives, because they didn't know they existed: the Fairburn *Letters* and all its networks, my own writing, my close and passionate friendships. I lived in all these spheres far more vitally than I did as the office worker and editorial manager they saw, though in fact my office life and its connections had itself created others. I met the playwright Roger Hall, for instance, sometimes had hilarious lunches with him – he too worked as an editor in Wellington, for School Publications, and he taught me more than anyone else the art of being serious and frivolous at the same time about the job. We both took it seriously; he showed me how to enjoy its absurdities.

But home, literally, was still what I went back to at the end of a working day, and a cold, jarring, inhospitable place it was. Trevor and I hardly even tried to maintain the pretence of sharing our time and ourselves, though we continued to eat together, talked superficially of the day's events, very occasionally went out together. He drank a good deal, looked unhappy, though, with the giving up of his cursed headmastering, he had ceased his overt rages. I usually arrived home after him; he would be standing in the same place, by a shelf in the living room where his glass of late-afternoon wine or beer stood, and as he sipped he made morose or hostile observations. I answered with surly mutterings; unable to tear ourselves away from the disastrous scene we had created, we seemed intent on making it worse. Was this a dreadful kind of power game, the only one left to us? Like fretful fowls, we pecked away, hoping to snatch some meagre victory from these fruitless exchanges.

But if that was our common situation, our separate lives and purposes were dramatically different. I found newness and promise in whatever I did – balancing and arranging the *Journal* each month, drinking with friends in the pub on the way home from work, lunching with Denis at the University Club, laughing and flirting there with new friends. It was all new, slightly inadmissible, wonderfully interesting. I listened, joined in, learned with the pleasurable simplicity a child practises, taking in my world through every pore.

There are times in people's lives when they are driven by forces they do not understand, or even know about, till long afterwards. I could not know that the strange mixture of exhilaration and despair that spun round in me was a kind of propulsion working to push me outwards from the group life in which I had been embedded, and towards the first truly individual life I had known. Trevor must have sensed the strength of the impulse that made me pull away from him, and, not surprisingly, he disliked everything that he saw appealed to me. He didn't really know what it was, the lure of my new life, and I didn't either. But I had for some time realised that for too long his work, his future, his place in the world, his reputation and professional well-being, had been the only version of these things there was, and I now could not summon up an interest in any of them.

Sometimes I stayed home all day (my job was supposed to occupy twenty hours a week) and worked on my own writing. Poems first, of course; hundreds of them. Now they'd started it was as though they had waited for this, as I had, all those years when I talked of writing but went on doing something else apparently more urgent, more necessary – my children, the household, the life which was now breaking away from me, or I from it. I would sit down at my desk by a window overlooking the sea, or outside on a step or ledge in my rough little hillside garden, and write and write, losing sight of everything except the inner prospect. It was as though I went alone into the vast echoing chamber where the words of new poems sounded, mine and those of everyone else who'd ever written, and who now constantly scribbled and scratched out line after line, as I did, and felt in themselves the tingling current of the new vision a poem confers.

One day I took some draft poems to Alistair Campbell; we met often for a drink after work in the pub midway between his office and mine (he too worked as an editor, for the Council for Educational Research). He read them through on the spot, and then said, 'You aren't writing about what matters most. The worst and hardest thing to write about is what you must choose.' Crushed, I hung my head, my eyes filled with tears.

'It's true,' he said, without a shred of sympathy. 'What about Trevor? You're unhappy about him, why don't you say so?'

I mumbled that of course I couldn't, it was all too awful.

'What is?' he demanded.

'Well, that we're so miserable and yet we stay together and we can't – ' I gulped and spluttered.

'Real poetry is about the thing you can't say, can't bear,' he said sternly.

It was a crucial encounter, of continuing value to me even long afterwards when I'd learnt to shape and interpret his advice in my own way.

During that year I realised that I had enough finished poems for a new collection – indeed far too many. I wanted to call it *The Pear Tree*, the name of one of the elegiac poems about Rachel that made up the first part of the total of forty or so. In dedication to her, I put a tiny unnamed poem in the front of the book, as an epigraph.

> She was so slight
> merely to hold
> twenty years' load
> of living

>   bent her
>   a green blade
>   early dew
>   huge
>   on her back

I was much more confident this time, and without Denis's help sent the manuscript to Albion Wright at Pegasus Press. Because it was so full of my grief for Rachel I wanted Max, who was an original and sensitive artist, to design a cover. He drew a pear tree in charcoal, spare and shapely, perfect for the purpose. Alas, the outcome was a literary disappointment of a kind that was new to me. Albion didn't say much about the drawing, and I assumed he liked it as much as I did. I did wonder why publishers didn't tell authors much about their own books while they were being put together and printed, but I was so new to the game I supposed I had no licence to ask.

One day a parcel arrived with my six free copies of the completed article. I opened it, trembling with apprehension. I was so horrified by what I saw that I could do nothing but burst into tears. Albion (he told me later) had decided without further consultation that Max's drawing, charming as it was, was on the wrong sort of paper so he himself copied a sketch of a pear tree from a horticulture catalogue, put a line around it and coloured the rest of the front a hard bright orange. Everything about it was an outrage. Clearly I had much to learn. Did writers have to adopt something like union tactics in negotiating with publishers? I began to think of PEN, which was a union, as potentially useful and practical, not just a matter of new friends and literary shop talk.

As it happened, Max did me some compensatory pear tree designs in crayon. I put these up on the wall near the desk where I worked, and found them a daily pleasure. The sky did not fall on either Albion or me, and nobody else made any comment at all about the cover of my book.

Working at my desk, engrossing as it was, could not go on all day without pause. From time to time I went outside to wander about my shaggy hillside domain – partly to inspect the fruit trees Max had planted, in the months after Rachel's death, when he had often come to stay. I felt his presence in the household as a gift – that peculiarly gentle kindness the young sometimes confer upon those much older – and I had enjoyed the project, a minor social experiment in that we intended the fruit crops for the benefit of the whole neighbourhood.

And the trees, beset by gorse and blackberry, beaten by violent winds as they were, survived for several years. Then a fire swept over the entire hillside and demolished everything, wild and cultivated. Max wrote me some wonderfully wry and funny letters; we supposed we had been tested in the techniques of social management and rather spectacularly failed. By then he had taken up his own life and career again, and for both of us the orchard fell into the past, a small bright island of endeavour, lit up by a misconceived yet heroic optimism.

'My own work', as I was beginning to call whatever wasn't for the *Journal* or the Fairburn *Letters*, was not poetry alone. Somehow declaring yourself a writer creates ripples all round, and these in turn produce other movements, writing possibilities and experiments. One of mine was a series of short essays for the 'Last Word' section of *Thursday*, a 'Magazine for Modern People' published in Auckland. I discoursed in what I hoped was crisp prose on prison reform, homosexual law reform, sex discrimination, human development courses in schools and many other matters. There were similar improving pieces for *Affairs*, the journal that had brought me to Denis's notice and thus to the *Letters*. As well, Denis himself generated projects, first by asking (or instructing) me to edit a collection of his poems and stories.

To be in Denis's confidence was to circulate in his orbit, and this I undoubtedly did for several years. His routine was a precise daily programme to which, at the proper point, I would be written in. He woke at 3 am, as he often reminded me, worked till seven, consuming a flagon or two of beer the while, then he made tea for Lyn, his patient, cheerful – and, necessarily, managing – wife. He then slept till 10.30, woke up ready to begin 'day two' and rang me in my office to tell me to come to lunch at the University Club.

Usually I went. I couldn't have said where my idea of club life had come from, but supposed that glimpses from English novels and films had clustered together to make me expect exactly the armchairs, the bar-counter conversations, the staid familiarity of groups of 'regulars' that I found. These daily arrivals were mostly elderly educated men who, like Denis, liked to talk about the war, but also had time to read the newspaper and hold forth on its contents. They prided themselves on liberality of outlook, but were unfailingly (if jovially) condescending to women. A slightly musty smell pervaded the room and everything we said and did in it.

Denis had a special character, something between aristocrat and buffoon, among club habitués. Everyone knew that to buy him a drink meant to conspire with the barman to make a double vodka look like the triple he'd ordered by adding a judicious quantity of water. He was by far the best raconteur in a crowd largely given to reminiscence, yet many avoided his table to escape the stories they had heard hundreds of times before. They were proud of his fame and distinction, even a little possessive about it – I often heard bits of boasting about 'our great poet' – and usually tolerant about helping him into his taxi at the end of the afternoon when alcohol caused a failure of the legs. They loved, and were exasperated by him, as I was.

I agreed to edit his collection of poems and stories, but reluctantly. We were an old river by then, Denis and I, spreading out into separate channels. I wanted to finish the Fairburn book, not manage his other projects. In fact the same process that eventually brought my *Journal* editorship to an end was also operating in this occupation of being in Denis's orbit. I began both in great humility; I had everything to learn, and an almost physical sense of putting my foot to the lowest step of a ladder that stretched upwards to infinity.

But as the years passed, the years of the late seventies, the time when my life seemed every day to change its skin for a new one, I became restive under tutelage, however benign. I was more interested every day in the questions raised by my own writing, and this undoubtedly made me a less satisfactory companion or, in the case of the *Journal*, employee.

I finished Denis's book, though, and it was launched with modest panoply, and an expansive flow of alcohol, at the club. Some time afterwards the club hosted a reading of my poems by Frances, Prue Langbein, a friend of hers also working at Downstage, and Anne Flannery, an established actress, and Denis had nothing to do with this at all. Perhaps it is always like this, the gathering of enough courage to take hold of your own life and work: you begin with a fascination with other people's projects, but gradually your own grow and take you with them, as in a rising lift, while the others, once so compelling, go quietly down another shaft and you don't even notice.

I made a trip to Masterton not long afterwards to share a poetry reading with Alistair Campbell and Rachel McAlpine. Reading to an audience terrified, excited and unnerved me. A poem was my most secret utterance, the thing it mattered most to say, and say accurately, yet the very reason I wrote it down was that there was never anyone to whom I could possibly tell this particular, precious truth. Suddenly, in front of an audience, I could. I had a wonderful sense of having wanted all along, through all the drafts, the endless scribbling out and rewriting, just this, to say it out loud to just these people.

There was another more practical lesson in reading to audiences. I already believed that poetry existed first and most fundamentally in the voice; its rhythms and cadences were those of real speech, not some special literary language. If I tried out a new poem, as with great boldness I did occasionally, and it didn't read easily, I knew that the stumbling of my voice uncovered a rough patch in the poem. In fact it wasn't finished at all, and I must take it home and do more work on it.

The Masterton audience behaved perfectly, it filled a large room and was attentive and appreciative. We glowed, each of us, standing about afterwards while individual enthusiasts came to talk to us. One who approached me was a man with an eager face, rather broken speech and a strong foreign accent. He had particularly liked my *Minas* poem, he said. It was:

> Sunset comes early in July
> and on the road there are minas warming
> their bare feet, savouring as cars
> approach the small dangers of delay,
> then cavorting upwards into
> a walnut tree to sit in its arms
> and laugh, their white fingertips winking;
> thin brown magnolia of the winter
> briefly flowering before the dark.
> They are like lovers who meet first when
> they are old: impatient, selective, and moved
> continually by an absurd delight.

'Good,' said my new friend, 'I like – I used to be a miner myself, once.' And he grinned broadly. Well, so did I.

Rachel McAlpine had invited me to stay the night at her house; I would drive back to Wellington the next morning. We were shy but talkative, fully aware of the interesting similarities in our histories. For many years her central occupation had, like mine, been creating and caring for her family. For her, too, writing had simmered just below the surface and was now erupting into real poems. We shared a strengthening sense of our own powers and a new right to exercise them. I confessed to her that I had a voice in my head that crowed exultantly from time to time, 'I'm allowed! I'm allowed!' She understood exactly; we laughed and laughed.

The next day was a Saturday. She had to go to an all-day course for Massey extramural students – another parallel between us; for her too adult university study nourished a long-unsatisfied intellectual curiosity. Over breakfast with Grant, her husband, I admired a splendid oak tree standing very close to the house. Near enough to touch, I said, and in fact from the breakfast room you could walk straight out to it. 'Just before I go – ' I began, and walked quickly forward. Something stopped me, an invisible barrier.

Suddenly I was standing still with blood pouring from my hands and knees, filling my shoes and splattering on the floor. It gushed out of me extraordinarily fast; since nothing hurt, and the whole world had gone into slow motion, it took a long time – a few seconds anyway – to realise that I had walked into a very large, very clean plate-glass window.

Grant was kind and prompt, but by the time I was on an operating table in the hospital the stitching up of my wounds was so urgent, the doctor said, that there was not time for anaesthetic. It didn't matter much; I was beset by a greater malaise than the pain of needle pricks. It was a kind of total body thirst. Could I have a drink? Water, tea – anything? Not yet, there wasn't time for that either, but I did learn that this curious and ominous sensation is the result of using up your natural reserves of blood, which I had apparently done.

Plastic bags of someone else's blood were suspended, one after another, above my hospital bed and dripped into my arm. It was given, I saw by the label, by Mr Constable. It seemed like a personal gift. I reflected with satisfaction that from then on whenever I behaved badly I would have someone to blame, the stranger in my veins; my private lifesaver who would always remain invisible.

A measure of the change in the course of my life was that the news of such events, which once would have been given first to Trevor, was not now for him at all but, except for brief necessary bulletins, kept for my friends. Marriages don't end at the same time for each participant and part of the profound *wrongness* of our hopelessly divided yet miserably together cohabitation in those years was that 'my' marriage had ended, Trevor's had not; or not yet.

Not that I fully understood this fact, or its implications. My mind was too scattered. A room full of leaping dancers who might one day coalesce into a chorus. So snatches of being married gave way to glimpses of the writer, reader, traveller, partner in various new friendships; everything was provisional and incomplete. Perhaps changes as fundamental as mine bring with them a state of shock in which all you can do is try out many new ways of being. I could not bear to stand still and contemplate the pain and despair of my old life, but neither could I settle into any one of the new possibilities, or connect them into a single whole. I sometimes looked at other people – the happily married, those confident in their work – and wondered if I would ever attain the internal harmony that I could see held them together.

But for the present, unexpected new directions kept appearing, leading I knew not where: always, and usually after only brief hesitation, I took them. One was a request that I join the Indecent Publications Tribunal. I worked on this committee for six years, surprised to find that pornography, closely examined, is more sad than shocking. I was glad when my term was over.

In 1977 the PEN International Congress was held close to home – in Sydney – and Bruce Mason and I were asked to go as the New Zealand delegates. I was overcome by the enormity of such responsibility, but in the event greatly enjoyed the high drama of international gatherings, especially the debates. These were largely political, dealing with the dilemma of writers living under repressive regimes. My Czech experience had a place in such discussions, and Bruce and I, who had once talked so eagerly of plays and performances, planned our public statement – on that and related subjects – with due solemnity.

As the week went by, I began to forget that I had ever lived any life but this, slept anywhere but in the Chevron Hotel. And then, of course, I wasn't there at all, but blowing past the grey trees at Sydney Airport in a fur-lined limousine provided by the sponsors of the congress, Stuyvesant Tobacco Merchants. The centrifugal force that possessed my life, shooting it further and further out to new perimeters, had exhibited another burst of activity.

My arrival home offered me, first thing, a curious little lacuna, outside both the 'there' and the 'here' of my journey, a spare piece of time, motionless and clear. Trevor and Frances were a few minutes late arriving at the airport. I stood beside my luggage feeling quite outside this solitary explorer, myself, who had journeyed from one country to another carrying out those small momentous missions – the letters from de Montalk, the Czech visit, the Sydney deliberations – and I saw that I had already moved a long way from the group life, the habits of family reference, that had held me for so long. I was on my own, at least intermittently, and I had been moving towards this separateness through a whole series of decisions, chances I had been afraid to take yet determined not to let pass. The *Journal* job, the dangerous alternative relationship with Arthur, the Fairburn *Letters*, my entry to PEN. It was a charged moment; there was no sense of arrival, no idea of a direction ahead. I saw myself rather as someone picking a path through a maze and finding, here and there, things lovely in themselves, though I didn't know their purpose, or what they might make if fitted together. Only, now, this – that I had taken a first lesson in being, and acting, alone. Then Trevor and Frances arrived, and I went home.

As soon as I decently could, and after Frances had gone to her own house, I began to telephone my friends who were members with me of the PEN Executive – Fiona, Alistair, Beeb. Dr Beeby, that is; he admitted to no Christian name (or not one he could bear to use – it was actually Clarence) but encouraged friends to use this amiable diminutive. In no time these eager conversations felt like my real homecoming, and almost as quickly they made Trevor feel angry and excluded.

Nothing is simple. Despite its crippled state, our marriage still rehearsed some old habits, like tunes we couldn't get out of our heads however hard we tried and however we'd come to dislike them. Going out together, for instance. The previous summer we'd gone to a PEN party, a Sunday in the country, at Sam Hunt's place at Pauatahanui, and Trevor had actually seemed to enjoy himself, though it appeared necessary for us to quarrel all the way home. When Denis visited us he devoted himself almost exclusively to conversation with Trevor, usually about football. Trevor must have felt that there were after all a few glimpses of sanity in the new world I was so mad about.

Sometimes I too behaved politely and accompanied my husband to parties and gatherings peopled by teachers and Education Department officials who could be, whether I admitted it or not, pleasant company. But these dinner parties, however tolerable, came to seem like a circuit, a part of a set programme for middle-class behaviour, not unlike the predictable social events I'd known in my long years among teachers; I began to resist them. Occasionally I thought I glimpsed the shape of a fundamental barrier forming between Trevor and me, like a hedge we both cultivated, but from opposite sides. I don't mean an emotional divide – that was clear enough – but a philosophical one. He really believed in groups, he was nourished and reassured by them; service in a collective mode, which he'd practised for most of his life as a teacher, was his glory. There is on the other hand – and it must have begun to show in me – an I-I-I quality in all writers. It's the individual vision that compels attention and every now and then wipes out every other; I suppose it often makes them tiresome company. There is no doubt that my writing lay at the heart of all my new enterprises, and my fascination with it made me impatient of the system of shared action into which I'd fitted for so long, and to which Trevor still belonged.

I wanted to disagree with everyone, and *always* disagreed with him after such occasions; most of all I didn't want to enter them at all, or if I did, I preferred to stand aside and contemplate how one might chronicle the patterns of their conversation and behaviour. I hardly needed to say any of this to appear insufferable to Trevor; moreover, the contrast implied by my new attitude, which put the individual vision, the desire to create new worlds of the imagination, ahead of his old life of service, was not in the least fair. He too had fine aspirations, and in his teaching had realised many of them, as visits from grateful and admiring ex-pupils often testified. But whatever it was, I wanted to do it myself; do it, do it, and alone. Writing is solitary and is much taken up with listening, an inner listening, secret, mysterious, urgent, unshared.

It wasn't just the dinner parties I wanted to repudiate, but everything that interfered with this newly found and deeply satisfying process, which I seemed to believe I had to guard with my life. I must have been less and less bearable to a troubled, middle-aged man whose own sense of direction was by now dreadfully obscured.

But this was only one aspect of the *danse macabre* of those years. The pent-up urge to say it – say, that is, everything that it had never been possible to say before – didn't simply arrive by itself. The habit of years, of maintaining a calm surface no matter how great my hidden turmoil might be, had led to a kind of constriction that hampered me like tight clothes; some of the 'un-disciplining' I did was active and conscious. I said to myself, almost peremptorily, 'If you're going to be a writer you have to let things happen, not shut them off to avoid trouble', and I deliberately allowed events to work their effect, sometimes their havoc, in me. Rachel's death had wrenched me open to a large and hurtful world of direct awareness, but I had to continue the process long afterwards, and consciously. One of the consequences was that, along with all the other eagerness that began to flood through me (instead of being hushed up for the sake of family peace), came one I hadn't expected. An urgent, more or less unlimited, and often erratic, impulse to fall in love.

Perhaps there was an 'in love' quality about all my new friendships – I think there was, even those with women – permeating every other new experience, event, place, or moment of fresh understanding. It would probably have been surprising if I had not fallen in love in the obvious, sexual way as well. It was as though this, like so much else in my working, writing life, had been held up, delayed, put aside, despite the evidence of a married life that had long been affectionate, even if it wasn't now, and a large number of children.

Whatever the inner working of the process, I fell in love over and over again, sometimes with great confidence and delight, and with one person in a way that changed the shape and pivot of my whole outlook. The first of these magnetic events arose, perhaps appropriately, out of the very system of educational bureaucracy I had come to detest yet benefited from in my job as *Journal* editor. This existed, after all, to discuss and promote matters educational, and in my first issue I published an announcement about a reading conference held by the International Reading Association. I would attend this gathering – indeed I had been invited to chair one of its sessions – and report on it the following month.

Chapter 38

'Speaking to the recent International Reading Conference in Wellington,' I wrote in a *Journal* editorial, 'Dr Beeby considered current threats to the continuance of the reading habit. He quoted George Steiner, who calls American education an "organised amnesia" and thinks the reading of books in future may become the province of an educated élite.' Yes, this was how you did it, being a journalist; you quoted people's exact words, but picked the eyes out, so your readers were instantly attentive. The book, said Dr Beeby, was 'the first defence of the intellectual freedom of the individual . . . and the first defence of the cutting edge of language'.

I liked that. I could go straight on to freedom of choice, the civilising effect of knowledge, breadth of outlook . . . and then finish with my old friend Arthur Sewell talking of different views of life 'engaging in neighbourly debate' in our minds. When Dr Beeby read my piece he was interested in Arthur's presence there, and as we got to know each other better he often talked of him. But first, at the conference itself, the great educationist was simply an august presence for me, as for everyone else; an eloquent speaker, a tingling battery charge of ideas, a charmer of crowds, before whom he postured a little if he thought it necessary to sharpen up their attention and their appreciation.

I was an untried journalist, lacking all training and experience, but I was fascinated by ideas and graceful language. My interview with him was notable for the wondering respect of its questions, the charming (if disingenuous) modesty of his replies. We had every reason to be pleased with each other; when I left his office in the Council for Educational Research, took myself down in the slow lift, and walked round a corner and along a couple of streets to my own office, I felt splendidly dignified, expanded, to have been permitted such intimate access to a famous man.

I was surprised all the same when he rang up a week or two later and invited me to have a glass of sherry with him at five o'clock when his office closed, and mine. Of course I agreed at once, prepared to be dazzled, and quickly found I was. He was as sparkling a talker in private as he had been before a crowd, and quite without inhibitions about relating events in his past life, many of them showing his own distinction, though he sometimes added modest disclaimers. I knew already that he had relinquished a remarkable Directorship of Education to go to France as New Zealand Ambassador, and thence to work on various Third World education consultancies. He had a wonderful dramatic sense and told stories that were both funny and informative about visits to Libya, Indonesia, Western Samoa; I listened, entranced.

As my visits to his office for a drink after work became more frequent, I gradually acquired a whole map of his former life. It came with a kind of practising of theories that seemed like discussion but was actually a long informal lecture. It didn't matter – I was so excited by his ideas, and the vitality of his presence, that it was a long time before I began to object to the slight smothering of my own opinions these thrilling conversations imposed – or even to admit it was there. 'I noticed you at the reading conference,' Beeb said one day, 'because you took such an intelligent interest in what I said.' Undoubtedly I was using to advantage, in the new life, habits I'd learnt in the old. From my long experience of family living I knew very well how to listen, prompt, encourage, enjoy another person's revelations. I'd noticed other women do the same when they weren't confident enough to command much of a share of the conversation with men who assumed, and held, the initiative.

Sometimes we met in bars or restaurants; invitations for these outings he issued with wit and style and a confiding pleasure that was irresistible. I received them all with a slightly arch compliance. I often found he had a new idea, or a subject for a lecture, that he wanted to try out on me; gratified to be consulted on the exalted subject of educational planning, I listened eagerly, my own teaching experience too meagre to permit much comment. However, there was another kind of planning that did include me. Beeb was a member of the PEN Executive, and brought to its modest deliberations the skill he'd learnt in more august forums like UNESCO, of which he'd been Assistant Director General (stories of its occasions and crises bristled with famous names; Julian Huxley, for instance, had been his friend). He decided to promote my editorship and management of the Young Writers' Award, and thus my own status in PEN; with a procedural flourish worthy of greater matters he prepared letters, memos, motions for meetings, on my behalf.

Even these prosaic dealings became for me charged with intensity, and he remarked at times that he 'lived in tension'. No doubt this sharpened both his magnetism and his dominance. He said too that it was his way to build whole intellectual systems out of crucial experiences; not to write novels (which he had once wanted to do) but to form theories.

I could have observed that in the panoply of his brilliant talk it often seemed that the subject that most fascinated him (and for a long time me too) was his own story, the evolution of his ideas and his time, in which, at least in education, he had played a central part. The logic of this was that his life and work were formed, fulfilled; he was more than twenty years older than me and in every way more embedded in his experience, the product of his achieved aspirations. I, by contrast, was in a state of rawness and uncertainty, full of unexplained – and unrealised – drives towards new ways of being, yet still shaken by the loss of the loving safety of marriage and my own awareness of betrayal of old loyalties. Perhaps the very fact of his immense assurance was comforting to me; lacking my own, I was glad to 'borrow' his.

He was used to power and authority; his personal style was consciously charismatic, his conversational armoury held every weapon known to the world of sophisticated diplomacy. He was socially as well as intellectually formidable.

I stood on the threshold of a way of life I barely imagined, and certainly did not understand. To take hold of it, knit it into my other, earlier selves, I naturally used my intuition rather than knowledge or experience. I followed my emotional nose, if there is such a thing, fell into the deep places it led me to, somehow trusting those ahead of me – like Beeb – to help me flounder through them.

There was, for all these marvels, a fundamental limitation to our friendship – two, in fact. One was that I was prepared to invest a good deal more of myself in it than he would ever have considered. While my marriage had been sustained by affection and a sense of common cause, I had felt no temptation to enter other relationships. Once it ended – emotionally if not quite geographically yet – anything seemed possible, including the wholehearted devotion I now felt. He, on the other hand, had not questioned, and did not intend to disturb, the system of loyalties, affections, obligations, by which he had always lived.

The other limitation was that our being together rested, at a profound level, on his pleasure in being so fully appreciated and mine in learning a new world from him through that appreciation. Desdemona and Othello, grown middle-aged, grown old. But I too came to want recognition; I grew tired of the wondering admiration I'd practised – and felt – in our first years. I wanted, I'm afraid, to teach him feminist principles, to cure him of attitudes towards women's lower standing and value that he had held all his life.

So did some other younger friends, he rather irritably observed; I felt suddenly close to them, more securely a part of their generation than his. And Beeb himself began to feel the oppressiveness of the expanse of years between us. The most ageless of men, he began to tire. Lunching in town one day, we sat quietly while the waiter poured our wine (he taught me that too – how to eat out in style); then he leaned towards me and said, 'I have to tell you, very soon I'll be an old man. You must understand . . . ' In a rush of tenderness I put my hand on his. There was no answer, of course.

On a weekend trip to Taupo, we quarrelled. He undertook to teach me how to fish for trout, but each time I held the rod he seized it to demonstrate how wrongly I was doing it. It all ended in a great piece of childishness: I took my suitcase and set off down the road, he caught me up in the car, I huffed and puffed, peace was restored. Despite all that, there were shared moments in that beautiful place that held the luminosity of light over the lake. In a hushed reverence for the natural beauty of lake and sky, we seemed at times to enter some other-world where talking, our usual obsession, was beside the point.

A year or two before I met Beeb I had gone one day into the Manuscripts Section of the Turnbull Library to ask for the file of Fairburn correspondence. If I was to learn how to be a scholar, this was the place to begin. Tentatively I approached the desk through shaded, book-smelling spaces between tunnels of library catalogues, and asked my question. What an impassive expression, I thought of the woman at the desk; and at the same time, how immediate and intelligent her reply, how in the first few minutes she established an extraordinarily intimate comprehension between us. Even as I beetled off into a corner with my files, we both understood we must meet and talk again, and soon. We had to put to the test some instantly recognisable tone or flavour in our first encounter. (She later called it irony, wit, a shaft of illumination we caught from each other in the first few minutes we talked.) This was Margaret Scott.

She was a friend of the poet Charles Brasch, and in fact was just about to visit him for what turned out to be the last time. During the first months of our getting to know each other I wondered if her raw awareness of his death was one of the reasons she could lay herself open to someone searching, as I was, for a map of the literary territory he had occupied and she knew well. In no time we had established a system of regular visits; they took place always at her house – she seemed reluctant to visit mine – and on Friday evenings. Like lovers with tender rules for assignations, we made sure that Friday was always set aside for our meetings. We developed routines, and as each crystallised I found myself devoted to it as to a precious talisman. I would arrive between five and six o'clock, sit always in the same chair in Margaret's sitting room, we would have a glass of sherry or, later, a large lemon-flavoured gin and tonic. The late light faded slowly from the sky outside her window – her house was on one of the Wadestown hills – and we would talk. And talk – and intricate, detailed, subtle talk it was, full of nuances of shared amusement, instant surprised understanding.

Like Beeb, she had a history crowded with significant events and compelling people. I never tired of listening to her stories of the poignant relationships she'd had with men I knew from reading their poems or stories, but had never met. I saw myself hovering about these narratives like a child shut outside when the lights go on. Here was someone who'd been in there talking, laughing, loving, among this favoured company. It seemed at times that she'd had a special friendship with every writer I knew of; this, she explained modestly, was because of Charles. He'd been not only a central character in the writing community but a lifelong friend of Harry, Margaret's husband. His, too, was a name I'd known years before, when I first went to Wellington Training College and Victoria University. Harry Scott, much talked about, a young man who was a distinguished mountaineer, a pacifist in wartime, a political radical, a leader. Years afterwards I'd read of his death on a climbing expedition to Mount Cook; now, twenty years later again, I found my new friend still grieving for his loss. The love affairs were really a recurring attempt to find another person who might come somewhere near his high quality; none did, and she had brought up her three children, one of whom Harry had never seen, alone.

There was a marvellous expansiveness in the way she gave me these long and carefully catalogued reminiscences. I did not realise till the process was far advanced quite why I was so eager to explore the strange terrain of another person's experience and, by exercising the fullest possible comprehension, to make it mine. I saw Margaret as the owner – and now the giver – of a pattern of life that seemed exactly to fit my literary enthusiasm as well as hers.

I thought at times that we stood together on some invisible railway platform, at which we had arrived by taking different trains. She'd been on the main line; I'd come from the country, past small stations whose names nobody knew, stopped at this junction and here she was, able to tell me everything I longed to know about the main route. Hers was a private, individual impression of the journey; others gave me different views. There would be talk of a writers' meeting, a famous reading by Baxter, an address everyone had heard, or heard about, and the other kind of address, a house, like the one Alistair Campbell and Fleur Adcock had lived in while they were married to each other, in Tinakori Road. Nobody asked if I remembered any of this because, as I put it myself, I 'wasn't anywhere' then. I'd come from a blankness that was puzzling at first, but quickly became accepted as a sort of idiosyncrasy of mine, like flat feet or left-handedness. Nobody asked for details, and I gave none.

Only years afterwards did I see that I did have more in common with these new friends than I had, in my self-consciousness, allowed for. Margaret and I, after all, both had children, of comparable age; and we swapped ideas about books and writing and reading and scholarship – those, for instance, that lay behind the writings of Katherine Mansfield, whose letters she was editing, and Fairburn, who gave me my similar though slighter project. And of course important friendships form their own milieu; our shared experiences grew and accumulated, making a world we both occupied. Nevertheless, at first I was in a real sense the receiver, the suppliant, the student. Margaret's story was not mine at all, yet knowing her made me more secure in the fast-changing present I was busy discovering.

As well as this, I found in her the first woman friend I'd ever had who talked frankly and naturally about sex. Part of my delayed development was, apparently, that I had come to the middle of life with slight sexual experience, even less confidence or knowledge. I had in one way been far more fortunate than Margaret in that I'd had many years of marriage that had contained within it a consistent and affectionate love-making. The shy, untutored, inarticulate marriage that was characteristic of my generation had probably served me better than it did many of my contemporaries, who could do no more than drop occasional hints of distaste for 'that sort of thing'. I'd felt no such distaste, yet I was aware that a part of that undeveloped, waiting self that I now occupied, and in which I charged ahead with such zest, was an emotional and sexual adventurer, looking to improve on the muted and conservative experience of the past.

Margaret talked with refreshing candour about women's natural desire, and capacity for desire; she was not guilty or apologetic, neither tortuous nor twee; and with all this she could be very funny. We laughed a great deal.

Everyone else I met seemed to be as interested as I was in how to live independently (Margaret had been doing it for years), whether or not that meant literally living alone, and this perhaps left a large place for friends to occupy. Certainly the work-and-friends networks that more and more overlaid my old husband-and-children ones taught me a new way of regarding friendship. It had always been subsidiary to my main enterprise; interesting, reassuring, an aid to sanity and peace of mind, but not in the end actually necessary. Now, in the unaccustomed solitariness of writing, and lacking a day-to-day partnership, I saw it almost as a way of survival. No relationship could have the binding quality of my love for my children, but, practised in that mode, I certainly looked for new versions of the complex intimacies I had come to depend upon.

I had met Vincent O'Sullivan at Arthur Sewell's house. I well remembered the witty, erudite, high-powered conversation between the two of them, the old cosmopolitan and the younger. It had been late summer, the mellow light that filled Arthur's living room at the end of the day pervaded also the knowledgeable but loving detail of their reflections about paintings they both knew in the great galleries of Europe. Feeling desperately provincial, miserably untravelled, I got up and went outside to sit on the steps at the side of the house and nurse my ignorance alone.

Now Vincent began to appear at Margaret's in weekends and often she asked me too; we drank her large cold gin-and-tonics, we indulged in high talk that Vincent sometimes referred to as 'silliness'. I knew of his European sensibility, but all his scholarship was impressive; he had a wide knowledge of Australian writers and university teachers that came out in conversation as a system of highly masculine loyalties, a camaraderie I did not yet know to call 'mateship', but instantly recognised when I went to Australia myself. He knew Alistair Campbell well, and the two of them together exhibited a boyish exuberance – a sort of educated matiness – that interested me as yet another view of the bright pageant friendship formed around our working lives. One reason for their significance was, I think, that for all of us work was so closely entwined with questions of how to live. Why one made one choice rather than another, and what kind of behaviour appeared as a result; how to express, understand, define the daily dilemmas of solitude and marriage and parenthood and independence and loneliness and love and despair . . . these were the subjects writers everywhere thought most about. Our work was our life, and friends were a natural part of it, especially if they too were engrossed in books and the writing of books.

There was an urgency in us, as though we were all emerging from some earlier state in which writing had hovered about, in preparation for moving into the centre of consciousness. This was certainly true for me – did I imagine it for the others? I don't think so; there really was an electricity darting among us, lighting us up, making us eager, voluble, sometimes excessive, almost mad. However, not quite everyone I came to know well was fanatical about the act of writing – each poem, word, phrase, each rise and fall of a rhythm, each semi-colon (and I *loved* semi-colons). Alistair of course had had this condition for years; so had Vincent, so had Fiona Kidman, with whom I began one of the first of the new friendships.

It was in Fiona's company that work and friendship came so close they seemed to merge into one process. She was in a phase of her life that paralleled mine in interesting ways. More than ten years younger than me, she already had an established reputation; nevertheless, she too felt a sense of having come from 'nowhere'. Hers was Rotorua, and she was married to a teacher, but the mutual recognition we felt did not really rest on a common history. Rather it was a shared awareness of insecurity in the new world of letters we'd found in coming to

Wellington. There was a thriving literary community here and we were both drawn to it with an eager, nervous attraction. Writing wasn't our daily job – Fiona worked for Radio New Zealand, I for my *Journal* bosses – but writing was our vocation and we dreamed of one day working at it full-time.

If you are inclined towards excessive enthusiasm, as both Fiona and I were, it is likely that you will see in an interesting and congenial new friend every quality you love and admire. This amazing person will seem more yourself than you are, yet better, grander, more advanced in the ways of the world. This is what falling in love really is, I suppose; and in those years I often, almost habitually, leapt into its whirl of sensations and discoveries. Certainly getting to know Fiona was absorbing in just this way; and if with other friends I was aware of a general literary ambience, with her it was precise, actual, real. She wrote poems, as I did, but the special acuteness of her judgements was always part of some story; it was the 'what' and 'why' of people's actions, the drama hidden in trivial words and gestures. Such speculations recalled for me the marvellous expansive conversations with Fanny, now far in the past; reminded me, too, of Fanny's moral strictures against 'gossip'. 'Trying to understand' was the proper way. Yes, indeed it was.

This led us to sober reflections on how writers must place themselves somewhere outside ordinary experience, in order to observe it. And that, in turn, to the risk we saw of supposing that this in some way excused writers from the rules of good behaviour which bound everyone else. Or, perhaps worse, permitted them to distort their relationship with the world for the purposes of their writing. These discussions absorbed us intensely; they also led to a kind of tacit understanding that we would remind each other of such pitfalls inherent in the work we had both chosen to do. An unusual component in a friendship, but precious and, as it turned out, enduring.

Sometimes we met in the Western Park, a pub in Thorndon, in the afternoons. This was a new thing for women to do in the early seventies, and in fact we had heard of a sociology student who was said to be spending his entire time browsing in Wellington pubs and observing their clientele, paid to do so by a grant from a benign university department. One afternoon we saw two ladies with matching hats and gloves, and handbags – pensioners, the kind of person we had both seen catching the bus into town for tea with other ladies. Here, they were the real adventurers; we were bluestockings, literary cronies, living out a phase in a long tradition (even if mostly inhabited by men) of writers meeting in cafés and bars all over the world, and writing there too. We just talked. And drank – a glass or two of gin and tonic, brandy and ginger ale. Smart, that was.

There were others in the starry firmament into which I had floated and where I now darted about bumping into new constellations at every turn. Part of the allure of such companionship was, I am sure, that I was not used to being 'out' in this sense. Trevor and I had embarked on a dinner-party phase, when we and other New Zealanders learned to drink wine and dine out, but only now, middle-aged and unofficially single, could I contemplate the kind of outings that were commonplace to my own grown-up children.

While I lived in my country towns and enjoyed my children, the world had changed; for many years I continued to feel a frisson of childish excitement every time the doors of a restaurant opened to me and a friend, and a warm gust of chatter and light blew us in. I was my new, individual self – I who had not seriously attempted individuality till now – but I was also my young, silly, adolescent self practising grown-up manners in a world that had taken to saying, 'You're allowed!'

Gradually – and in some cases suddenly – friendships that were to some extent literary collaborations grew larger and more secure. Roger Robinson, one of that company and a new arrival in Wellington, to the English Department of the university, had the knack of naming things. A mysterious chemistry bound us to one another, he said later, and worked so strongly in each of us because we were all looking for second-chance lives. We were student revolutionaries long after our time for being students had passed. Yet historically, as I'd already noted in seeing the breaking up of my own old certainties, the revolution we called 'the sixties' was still working strongly in New Zealand. Now, more surely every day, it was there for us, the young-old, the suddenly adolescent middle-aged, as it was for the genuine, first-time discoverers of the shape of adult experience. Part of my eagerness and delight was in recognising a new community which could apparently accommodate the new shapes and angles knocking about in my psyche, because the same thing was happening to each of its other members.

For all that, each friendship had its distinctive flavour. Bridget worked as an editor for Oxford University Press where, by that time, my poems were being published, so from the beginning our association was partly a professional one. But we spent far more time exploring personal questions, chiefly those that appear in the wake of broken marriages. Her habits of mind were searching, powerfully analytical, abstract; we sat over dinner through long evenings, examining again and again one absorbing, elusive subject. It was really the philosophy of relationship.

How did you judge degrees of loyalty, degrees of intimacy? Was there a kind of integrity that allowed scope for many relationships of different quality, without ordering them on a scale of better or worse, false or faithful? How much, or how little, should you be bound by the conventions around you? Could you, honourably, form your own morality and live by it? We felt the same confusion, the same eagerness for solutions – and perhaps the same faith that they could be achieved. We talked as though our lives depended upon it.

Chapter 39

For all its variety and challenge, my life was still incoherent and contradictory, breaking up like an iceberg into separate floes which in turn took off and connected with others, none knowing their final shape. My marriage officially, if skeletally, still existed; the same walls enclosed us, we often ate together but talked in a brittle, misleading fashion, if at all. Occasionally I asked myself, appalled, how such emptiness could look itself in the face every day and not run away and hide – in other words, send us off to pursue our different courses decently hidden from each other in separate houses. The reason we didn't was that, despite everything, we both felt, in some unadmitted, untouched part of ourselves, a kind of panic at the prospect of finally being cut off from the 'Lauris-and-Trevor' we'd always been, though God knows that whole was by now the merest skin, seeds and flesh having been long ago scraped out and devoured.

In the end some mindless force moved in me; without preparation or warning, I began to cry. When I came home from the office, I sat in my car and cried, and could not make myself get out and walk the long path to the house. It was a kind of paralysis, as though marriage itself, terminally ill, had finally entered a coma. I realised that we who had once so helped and supported each other were now doing some positive, active harm by staying together. I talked to my old friend Bruce Mason – these days we met for occasional lunches in town – and he said, 'You must come and have a meal with Diana and me.' This, to be honest, didn't help much, but it was a beginning; Alistair and Meg Campbell, experienced in suffering, were, over our next drink, much more emphatic. Meg was a remarkable person; she had a capacity for strange, sudden insights and a way of uttering them, a sort of inspired blurting out, that made her as prophetic, and as uncomfortable to listen to, as any Cassandra.

'You can't live like that. You're doing terrible damage to each other and yourselves; you have to leave. At once,' she declared.

How was I to do that?

'Doesn't matter. Just do it.'

Ironically, when I arrived home that evening, Trevor was already there and there were 'letters from the kids' to read and discuss; a kind of normality re-asserted itself. Like many other grown-up families, ours was actively scattering itself about the country and beyond; there was much travelling abroad, occasional meetings in foreign cities. Trevor and I were the parents left behind, our role to answer mail, pay for collect phone calls, talk to other middle-aged parents about the latest adventures of the young. We did carry out these functions too, but behaving like decent parents didn't help us in the least as individuals. Writing about it was the only relief I could have, and Trevor did not even have that.

> A RECKONING
>
> You were my friend, accomplice in
> the copious plotting parents are a party to;
> through centuries of jovial boredom
> on the beach we stuck it out together
>
> then separately awake hallucinated
> over teenage accidents in cars, until
> a door at last breathed out and cracks
> of guilty silence shot us dead asleep.
>
> Our fears kept us close; pride too,
> and the small events' unmerciful momentum.
> It was a walled garden, safe to quarrel in,
> love coming down on us reliably as rain.
>
> We were its keepers, so intent we did not see
> the change of sky, the gradual departures
> – then there was just a man, a woman
> slamming some old gate on a quiet plot
>
> ill-tempered without learnt weather
> and the rule of law. Who were
> the guardians then, and who, despite
> that virtuous authority, the guarded?

I had made occasional speeches to Trevor about this dichotomy: perhaps being parents could be the basis of a new, slighter kind of relationship between us? But that made him seethe with rage; his sense of a separate direction had not formed and cohered as mine had, and these proposals – to me so civilised – no doubt seemed to him trivial and evasive. Failing to recognise the real gulf between us, I persevered. I was, after all, Fanny and Lewis's daughter, with a long training in 'positive thinking', and the wilful blindness it so easily induces. But now, prompted by Meg, I had an idea that actually might work.

I suggested we finish building the downstairs part of the house (we already had a staircase), construct a new kitchen and thus make two establishments, one for each of us. We would then be formally separated but within easy reach of each other. It had become urgent, for me, that some change should occur. A new and more hopeless phase had begun – I not only sat in my car in tears, I began to cry as soon as Trevor came into the same room.

Why do marriages cling so desperately to their own ruins? I tried to explain to my sister Lindsay: 'Each time I have wanted to do something like this before the financial problems, as well as the enormous opposition Trevor has put up, and a feeling of panic too, in myself, have all conspired to stop me.'

But in the end Trevor did agree, builders came to spy out the land, timber was again pushed and slewed and shunted down our steep hill, plans were made and discussed, amicably enough, and a more humane and practicable future began dimly to take shape ahead of us. 'We have very little to do with each other, but all the family connections are there, and we do share those,' I wrote to Lindsay, relieved that there was, at last, some news which was not simply desperate.

Lindsay and I had found, these last few years, that as our children grew older and our new families (but they were long-established by now) progressively displaced the old, our intimacy diminished. Our parents were dead, the Scott connections fading, the present always large and demanding. I thought her husband Doug bossy and arbitrary; she had goodness knows what opinion of Edmond style and habits. We wrote less often, more superficially. At the same time my sister had been wonderfully gentle and kind to me after Rachel's death. She had come to stay and for days together was simply there, offering a sensitive, often wordless sympathy for which I had been very grateful. Her life, her marriage, had a stability I could only admire, and now my present sustained crisis made me turn to her again and again.

Our inching apart, Trevor's and mine, gave us a way of behaving that restored some of the self-respect that years of humiliating quarrels had eroded or destroyed. But for me the change brought a curious blankness with it, a kind of amnesia, as though in order to achieve separateness (however limited) I had to blot out every remnant of the old shared life from my mind. Trevor sometimes said, 'Do you remember . . . ?' or 'You know that time we went . . . ?' – but I never did. As mystifyingly to him as to me, I'd forgotten.

It wasn't true, of course, or not permanently so; but for the time being it appeared that the silent, potent manager of the organism of myself, lying deep in the canyons of the mind, decreed that a loss of memory would help me to step safely ahead – like a mist obscuring the precipices, it would clear over the next two or three years as I became more sure-footed. There was one sign, however, that came up in a powerful surge from the lost years of harmony, and the hurt and destruction that brought them to an end. Mungo, Martin's dog, had long ago become a sort of resident pensioner; like most family pets, he stayed at home when his owner left. Those going off to seek their fortune in the great world don't want the appurtenances of childhood with them, especially if they want to eat, sleep, squeak, bark or in other ways assert their presence.

Mungo grew old and sick. Eventually he could not climb the stairs between Trevor's half-house and mine. We watched over him, debated endlessly whether we should engage a vet to 'put him down', but even the euphemism upset us; to speak directly of killing was impossible. We cared for him with an elaborate concentration, every gesture unmistakably suggesting that we felt ourselves to be facing the terminal illness of something far greater than the poor old mongrel lying in the corner of Trevor's living room. He gazed mournfully at us as we offered food he could not eat and sips of water he could not drink. When he died we wrapped him in an old sheet, buried him in the garden and planted a crimson rhododendron over him. When we came inside to have a drink, I sat on Trevor's couch by the window and cried and cried and could not stop. For once we did not need to disagree, expostulate, nor even explain; that afternoon at least we both knew what we had lost, and grieved for its going.

Declaring myself a writer had one effect I didn't expect: it made me a member of a sort of nationwide action group, or committee. I already occupied a tiny, useful place in the national literature, a stall in the corner of a market, by managing the Young Writers' Incentive Award. Indeed, I'd extended it by putting together an assortment of winning entries and persuading PEN to publish them as an anthology; *Young Writing* came out in 1979. It had a mild flourish, was launched in the conference room of the Council for Educational Research where we had our PEN meetings, and crowds of established writers gathered to acknowledge the arrival of a younger literary generation.

But I also found that becoming even modestly known in a small country, you attract offers and invitations to write in ways you might not have thought of yourself. *Landfall,* for instance, suggested I act as guest editor for one issue. This offer rather went to my head – could it be true that after ogling that attractive but unattainable authority for so long I was to be summoned into its very presence? I knew, of course, that poems went out into the world and wrought all kinds of changes, but I associated the phenomenon with other people more than myself. Hone Tuwhare was one whose poems filled my consciousness to overflowing with their compassionate resonances. Since our first solemn meeting in the hospital ward where our children were being cared for, he had become not only a dear friend but a poet always able to move me profoundly with his writing. His line 'I am at one with the wind' we had chosen for Rachel's epitaph. This was the universal work of poetry, its influence, its power.

In 1979 there was still some uncertainty about how you referred to someone you lived with but to whom you were not married. This person was your 'companion', your 'friend', your 'partner' or, as some older people who still disapproved of the practice would put it, your 'de facto'. Vincent chose simply to say 'this is Caroline' when he introduced to his Wellington friends a robustly beautiful woman with a profusion of auburn hair, gold-flecked brown eyes and a ready laugh. They had known each other for years and were now to buy a house and settle in our city. Her arrival caused changes for us all – indeed it *made* us an 'us', far more of a group than we had been before.

The real influence was probably Vincent, with his taste for establishing limits round friendship and close ties within it. Permitted a place in this charmed sphere, you felt yourself marked for distinction; but it was Caroline who made occasions. Dinner at their house was elegant, and quirky; she had a fine sense of how to run with the mood and temper of any gathering, but she specialised in knowing Vincent's own. Later, however, when the momentum of the evening had gathered way and we had merged into a single composition, separate outlines blurred, her presence grew and intensified. If the first serious move to go home came after 3 am, Vincent insisted I stay the night; I would wash briefly in their crimson bathroom and sleep, suddenly and deeply, in a spare room till morning. One of the accidental luxuries, I told myself, of living like a single person.

There was magic of another kind in some winter evenings. Their house stood on hills facing west and looking across the tops of pine trees planted far down on the lower slopes. Uncharacteristically for Wellington, there was often a strange stillness in this enclosure of hills and trees, and at times a mist came and settled in the treetops like a gathering of great soft white birds. We could stand on the balcony, silenced to a whisper, and imagine ourselves in Norway or Iceland, seeing the legendary pine forests known from childhood stories, the mist like snow whitening their high branches.

There were others in what for a time felt like a 'circle' – Alistair and Meg, sometimes Margaret, nearly always Frank McKay, a Marist priest who taught New Zealand literature at the university and was Vincent's close friend. I'd met him as a contributor to the *Journal* (writer of a little poem about the yearnings of those who go out with a rod and line, ending, 'and Lord, one fish, but not too small'). Now he lived, not in a monastic establishment, one of the households his order ran for groups of young priests, but independently, acting as host to visitors from within the order, but preserving the freedom to move among his own friends – to eat with us, cook for us, drink and talk through evenings of a charmed familiarity.

Writing is a solitary act. So, of course, are many other occupations (including the one most familiar to me, child-rearing), and the camaraderie of shared understanding, even if most of the time we didn't exactly 'talk shop', was not very different from the Friday evening drinks at the pub so relished by office workers or teachers. Teachers – ah yes; I wished now, too late, that I'd been more amiable about Trevor's weekly boozing with the boys in Ohakune or Greytown. Work generated so much of my present energy and zest I couldn't help looking back with regret to the beginnings of our troubles, Trevor's and mine, and the old confrontations between 'home' and 'school'. I even remembered saying with great sententiousness, 'It's not what you do (working, presumably), it's what you are that matters!' Good God, I proved every day now that they were aspects of the same thing. But how could I possibly ever explain this to Trevor or anyone else?

Part of my changed view of 'work' was, of course, that now it richly overflowed into all other occupations: my own, not those carried out by Trevor, to which I was connected merely by association, or duty, or loyalty. A national writers' conference held in Wellington in 1979 was a perfect example. Organised by Roger Robinson and full of intellectual and social fizzing, it was a pleasure to me in ways that no doubt had their parallel in the sporting or teaching gatherings Trevor had relished for so long. It ended with a party which I, exulting in my sole occupancy, insisted must be held at my house.

Behind all such events stood always the spectre of the unfinished Fairburn *Letters*. How could a project go on so long and so inconclusively? It seemed to have followed me about for ever. The floors of my bedroom and living-room were so constantly covered with Fairburn papers that it seems they had achieved total occupation. But in fact I did inch forward. My friends Bridget and Vincent, who had scholarly experience I lacked, both helped; I learned how to do footnotes, I gathered more letters, made my selection and wrote an introduction explaining my reasons for it.

Denis and I saw less and less of each other; I was too busy to go to the club. I'd heard all his stories, some many times; now there was nothing for it but to finish the wretched thing. Moreover, I had younger friends for whom I was not the pupil-nursemaid-admirer-secretary I sometimes felt I'd become in Denis's company. Yet he'd been a major liberating influence, and if our time for being valuable to each other was gone, I still felt a good deal of gratitude, and an exasperated tenderness for him, when we were together.

I think I didn't realise how much he taught me of the craft of poetry, and the honesty and good sense one must bring to it, till after his death a year or so later. Writers then gathered from all parts of the country to do him honour, as well as friends from earlier acts in his own life drama ('I have gone through life shedding printing presses, wives and books'). But it was a dreadful occasion, dominated by the speeches and rituals of military men, especially from the Navy. We, his writing associates, grieved almost as much for the inappropriateness of this warlike panoply as for the loss of our friend. In the pub afterwards Vincent and I had our first (and only) quarrel, and perhaps that was our excuse.

However, I also met Dunstan, an elegant expatriate who said, 'Come and visit me in Paris', and, lying eagerly, I said I would. Vincent had in fact suggested that I apply for the Katherine Mansfield Memorial Fellowship, which sent a New Zealand writer each year to work in Menton, where Katherine Mansfield had written some of her famous stories. I remembered my encounter with Barry Mitcalfe with an affectionate pleasure, and after a few fits of fright and hesitation I sent off my application. My year was to be 1981.

Chapter 40

One reason I wanted to go was that among my exhilarating new friendships there was one that caused me an acute anguish. It had begun a few months before I left for Africa and Europe, in the apparently accidental way momentous events often do. There was a routine book party to present awards to writers, and among the guests was a tall, serious, dark-suited man, a university teacher from somewhere in the South Island; he had retired early, I learned, and often came to Wellington for research consultations, had been brought to the party by some friend. His conversation, which I joined by accident, was measured, informed, sedately playful, astute. I began to lose interest in the book party proceedings – a surprising deflecting of my usual attention. His name, I heard as he left, was Edward Green. I hoped I might see him again.

Before long I did. We lunched together in a small restaurant near one of Wellington's beaches, politely conducting a conversation like a ball game, really designed to reveal the aspects of our history and habits that each might find promising in the other. In short, we discreetly paraded ourselves as likely friends, possible lovers. The undercurrent of excitement was intense; it caused us both to order fish and then fail to notice it was there to be eaten. Outside on the pavement we kissed with an astonished tenderness and walked away in opposite directions, filled with the reverberations of the encounter.

That is to say, I was and, since over the next few months we went on conducting ourselves in much the same way, I supposed he was too. We made shy declarations to each other, both terrified of misusing the hackneyed phrases of lovers' dialogue, especially when we began to compose poems for each other. We discovered that we were almost the same age; we knew already that we were both in the process of abandoning old but now unbearably constricting marriages. We recognised a shared craving for new experience, new ways of loving and working and living, but didn't know exactly how to find them.

Some of this we could explain to each other, some we could sense; perhaps it was the force that gave such extraordinary intensity to the time we spent together, in those first months. Breathless encounters, when we could manage them, then phone calls, notes and poems in the mail; silences, when Edward returned to his family, tortured reflections while I waited to find out why. This was being in love on a different scale from any other I'd known, and there were dangers in it for me, as well as delights. One night, carried along by a rush of happiness, I was suddenly in tears, wracked by sorrow I could not understand and Ted, with all his sensitive ways, could not at first assuage. It was impossible to stop; we were both almost frightened at such violence of feeling, but of course there was a reason for it. The profound loss of Rachel's death, and the knowledge of loss that since that time had been constantly with me, had opened up wells of feeling that had probably never been touched in my whole life before. Some special abandonment in the drama of my relationship with Ted had swept me into this far region of the heart. Fortunately for me, he had an emotional wisdom that went beyond ordinary comprehension, and this in the end allowed me to be comforted. I was as helpless as I had ever been in the hands of another person, and afterwards a little healed, as I probably could not have been in any other way. No matter what else might happen to us, this gave me a kind of faith in him that no disappointment or betrayal could entirely destroy.

This was just as well, since one of the conditions of this enchanted discovery of each other, and of ourselves in the other, was that we were both in a state of beginning, and it was inevitable that we would move in different directions. Into the heedless, ill-judged excesses of adolescence, in fact. The second adolescence, a foolish business.

It began quite soon. Edward was geographically removed from the new friends and opportunities that Wellington (or our part of it) was teeming with, so the old/new dichotomy was for him a matter of actual journeys, flights between Christchurch and Wellington. Meetings and outings couldn't happen spontaneously; they had to be arranged, and when he began to choose other people for these, as well as me, I had fits of jealous despair. My journal, essential as a repository for emotional excess, tingled with manic intensity. Page after copious page addressed him, admonished my suffering self, apostrophised a confusing universe in which love perfectly acknowledged and consummated could, the next moment (or the next week), be tossed so lightly aside. Like any other adolescent, young or old, I could not imagine purposes and desires that did not match my own.

Not that we didn't explain – heavens, we never stopped explaining ourselves, in letters and in the long eager conversations we continued to have. There appeared to be a pattern of events, an emotional choreography, composed of passionate encounters, strained withdrawals (his), earnest inquiring (mine) and painstaking redefinitions (both of us). We began to recognise differences that underlay the similarities that had so pleased us at first. However the later phases of marriage had denied the separate self, Ted's work, his profession, and the intellectual experiment it entailed, had proceeded confidently. That, under the old rules, was how it was for men. My writing, with almost no scope at all, had remained a scrappy, unfulfilled, clandestine affair. On the other hand my married period had offered much greater emotional freedom than his, in relationships with family and friends.

We were endlessly interested in these definitions of ourselves as man and woman typical of our time and generation. We had both grown up in small country towns, and this pleasing fact somehow added substance to our theorising. I would not by myself have been able to abstract my historical placing, or anyone else's, in quite this way, but Ted's way of arguing his way towards a shaping vision drew me into the process. When intellectually excited he could draw on a long scholarly training, his mind opening further and further like an echoing chamber.

But the violent fluctuations continued, and with them my recurring private panic. We were trying to change a whole system of living, to shift house, as it were, in mind and heart and body, and for all the watchfulness we could induce in each other – or achieve alone – some items were overlooked, and remained just as they were. This too I came to think of as typically adolescent – leaving home with some, but not all, of the treasures one so emphatically declares to be one's own responsibility. One, for me, was something I called loyalty but which was more like possessiveness, thinly disguised. I had complex webs of relationships with family and friends myself, yet I made a very undistinguished attempt to allow this for my friend. Similarly, I flew at each new experience like a starved gull after crumbs, then suffered agonies of betrayal if he did the same.

In occasional calm moments, however, I could reflect on the

advantages of this second-chance living we had embarked on. Without our long and tangled adult experience – if, in fact, we'd been genuine fifteen- or sixteen-year-olds – we could not possibly have found in our love-making the intense delight that always danced round us like clouds of brilliant fireflies, wherever it took place, and however we might posture and fuss when we had our clothes on.

Of course I wrote poems for him. They seemed at first to glow with the radiance of real places, weather that reflected a mood, details of breathless arrivals, poignant climaxes in our talk. However, they gradually shrank on the page – an odd contrast with the more authoritative verses I'd written for Beeb. Did love poems need distance then, rather than immediacy? Events seemed to prove they did. Only after the first heady rush of intimacy was over did I begin to write of it with a fair degree of control.

Then he fell in love, and very thoroughly too, with someone else. By a bizarre yet appropriate coincidence it was one of the 'new' people in whom I was interested myself – a young woman of literary tastes and, I had to admit, great charm and intelligence as well. It was at this juncture that the idea of going away – to France, if I could – began to look like a merciful escape from torment. Apparently the new 'good life' was no better than the old at offering unmitigated happiness and fulfilment. My private journal proliferated, page after rapid, overheated page. It was all very well to speculate poetically about detachment; it didn't do much to induce it in real life.

And then we all made an interesting move. Each one, observing the shift of position that had made us look like any old eternal triangle, made a kind of declaration of allegiance to the friendships that already existed. My knowledge of Ted's adored one was still recent, but it was she who came to see me, determined to say some of the critically unsayable words that lay like big rocks between us every time we met. 'We are just becoming friends, you and I,' she said, 'we already have an understanding that neither Ted nor anyone else should be allowed to destroy.'

I was silent, concentrating as though on a high wire; was I to shake, perhaps fall, to jump; or keep my head and hold on? I looked at this beautiful young woman who had, in one sense, taken from me something I had powerfully wanted to keep, yet, in another, had simply followed her own impulses as I had followed mine. I felt almost physically a wrench, a kind of separation of particles within me. If the old coherent system of living was breaking up, was this the moment to look for different qualities in each part?

More haltingly, Edward and I made gestures I interpreted as salvaging acts, but inevitably we drew some distance apart. At our last meeting before I left for Menton, he gave me his address in London, where it appeared he would be going to do some work; it would be June, about halfway through my own year in Europe.

Chapter 41

March 29 1981: 9.30 pm. *I'm here! Not in the frying desert, not in dirty, beautiful, dangerous Damascus, not at Charles de Gaulle airport racing from desk to desk through that maze of miraculous constructions; not even in Nice where the little French bus waited while I struggled with my appalling luggage . . . Here. In Menton. In a safe, clean, courteous hotel – I don't care if it costs a million francs a night. And it's raining. Cool, soft, singing rain; I feel like a dying plant suddenly allowed to drink great gulps of fresh water.*

There are enormous palm trees in the little square outside my window, tubs of primulas and cyclamen, a fountain. A man riding a bicycle has just bumped into a car; he fell off, but it was all very mild and moderate, acted in slow motion – the two navigators exchanged a few words, then both set off again (in Syria they would have shot each other). Everything already seems easy, wonderfully arranged after the chaotic and violent streets of Damascus, and the queer watchfulness in that hotel.

April 1: *I'm more than ever here – right here, absolutely inside, living in the KM room. It's an elegant place; pale cream walls, aristocratic furniture, subtle lighting that flows magically out of panels high up on the walls; leaves across the windows – flax, good green New Zealand flax, at one, palm leaves like green fingers spread out at the other. A small pebbled courtyard, a craggy tree (is it a loquat? I haven't seen one for years, but I think that's it), and the soft pouf! pouf! of doves floating over the garden next door. It's all exactly right, and I am amazed and delighted that it is mine. There are daffodils in that garden too. I shall plant a red geranium in my corner plot, if I can find one.*

But the getting here . . . I see myself standing helplessly in the Office de Tourisme while the briskest officials in the world plan my stay. They must find me a small cheap studio for six months; one of them begins ringing up. Alas no, the season will begin soon and who wants small cheap tenants then? They look at me despairingly. I could stay in the room, I murmur hesitantly. But why on earth hadn't I said so before? Oh, of course, no French. I am hurt by this and explain in their wretched language that I thought the mayors and councillors didn't approve of such an arrangement. Ach! It is sensible – a nice place – the best I could have – and so cheap, it will cost me nothing! Exactly, I think. I know there is no kitchen? I do, and expect to be able to manage.

Everything has become simple. We race off in the Mairie car to another office, collect the keys and another official who accompanies the driver and me to the room. There they carry my bags, switch on power and water, open everything, all in a moment. Then they lift up the corner of the bed cover – but I have no draps! They will return soon. They extract my mail from the locked letter box, and vanish. I begin to read my letters, almost crying with relief and pleasure at finding that New Zealand did not after all drop off the end of the world, as in the Middle East it seemed perhaps it had.

In no time they are back with two enormous hem-stitched sheets, two satin-edged blankets, towels and a tubular pillow slip to cover the sausage body of my bolster. I cannot guess where it all came from (there are drycleaning tabs on the sheets – did they steal them?) but am grateful. We all shake hands. Then they remember something else, and out of the back of the car is drawn a tall, curly, polished wood umbrella stand. Since I have no real life-support system, no stove, bench, cupboard or refrigerator, not a cup or plate, knife or fork, this strikes me as a gloriously funny gesture. I smile broadly, we shake hands again and with manifold courtesies part at last.

How I luxuriate in being at home – my small, beautiful, secret home for months and months. No doubt I shall be lonely and unhappy, no doubt I shall wish for many things I haven't got, but for the moment there is nothing, nothing, nothing. There is no past and no future, only this island in time, light as a bubble and shining with rainbow colours.

April 2: *My birthday, but I have positively no expectations whatever for this occasion. I can see the sea this morning, through the trees; it's cold and early and I'm sitting over my hot little electric heater and looking out the window. If I'm honest I'll admit that I'm partly looking at the letterbox because yesterday I received two birthday telegrams and today I hope there might be more.*

Something did happen! Better than mail, a little fat jolly man coming through my gate with an enormous bunch of flowers, shiny paper and miles of ribbon – Pour vous Madame, de Nouvelle-Zélande . . . my dear, dear family – I can't think what it will have cost them, millions; but what a delicious thing to do. Tiger lilies and tulips and clouds of asparagus fern – and I can find two large inelegant jars to put them in. Pure happiness.

April 9: *I'm sick. I think the honeymoon must be over. For twenty-four hours I've had the most disgusting, humiliating, debilitating diorrh – can anyone spell that word? – diarrhoea. I am weak, miserable, depressed, homesick, disconsolate – I have all the sicknesses I supposed might attack me, without ever believing they would. I am forlorn, I want someone to be kind to me. I want to be noticed, protected, attended to . . . living in this hole alone is hard. Well? says my other, severer self, isn't that what you came for? It is, it is, but that doesn't, today, give me much saving resolution. It doesn't do anything – it kicks a sick horse who rolls his horrible eyes and tries to get up and can't. Useless to say I'll emerge stronger for my trials – or at any rate I'll emerge; for the moment I just want to burst into tears. And indeed a few tears do swim into my eyes – but why shed them? Who's going to do anything because I do? Who's going to see, even?*

My briskness – my going for tremendous walks when I felt confused – even that's not there today. For one thing I can't, because I keep having to run for my life to the toilet to perform ignominious acts there. Anyway I don't want to. I don't even want to go to the post office – the ultimate expression of defeat. I just want to go to sleep and wake up to find everything different. There's nothing impressive about this malady – it leads to no great insights, no clearing away of the trivial distractions of existence. On the contrary, it overwhelms me with the most boring and constricting of my own personal trivia – physical, first, but it's all one. I'm no better than my illness, I'm turning from solid to liquid in body and soul. All my reassuring habits of thinking, my response to the bright and tingling world, my power to make up my life as I go along – it's all flushed away as though down a lavatory pan.

I suppose my silly body is having the same problem with French bacteria that I have with their fierce and threatening language. In both cases what's needed is a slow, gently increasing intake, but instead there's a mighty rush.

April 13: *Two ladies appeared at my door this morning. One French, one*

English, both teachers of English to graduates and other adults; they had seen my picture in the local paper as I shook the hand of Monsieur le Maire. Would I like to ride to Nice in a bus to view a museum there? Closer to home, would I like to borrow a camp cooker, some cups and saucers, an electric jug? How disgraceful that the town had not better provided for me. It's done quite a lot I said, waving my hand towards the umbrella stand.

Also, I felt better and went to the bank. A gentleman from Mauritius who works there told me I must join the British Association, so with his card of introduction I went to the bar where they meet. Two elderly gentlemen were sitting in a corner standing tiny flags up in a bowl – flags of Empire, they explained; a pity they didn't have a New Zealand one (did they say 'colony'?). There was a long conversation about the quarrel that has divided the supporters of the English Library; the vicar had been most unreasonable . . . no, say the others who have since arrived, it wasn't his fault. Fancy that man taking those books and . . . It is a present crisis? I wonder. Oh no, it happened four years ago. When I was in Indiah – begins a white moustache next to me; someone else is talking sorrowfully about Princess Margaret.

I went outside into the French street and walked away under the leafy French plane trees, wondering why these people elected to live here. Came in the nineteenth century and lingered on; for the climate, I suppose.

April 14: *This is a kind of solitude I have never known. Being alone, with your familiar world 'out there', is quite different – friends and family, the networks of claims, desires, ambitions, temptations . . . they are indeed like a net, they spread out to catch you whenever you're ready to jump. Here there's nothing, so I can't jump at all. What do I do instead? Construct a routine – yes, I can see that's what I've been doing. In the morning I make tea, turn on the BBC news (I listen to Paris and Monte Carlo later in the day, but I love the BBC – it's like a secret vice), dress, unlock the gate, eat my breakfast out on the battered old green seat under the loquat tree. When I can't put it off any longer I sit down at my desk and read over the last bit of yesterday's work, and begin today's. You're a different creature writing prose – I am amazed at how unlike writing poems is this systematic daily production of the Ohakune stories (which I can't keep separate – more and more they're running together into one story).*

It's never simple. Yesterday I'd left a scene in the middle (I work in scenes – does everyone? I'm devoured by a desire to talk to other writers; but perhaps it's just as well I can't. I guess everyone has to grapple with these mysteries alone) so today actually did begin easily. The second half of the scene was there waiting to be written. But if I've got to the end of one on the previous day, I have to spend a lot of time and concentration on the new one to make it come into focus. It's there, but it's dim. I'm astonished how much detail has to appear on the spot. It seems, for me, to be the only way. What do I mean? The only way for it to be fresh and interesting, to me, is for it to be right there happening in my head while I'm writing – though, of course, I have a guide, a plan. The few times I've concentrated on the entire detail of a scene before writing it a strange thing has happened. It won't allow me to do it that way. It simply changes in the writing – it's as though something in the story itself, in the people, says to me, 'You just wait and see what we want, don't tell us beforehand.' Extraordinary.

When I'm stuck I walk about, in the courtyard or up and down my little hill road, the Chemin Fleuri, scowling. If it's very difficult I lock up and go for a real walk, but as soon as it's ready I come back quickly and start. I mismanaged it today. Thinking about the new scene I went way up past the Jardin Exotique without noticing what I was doing, and then had it clear enough to start writing and was too far from home. I had to fly back like the distressed ladybird. Quite like the days when I had diarrhoea.

I can't work all day and all night of course. The 'free' parts of my day are strange and somehow fragile. In some ways it feels like being in hospital – your conditions are unusually neat and refined, you are surrounded by flowers you haven't had to grow, news of the world comes from a long way off; visitors pass and stare, nodding at you tactfully. Only one couple, so far, has wanted to come inside and they were curious, not about Katherine Mansfield, nor New Zealand, nor my residence here. It was simply that they had visited every other monument mentioned in the guidebook, and wished to tick this one off on their list. They would like to read the short résumé of her life? They liked her work? No, no, none of that: they glanced vaguely about and went away, mysteriously satisfied.

Afterwards I sat on the brick ledge beside my minute garden; a lizard joined me for a few moments, his tiny pulse beating warily – there are dozens of families of them, this was a young adventurer from a minor clan. There was a film over the sun but the day was warm and still; there's *a clinging quality about the air here, it's like fine muslin lying always against your skin. Jasmine is in flower in the garden next door, and some sort of mock orange that grows everywhere and is full of a heavy sweet scent. But you don't fully experience a spring that follows a winter you have not known. I have impressions, sensations of pleasure; but that poignant awareness of new growth that you feel in the air when it is still cold in New Zealand – that I don't have.*

April 15: *I have just begun to wonder who are the real Mentonese. Not the rich geriatrics who crowd the waterfront boulevards with a sort of stupor of resignation on their faces; not the annual tourist crowd that is already trickling on to the beaches for Easter and which will come in thousands in July and August. A few of them I watched today, lying face down and motionless while the sun slowly fires their bodies to the right colour and crispness; one couple was stretched out, leaning back on a seat, eyes closed, their faces set in the dazed melancholy fixedness of sun worship. But there must be people who really live here, who haven't come to be cured or to die, or find a soporific for the restlessness of being rich.*

April 16: *I've met one. A genuine native, born here seventy or more years ago. He's a shy, courteous, bent old man who was wearing his dressing gown at five o'clock when his wife brought me to call (the ebullient Madame Bosano, one of my callers). He left his study and disappeared (to shave, but the dressing gown remained), then came back and slowly, with great deliberation, served sweet Martinis and tiny salty crackers while he talked in soft, beautifully gentle French. (Usually I am struck by the energy and enthusiasm of French conversation – they agree with one another, or perhaps disagree, so tremendously, so repeatedly; are there no calm or taciturn French, I have wondered, who leave an occasional word to be understood by silence?) Their house stands high on a hill on the west side of the town and looks up towards the ancient monastery of l'Annonciade, or across to the high peaks further up the valley with a glimpse of one of the old villages, once forts built as protection against the Saracens when they swept across these mountains with marauding armies in the tenth century.*

April 18: *Easter Saturday. I wake to the sound of rain; if this is the best climate in the world it rains surprisingly often. Not that I mind – it always brings a delicious freshness with it. Madame Raynaud, with whom*

I am to lunch, arrives at 10 am, bringing me a crocheted shawl as an Easter present. Then we walk, slowly, since though spry she is very old, to the other end of town where she has an apartment in one of the huge nineteenth-century palaces whose sweeping staircases and marble pillars are now thoroughfares for hundreds of tenants. Madame belongs to a family that traces its ancestry back to Joan of Arc; her husband, who died recently, was a colonel in the French Army. Naturally her opinions are unshakeably conservative, but her manner while she dismisses unsuitable persons or practices is urbane, her conversation witty and stylish. Her English, which she learned in childhood from a governess, is excellent.

She lived for ten years in Romania and tells me that the Romanians are charming but have no morals whatever. They change partners, they marry and re-marry, they have a different father for every child in the family. When you ask a Romanian woman to sit down, she lies down, it's what she thinks you mean. When Madame left she was complimented on having remained happily married and caused no scandal. It is because I have l'équilibre, she says; that is what one needs.

Simone de Beauvoir is mentioned. Madame has no time for her. Sartre? Worse. He caused nothing but trouble. She talks of the church, has several nephews who are priests. Celibacy? It is a practical matter; there is the expense of supporting wives and children – a priest is always poor. More important, he holds the secrets of the confessional; if he were married he would tell them to his wife and then everyone would know. Only if confession were abolished could priests marry. However, she adds, many in France are married because they come to the priesthood from other professions. Do they keep their wives? Well of course. We are not careless.

Nor are they dirty and untidy like the Italians and the English who are absent-minded as well, and terrible gossips. Indeed, it seems there are no other races that measure up. The Russians are morose, the Swedes drink too much – everyone is drunk in Sweden; if you sit down in a public square in Stockholm a policeman comes and shakes you because he knows you must be drunk and he wants to know what you're thinking of doing. And the Central Europeans, the Croats, Serbs, Bohemians, Bulgarians and the rest – they are all like the Romanians, entirely without morals. The trouble is the Greek Orthodox Church, it allows anything, has no standards, no rules. People think this about the French but it's not true; they are a very formal people with a great respect for their institutions. When Monsieur was in a German prison camp during the war Madame worked in an American canteen; as soon as the men knew you were French they would begin shouting 'coucher! coucher!' at you. The very idea . . . she is full of scorn.

It is all delightful. Before I leave I learn too that there are hotels in the town to which one must never send one's friends because they are fit only for those particularly despicable creatures, the English railway crowd. Also that the English postal service is so complicated that every postman has to stay in the same job for the whole of his life, because no one can learn it twice. She sees that I am enjoying her prejudices, and of course enjoys them a good deal herself. We will meet again; she will take me to a concert in the Chapelle des Pénitents Noirs, there is a fine local flautist whom I must hear. When I leave I am permitted the French kiss on both cheeks, and a final piece of instruction. Some vulgar people overdo this salutation – they do it twice on each cheek, without expression, without enthusiasm; you can tell they come from the lower classes.

April 19: *I like the French – today, at least. Along the waterfront boulevards there are couples walking at all hours of the day and night, men and women of all ages, together and at ease in a way I think is rare in New Zealand. They neither ignore nor overly concentrate on each other, they simply behave – walking, sitting, eating and drinking, shopping – in a way that makes being together wholly natural. As natural as being alone, yet more sustaining. More often than not they link arms or hold hands; there is something very touching about two of the very old wandering along hand in hand – but none of them are conscious of it in the way we would be. The local supermarket emblem is a couple holding a basket between them.*

Of course many are retired people. There is too the different organisation of the day; there's a morning which starts early and ends at 12 or 12.30, lunchtime, when only the restaurants are open and everyone falls to with great seriousness; and the afternoon which begins at 2.30 or 3 and may last till 7.30 or 8 in the evening. After that there's the promenade. Dogs take part in it too. There are nine million dogs in France and I am convinced that eight and a half million of them live in Menton. All are on leads, all docile, as decorous as their owners, except that they shit in the street. Sometimes I have a desperate longing to see an animal running free or a tree, unpruned, growing wild and spreading itself copiously about the sky, or even an untended garden. Then I walk across the border into Italy. At once the paths are cracked, the geraniums and arctotis sprawl, passers-by greet you like amiable villagers; the beaches, unimproved, are rough and beset by rocks, bottles lie in enormous piles under stone arches that support the railway line.

April 26: *In the meantime, my stories, my book. They're all one now; if I had the nerve I'd call it a novel – but I'd say it almost inaudibly, write it very, very small. I'm very fond of my characters though; I think they're becoming substitutes for friends. The place where they are – how clear it is in my mind. It's a sort of plateau, an open grassy place where we can walk about, not talking much but* being with *one another very strongly, all of us. I'm one of them, yet I'm also watching them and thinking, trying to be fair to each one. But I have to do it carefully or they will see and then they will be embarrassed and not act naturally. Well, they are my friends now, we've been through a lot together. I can't be rude. So if T is going to be an ass I watch him covertly, not to laugh in his face. I positively hide when I'm seeing what that awful creature MM is going to do.*

I think I'm becoming absent-minded (like the English!) – it's because I keep going back to my people. For the first time I thought today that it's wonderful to be so alone. How do people ever write anything unless they're all by themselves in a small room for months on end?

I've got a title. I'm going to call it High Country Weather. *Sounds like one somebody's used before, but I like it, and it's right. I'm going to use it for the present anyway.*

May 7: *A day of crisis over* Weather. *It began yesterday – I seemed to have come to a stop, though I knew I was only half way. It's been a wonderfully good few days, every word just bounding out and onto the page as though it couldn't wait to get there. I've been so excited I couldn't sleep. But I must have rushed ahead without watching because suddenly I felt as though I was at the edge of a cliff. So yesterday I stopped after only an hour. When I came to it today I couldn't get it back. It had all gone completely dead, simply lain down on the ground and wouldn't move. I walked about feeling frantic for a while. Then I had a brainwave; I decided that this was the halfway point, and I could say so. I could finish off that scene and put* End of Part One. *So I did. Felt great. Smiling all over my face, I leafed through – yes, it hung together, it was the place to stop. The second half would be different, and I thought I could see how.*

But could I do it? I've been all day making notes and screwing them up. It's the panic that's worst – what if I've got this far and can go no further? How I want someone to talk to! Here I am cooped up in this little cave, and one day they'll come and take me out and say What did you do, and I'll say I started something and I got halfway. Then the kind ones will say Oh but you had the European experience – but I *haven't had the bloody European experience because I've been tied hand and foot to this horrible story, and now I can't finish it.*

May 8: *Started again.*

May 10: *Madame Raynaud came to see me this morning. She has another crime to add to those committed by the English. They take the combings out of their hair brushes and roll them round their fingers and then put them carefully in a drawer! She's seen them do it. Oh I love her – she's superb.*

May 22: *I've been to Cannes. Wonderful to be able to say it, and wonderful in truth it was. Those good films . . . all that unexpected national pride . . . that glittering crowd. Being among those other New Zealanders did something strange – it lifted off the weight of solitude like the peeling off of one heavy garment after another on a hot day. Now I'm back I have an almost physical sense of turning inwards again. I have waved goodbye, smiling brightly, I turn at the door, I begin the concentration that will slowly bring up the outline of my own mental furniture. It's like learning – or waiting to be able – to see in the dark.*

But coming home was a special thing in another way. For the very first time my little house actually represented home (I don't count the initial euphoria when I rhapsodised about it being mine, mine, tra la) and I came to it with keen pleasure. The datura was covered with richly scented trumpets, there were passionfruit flowers, exquisite as orchids, all over the vine on the fence – and at least a thousand letters from New Zealand in my mail box.

May 25: *I can't look at* Weather *and on a sudden impulse yesterday morning I decided not to try. So I've been writing poems. It induces a kind of ecstasy – for so long I've been tied to that book. I've done poems of course but usually in the middle of the night or in some oblique way, half pretending I wasn't. Now I'm not pretending. I know all over again that it's what I most want to do; it gives me a sense of coming home rather like the physical one on Friday.*

May 26: *Letter from Ted, he's coming to England, then here. Good, good. Last night a shadowy Algerian (I think) followed me home, and Peter Smith, my English friend from one of the mansions along the waterfront, appeared and saved me. Miraculous. I was terrified.*

May 29: *Now they've begun there's no end to my remarkable experiences. The woman who's said to be terribly literary turned up – she had T.S. Eliot to tea. And two terrible English ladies, one fat, one thin – Knife and Spoon – who discoursed for hours about the disgrace that nobody in England speaks English any more. Then they couldn't pronounce Salle des Variétés and had to point it out to each other on a brochure.*

Walked up the hill to the Old Chateau Cemetery, full of its English dead taking honours with them into the next world – baronets, colonels, majors . . . Dear me, the vanity – and all are becoming obliterated. Some are already dusty relics under pine trees, the stones cracked and pine needles swept by the wind into piles that cover the names.

May 30: *I've had another panic about* High Country Weather, *the worst there's been. I've had a long good spell away from it, doing poems, and felt ready to go back to it. So I did – read a few pages back and began again where I'd left off a fortnight before. Almost at once I became convinced that the whole thing was dreadful rubbish; I couldn't write a word, I was paralysed. So, last evening I sat in the bed, knees up on my chair, a glass of wine on the other chair beside me, and I read it, every word from the beginning. And I was pleasantly surprised, and reassured; I have no idea whether it's good or not, but at least it's interesting to read. I think so, I really do. On the other hand the very idea of having it read by other people makes me blush with fright – but I have to finish it first, and I'm slow.*

June 7: *A letter from the Paris Embassy asking me to go to lunch on the 12th. I can't possibly, I can't do any mortal thing till I've finished this draft of* Weather. *I'll write and explain. How many days are there? I wonder if I just write, night and day, from now till then and leave the typing till later, if I possibly could? Paris, for a weekend . . . It will kill me, but I don't suppose that matters.*

June 9: *I've finished! So many thousands of times I've thought it would just go on and on for ever – and now I've done it! I can't sleep, haven't* slept properly for several nights, but I don't care, I don't care about anything except that it's DONE. And now, I even like it – I came to love them in the end, Nigel and Louise and the rest. Of course I may be quite wrong, everything may be a mess, but I don't think so. I began to feel all right when I learned how to punish them, push them further, not just let them stand round and be pleased with themselves, which earlier they showed a tendency to do. I went to Italy and bought some shoes.

June 18: Well, Paris. It would be interesting, a useful experience, I'd thought, but I would emerge from it unchanged. Wrong. Wrong I suppose, from the moment I got Ted's card and wired back suggesting he should come too. I was pretty cautious still though, when I met him at the Gare du Nord; we had some coffee in a street café, went to the hotel, were hot and had a shower, dressed to go out for dinner – and I really did dress, in my new silk trousers, while he, reproached, changed into a posh shirt. It began to be fun. There we were, outside on the crowded boulevard at 11 pm drinking vin de la maison, and me telling him I wanted him to see Notre Dame lit up, and the square full of people wandering about in the warm air at midnight, as I had myself done the evening before.

We got as far as the Pont Neuf, the crowds thickened, the atmosphere grew magnetic, fireworks began to explode glittering flowers into the dark sky. It was all magical; we leaned over the bridge, I thought how betrayed I ought to feel by all his previous – well, betrayals. Any woman with reasonable self-respect would . . . but still, there I was, in a French crowd in the middle of a summer night on a famous bridge over the most romantic river in the world, fireworks blossoming in the sky, and what do we do? Cling to each other as though we could never let go, and then, arms round each other, pushed through the crowd, somehow navigated the dark and unfamiliar streets and got home where we could go, wonderfully, to bed. That's Paris for you.

Ted and I were unsophisticated travellers. Paris was for both of us a literary idea, theoretically familiar as the cultural and artistic nucleus of the Europe of our reading, but as a modern city, easily exasperated by its English-speaking visitors, it was a new and alarming prospect. We attracted catastrophes, we lost our way, were mystified by the Parisian telephone system, went into the wrong rooms in the house-hotel accommodation we appeared to have chosen. A rapid gunfire of French explanations (or accusations) followed us and our minor crimes wherever we went. We were often reduced to apologetic gestures and a helpless silence.

Yet we had a very good time. Our escapades, at least after they were over, seemed wildly funny to us both. And we did have, when we could get to the right address at the right time, a wonderful guide in Dunstan. The wise and witty Dunstan, New Zealand Parisian. He took us to parks and galleries and restaurants, to dinner with his friends; he guided us into events we would have had no idea how to create for ourselves, like drinking brandy at three in the morning at the Deux Magots, the cafe where Sartre had sat and worked at his famous writings. And he talked, of Paris, its richness, its magic, his reasons for choosing to live and work there; without our realising it, he brought our bookish knowledge of the city into a shared, living present.

Then Ted caught a train to England, I another to Nice and Menton. We said goodbye in a windy, gritty tunnel between the north and south lines in the Gare du Nord. It had been, he said, an exceptional time. He would come to stay later in the year and we would go to Florence. *Pourquoi pas?*

Chapter 42

Journeys, to Florence and beyond, grew and proliferated in the second half of my year in Menton. To go away – north, usually – was a natural thing to do in the summer; the Riviera became entirely over-run by tourists, prices doubled, the beaches, already dominated by rapacious café owners who demanded you pay for every square inch of sand you occupied, became an indivisible mass of roasting flesh, white if English, sizzling brown if from a more southern climate. Music designed to induce a desperate hilarity roared and shrieked from loudspeakers along the waterfront below me through all the hours of the day and night. The only way I could work during the day was to draw the curtains of my fiercely hot little room, shower every couple of hours and leave the cold water on my skin to evaporate slowly as my temperature rose again. Sweat rained down over me as though I was constantly in tears. The radio said there were fires in Athens, the temperature there was 41 degrees.

My finished draft of *High Country Weather* lay tied up in a corner (with string round manila folders) like a rampant animal finally tamed; but there were other projects. Poems of course, a report for the *Listener* of New Zealand films at Cannes (including *Smash Palace*), a story I wanted to write. And letters kept coming: Bruce Mason told me that *Foreskin's Lament* was sweeping all before it in New Zealand theatres; Kathy said she'd spent an idyllic weekend with Stephanie and Barry in a derelict house they'd found for lease in the Wairarapa.

Bridget was starting a new small press, Port Nicholson Press, and planned a miscellany, a book for summer reading, as its inaugural publication – would I be back for that in October? Fiona talked of contemplating, and then accepting, the presidency of PEN, but finishing a novel first. Stephanie, training as a teacher, felt 'less and less enthusiastic about teaching' but liked the idea of being a music specialist and could she borrow my piano? And Ruth wanted to come and stay with me the first night I was back in New Zealand. Anne French, working at Oxford University Press on details of the Fairburn *Letters*, which would finally be published at the end of the year, talked of jacket designs and footnote references . . .

Then Mrs Thelluson, an English lady I knew, tiny as a child, ninety years old and full of a zest that in Menton was uncharacteristic of the English, knocked at my door. She was going to England for the worst of the summer, and wanted me to do something for her while she was away. It was, she explained in a perfectly nonchalant tone, to take a brush and dustpan up to the cemetery every now and then and sweep the pine needles from Aubrey Beardsley's grave. I swelled up with the magnitude of this poignant commission and, as soon as she'd left, hurried along the waterfront to the supermarket to buy the implements for my task.

Twenty-nine, he'd been, the creator of those elegant, unnerving drawings, when, like Katherine Mansfield and all the others, he had come to Menton to seek a cure for his consumption and instead had died of it. He'd lain ever since up there under the whispering pines, where I did indeed several times perform my small act of worldly housekeeping, reverently keeping his stone face clean for another few days in his eternity of dust.

In August Ted came. My English neighbour Peter Smith secured a hotel booking in Florence for us at short notice and at the height of the tourist season, so as Mr and Mrs Smith (which for some reason I thought much funnier than Ted did) we roamed the streets and galleries of the world's most beautiful city. We would wander home in the afternoon along the banks of the Arno, emerge again at eight or nine in the evening, and go to join all the other tourists who were sitting out till midnight and after at little tables round the edges of the great piazzas, eating their dinner and drinking chianti and watching the entertainers, the violinists, dancers, magicians, clowns, who came to amuse the summer crowds.

Margaret Scott came from New Zealand to visit me – or, more exactly, so we could take together the European journeys she had been unable to afford on her much smaller fellowship grant, ten years earlier. We knew very well how to talk of everything under the sun (especially ourselves); to travel together would be an entertaining extension of our habits at home.

And so it was. We sat or lolled our way across Europe in a dozen hot trains, sleeping in shabby and uncomfortable hotels, battling with rascally taxi drivers, eating unrecognisable (though sometimes delicious) food. We went to Delphi, because I wanted to hear the Oracle speak – as it surely did, high up in those echoing hills: to Rome to gaze at the Colosseum, the Sistine Chapel, to Barcelona for the famed Gaudi Cathedral . . .

In Venice we sat on the Rialto and said to each other, as though we had waited for ever for the savour and relish of it, 'Signor Antonio, many a time and oft / In the Rialto . . . ' And one morning we stood on a bridge leaning over one of the canals, and almost cried when a fine rich soprano singing *Barcarolle* burst out from an upstairs window nearby. We were, we were sure, performers ourselves in a small dazzling opera that sang of our own lives, and the whole span of European history. Then Margaret went to America; we promised to meet again in New York, before she went home and I back to France.

But my annus mirabilis wasn't over yet. In September I went to London, and there I found a little cartel of New Zealanders temporarily separated from cataclysmic events at home. It was the Year of the Tour, the arrival of the Springbok rugby team, the huge anti-apartheid, anti-tour marches in the streets, the eventual cancellation of a match – after flour bombs were dropped on the ground in Hamilton – and the violent clashes between protesters and the police Red Squad. Even London newspapers thought it was news; as for us, the New Zealanders (or those I knew), we met constantly, talked of it obsessively. Ted was there, and John Thomson, Bill and Marion Manhire, Bill Pearson; all our conversations were the same. We would meet, John and I for lunch perhaps, or several of us to drink brandy in the Manhires' flat at William Goodenough House, and would begin as civilised folk should, to talk of books, plays, the weather. Almost at once we would abandon this attempt and fall to, like starving creatures offered a meal, on the one subject that held us, the state of near civil war in our remote and peaceful little country.

Everyone had letters from home telling of the brutal stampeding of protest crowds, of sit-ins across highways, of quarrels making uncrossable divisions in families; my news came from Trevor, Stephanie, Kathy, who was now a trained journalist and had to suffer the pangs of official neutrality in reporting events in which she felt, as everyone did, a desperate involvement. Why was it happening, we asked ourselves and one another, in our anxious (and somehow guilty) isolation.

Was it really about rugby football and apartheid and South Africa, or about something in ourselves? Perhaps the long period of oppressive and insulting authority under Muldoon governments that seemed to assume that 'the ordinary New Zealander' was a narrow and infantile bore, incapable of adventure or altruism? Had the divisions in our society, praised for its egalitarianism, run much deeper than we realised, and lain there, waiting to erupt?

The protesters who were out in their thousands in the streets were not the protesters we knew – students, women for or against abortion; this was more comprehensive by far – it was more like the Vietnam War protests. Indeed, it looked as though it was a war. We talked of loss of innocence. The country would be changed.

I met Chester Wadsworth, a New Zealand poet whose work I'd admired for years; he now lived in London and came to a New Zealand expatriates' party – but he had left his country behind more than twenty years before, and could offer no particular insights. It seemed, he remarked, that New Zealand was no longer a place he knew; he would retire the following year, and might come on a visit. I gave him my address, thinking it unlikely that he would keep or remember it.

When the time came to leave, John and I had a final lunch in one of his familiar restaurants – he had been living and working in London for twenty years – and made plans for him to visit me in Menton. He would bring his cousin Elizabeth and they would stay in the Hotel New York, a tiny villa at the end of the Chemin Fleuri and a few minutes' walk from my one-roomed house.

John and Elizabeth and I made forays into the old cobble-streeted town, across the border to Ventimiglia, the little Italian market town that contained among other things a vast warehouse full of silk, cotton, gauze and linen flowers, a display of local magic. We went to Nice, and its exquisite little Chagall Museum; we drank late brandies at the waterfront cafés, or lunched in the garden of that small public cottage, the Hotel New York. For some of the time Dunstan was there, and with him we walked the craggy hilltop paths and dark beaches of the Italian coast, talking, constantly flexing the new (for me) intellectual muscles with which we tried to shape an international consciousness out of our island habits of mind.

Ted and I had talked of this too, in a sudden burst of shared discovery the morning we left the hotel after our weekend of Parisian adventures. However ripe and expansive European culture, we energetically, even passionately, declared ourselves for our own younger, more unformed community. We didn't want to observe, we wanted to act, to belong, even (in a rush of excitement) to change things, we said.

But my own awareness of the end of the Menton year came privately, gradually, and tangled by contradictions. After all the journeys I had a spell 'at home' alone which began with the disillusioning discovery that working each day at my desk – the habit which had saved me from absolute despair in those first precarious weeks – had itself become tentative and unstable. For one thing, the recurring whizz and bluster of the trains – there were forty-five every day, passing only a few yards from my door, on the other side of the Chemin Fleuri – seemed louder, more insistent, in some inexplicable way sadder. Unable to settle to steady work, I wandered about, stared at them forlornly.

Menton had done all it could. I felt bored, irritated, vaguely disappointed with everything; yet the matchless physical beauties of the place were more present than ever. It was autumn, the jacaranda trees were out and their great arches of purple stood on the hills above me, in that attitude of blessing the land that they give with the lovely drooping of their leaves. Oleanders were in flower too, little bright buttons of colour, and the astonishingly vivid bougainvillea – there was warmth and ripeness all about me. It was just that it had become somehow static, as my visits to friends now seemed. I could feel the autumn, the fading of a season, in my bones, my very cells.

To start it all again, I thought, would take a new effort, a joining of myself to what was there – some big step forward in my language competence, for one thing – a beginning of something I knew I could finish. Instead I frittered and yawned; when I worked it never seemed right. Robbed of this saving anchor, I thought about it, tried to see its shape so far.

My 'life as a writer' is strange, it's so short – I wonder if it has a future, if I have the power to take hold of my experience, and give it one? A woman of fifty-seven is beset by vanities, pretences, fears, protections – well, I am. The thing that concerns me most constantly and most painfully is growing old. And being alone, of course. But I don't write about that, yet – there, I think, is where my next conflict lies. At the moment, whenever I try, I skulk around the question, eye it balefully, too frightened to close with it. I believe I have to move outside myself, yet hold to myself – it's always the same thing, always. Not just the excitement, or the pain, but finding the objective evidence, the detail. All my life it's been the same – it's been hard work to find the substance, the things in experience. Trevor never has intuitions, but he sees the stuff of his life. If only his sturdy matter of factness could have joined with my love of the essence, so we had confluence and fertilising, instead of boredom and dislike. I can't write of this, it makes me cry. I am weak and sad altogether; these last few days I've been tired yet restless, inclined to wander from myself like a broken needle in a compass, losing the north.

I've recovered. I am what I am, I work as I can – harder, often fruitfully. And today I read Wilde's De Profundis and was again greatly moved by it. 'Pleasure for the beautiful body,' he said, 'but pain for the beautiful soul.' It's full of the discovery of humility through the most appalling hardship; he emerges as himself, in love with the world and entirely free of claims on it. It's helped me to give up my posturing, to feel again my place in the world and myself fitting into it. I'm here to work, but I am here too to know I am here.

So I've walked about in the caressing late summer air, watched the dancing down by the boat harbour, and thought myself lucky to be part of this summer on the Cote d'Azur, this crowd of festive French holidaymakers. Wilde says at the end, 'All trials are trials for one's life, just as all sentences are sentences of death . . . '

John and I said goodbye in a queue at Nice airport; he thought of coming back to New Zealand to live, I said he must do so. New Zealand was . . . and all the way to Paris, to America, the Pacific, in planes crossing the world, I thought about that, what it was. I realised even before I arrived that absence had produced a curious effect – it turned distance, like a telescope, on to my country. I looked down its long tunnel and through the lens at the end I saw not only my children, my house, family networks as I now knew them; New Zealand itself was there, its land and history, all my experience of it and, dimly, everyone else's as well. I was a New Zealander, and knew it with a sharp new consciousness. Simply by the act of separation I had made my own country a single whole, round and complete and graspable at the end of the long corridor of distance.

There it was, holding within its compass each of the places and times in which I had found a home, right up to the present, still charged as it was with the pain of separateness and the fierce excitement. There was my new population, the community of writers, those with whom I could talk shop (though writers didn't actually talk about work in hand – they couldn't, and neither could I; it had to be private and secret till it was done). They stood about this telescoped landscape, the dearest, closest to me, in the foreground, others in their place, nearer or further away, and I watched them grow slowly larger and clearer as my journey stretched out and brought me towards them.

This, and all my earlier lives, had their place in the capacious expanse of my own country. Islanders we might be – yes, occupants of a small island nation, remote and self-conscious, struggling to separate itself from the old cultures from which it had sprung – but our vision of ourselves and the world could encompass, if we chose, the most far-reaching of human possibilities. Once I had lived in family households in small country towns, behaving, as it were unconsciously, like a New Zealander. Now, having left home for long enough to develop, however slightly, a more detached mode, I had become a conscious, active, deliberate part of the whole. I came home to live by choice. New Zealanders travel widely, this experience must have been familiar to thousands; well, now I had it too.

A week after I arrived the Fairburn book, finished at last, was launched in Auckland. At home, a greater climax awaited me: Trevor announced that he wanted to move from Grass Street and buy his own house in Greytown; and in Mount Maunganui, where Lindsay lived, Doug was lying mortally ill, too weak to be visited. I spoke often by phone to my sister, but I did not see him again. He died just after Christmas.

Publicly the country was still writhing from the effects of the Springbok Tour. This, I thought, was a nation with the beginnings of a new political consciousness, a new awareness of being divided, a willingness to contemplate the unpleasant facts of violence and prejudice so long hidden, evaded, or excused. Every New Zealander would from then on be a little more separate from every other one, slightly more responsible for taking political positions, having opinions. I felt myself to be, probably permanently, part of a minority that would always have to form its own ideas and convictions and be prepared to defend them. I couldn't rely on being vaguely sanctified as a member of a 'good little country'; I had to think for myself.

And then the electorate returned the same old Muldoon government that had allowed the South African footballers to come in the first place. A minority vote, certainly, a tarnished victory, but a victory nonetheless. I was amazed, then profoundly depressed; it seemed that the well-talked-out conclusions of our little enclave of morally anxious expatriates did not have much to do with the political clout of the Rugby Union, or the widespread impression, fostered by Muldoon himself, that protesters were nobodies, weirdos, trendy lefties, not real New Zealanders, ordinary rugby-loving blokes, Rob's Mob, as he horribly called them.

However, my private homecoming held reassurance, as well as change. If Menton had steadily disconnected my known networks, Wellington in those few months did its best to join them together again. Frances and Stephen were in Australia, Martin and Jan in America, but I saw Stephanie and Kathy often and, with them, helped to find Trevor a house in Greytown. It was exactly the right place for him to go, the last of the small towns we'd lived in where he had been really happy. He would be a revered elder, held in special regard by a generation of Kuranui College ex-pupils and parents.

In promoting the in-house separation that had somehow carried us through the final stage of our marriage collapse, I had insisted to myself and everyone else on its suitability and success. Now that it was over I was forced to confront its insufficiencies, largely because Trevor talked to 'the kids' (who then talked to me) about the miseries of being almost in the presence of my separate life, yet not a part of it.

There is no way to hasten the healing of that slow, hurt, lopsided grief at the loss of a marriage. Perhaps by insisting on the shared separation we practised in those hard years I made Trevor's slower accommodation more painful; perhaps it was all we were capable of achieving. Who could tell? Some of my sorrow and perplexity found its way into *On the Te Awamutu Road*, a poem which for a long time I could not read without coming close to tears.

> It was a dark bird, silvery
> in flight, coming quick
> and awkwardly – low too, as though
> already maimed; but that is useless
> now to think of since without
> apparent impact, no thud nor
> syncopated interruption
> of the wheels, I killed it.

> I saw a turning tuft like black
> and silver petals in the wind
> and thought for something like a mile
> that I should stop – and then
> forgot. So it lies
> without reproach, without defence
> among the larger carelessnesses
> left about my life.

We advertised the downstairs half of the house, received thousands of applications and chose two young men in flight from the imposition of martial law in Poland.

Chapter 43

After Trevor's move to Greytown, and the installation of the Poles, I had a kind of relapse, as though marriage, and the separation it had led to, were a psychic malaria whose symptoms never entirely left the system. When one was weak and without resistance they recurred. Alone in my half-house, with strangers downstairs, I was lonely and forlorn. I called up the habits I had learnt in Menton, reminded myself with furious insistence that the solitary person must initiate saving social projects. There, week by week I had done so, carefully placing outings and visits at intervals through my quiet days, but I had always been a foreigner, everything had been provisional. This was permanence. I lived in my own town, among familiar places, expected gatherings – and I was alone. The giant fear that had waited outside the door for my whole life at last turned the handle and came in.

I had no money. I might feel ready for the 'freelance life', but there was no sign that it paid a steady income. I cast about, managed to get a job for a few months investigating literacy levels for the Education Department, and began to pursue my research with the zeal of a conscientious (and financially anxious) journalist; I gathered facts, I interviewed experts, compiled my report. There was also, of course, the work that I called 'my own'; poems written, or begun, in Menton to be shaped and polished for the collection I saw they could become. But without the ballast of a long job like *High Country Weather*, my working day became sporadic and elusive. It slipped through my fingers in unaccountable ways, found me working urgently in the middle of the night, or at first light, yet restless and ineffectual during the hours that the whole world knows are to be apportioned to work.

But however the day managed – got to its feet, tripped, fell, struggled into position again, rushed ahead, flopped – inescapably it advanced to five o'clock; and there it was. Five o'clock. The time, once, for going to the street bar of the Abel Tasman with Beeb and Alistair, to tea with Madame Raynaud or for a gin and tonic with my Menton neighbour William in the garden of the Clos de Peyronnet . . . a brandy with the Manhires in their flat in William Goodenough House . . . a brandy and ginger ale with the General Secretary – yes, even this – in his office. All these versions of the five o'clock finishing line that a working day might reach, whatever its speed, had vanished, while five o'clock itself – or 4.30 or six, or any other time when the season of the day enters its decline – *that* remorselessly remained. The time when the solitary day has to look in the eye that silent beast that has sat out the action, the lassitude, the urgency, and now when it all ends is ready to spring.

I paced up and down. I learned to pour a drink (if I had any wine – it wasn't as cheap as the five francs a bottle the Garavan supermarket charged) and drink it alone, I listened to the radio, I read the paper. I began to think, and understand, more about other people living as I did, and sometimes we rang each other up. Beeb's wife was now permanently in hospital; he was learning to cook; he claimed solitude suited him, yet he too seemed to need the precious telephone.

Margaret, alone among the network of the similarly solitary that interested me now, did not find the condition strange. Painful at times, of course, but not unfamiliar; she had had most of her adult life to learn its mercurial, perplexing quality.

My visits to her began again, and continued as regularly as before, except that now we had our shared travel dramas to recount. In the middle of one of these satisfying reminiscences she said, 'I'm going to give you some money.' She couldn't do that. Everyone knows you don't just give money away.

'You made me stay in all those dreadful hotels,' she said firmly, 'and I saved thousands, and you haven't got anything. Don't fuss' – and she wrote me a cheque for $1,000.

I expostulated, insisted this must be a loan, that only families made such gestures; she said that money wasn't nearly as much to do with morality as most people thought. You could do what you liked with it. I listened admiringly; she was right, of course, she was inspired. I pocketed my perfect gift.

Sometimes when I visited Trevor in Greytown he talked as though we would in some pleasant future be together again. But what surprised me even more about the months following his departure was that I myself was after all quite poorly prepared for it. I missed him. However slight our upstairs-downstairs meetings had been, they represented a link with our richer, warmer past, and some of the sharpness of my new solitude came from the severance of that tie. There were times when I sat at my desk and stared out the window over the harbour, the place where the centre of the house (if not my entire life) somehow lodged, and felt myself to be truly removed from every other human being on earth.

Tristesse d'animal

Here, yes, I am here –
don't you see my hand at the window, waving?

It's all still the same,
tremulous water lifting its face
to the wind, a clock calling over the city

light late on the hills –
and I'm alone, as before.

Where are you, companions
who promised to come
to the very door of the grave

– where did you turn back?
Are you dancing somewhere nearby

or is that only the neighbours?
I might call you
but what language is there for it

– the blood-smear we were born in
the gasp of that strong bitter oxygen
the first taste, the last we shall have.

And then one evening there was a knock on the door and there was Chester. 'Oh,' I said, 'you've come to the back door. Nobody does that.' He brushed aside these idiocies and came in as though he meant to stay – which, as it turned out, fitted the facts.

After our meeting in London I had not thought about him at all, but I was delighted at this surprise appearance. Not merely because he was a writer I admired – though I did – nor because we'd exchanged a few friendly sentences on the other side of the world. The truth was, rather, that he had by chance chosen the very moment of all others when I was least assured in my solitary state. If he'd come before the Menton year Trevor would still have been close by; if he had arrived a few months later I would have re-established my Menton practices of a disciplined routine. Just then – it was March – I was still so deeply dismayed at the sheer *extent* of the solitary life, the huge unchanging silence of it, that his arrival was the advent of a saviour.

He too must have been in some sort of shock; the New Zealand he returned to offered only tiny islands of homecoming in a wide expanse of foreign-ness, and I perhaps was one of them. The result was that we inspired in each other a state of purposeful euphoria which relieved us for the time being of every kind of normal responsibility or rationality.

It seemed that we must talk, eat, sleep, walk, live every moment together, even write our poems together (or at least under the other's eye). Clearly others would understand this necessity, including Chester's wife, my family, Ted – who after all had fallen in love plenty of times himself, and would perfectly accept the undeniable truth of our new state of being. Did we really believe all this? Or was the mere saying of it so delicious, so funny, that we didn't care?

We stayed home; we went out. Suddenly I had a natural partner for all occasions. Chester's presence cured me of the minor anxiety of always having to search for a companion for theatres or restaurants – now I had acquired a taste for them – or go alone. It was a comfort amounting to luxury. Indeed throughout the weeks our shared excitement lasted, it acted, at least for me, as a sort of alchemy that dissolved all the risks and threats of solitude, and even transformed established friendships into minor frivolities; one could take them, or leave them. Chester seemed to think there was too large a social population around us anyway. Some, like John, were wary of him but I shrugged this off with perfect ease; John didn't know him as well as I did, that was all.

My dear friend in Radio Drama, Fergus Dick, also gave a kind of warning.

'I've fallen in love, Fergus,' I said.

'Oh you poor thing. Sit down, I'll get you a glass of water.'

Trevor couldn't bear the sound of Chester's name, and this I did take seriously; indeed, going through the gate of his Greytown house one day I thought, 'This is the house in which I always cry', but even so I thought that, like rough weather, the turbulence would pass and Trevor accept my changed state more calmly.

Then Chester left. He would go home, arrange with his wife and his 'other friend', with whom he partly lived, to leave, return to New Zealand and live with me instead, for ever and ever. For three months we wrote constantly, long, confiding, passionate letters full of plans and literary references; we made tender declarations by long-distance telephone, induced in ourselves and each other a delicate waiting poise. Everything else waited for us too – for the spring, when our true lives would begin. I told Chester carefully of the shedding of the leaves of a silver birch across the valley from my bedroom window; when its new green appeared he would be here. This gentle, luminous image of ourselves, the parted lovers comforting each other, became our reality; we were as convinced by it as if we had pieced it together out of the daily grind of twenty years of co-habiting. Our future was assured.

And so it remained for several months after his return. A long time, really, longer than we deserved, considering the infinite artlessness of the beliefs on which our union was based. We began blissfully – also properly, in that I arranged for him to meet my friends. We went for walks, prepared dinners, whatever seemed appropriate for the main figures in my private landscape. Beeb, Fiona and Ted were the first to be drawn into this carefully contrived social operation, and each performed with valiant good humour. Yet the occasions laboured through a haze of artificiality that everyone seemed helpless to lighten or disperse.

I observed that other friends regarded Chester and me with an odd kind of smiling, rather indulgent detachment, as if we were children playing house. Yes yes, this toy kitchen was perfect for cooking, this imaginary bed just right for sleeping, our bright vision of our own happy-ever-after touching, and sweet. There there dears, they almost said. I was puzzled by this attitude, and suffered from an urge to explain how deeply, permanently authentic we were, but these attempts never went well. 'Of course if you say so . . . ' hung unsatisfactorily about in the air afterwards. More and more often we were left alone, which rather suited Chester because he was far less gregarious than I. We could turn our attention to educating our families in the new way.

When he visited his clan, they appeared to conduct dignified conversations about books, films and the state of the country. My visits, held in Greytown, were, on the contrary, fraught with tormented accusations, angry repudiations of my present state. I could of course do what I liked, but I was not to think anyone would ever visit me at Grass Street, or regard it any longer as home . . . Trevor thought I should not continue to live in a house he partly owned; I should pay him for my share and move out. I was dismayed by this proposal, though I did come to acknowledge a kind of justice in it.

In the event it led to our first unsettling, our first awareness of the repercussions Chester and I might expect, as our joyful rearrangement of destiny settled into the minds of our friends and families. When he returned after a family weekend visit, I told him of Trevor's sobering proposal and suggested that perhaps it was time for us to talk of money.

We did – or we tried, but almost at once we were stuck in a morass of prosaic realities; confused ideas of 'fair' and 'unfair' rocked our loving equilibrium. The unpleasant possibility that we might be selfish, disloyal, superficial, flowed into our conversation, leaving dark streaks on its attractive surfaces. Miserably, Chester went to the kitchen to prepare something for dinner and put a plate for warming straight onto a live element. It broke. I burst into tears.

Nothing went right. I returned from my next Greytown visit to meet Chester on his way to a restaurant because I was late and he was hungry. A week before I would have laughed and cajoled him; now I wept again. There seemed no end to the trivialities that could ensnare us; it was as though we'd both forgotten that life could contain housework and shopping and bad temper and bills; they crowded round us like a hostile gang coming out of its ambush.

However, we didn't quarrel, or not much. Our ending was as gentle and childlike as everything else in our sparkling, opinionated, doomed association. We cried a lot, we talked and talked about our failure without in the least understanding what it was – indeed I only discovered long after Chester had gone back to England the real character of my own hopes, the aspirations that had propelled me into my 'year of the spectacular mistake'. A first glimmer of understanding came out of my unexpected relief that life had returned to normal. So, it had a 'normal'? Something in me sat down, fluffed its feathers, settled into position; my friends moved back into the positions I recognised, my family shrugged and began again to visit me. Even my solitude, though I still thought of it as 'unnatural', began to look like a comfortable place to be. Chester had brought with him, and left behind, some final proof that I no longer wanted to arrange myself, my time, my thoughts and feelings, into a mosaic shaped with some one else – however beautiful and intricate the result might be.

I had carried with me like a hidden germ some old idea of love-for-ever, a kind of birthright, always possible, always precious, the only real insurance against the loneliness that lay somewhere ahead when one was adrift in old age. There, in a dim beslippered place, would be a familiar loving person making tea, lighting fires, keeping an unfriendly world from the door. I looked askance at this vision and asked myself if I had projected Chester into my own future. The future? Did it exist? If you tried to learn to live in the present, as I had been doing in discovering the 'life of choice', did the future then fade away into obscurity, where perhaps it belonged? The life together Chester and I had imagined – was it a mirage, and this the real reason it had vanished as soon as the mean particularities of money and obligations touched it?

To sleep and wake with another person, to breakfast together and plan the day, to laugh at discrepancies in plans and purposes – and Chester often made me laugh – to fall easily into the words and gestures of love: all this had at first been an endless delight. Best of all was the agreement to allow without comment – by a sort of literary tact – the private periods each might suddenly need to have for a piece of writing, a poem. To work at my desk in what had become 'our' room while outside the window my friend also wrote or read, exposing his pale now-English skin to the good New Zealand sun – this had been a delicate pleasure. To read drafts of poems to him and consider his astringent comments was another; sometimes in those months it had seemed to me that the poems I wrote were becoming shorter, more pungent, more like Chester's own, but he maintained that our separateness in style and outlook remained intact.

Certainly he was a crisp and clear-headed critic, and addressed the poem, not me, when I asked for his opinion. Sometimes his questions made me bolder, more brave in the next draft. It was a kind of collaboration I'd never dreamed of, to spend my days with a poet of distinction who didn't mind acting the useful critic. Our shared ruminations about writing became at times wonderfully knitted in to our ordinary life; one day as he was brushing his hair after shaving I came to the bathroom door with a draft of a very small poem I called *Signs*, a reflection on the breaking of a marriage, a subject with which I was always preoccupied.

SIGNS

> The pronoun is
> a tiny instrument we use
> to unpick our lives; so 'I'
> and 'you' begin to show
> beneath the old shared knots
> of 'us', so 'ours' is spoilt for 'mine'.
> We do not know the dreadful pleasure
> of our industry until
> the rag's too weak to take
> the weight of joy or compromise,
> the pull and tear of love.

'Why compromise?' asked my consultant; 'why the *weight* of compromise?' I could not answer very coherently, though we might well have pursued the matter. Neither of us realised its connection with our own fragile circumstances. Nor did we notice that in middle age (Chester was in his sixties, I approaching mine) settled habits filled us up like old clinkers in a newly lit fire.

This moment of mystification about my scrap of a poem was a pivot on which the larger issues of living together invisibly turned. The weight of compromise it was that came down on us and crushed the shaky harmony we'd composed. Neither of us observed the evidence, obvious to everyone else, that after whole lifetimes of different ways of living and thinking, the only possible way to live together would have been to allow immense distances around each other's separateness. We'd believed instead that love by itself wiped out all other habits, all familiar patterns. Love . . . Heavens, we might as well have made our vows on a Hollywood film set.

I was in the end ashamed of the cavalier way in which I'd hurtled in and out of this relationship, and appalled at the unreality of its shape in my mind. Second adolescence indeed – it looked as though I'd never left the first. Chester himself was for a time very angry; the disruption of his life had after all been much greater than any I'd suffered. But he was a gentle, intelligent man and we did afterwards meet in London and manage to make a milder judgement of our shared absurdity, to forgive and be forgiven.

I came eventually to realise that this episode, more than anything else I did, shook me out of the confusion and abandonment of those years, and brought me to a sober acknowledgement of a new reality.

My independent life was not after all a simple reversal of all that had gone before. Living freely was not a matter of doing what you liked; it was a way of understanding a different system of living, with new limits, new disciplines. You had a larger share in making the rules, that was all. The second adolescence, like the first, had to move to adulthood to achieve its merely sketched maturity; experiment had to be judged, and perhaps put aside.

Stung by the thrust of my own mistakes I found, however, that my Pandora's box, like all others, contained a whisper of hope and reassurance. For one thing Chester and I, unfitted as we were for our great adventure, yet retained a small residue in the form of a correspondence and the exchange of poems, sometimes written for each other. And I discovered that, despite everything, I had learned my impossible lesson – or at least come close enough to it for my life to acquire a sense and stability it had not had for all those 'new' years. I had found out, probably as much as I ever would, how to be alone. While I wrestled with the question in Menton, then abandoned it with Chester, it appeared to have worked away behind the scenes and found its answer. Provisional perhaps, but more real and certain than ever before.

I remembered how I'd learned, day by empty day in Menton, to hold on, stand my ground, to survive; nothing more. And now it seemed that survival had given me a new kind of skin, slightly stronger and stiffer than the old one, one in which I could stand up without too much wavering, in any weather. Life like a well-tailored suit instead of the soft blouse of my enclosed, complying years.

As if in confirmation of this phenomenon, the detachment I'd for so long wanted in my writing (coupled with immediacy, of course) now appeared, said critics and readers, in the *Catching it* poems, and others that followed. Some new knowledge – an inkling of the way to stand close to friends and family without needing them too greatly – had, by a mysterious process, communicated itself to the page on which I wrote. I had often said that a poem was itself a gift, not an accomplishment; so, now, was this long-hoped-for balance, or poise – whatever it was – which had crept into the words and phrases and silences of poems and given them a little more of their own authority, a little less of mine.

The year after Chester left I re-wrote *High Country Weather*. My frantic excitement at finishing it in Menton had been followed by disenchantment and unease; for months it lay ignored in its box, occasionally I took it out and scowled at it as at a recalcitrant child who refuses to admit to gross (though hidden) misdemeanours. Then Caroline lent me Salman Rushdie's *Midnight's Children* and about halfway through this enticing fantasy my problem with my own book suddenly leapt into focus. Here was a story in which the teller stood outside himself, making surprised or ironic comments on his own past – that was it! I could do it too. Without so much as a grateful thought for Rushdie, I tossed his book aside and pounced on my own.

After several months of hectic engagement with it I emerged to look the world in the face again. Bridget had successfully established her new firm; when I asked her who I should give my manuscript to she simply answered 'me'. My book was launched at a summer Sunday party at Bridget's house on the other side of the harbour.

Through all this time my family friendships, as I liked to call them, expanded their margins as new partnerships were formed, journeys made and returned from, children born. I eagerly corresponded with those who travelled – far more eagerly indeed than they felt the need to do – felt again with each new birth that keen stab of amazement, the surge of love, which had so shaken me with Ruth's arrival. The next baby bore an Arab name, Jamil – the beautiful. When we first saw him at a few months old he was lovely indeed, a pale shapely flower fast asleep on a small canvas as he was wheeled towards us at the air terminal. And the third grandchild brought my new three-tiered family condition even closer. Crispin was born in Wellington and lived the first few weeks of his life in my house – a more immediate miracle than the first two births, which had taken place when I was on the other side of the world. This infant slept and woke near me, cried when I could hold him, stretched, curled up again, began to focus that faraway wandering gaze within which a baby prepares for its entry into the sudden world. When the family left I recovered only slowly from the dismay and melancholy of a return to silence and emptiness in my house.

When Frances and Stephen returned from their journeys to England and America they too decided to have a child. Frances by this time had a significant and growing reputation in the theatre; her life had a rhythm which quite startlingly removed it from all others, except those of her own kind. She, like other actors, appeared to work all day at rehearsals, singing or dancing classes, or other kinds of limbering up, then perform at night and at last have time to talk to friends in the theatre bar after the show, at midnight, or later. I supposed they slept in an exhausted trance through the hours left before morning. Suddenly Frances announced that she wanted to change all this 'unnaturalness'. The time had come to live at a lasting address (they had moved house often), take on a permanent phone number, grow a garden, buy a car that didn't break down; above all, have a baby.

After Tess was born Frances told me that motherhood was fantastic, exhilarating (my own feeling exactly) and that this was the best role she'd ever played. When Stephen rang up with news of the birth of their baby I said, 'How do you feel?', and in a low-key laconic tone he replied, 'I don't suppose I've ever been so happy.'

Family gatherings, however, were another matter. Christmas could be terrible. The deep divisions between Trevor and me, covered over by constant acts of co-operation during the year, erupted into violent quarrelling when we came together for the express purpose of celebrating family connectedness. Usually we began well. The events of the year – mainly visits to Trevor's new ménage, the elegant old house which I often cleaned and tidied for him, the garden where I weeded and planted – gave us a convincing enough vocabulary to begin the intense proximity of several days in the same house. But as the level of conviviality rose we each began to assert our real selves, more and more at variance with the other and, worse, in some obscure way in competition.

Of course the reason, or at least the source, of competitiveness between Trevor and me in the presence of our children should not have been obscure to anyone. We'd practised it for years. Nevertheless each time we were blown together by a gale of familiar Christmas eagerness, childlike Christmas secrecy and planning, I for one was newly hopeful, newly convinced, that not a single cross word would pass between us. That's what separation was for.

By the second or third day – if not before – we were in an uproar. The others joined in or drew back according to temperament; children cried, or gave a collective shrug of resignation and played with their new toys. By the end of the festivities we were all rather ashamed; resolutions would be talked over and half formally made, to ensure that such inglorious performances could never be seen again. And then the next year it would be the same, or worse.

Looking back, I could see that an aspect of our infinitely slow, infinitely contradictory moving apart had been our poor performance for each other. Trevor was thought of by his friends in Greytown as a warm, compassionate, thoughtful man; to me he seemed characteristically churlish and complaining. There is no doubt that I too offered him the worst self I could muster. Perhaps it was a measure of how long and hard had been the route to a real separateness from each other, we who had so assiduously bound our lives together over many years, and begun to do so when so young. Had that been our first real mistake?

Occasionally I asked myself why it mattered so much that Trevor and I should try to be friends at all. There was one simple reason, that he needed help in setting up his own household and I believed in a kind of family loyalty that could survive such changes as marriage separation. I knew too that the shared habits of our past had taught me a thorough familiarity with domestic management but left him with almost no knowledge of it at all. The washing, ironing, cleaning, planning that were almost automatic for me were to him a great labour.

The division of our occupations into those proper for a man and a woman had been even sharper than I'd thought, more mutually exclusive. In retirement, alone in his own house, Trevor was endlessly perplexed. Often he rang up to ask for advice; I fell into a habit of support and encouragement that was not unlike the one we'd developed years before, when he'd felt that first dismay at the alarming requirements of headmastering. I felt virtuous, useful, good. But there was, could I have listened to it, behind the voice of this respectable friend, a cry from the anxious wanderer who still lurked in me, still keeping home in mind. On that level I had not yet distinguished between Trevor's home and mine; they remained the same. I walked in as of right, to help in the house, to plan or plant in the garden. It was clear that he was now learning my job, as I was learning his, and, as though naturally, I helped.

There were crucial differences, of course, and one was in our patterns of friendship. Teachers in the time of Trevor's career had moved about a good deal, but in each place they had come home to the same compelling milieu of class relations, staffroom shop talk, the conviviality of sports teams and education politics, the companionship of drinks together in the pub or club at the end of the week. Friendship was another name for the fullest experience of working together, being colleagues. Trevor had understood it well and practised it so successfully that now, without this natural overflow from the routines of working – and of course without work itself, in the old sense – he had lost his community, and could not for a long time see how to find or create another. In Greytown he was, as before, liked and respected, but he had no habit of spontaneous association, seemed to know nothing of the arrangement of visits and occasions. When we lived together I had done this for us both; school had produced its own.

We talked of this question a great deal. It seemed to me that if I could only convince him of the great rewards in organising one's life to accommodate and include other people, his loneliness would be solved. I talked in eager proselytising bursts of my Menton experience in learning the trick of solitude. Trevor portrayed himself as an uncompleted circle, I sometimes thought, then turned and handed you the chalk. It was very inviting. I felt useful, he appeared reassured, though few of the changes proposed ever actually occurred. Advice-giving had become a habit that sustained me and appeared to do him no harm.

Later I was chastised by the family, or some of its members, for this helpful involvement in Trevor's struggles. My reply, when I had one, was that I believed that late friendships were possible for people like us who could no longer meet each other's more intimate and fundamental requirements. I did believe it too; I preached a sort of continuing, if intermittent, sermon on the subject in a thousand conversations with Trevor in Greytown, on the phone, or on his much rarer visits to my house in town. The breaking apart of a marriage, even the separate living it entailed, were not enough, apparently, to scotch my long-held faith in the power and centrality of the family. We had come to an end as husband and wife, but were we not parents still, old friends who had shared the largest part of our adult lives, devised together our earliest and most far-reaching aspirations? We surely could not disentangle our mixed destinies entirely, even if we wanted to – so my argument familiarly went. But the wariness, and sometimes the indignation, of family members worried me. It was as though they wanted us above all to finish our separation, however little they liked it, and be done with it.

There were times – usually when I was at home, not in Greytown – when I felt a rush of admiration for Trevor, simply because he did manage, however incompletely, to conduct his own household and live in it, in the state of solitude he hated but could not change. Men of his generation, leaving a marriage, far more commonly formed new alliances, usually with women years younger than themselves. Trevor simply battled on. He complained a lot, grew depressed, asked for advice he never took, continually resisted his fate – and yet, as months and years passed, there he was, doing his daily shopping, choosing carpet for an upstairs room, buying a winter heater designed to warm large old houses, never actually letting go of the daily complexities thrust upon him by an unkind destiny.

I sometimes thought of his powerful resistance to every kind of risk or change when we had lived together, and how maddening a quality I had found this to be. No doubt he had it still, but it seemed to me that later life, his as well as mine, had a way of requiring, beyond all refusal, that you attempted what you had failed to master earlier. For him this meant change of the most central kind, constructing for himself the machinery of daily life which the two major institutions he'd known, school and home, had always before provided.

My good fortune, which I shared with thousands of other women who were feeling their way into independence, was that 'work' could easily be grafted on to old habits of domestic planning. Women everywhere were by now managing separate lives and occupations; some marriages had survived the change, others, like mine, had not. But in either case women, however they lived and worked, could not lose their long-practised habits of sustaining those close by, including themselves. You might become lazy or preoccupied, but, as with the riding of a bicycle, you could not actually forget how to cook or clean or wash clothes or go shopping, to keep the enterprise of being alive up on its feet and in some fashion moving forward.

The difference for Trevor was that his second life, the one after marriage, was something he didn't want and didn't really believe in. It wasn't a matter of new opportunities, adventures, experiments, as mine was; in a quite fundamental way I think he felt that he had done his work. Keeping house was minor and trivial. A man of his time, he probably thought still that it was a woman's work and only an unfair world could expect it of him. But there it was. I too could see that the logic of his life asked for a far lower key than the grand chorus of earlier phases, and I was sorry for it.

I was, of course, very reticent about the much more adventurous weather in which my daily journeys were made. However frightened

I might be, however hidden and incomprehensible my direction, the awareness of possibilities greater than myself, or my own powers, never left me. Trevor, already by temperament inclined to hold to familiar things and repudiate change, could not fail to see that his time of achievement by now lay far back in the past, and though reminders of it recurred, in visits from ex-pupils and in the affectionate appreciation of Greytown parents he still knew, the good years, as he sometimes called them himself, were slipping further and further away.

The axis of the family had changed too. Some of this was the natural shift of emphasis that comes with aging, the establishment of later loyalties, new families, fresh adult perspectives that take little account of the old family, now come to its decline. One Christmas that actually did proceed to an exhausted but not acrimonious end suggested that this was an easy transition. It was held in Hawke's Bay after Kathy's marriage to Bruno, that highly civilised young man, member of one of the old landed clans of the district but with an adventurous rural consciousness of his own. They were warm and generous hosts; the occasion was for me a kind of rite of passage, however troubled other aspects of the growing of the family and the breaking of its patterns might be.

But behind this natural movement of the generations, appropriately enacted in the pastoral setting of the Hawke's Bay countryside, divisions persisted. Some grew more complex and intractable as the years of our separation continued and, not having been recognised or understood, they could not now easily be healed.

Chapter 44

The day of the 1984 election in New Zealand I went to Australia. I had not meant to be away for what I believed would be the most significant electoral drama since 1935, it was simply that, like everyone else, I didn't know it was to happen till a few weeks before it did. The National government that had allowed the 1981 tour without being driven from office was three years later so tarnished, the Labour Party so convincing under its large and eloquent new leader David Lange, that a Labour win seemed inevitable.

I was only one of many thousands who saw this as the rightful fulfilment of a process that had begun with the 'civil war' of the tour. If I had regarded myself then as part of a thoughtful minority, hitherto largely unheard in the rugby-racing-and-beer culture we had inherited, by 1984 I believed this had changed. We had emerged from our confused and inarticulate silence into a proper consciousness of national aspirations, and the election of a Labour government would confirm our maturity.

Mine was a working, which is to say a reading, tour, the first I had ever made. Australian audiences taught me how to read – publicly, from a platform. It was impossible to remain self-conscious among people who laughed and clapped so readily, commented and agreed or disagreed with such amazing immediacy and directness. By the time I came home I knew there was a good chance I'd be offered a term as writer-in-residence at Deakin University in Geelong, an hour's drive from Melbourne through the grey, spare Australian countryside. One journey seemed to breed others, in the most remarkable way.

And indeed once you'd embarked on this game of New Zealander Abroad it revealed a whole set of rules and conditions I had never supposed could apply to me. Nor did I think that my longest and most crucial journey, the year in Menton, had itself generated others; no, it was this business of standing up in front of foreign audiences and saying (in some fashion), 'This is New Zealand, we write poems, some of us, here are a few of mine . . . ' When you'd done it once, and learnt how not to die of fright every time you saw a microphone, you were on the way to knowing how to do it again, somewhere else. You were on the board, as it were, had passed 'go', and the hazards ahead were whatever a dice throw might decide for you.

In just this way the Cambridge Poetry Festival blew up, apparently out of nowhere, the next year. Cambridge. Cambridge England, that is, the legendary city. Reading the letter of invitation I felt like an All Black summoned to his first trials. Miranda was staying with me, I was busy and left opening my mail till late in the day; when I read the incredible statement I called out to her, occupied in the kitchen preparing children's tea, 'Hey' – in a dry squeak of a voice – 'I've been asked to go to Cambridge – ' Nothing changed, the household went on functioning prosaically, but in that bemused moment standing in my room, with the late light rolling its mellow pageant across the harbour, and the mild sound of children's chatter coming from the kitchen, I felt something new turn over in me, stand up and stretch, ready for whatever was to come.

There had been so much that was new and strange, I could now hardly remember the condition of habit and predictability, the settled expectations of those family years I'd now moved so far away from. Each day could produce a letter, a phone call, a message, even a sudden impulse in myself, that could shake the ground I stood on, perhaps alter again what had just settled the day before. And here it was again, a different kind of jumping off into the void. If journeys are to be taken, I thought, standing there with my letter and staring out the window, if that's it, all right then, I'll take them.

I had always wanted to go to Russia, Tolstoy's country, and Chekhov's. Now I could do so: Air Japan flew to Moscow on the way to London. I entered an airport that felt like a vast, chaotic country market, and went to live for a week in a city of nine million that still seemed like a country town, though one filled with ancient treasures and amazingly eloquent people. Tolstoy was there, in bronze in the garden of the Writers' Union, and a modern poet, Kuprianov, also en route to Cambridge, who read me his poems late one night at supper with his friends – potatoes and sardines and cognac, and wonderful conversation, vivid and cultivated, yet intimate too, and full of laughter.

Cambridge held revelations of a different kind. In rooms of stately splendour ('cathedrals you don't go to church in,' said my Russian friend), I listened to poets from Europe and the world, performing, in a hundred different ways, poems resounding with an infinite variety of meanings and echoes. Still tingling with these dense and exhilarating exchanges, I went to London to read at New Zealand House, then briefly to the strange, darkly beautiful north, to Newcastle.

I came home to New Zealand to a still-tenanted house, so moved about the country, staying with Frances in Auckland and Kathy in Hawke's Bay, Stephanie in Wellington and Trevor, briefly, in Greytown, waiting to go to Australia. Lifting a pram down some steps at Frances's house I slipped and gashed my shin, supposed so slight a wound would quickly heal, ignored my daughters' advice about medical help, and in the end nearly lost my leg. I spent three weeks in the orthopaedic ward of Wellington Hospital and went to Australia festooned with skin grafts.

There, when I wasn't working or talking, eating, drinking, often laughing with Australians, I explored Melbourne and its bizarre countryside of sudden rocks and mountains, including Hanging Rock (where I went for a picnic with friends from the university). One night when I went home, as always, to my small lace-decorated suburban house to read and potter, the phone rang. Vincent. He was working in Adelaide so this was not too surprising.

'What are you doing in November?' he asked.

'Going home.'

'No you're not, you're going to London.'

I'd been to London, I told him, once a year was quite enough; I'd finished with travelling.

He went on anyway, telling me with a wonderful selfless excitement how overjoyed he was that my book *(which one?)* had won the Australasia-Pacific section of the Commonwealth Poetry Prize *(the what?)*, that it had been a tough field but the judges *(who?)* had been unanimous. He kept repeating this, but since I'd never heard of any such event, or been in any way involved with prizes or competitions, I found it hard to take him seriously. However, Vincent was so exuberant it seemed tactless to say *Oh yeah?* so I just thanked him, and privately resolved to go home as I'd planned in November. When they rang in the morning to tell me officially, I was to sound surprised (that at least was easy); his call was that of a friend keen to be first with the news. Dear Vincent, what nonsense, I thought, pacing round the house afterwards – and what was all this talk of thousands of pounds? Was he hallucinating? Was I?

Well, the call came; a Dr Syd Harrex, chairman of a panel of judges, experts in Commonwealth Literature, told me they'd met and held long deliberations with the result that my *Selected Poems* (entered by the publisher, I discovered) had indeed won the £1,000 that was the regional prize for this part of the world. The world, or the Commonwealth, had been divided into five: Australasia and the Pacific; North America; Asia; the United Kingdom and its territories (Gibraltar, Malta, the Republic of Ireland . . .); and Africa. The system was one of local judging by a panel of academics, followed by a final when representatives from each region would meet in London and agree on an overall winner. It sounded inescapably like a Miss World contest. In order to win the big prize – £5,000 – would we wear svelte bathing suits, glittering high-heeled shoes, posh coiffures?

It was hard to associate any of these fancies with the writing of poetry but the very absurdity of the thing began to be rather a pleasure. I had to have my photo taken with the local manager of British Airways, and one afternoon in their Melbourne office on the corner of Elizabeth Street I stood with him in front of a large plastic model of a BA plane, held a poetry prize brochure in my hand and faced the camera with a wide asinine smile. I never saw the photo, which I suppose was destined for an in-flight magazine, but I imagine I looked incapable of writing a nursery rhyme, let alone a whole volume of poems.

Gradually I came to believe in the ridiculous affair sufficiently to make plans to leave. I gave final readings in Melbourne, said rather preoccupied farewells, made my way to the VIP lounge in the British Airways quarter of the air terminal. There I was invited to drink unlimited gin-and-tonics, read *The Times* or the *Daily Telegraph* and sit in a leather armchair among unmistakably British businessmen. I had with some difficulty changed my flight, going a day earlier than I'd planned, in response to a letter from the librarian at the Commonwealth Institute in London. It said that the five finalists were to gather there on Sunday 24 November, four days before the presentation ceremony. Did this give the judges time to look us over thoroughly? Would we give sample readings? Hold forth in our local vernacular? Dance and sing?

Actually, for several days we did nothing at all, not even meet each other. I stayed in a cramped little hotel in Kensington, a block or two from the Commonwealth Institute, in a state of complete anonymity – except that it appeared my bill was being paid by some nameless authority. Phone calls to the institute were met with an inscrutable silence, no messages came, I was left to observe, as best I might, hotel guests who might turn out to be the other finalists. I didn't ever find the courage to approach any of them, so by the time I arrived at the reception I had met nobody, and had not the remotest idea why I had been so urgently summoned days before the event. (In a mood of slight truculence, I had, in the end, spent my time going Christmas shopping in wintry, Dickensian London.)

I did meet Fleur Adcock, who seemed to know a good deal more than I did about the Commonwealth Institute, the prize and the secret deliberations connected with it. The panel of judges, drawn, as we finalists were, from all parts of the Commonwealth, had, it seemed, been holding meetings right through the days of silence. In the interests of neutrality they had been instructed not to meet the contestants themselves, while they were discussing questions of local validity and universal significance in the poetry before them. It did occur to me that it could not be beyond the scope of some organiser to have arranged for us to meet one another, but this, apparently, was not the English way.

On the afternoon of the party, due to begin at five o'clock (I never received an invitation but Fleur gave me hers as a souvenir), I crouched on the bed in my tiny hotel bedroom paralysed by fright. I worried about my Melbourne-bought blouse, about the weather (it rained), about how to get into the institute, which I had skirted nervously round a day or two before; most of all, I worried about how one was expected to behave. No, most of all, I wondered about who would win the prize, since I had convinced myself absolutely that it could not be me.

When I crept in through an entrance of some sort I found myself in the photocopying room. A languid young man (who turned out to be the secretary) said, 'You can't come in here.' I withdrew hastily, and tried a woman behind a desk. 'You're the winner,' she said. 'Yes,' I assured her, 'we're all winners, so far.' Then some large doors opened, someone gave me a drink and I went into an enormous room crowded with strangers.

And then everything changed. For one thing, the drooping secretary came up to me, now that recognition was, it seemed, allowed by the rules, and summoned me to a corner of the room where he whispered, kindly after all, that he didn't think it fair for me to be confronted with the news at the moment it was announced so he would give me ten minutes' warning – there it was – congratulations – was I all right? I suppose I answered him, but from that time onward I was in a kind of trance, a hypnosis for which the instructions came from public occasions I'd known. I met the others, we chatted, sat down in the front row for the speeches, did our own readings, I looked casual. We all did, I think. There was a big, handsome, easy-spoken North American called Gary, a rather brusque white African from Zambia (he had won the old Commonwealth Poetry Prize for a best first book, and was to tour with us the week after the presentation), a tiny delicate Indian gentleman with a beautiful smile and, I later discovered, a string of degrees including a high-powered one in economics, the Irishman I'd heard about – bearded, shaggy, very engaging, with a musical Irish lilt to his speech. There should have been someone else, a black poet from Ghana, but he arrived later and differently, coming down the aisle just before the ceremony in a white toga with a splendid embroidered swathe across his shoulder and a retinue of followers. The finalists were all men except me. Fancy that.

For the rest of the evening I only knew what happened by watching: someone was there, performing like myself. Here she was, this creature in the silk blouse moving forward to read the prescribed number of poems, listening to speeches by the Director of the Commonwealth Institute, someone from British Airways, the chairman of the judges' panel (the Australian poet Peter Porter). In a dream-like sequence others went to receive envelopes containing their £1,000. Beautiful Vikram from India, Gary the amiable Canadian, Kobena in his white robe and orange mantle and Michael, sturdy and grand all at once, my Irish rival; and Tim, the stiff but stalwart African who sounded like Ian Smith (but had radically different opinions). Finally, there was this facsimile of myself, walking slowly forward to take the blue envelope labelled 'Overall Winner', then standing for cameras with Sonny Ramphal, smiling, shaking hands, listening to journalists making appointments for interviews, smiling at congratulations, answering small questions, smiling again, smiling, smiling . . .

One reporter insisted that we go into a quiet room and tape an interview at once so he could get it into the overnight news to New Zealand; so the zombie who looked like me followed him obediently, sat down and began to burble on about the implications of the new prize, the state of New Zealand's literature, the place of her work in it, the role of women, and much else besides. (For several months afterwards I dreaded any mention of this news item, and my no doubt fatuous share in it; eventually I heard it and found to my surprise that the automaton who functioned for me that night actually spoke quite realistically and sensibly, committed no extravagances: the ways of the human organism are more devious than I had supposed.)

There was a buffet dinner somewhere in the institute and I met the panel of judges at last; women were not much in evidence here either. Out of a total of ten there was one, a professor of English from the University of Hyderabad, small and charming in a gold and black sari. But the person I most enjoyed talking to was Lewis Ncosi, a professor of literature from Lusaka where he taught at the University of Zambia; he was a handsome black man, twinkling, quick-witted, full of fun. When we left – I was to go to a nearby pub with some of my new friends – he kissed me enthusiastically and asked me to come to Zambia. What a good idea.

The pub was so packed you couldn't move and so noisy you couldn't hear a word, just the roar. Again I saw myself as from a distance, jammed into the crowd in this unknown London pub, half listening to the erudite conversation being either muttered or shouted beside me, staring about with a glazed expression, incapable of any more intelligent contribution myself than 'yes, very hot . . . yes, quite tired . . . ' as Gary the Canadian, on my other side, began to talk of going home (he'd been in the hotel for days too, as anonymous as I).

When I got into my cell I rang reception and asked if I could call New Zealand. 'Oh God!' he exploded, 'that's the limit – I've already got calls in to Taiwan, Saudi Arabia and Malaysia. What's the matter – have you all gone mad?' 'I'll wait,' I said humbly and sat down to open the blue envelope. The cheque had a big blob of white ink with '5' typed over it before all the 000s. This amateurish reminder of the arbitrariness of my elevation to great riches suddenly brought it home to me, and there, in my little cubby hole with a London winter fog thickening outside, I laughed and laughed.

And then we all went on tour, a curious and often poignant connecting of our widely differing experiences, and the poetry we had created out of it in our various English languages, with the place where English began. Belfast, still troubled in the present by divisions begun centuries before, was our history too; so was quaintly eighteenth-century Tunbridge Wells; and Hull, where Philip Larkin had just died. Indeed, there were three deaths of notable English poets during the week of our tour – Larkin, Geoffrey Grigson and Robert Graves. It almost seemed as though an old guard had thought it time to make an exit, now that newer, younger Commonwealth voices had come to be heard.

We separated at Belfast, as regretfully as if we'd known one another for years. In London Fleur made me promise to bank my cheque because she said if I kept carrying it round and looking at it I'd lose it. Oxford Street was a huge Christmas fairyland, all the decorations in the world in one place, and frosty weather as well. I saw two robins. Then I came home to celebrations by summer picnic of a festival that seemed to have lost its meaning without the winter solstice with which it began, long before Christianity took it over. But there were pohutu-kawas ablaze on Oriental Parade in a hot Wellington December; I was glad to be home.

I took other journeys – to America, Germany, Canada, Australia again – but the end of this one really marked the close of a cycle. The new life now seemed a good deal less new, more habitual, though it hadn't done away with its capacity to surprise; rather, as I'd realised in London, one could get used to the recurringly unexpected. And mine did continue to grow. One of its new components was the experience of performance that I thought I'd learnt in Australia, but had now practised much more extensively on platforms and stages and steps, in rooms and cafés and seminar cubicles, in unfamiliar corners of the world and far from home.

This, of course, was a version of a 'literary circuit' which many thousands of writers had already traversed; I hadn't discovered it. Indeed, if the second life I'd now been living for ten years or so was built out of rules and conditions I made up for myself, not those dictated by parents and teachers, how did it happen that I found myself not making up, but simply joining, occupations that had always been there? Perhaps all one did was to interpret experience, to be there, watch, be ready to recognise and understand the world, and take part in its carnivals, its crises. These journeys, for instance, had appeared from nowhere, yet perhaps it was some new readiness in me that allowed them to happen. No matter how terrified I felt, I did after all always say 'yes'. Dunstan had said that the French have a good word for this state of mind – *disponible,* the being available, ready, disposed towards. You have to be that, he said, before even the most apparently accidental events can occur.

And then came one that could not have been accidental at all, but must have been lying in wait for a long time before it leapt out like an angry stranger and dealt me a sharp blow. It was not actually an event, though some of its impact came to me by letter, but a dramatic change of position within the family. Two of its members suddenly – and then persistently – expressed such rage towards me that it took me a long time to grasp the fact that it was happening and longer still to understand the reasons for it.

The difficult process of doing so became a reckoning, a reappraisal of the whole shape of my later life. The expanded opportunities, my sense of the stretching of powers long unrealised, aspirations long denied, all the rich, risky joy of these last years had, I'd thought, been fashioned out of a newly found present, the immediate moment that gave me its full flavour if I knew how to take it. I'd learnt, I believed, to do what is called living in the moment – indeed poetry was a quintessential expression of this very act, or capacity. Suddenly I saw, or painfully began to see, that this new life of mine was in reality built out of old materials, that it was as deeply connected with the past as every other phase of growth. No child can stand without first sitting, speak without listening, chattering, babbling; each is a gathering together of old experience and moving ahead to new and more interesting ways of using it. It's a departure into a new solitude. I'd thought I understood solitude to the last degree, but I was wrong. The rough, sometimes cruel teaching of my children told me why.

Chapter 45

In one sense nothing much happened. I had a few encounters, a phone call or two, angry letters; but most of the period of estrangement was simply a silence. I spent much of the time in intense turmoil, I talked to my compassionate friends, sometimes to sympathetic members of the family – till this made them impatient too, and I had to wrestle with the question on my own. I asked myself a thousand times what could be the reason for this shattering of an old and natural affection; parents and children grew away from one another of course – but surely this had already happened years before . . . the journeys, the living in other countries, did these not confirm such a separation? Such reflections, however logical to me, changed nothing. I remained as I was, distressed and mystified.

There was Trevor to talk to, of course; as the other parent he could be expected to have useful insights. However, he did not have any such thing. His own family relationships were in a simple unruptured state. Did he sympathise with me in my misery? I wasn't sure. Certainly he grew tired of my insistence, as others had, and that cautioned me. We could still quarrel, and dry, hard, hurting affairs quarrels were, a hacking cough of the emotions.

At home, I began a practice of scrutinising the recent past, looking for clues. I surveyed as critically as I could those first jazzy years when in the eyes of my children and their friends I had been the only liberated woman for miles around, if not anywhere on earth. I thought of the youngsters who had wailed, 'Why isn't my mother like you – we can *talk* to you . . . '; and how open and intimate that talk had been, how pleasant a contrast, it seemed, was my tolerance with the surly silences of their own mothers (nobody thought you could talk to fathers at all).

This was all very well, but, scowling at these scenes passing before me as I sat huddled in my present disillusionment, I saw that with my own children I had gone much further: I urged, encouraged, gave advice, held before them an ideal of maturity (open-minded . . . tolerant . . . yet achieving, resourceful . . .) as earlier in their lives I had propounded an ideal of superior childhood. Was it possible, I began to ask, that I had been not merely an idealistic parent, but a *moralistic* one, urging my developing children to be like *this*, like *that*, because there lies the way to the best and noblest behaviour? I had overlooked – as perhaps a whole generation of well-intentioned parents had done – the fact that each child must find its own way to whatever version of perfection it conceives, and can attain.

I reflected too, with a sort of surprised humility, that my own children as parents (the third generation being far enough advanced for me to be able to observe them) more typically said to their young, 'Be yourself . . . ' In this later milieu there was a rhythm and flexibility that I had not known. I had embraced without hesitation the goal of good parents – to make sure our children excelled at everything, that they were both virtuous and impressive. Now, I could watch while children, and parents too, far more often followed their natural inclinations, being awkward, reluctant, untidy, ill-tempered. I noted that the sky did not fall on any of them; on the contrary they flourished. Even quite small children had a sense of individual quality and style.

Something of this lurked, I knew, in the thunder clouds that had gathered over some of my late parent relationships. Yet, if this was merely a way of withdrawing from an old style of too-insistent interest and control in parents, why was it so angrily directed at me, and at Trevor not at all?

A good deal of my agonising took place at night. Days continued to be eager and various, but nights could echo horribly, cavernous tunnels where past and present reverberated round and round, and morning remained a distant and unattainable glimmer. Frowning over midnight cups of tea I chased my theories up and down like rats in the dark. Some turned into furies against Trevor. There he was, making everyone sorry for him, inviting their help with the simplest operations, encouraging them to like him! This bit of venom had the merit at least of making me laugh and therefore fall asleep at last.

But I returned to the idea, and eventually it led me to a new and salutary questioning of the whole system of social laws by which Trevor and I had lived, and which was now called our 'conditioning'. I was used to thinking of the changes in these laws as 'mine' – mine and other women's; we were the ones who had been offered larger freedoms and greater fulfilment, a more ample territory for our separate growth. Men, I knew, had changes to contemplate too – indeed, I saw them with painful immediacy in Trevor's domestic struggles. But when I brought our children into this calculation, as now I must, I realised that behind those changes lay, unobserved, a request that embraced both parents equally: that when their work was done, and at the proper time, they would themselves decently decline.

Yes, that was it – instruct the young in the wisdom of their time, the cultural inheritance; hand on the baton if you like, and then go away; subside, run off the track. Applaud the new performer from the sideline. And Trevor, by circumstances if not active choice, had done so. I had not. While the marriage that had established and then sustained this family slowly disintegrated, I had followed with obsessive concentration the emerging star of my own independence, my chance to work, to write.

I looked back to those first years of change, and there I saw a small, clear scene. A woman chatting with her young adult children; Sunday night, the week's ironing strewn about . . . the talk is eager, confident, informed – books just read, poems, ideas, theories . . . But the style is hers, the thoughts follow her lead, the momentum is at her direction. None there realise that this is so; they are warm and close – closer perhaps than a middle-aged parent and young adults, beginning to form their views and vision, have any right to be. A keen affection binds them – and blinds them, I see from my place in the shadows of time to come, to the breaking apart which must come and may be all the more harsh for having been delayed.

I pondered this, and other such scenes which passed through my consciousness, and I put them against a sort of graph of the generations. I had been a mother who managed, but also served; I had claimed little for myself, except that I wanted to be loved. Yes, loved – and all the more, perhaps, as Trevor's increasing absorption in his 'real world' of school took him further and further away from any shared life we'd once had. And then I had acquired my own 'real life', the one I now enjoyed, indeed gloried in. It did not fit the generation graph, as Trevor's did; but there was also this question of wanting so badly to hold my children's affection, through all the changes I made. Was I really clinging to a part of the old system? Had I, below all the high excitement, the pleasure in being tested, clung to something of the past that I was afraid to lose? Was it even possible that a stratum of guilt, that favourite woman's means of self-laceration, had lain deeply buried in me all this time? And was that in turn related to a very old habit, reinforced by Trevor's tendency to blame me for whatever went wrong, to expect punishment for my adventuring, and thus, sooner or later, to court it?

Having come upon this remarkable idea, I took it further and speculated that here too perhaps lay the clue to my persistent desire to help Trevor; as though a voice in some secret chamber of the mind had said, 'You were wicked to desert the husband who so needed you, and only by a desperate attention to his present requirements can you hope that he and his children may in time forgive you . . . '

From the earliest years my woman's habits of mind had been underlaid by a dim – and not usually conscious – sense of being accountable. To someone – my parents, occasionally to a teacher, friend, lover, certainly to the man I married, finally and perhaps most powerfully, to my children. Now, at long last, I was ready to enter a larger inheritance. I had already become, and would now remain, most fundamentally accountable to myself, and it was time to acknowledge it.

This had nothing to do with loving my children – unless it was a final act of love to embrace the mature detachment such a realisation implied. I hoped they would in the end (and some already had) do as much for me.

And then Trevor died. Suddenly, easily, at home in his little town and long before any of us could go to him, or know he was no longer there. Old friends, ex-pupils, teachers, neighbours, relations, gathered to mourn. His old life of educational vision, his consummate teaching skill, and his later years of struggle, sickness, submerged rage – and partial resignation – all came together in the respect and compassion of this company; in their reminiscences, in formal speeches and reverent farewells.

As for me, I entered the first days of mourning believing myself to be part of an indivisible unit, his family, drawn together in a common wish to express a common sorrow. I was wrong; it was not so. Disbelieving, hurt and shocked, I had to acknowledge that my children saw me, for this occasion at least, as an outsider. One even said, 'Lots of people in your situation would not be here at all.'

This view did not appear to be shared by friends and other visitors who had come to say goodbye to Trevor. They took it for granted, as I had done, that I was quite properly, and with great sadness, relinquishing a person and a connection that had been central to my whole adult life, however it had diminished in recent years. I spoke to these people, I welcomed and farewelled them, I sometimes wept with them; but inside I was in a state of emotional panic which I could not declare and whose cause I could not find.

It was of the greatest importance to me that I should do so. As declarations were made, tears shed, farewells expressed and honoured, I watched and listened with close attention. And I saw that what these people recognised and celebrated, again and again, was the long natural flow of a life, its continuity, its logic, its predictable direction. Old friends who came, the now middle-aged men and women Trevor had taught when they were children, all told stories of famous events from a time when everyone was young and he a favourite teacher. The tender laughter at his foibles between Frances and a girl from an old fourth form class, the shared reminders Martin exchanged with youngsters from a past now made present, kids who shed for the moment their later lives as strangers and went back with us to halcyon summers in Ohakune or Greytown . . . there was a melancholy happiness in it all. Trevor, who had lived much in the past, would have enjoyed the talk, we said. All was as it should be.

A man has his career, his full flowering, his influence, his decline, his support in illness and in the necessary weaknesses of age. And then he dies. My life by comparison suddenly seemed rootless, precariously assertive, without the deeper definitions in the world around us that were Trevor's by right of his faithfulness to its laws. I, having broken them, must fight for my place and whatever recognition it carried, on my own. I saw that it had always been so: from that first breaking out of the acknowledged pattern of women's lives, my new growth had contained within it the seeds of this ultimate loss I now felt so keenly. My children by contrast mourned their father, at home with the assembled characters of his past, and theirs.

Why was I not there, with them, supported by the sharing of our grief, respected as the one parent left, guardian of family traditions we had established together nearly half a century before? Well, I reflected soberly, he hadn't left home, and I had.

Yet my grief was real, and I was profoundly shaken by it. The day of the funeral I went outside for a while, alone, and there, in a corner of Trevor's problematical garden, I sat down and thought, I put down my threadbare old loyalty, my anxious regard for the opinion of the other parent and my more recent longing to be understood by my children. There, alone, without those young people whose direction, and in the end comprehension, pointed elsewhere, I wept with a wholesome natural sorrow for the end of a life that, almost as long as I could remember, had been bound up with my own. It was an association, I saw, which, passing through every possible phase from ecstasy to despair, had truly ended only with his death.

In marrying a conventional man, at a time when the 'bourgeois' habits of mind of his family were very attractive to me, as a reaction against the oddity of my own family, I had, without knowing it, agreed to establish a conventional family. We would bring our children up securely within the social expectations of our time. Indeed, I'd wanted to do this, and if I then wanted to abandon the wife-and-mother docility these conventions imposed upon me, that was later, and I had to do it alone. The idea that I could have taken with me, as it were, my children and their loyalty (the kind they have for parents) was absurd. I had, it seemed, tried to do so. Why else should I have revelled in those exciting and influential conversations with their younger selves that I now remembered with such chagrin?

I had begun my adult life trying to solve the problem of 'difference' by joining forces with a man who understood how to be 'the same' – as the world and its institutions, that is. Now at long last I was truly myself – some amalgam, no doubt, of the rule-keeping central to Trevor's family, the fragile maverick enthusiasms of mine, the experience of parenthood, and, now, the outlook and habits of a solitary person, a worker, a writer.

Driving home from Greytown for the last time, I felt a lift of the spirit. As the afternoon light deepened the severity of the valleys and spurs of the Rimutaka hills, I had an unexpected sense that I was now freer than before to navigate my own difficult terrain. If I grieved at the ending of Trevor's life, I was also in one way liberated by it. The divisions between us had, in some form, remained also to haunt our children; I thought at last I understood the painful, and it had seemed punishing, family silences towards me.

Trevor had always projected (and perhaps revelled in) an image of silent reproach, of injury at my choice of another life in preference to the one I'd shared with him. I did not believe I deserved this implied accusation, but neither had I been able to free myself entirely of the burden of anxiety it placed on me. Now it had gone, and I breathed more easily.

I thought about Trevor himself, in ways that my children could neither understand nor share, as I could not comprehend their sense of the loss of a father, except perhaps by thinking back to Lewis's death, now more than thirty years in the past. Trevor's death suddenly seemed to place in my hands a kind of posthumous gift. It freed me from some old idea of family solidarity and released me into an awareness of profound, but peacefully contemplated, differences amongst us.

It had occurred to me some time earlier that, despite family conflicts, my life had in a broader sense come to a kind of resolution. It had emerged from the hot and risky turbulence of those first years of knocking about in the chaos that lay outside marriage, its settled systems and groups. I no longer fell violently and repeatedly in love, nor did I wake up in the morning with a trembling awareness that the whole familiar world would have turned upside down by the time I went to bed at night. I had stable habits; working at my desk was fairly systematically relieved by outings, visitors, telephone calls; I decided for myself, mostly without panic, how the pattern of my days would evolve.

At the same time a sense of loss still underlay each step from the old secure predictions to the new and variable practices that I made up for myself. This had never left me; perhaps it never would. And of course I could still feel lonely and dispirited, I still occasionally looked with envy at the placidly married ('one person in the world for whom you know you always come first'); I had found no escape from the nervous blindness inherent in writing itself – the hurtling forward without knowing where you will get to; the wanting so badly to say something that is at first unsayable, and may remain so. And I had never quite cured myself of that sudden rush of sadness as I turned the key in the lock and came into my own house alone and silent, after being with friends.

However, friendship had a central place in this maturing I observed in my independent life and its system – for it had become a system. Those remarkable discoveries made, in my first years alone, of people with vision, intelligence, passion, who were somehow embarked on journeys similar to my own – these had become settled and familiar associations. They had their secure affections, their curious remembrances, their weird or funny stories to tell – in a word, their own past. Fiona and I had for years now talked often – sometimes daily – of our work, our families, our relationship with the world and responsibilities as writers. We had depended on each other, confessed a thousand times to fears, perplexities, sorrows, expecting understanding and intelligent analysis. From her, and other friends with her candour and courage, I had learnt balance, a way of waiting – especially in relation to family differences where we found endless reassuring parallels; and we often ruminated together about factions and fashions in the writing community, and affirmed our faith – easily shaken as it could be – in 'the work itself'.

Gabriel Garcia Marquez says in *Love in the Time of Cholera* that 'human beings are not born once and for all on the day their mothers give birth to them, but . . . life obliges them over and over again to give birth to themselves . . . ' I daresay this is what we were all doing together, as well as alone; others too appeared to have found that a burst of experience, exploding like new constellations, had settled into a steady, quieter illumination of some aspect of their lives.

Margaret and I had long finished with the drama of past exploits; we often talked of work which, for her as much as for me, had come to compose a pattern with its own disciplines, its own escapes. Though her scholarly editing was in its detail unfamiliar to me, I could understand its triumphs and frustrations, and I found constant pleasure in the subtlety and wit of her observations. We sometimes remarked that an event had not really taken place till we recounted it for each other.

And Ted? Well, this crucial relationship had, to our own rather rueful surprise, also proved that the second adolescence, like the first, does come to its end. Master as always of the exact phrase, he said he now knew you could learn to be 'a loving person' instead of one always erratically 'in love'. By surviving our past we had achieved a present, and marvelled still at the vein of common experience that connected our lives, despite the obvious fact that our second, and at last genuine, adult selves were vastly different from each other in temperament, and in many of our tastes and habits. We didn't give up constantly wondering about ourselves though, nor our old addiction to theories and explanations, not to mention our taste for going to bed together. Chester and I wrote friendly, shortish, irregular letters.

Those half-lives, half-loves that had so magnetised and possessed us in earlier years – were they real, or a childish pretence? Were we ourselves real? It seemed to me, as one by one we settled, found what mattered most and pursued it more sedately, that there had been a kind of mesmerising dance, a midsummer night's dream, in which we had found a more vivid reality than any we'd known before, or would have offered to us again. We were all in various ways emerging from a life of settled expectations which we had not actually chosen for ourselves. We were all writers, or connected with writing, and thus obsessed with coming as close as possible to our experience, penetrating it, knowing it from the inside.

Then there was that strange division between those who, like us, wanted to know the world in order to re-create it, and those who wanted most of all to live, and do that well. We – as Fiona and I had sometimes reminded ourselves – were in it for the knowledge; others were in it for the performance. None of us believed that wanting to transmute your experience into some other form labelled 'art' excused you from keeping the rules of civilised behaviour. Far from it; it merely imposed a double vision, so you had to keep one eye on the facts and another on the possibilities.

Falling in and out of love, leaning eagerly across drinks in strange pubs through hours of passionate conversation at all hours of the day or night, I think we had been living in that second world, the one of possibilities, exercising our power to live in the imagination, and to understand and control it. When we could do that we were satisfied, and as it were went home.

And I? Amidst the gentle dispersal all about me, the settling of brilliant particles, I acquired grandchildren. More and more of them, and divine creatures they were too. I had travelled, and returned; touched a world of strangers and come back to find strangeness itself familiar. The quick world after all was near at hand. I'd proved for myself the truth of the old Sudanese proverb I'd learnt in Africa years before: 'Salt from the north, gold from the south, and silver from the white man's country; but the word of God and the treasures of wisdom are to be found in Timbuktu.'

Knowledge is a pool, its ripples are endless, its connections subtle, its elements a moving current. From my grandchildren flow a thousand new signs and messages; some tell me how I might have been a better, more open kind of parent, less moralistic, more willing to allow each child to take a separate journey into an unknown, unprescribed future. But at other times the message says that parenthood is a system of morality, an institution dedicated to the growth of conscience, and that children, who haven't entered it, and grandparents, who have come out the other end, have a natural affinity for each other. In the anarchic state that childhood and age both occupy, they meet with easy pleasure. It's the kind of love that produces forgiveness before the crime, laughter before the joke, a giving before anything is asked.

There are others who have, with the matter-of-fact assurance young children possess – it's their trailing clouds of glory – taken me into worlds both new and familiar. Jamil, at thirteen, out on the porch of Trevor's house, holding me with a strong, comprehending embrace while I wept hopelessly and Trevor lay inside, dead. Tess, shrieking and hugging me, and I her, as we crouched a yard or two away from the cataclysm of the birth of her baby brother on a towel on her mother's bedroom floor. Carlos walking, still unsteadily, with me through the long grass and whispering about the young turkey which eventually ran out into the open and scuttled under a fence, so we sat there together, characters in a story as old as the telling of stories, at one with the grass, the huge sky and the gasping, running, feathery thing we had caught and held for a moment before we had to let it go.

To write your life story is to go down to the dark and steamy kitchen of the soul, to lift the lids of cooking pots and examine the contents, one by one. I began with fictions – for the past is the first and greatest fiction, one we create year by year and hour by hour, and the further back you go to find it the more complete it is, because you have had so long to remember and create it. My childhood seemed to me, as it rose, cleared and settled in memory and imagination, admirably finished and whole, requiring nothing but an act of will to pick out its entire contours.

My life as a young woman had been only imperfectly shaped when I went to look for it. I walked back through the slow weather of the years and peered about like a wanderer on a beach frowning at the tips of rocks and shells that showed through the surface of the sand. Patiently I uncovered each object, or the fragment I could find, and set about arranging a mosaic that would reveal their true character.

But all the time the roaring present continued on its way, as it must, threatening to steal the past tense from me and substitute the visible, tangible discoveries proliferating about me in an inchoate, unfinished, contradictory present. But before I turn back to them with the concentration they deserve, it seems worth recording the fact that the very act of making a record has itself become an instrument in the making of the pattern, the fiction that my life, like everyone else's, is constantly becoming.

Without the writing of this tale I could not have understood how it is that challenging the conventions of my time meant uncovering layer after layer of habit, each one demanding a fresh confrontation. Nor would I have realised how, and why, one must gradually separate the person from the parent if parenthood has been central to your life, as it has to mine. And I would not have known – which is to say remembered – how at the end of the twentieth century, and in this country, it is possible to create an image of the older woman who does not submit to old stereotypes, one who is mother-in-decline, grandmother, but also individual, new and separate and unlike both of these.

Ours is a society that does not value age, especially in women. There are vital and purposeful older women everywhere, of course, but if they are Pakeha they have been given as of right no kuia status, no natural rank; all have had to struggle for the place they have, and some have paid a high price for it.

Late one night I came home, after a bruising family encounter – one aspect, I thought, of the penalties inherent, for me, in changing old patterns rather late, and wrenching new ones out of them. I went to bed and in the most graphic detail dreamed my own death. I lay back, an object of professional (though I thought rather offhand) attention while my body was tidied up for burial. One or two people I knew slightly came and glanced at me, one put a few flowers on my pillow. Dead but conscious, I urgently wanted to get to the telephone – could I use it still, or was I past that? There were people I *must* talk to before it was too late. They were, of course, my children, the people I loved most in the world, some of whom were clearly out of patience with me, out of love.

As I woke up the real phone rang, and it was Kathy, sane and wise as always. 'You don't have to die just because you make mistakes,' she said. I hoped she was right.

In time the healing of family divisions I had hoped for did occur. I had acknowledged that my marriage finally ended only with Trevor's death; perhaps for others, too, family connections became easier when they were not underscored by the pain and irresolution of our last phase as parents. But out of this has come another story, not told here, of the delight of mature friendship between adult parent and adult child. If our history as a family was marked by the trauma of a long, late search for the respect for differences we failed to achieve when young, this has been followed by a mellowing of understanding that is all the richer for having been hard to come by. The poem I wrote, when this process was much less advanced than it is now, seemed to know this with the prophetic insight poetry sometimes mysteriously possesses.

FAMILY GROUP

The children of the family are playing families:
cousins brought up by the touchy sisters exhibit
a judicious bossiness the little ones swallow whole;
the smallest shivers with ecstasy merely at being
included by this beneficent authority. The sun
is hot on the hills: here by the walnut trees
we will light a fire in the evening, eat out on the grass.

Conversations bloom all about with instant colour
like nasturtiums sown in the wind. We have all
travelled a long way. The old jokes are heard
in echoes and fragments, as we see forgotten summers
in the crumpled rugs on the grass.
And of course she is here too, the one who
for ten years has set us the hardest lesson –

to find what it is even death cannot take away:
I hear a familiar cadence, see a still tenderness,
hand lightly placed on the arm of a tired young
husband, some poise in a seated figure –
these are the blends, the trace elements,
the life after death of her, now in our keeping,
mutely alive in our lives, like the threads still

bright in the old tartan rug where we sprawl.
I look round at these figures in a mellow landscape
and know we have passed our meridian; the precious
inheritance is being received, by unconscious
yet deliberate act and moment by moment, into
the proper hands. This is the photograph
of a notable occasion no one remembered to take.